CliffsTestPrep®

Catholic High School
Entrance Exams

CliffsTestPrep®
Catholic High School Entrance Exams

by

Fred N. Grayson

Contributing Authors/Consultants

Mark Weinfeld

Sharon Saranson

Elaine Bender

WILEY

Wiley Publishing, Inc.

About the Author

As an independent book developer and publisher, Fred N. Grayson has published hundreds of books in conjunction with many major publishers. In addition, he has written and/or coauthored dozens of books in the test-preparation field.

Publisher's Acknowledgments

Editorial

Project Editor: Marcia L. Johnson

Senior Acquisitions Editor: Greg Tubach

Copy Editor: Kathleen Robinson

Technical Editor: Clifford Hull

Production

Proofreader: Henry Lazarek

Wiley Publishing, Inc. Composition Services

CliffsTestPrep® Catholic High School Entrance Exams

Published by:
Wiley Publishing, Inc.
111 River Street
Hoboken, NJ 07030-5774
www.wiley.com

Copyright © 2004 Wiley, Hoboken, NJ

Published by Wiley, Hoboken, NJ

ISBN: 0-7645-4169-2

Printed in the United States of America

10 9 8 7 6 5 4 3 2

1B/SS/QT/QU/IN

Library of Congress Cataloging-in-Publication Data
Grayson, Fred N.
  Catholic high school entrance exams / by Fred N. Grayson ;
  contributing authors, Mark Weinfeld, Sharon Saranson,
  Elaine Bender.
      p. cm. — (CliffsTestPrep)
  Includes bibliographical references and index.
  ISBN 0-7645-4169-2 (pbk.)
  1. Catholic high schools—United States—Entrance
examinations—Study guides. I. Title. II. Series.
LB3060.24.G73 2004
373.126'2—dc22
                                                              2004002242

No part of this publication may be reproduced, stored in a retrieval system, or transmitted in any form or by any means, electronic, mechanical, photocopying, recording, scanning, or otherwise, except as permitted under Sections 107 or 108 of the 1976 United States Copyright Act, without either the prior written permission of the Publisher, or authorization through payment of the appropriate per-copy fee to the Copyright Clearance Center, 222 Rosewood Drive, Danvers, MA 01923, 978-750-8400, fax 978-646-8600. Requests to the Publisher for permission should be addressed to the Legal Department, Wiley Publishing, Inc., 10475 Crosspoint Blvd., Indianapolis, IN 46256, 317-572-3447, or fax 317-572-4447.

Trademarks: Wiley, the Wiley Publishing logo, Cliffs, CliffsNotes, CliffsAP, CliffsComplete, CliffsTestPrep, CliffsQuickReview, CliffsNote-a-Day, and CliffsStudySolver are trademarks or registered trademarks of John Wiley & Sons, Inc. and/or its affiliates. All other trademarks are the property of their respective owners. Wiley Publishing, Inc. is not associated with any product or vendor mentioned in this book.

For general information on our other products and services or to obtain technical support, please contact our Customer Care Department within the U.S. at 800-762-2974, outside the U.S. at 317-572-3993, or fax 317-572-4002.

Wiley also published its books in a variety of electronic formats. Some content that appears in print may not be available in electronic books.

WILEY

Table of Contents

PART II: PRACTICE EXAMS

Introduction

This book is designed to help you develop your test-taking skills, regardless of whether you're planning to take the Cooperative Entrance Examination (COOP) or the High School Placement Test (HSPT) for admission to a Catholic high school. These are the two most common exams that are used, although some schools might require you to take the SSAT or the ISEE instead. About 1,600 Catholic secondary schools exist in the United States. Not all of them require the same tests. However, because you picked up this book, we'll assume that either the COOP or the HSPT is the exam for which you'll be studying.

The testing requirements differ depending on where you live, and the level of importance that is put on these exams depends on the school to which you plan to apply. In any case, it is important to do your best—not only for yourself, but to demonstrate to the school to which you are applying that you've made the effort. Admissions personnel are able to translate the effort you make on the test into a prediction of how well you will do when you're in high school. Of course, they combine the test results with your grades to get the clearest, and most complete, picture of who you are and your potential for success.

This book is the first step on the road to success—at least in terms of doing well on these tests. A basic concept in all test preparation is the more you practice, the better you do on the actual test. We've tried to give you an in-depth look at both the COOP and HSPT, as well as provide you with extensive test-taking practice.

Subject Review

Two separate subject areas are covered: verbal questions and mathematics questions. Some of the material is the same in both the COOP and HSPT, and some is unique to a specific test. We indicate within each topic which exams require which material. For example, both exams have analogies, but the COOP uses picture analogies, whereas the HSPT uses verbal analogies. You get practice on both. You will find the material to review in the next part of the book.

Tests

The last section of this book features three complete, simulated COOP exams and three complete, simulated HSPT exams. By taking these exams, you get a feel for what the tests are like.

To help your progress and understanding of the material, each test is accompanied by fully explained answers. Every answer is given in detail; every mathematics problem is solved. All you have to do is check your answers, and if you don't know why you had an incorrect answer, you can read the explanation or go back to the earlier review section for a more in-depth explanation of the topic.

Let's take a brief look at each of these two exams before starting the review.

The Cooperative Entrance Exam (COOP)

The COOP exam is designed for eighth grade students who are applying to a Catholic high school. Your score on that test is used for both the admissions process as well as determining your placement in ninth grade. The purpose of the exam is to measure academic achievement and aptitude in reading, language arts, and mathematics.

The test is given once a year, in October or November, and you can take this test only once. You can register to take the COOP exam through your school. Ask your student advisor. After paying your fee and registering, you receive a complete booklet with sample questions, along with your admissions ticket, which you need when you go to the testing site.

The COOP Format

The format of the COOP exam changes every year. Currently, all the questions are multiple choice, with four choices each. The choices are labeled **A, B, C,** and **D,** or **F, G, H,** and **J.** This change in lettering is done to help you keep track of the questions you're working on, especially if you skip a question and plan to go back to it. Too often a student skips a question, goes on to the next one and forgets to skip a line on the answer sheet. In this format, if you're answering a question with choices **A, B, C,** and **D,** you are able to see whether you have missed a line on the answer sheet (because the answers will be labeled **F, G, H,** and **J**).

As of the writing of this book, these are the *approximate* topics, number of questions, and time limits. However, the types of questions are likely to be the same. Therefore, if you're familiar with the question types, it shouldn't matter to you whether you are presented with 20 questions or 30 questions, or whether you have 15 minutes or 25 minutes to answer them. The test developers (CBT/McGraw Hill) know how long it should take to answer certain types of questions.

#	Topic	Approximate # of Questions	Approximate Time
1	Sequences	20	15 minutes
2	Analogies	20	17 minutes
3	Quantitative Reasoning	20	15 minutes
4	Verbal Reasoning—Words	20	15 minutes
5	Verbal Reasoning—Context	20	15 minutes
6	Reading and Language Arts	40	40 minutes
7	Mathematics	40	40 minutes

COOP Scoring

As on most standardized tests, you receive a "raw" score that is then converted into a "scaled" score. This scaled score helps administrators evaluate your score with the results of the other students who have taken the same exam. You are also given a percentile rank, which is your standing in relation to the other test takers.

The raw score is based on the number of questions that you answered correctly. The good news is that you are not penalized for incorrect answers. What does that tell you? It indicates that you should take a chance and *answer every question* whether you know the answer or not. You have a one-in-four chance of getting the correct answer, and it can only help you. (More about improving your score is discussed later in this section.)

The High School Placement Test (HSPT)

Developed by the Scholastic Testing Service, the High School Placement Test (HSPT) is a multiple-choice exam, similar to the COOP. Optional tests also exist, which are not required by all schools—Catholic Religion, Mechanical Aptitude, and Science. The results of these tests are not included in the final score of the HSPT, and we have not included that material in this book. When you apply to take the HSPT, ask your advisor whether the schools to which you are applying require any of these optional tests.

The HSPT Format

The format of this multiple-choice exam is slightly different from the COOP exam. Most questions offer three or four choices, but they are lettered **A, B, C,** and **D.** Keep this in mind as you answer the questions. If you skip a question, make sure you skip a line on the answer key. Although the exam has five major sections, the questions are numbered consecutively from 1 to 298. Always make sure you are filling in the answer to the correct question. If you mark an answer incorrectly, all the answers that follow will be off by a number and, therefore, incorrect.

Although the number of questions and type of questions on the HSPT has remained fairly stable throughout the years, keep in mind that when you take the actual exam, some material might be different from this book. As we pointed out earlier about the COOP exam, if you know how to answer the questions, it doesn't matter how many there are or how long you're given to answer them. Following is a table of what you can expect on the HSPT.

#	Topic	Approximate # of Questions	Approximate Time
1	Verbal Skills	60	16 minutes
2	Quantitative Skills	52	30 minutes
3	Reading	62	25 minutes
4	Mathematics	64	45 minutes
5	Language Skills	60	25 minutes

HSPT Scoring

Like the COOP exam, your raw score is based on the number of questions you answer correctly. You are not penalized for incorrect answers, so you might as well guess at those you don't know. It can't hurt—it can only help.

The raw score is converted to a scaled score that ranges from 200 to 800 and is used by the admissions personnel in the school to which you apply. These scores include your ranking on both a local and national level, as well as your Cognitive Skills Quotient. Of course, the schools use this information *along with* your current grades.

Scoring High on the COOP and HSPT Exams

There are no secrets for doing well on these exams, but there are ways to do better and improve your score.

The first technique is to study the material in this book. We've tried to cover all the material that you might encounter on either of these exams. However, you should also have learned most of this in school. This is, after all, a review book and its purpose is to help you brush up on the subjects that you should have already learned. Perhaps, though, you will encounter some new material. Even better, you will now be more prepared than before you started with this book.

The purpose of reviewing the material is to help you recall some topics that you might have learned the previous year and that might not be in the forefront of your mind. These topics should become a bit more focused in your thinking, and that should be helpful when you encounter these topics on the exam(s).

The second technique to improve your performance on these exams is to be completely familiar with the exams and the directions. We have given you three full-length tests for each exam—more than enough with which to practice and become familiar. One of the most important aspects of doing well on these exams—or any other standardized test you take in the future—is understanding the directions. Why? Simply because each test on these exams is timed, and the *more* time you spend trying to figure out what you're being asked to do, the *less* time you have to actually answer the questions.

For example, if you have 15 minutes to answer 20 questions, that means you have only 3/4 of a minute—or 45 seconds—to answer each question. If it takes you 1 1/2 minutes to read and figure out what the directions mean, you have only 40 1/2 seconds to answer each question. If it's a more difficult subject for you, every second counts.

The message is, therefore, when you work on the tests, make sure you understand the directions—memorize them, and if you're not 100 percent sure of what they mean, ask your parent or teacher to help you.

The third technique for doing well on these exams is to understand how to answer a multiple-choice question. The better your skill is at this, the better your chances are of doing well. Follow these three basic steps:

- The first approach is to read the question. If you read the question and immediately know the answer, check the choices given, and mark it on your answer page. This is the easiest, and we hope that by the time you finish using this book, most of your answers will be that easy.

- The second approach is to read the question and if the answer doesn't immediately come to mind, as discussed previously, read the answer choices. If you know the material fairly well, the correct answer should be clear to you at once. Or, if it is not immediately clear, a little thought should root out the right answer.

- The third approach is to use the process of elimination. Very simply, it involves eliminating the wrong answer so that you're left with the correct one, or at least you've narrowed down the choices. When test developers create questions for multiple-choice tests, a process is often followed. In a question with four choices, like those you'll find on the COOP and HSPT exams, one answer choice is always undeniably correct. The other choices are called *distracters*. One choice is usually completely incorrect and can be quickly eliminated. The other two choices might be similar to the correct answer, but certain clues might make them incorrect.

In mathematics, for example, decimals might be in different places in the answer choices. For instance, there's a big difference between .106, 1.06, 10.6 and 106. Keep these things in mind as you solve math problems. They should all be labeled correctly and consistently.

Look for give-away words like *always*, *never*, and *not*. Most things in the world are not *always* or *never* anything, and you should be careful if a question asks, "Which of the following is *not*...?!

By using the process of elimination, you increase your chances of getting the right answer. Remember that you are not penalized for incorrect answers on either exam, so it's worth taking a chance. What this means is that if you just guess, you have a one-in-four chance of guessing correctly—25 percent.

But what if you are able to eliminate one of the choices because it just seems wrong to you? You now have a one-in-three chance of selecting the correct answer. That's 33 percent, which is surely better than 25 percent.

If you're able to narrow it down to only two choices, you then improve your odds to a one-in-two chance, or 50 percent. You just want to improve your odds of increasing your score, and you can see that it doesn't take much. It is definitely to your advantage that you don't lose points for incorrect answers.

As we said earlier, there are no secrets to successful test taking. There are, however, time-proven techniques, and this book provides them for you. Try to pace yourself as you go through the book. Review the material, answer all the questions provided, and go back and review anything you didn't understand the first time around.

Then take the practice exams. Try to take them under conditions that simulate the real exam. What this means is find a quiet room in which to work undisturbed. Ask your family or friends not to bother you during this time. Set an alarm so that you can know when to stop. When you're done, relax. The next day, go back to the test and mark your answers. Highlight those answers that you missed and didn't understand. Some answers might have just been careless errors, and you should just remember to work a little more carefully or slow down, if necessary. If you still don't understand why your answers are wrong, read the book again or ask for help.

This book has been written to make your studying and preparation for either the COOP or HSPT exam easier and more fruitful. We hope that you take the time to go through the book carefully and follow our suggestions for studying. You can't help but do well if you understand the material we've presented. Good luck!

PART I

SUBJECT REVIEWS

Verbal Review

Mathematics Review

Quantitative Reasoning Review

Verbal Review

This chapter reviews the questions on the COOP and HSPT exams. Read the directions for each type of question carefully. Knowing the directions and being familiar with the types of questions saves time when you take the exam and makes it easier to answer the questions. The review tests help you see how much you have learned and which types of questions require more study and practice.

Analogies

The COOP exam has 20 analogy questions. COOP items use pictures to form the questions instead of words. The HSPT has 10 analogy questions, which are part of the Verbal Skills test.

Answering Analogy Questions

Analogy questions are about seeing the relationships between two words and then applying that relationship to other words. To answer these questions, you need to figure out how to describe the connection between the first two words. What is their relationship to each other? After you have determined that, look at the third word and the answer choices. Which of the answer choices has the same relationship to the third word that the second word has to the first word?

Some general relationships appear frequently in analogy questions. They includes synonyms, antonyms, part to whole or whole to part, function or purpose, association, location, characteristic of, cause to effect or effect to cause, and degree.

The answer is always the same part of speech as the third word in the analogy. Here is an example.

> Sick is to healthy as poor is to:
>
> A. money
> B. wealthy
> C. poverty
> D. injured

It is clear that the first two words are antonyms. Thus, choice **C,** a synonym for being poor can be eliminated, as can **D,** which is related to the first pair of words. Choice **A** is tempting; if you have money, you aren't poor. But money is a noun, not an adjective, so **B,** wealthy (an adjective), is the better choice.

When answering analogy questions, if the relationship of the first pair of words isn't obvious, try to think of a descriptive sentence using the words. A person who is sick isn't healthy; a person who is poor isn't wealthy.

After defining the relationship of the first pair of words, eliminate obviously incorrect answer choices. From the remaining choices, choose the best answer.

Sample Questions

COOP Analogies Directions: Choose the picture that should go in the empty box so that the bottom two pictures are related in the same way as the top two.

1.

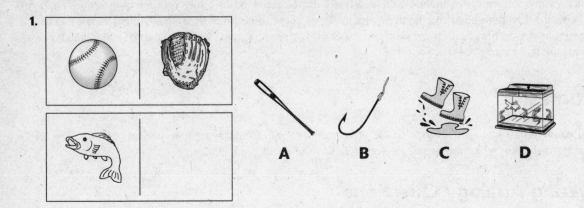

HSPT Analogies Directions: Mark one answer—the answer you think is best—for each problem.

2. Rare is to scarce as familiar is to:

    A. unusual

    B. friendly

    C. common

    D. excessive

3. Punch is to bruise as tickle is to:

    A. scar

    B. annoy

    C. funny

    D. laugh

4. Lemon is to sour as flea is to:

    A. gnat

    B. tiny

    C. bite

    D. bitter

Answers and Explanations

1. B. This is a relationship based on use or function. A baseball is caught in a baseball glove; a fish is caught with a hook. The baseball bat, **A,** is associated with the first pair of words. Choices **C** and **D** are related to water and fishing, but they do not have the same relationship to fish as a baseball glove does to a baseball.

2. C. The first two words are synonyms. Of the possible answers, *common* is the closest in meaning to familiar. *Unusual*, choice **A,** is similar in meaning to the first pair of words. Choice **B,** *friendly*, is a word you might associate with *familiar*, but it is not a synonym. *Excessive*, choice **D,** means more than enough, so it is almost opposite in meaning to the first pair of words, but it is not a synonym for *familiar.*

3. D. The relationship is cause to effect. A punch causes a bruise; tickling someone causes the person to laugh. Choice **A** is associated with the first pair of words. Choice **B** might be associated with being tickled, but it is not the effect of tickling. Choice **C** is the cause of laughter, not the effect of tickling.

4. B. The relationship is between a word and a characteristic of that word. As lemons are sour, fleas are tiny. If you think of the first two terms as a sentence, lemons are bitter, choice **A** can be quickly eliminated. A flea is not a gnat. Choice **D** is another word that could be used to describe a lemon, not a flea. Choice **C** is something a flea does; it is a verb. It is not an adjective describing a characteristic of a flea.

Reading Comprehension

Both exams have 40 reading comprehension questions. The COOP exam has 9 passages with 4 or 5 questions about each passage. The HSPT has 4 passages with 10 questions about each passage. The questions on both exams are very similar, although the wording of the questions might be slightly different.

Answering Reading Comprehension Questions

These questions demonstrate your ability to understand what you have read. Sometimes they ask you about the content of the passage, and the correct answer repeats words or phrases from the passage. Some questions have an answer that repeats the content of the passage in different words. For these questions, the correct answer is a paraphrase of material in the passage. Sometimes a question asks you to make an inference. To infer is to make a conclusion based on the information in the passage, although the passage itself does not state this conclusion. Some questions are about the meaning of words in the passage, but you are not expected to know the meaning of the word before reading the passage. You can determine the correct answer by seeing how the word is used. For all the questions, the correct answer is based on something in the passage. Some answers might be true statements, but if they are not in the passage, they are not the correct choice. It might even happen that you know something in the passage is untrue. Even so, if that statement is given as an answer choice, it might be correct according to the passage.

As you read the passage to get a general idea of the subject, focus on the first and last sentence of each paragraph. These sentences often contain the most important idea in the paragraph, and one of them might state the paragraph's main idea. Look for words indicating how ideas are related. Words like *but* or *however* indicate contrasts. Often, words and phrases relating to causes and effects (such as *because*, *therefore*, and *as a result*) indicate material that questions will focus on.

Read each question and all four answer choices. Eliminate any choices that seem obviously incorrect. If one answer seems to be correct, reread the portion of the passage that it is about, and if this still seems to be the correct choice, select that answer. If none of the answers seems appropriate, reread the passage to see if you can eliminate choices or find information to determine the correct answer.

If you still are uncertain about an answer, do not spend more time on that question. Because no deduction is taken for wrong answers, choose the answer that seems most likely, even if you are unsure. You can return to these questions if you have time to do so.

Some people find it easier to skim over the questions before reading the passage. This gives them an idea of what to look for while they read. As you take the practice tests in this book, try this method to see if it makes it easier for you to answer the questions.

Sample Questions

Essentially the reading comprehension tests on both exams are similar. Following are the two different sets of directions for both the COOP and HSPT exams. You should memorize them so that you don't have to waste time rereading them when you take the actual tests.

COOP Reading Comprehension Directions: For questions 1–40, read each passage and the questions following that passage. Find the answers.

HSPT Reading Comprehension Directions: Read each passage carefully. Then mark one answer—the answer you think is best—for each item.

Passage for questions 1–5:

Scientists have discovered the bones of what might be the largest meat-eating dinosaur ever to walk the earth. The discovery was made by a team of researchers in a desert on the eastern slopes of the Andes in South America. Besides the fact that the dinosaur was huge, more astounding was the fact that the bones of a number of the dinosaurs were found together. This discovery challenges the earlier theory that the biggest meat eaters lived as loners and instead indicates that they might have lived and hunted in packs. The Tyrannosaurus Rex, a previously known giant meat eater, lived in North America and was believed to hunt and live alone.

The newly discovered meat eater appears to be related to the Giganotosaurus family. It is as closely related as a fox is to a dog. It is actually not of the same family as the Tyrannosaurus Rex; they are as different as a cat and a dog.

The fossilized remains indicate that the animals lived about 100 million years ago. With needle-shaped noses and razor-sharp teeth, they were larger than the Tyrannosaurus Rex, although their legs were slightly shorter, and their jaws were designed to be better able to dissect their prey quickly and precisely.

1. The newly discovered dinosaur remains are evidence that it might be the largest:

   A. dinosaur ever
   B. meat-eating dinosaur
   C. plant eating dinosaur
   D. North American meat eater

2. According to the passage, the most amazing fact about the find is that this dinosaur:

   F. lived and hunted in packs
   G. had a powerful jaw and sharp teeth
   H. was found in the Andes
   J. was larger than Tyrannosaurus Rex

3. The scientists were astounded because before this discovery, they thought:

   A. meat-eating dinosaurs were small in stature
   B. no meat-eating dinosaurs lived in the Andes
   C. Tyrannosaurus Rex lived in the Andes
   D. meat-eating dinosaurs lived alone

4. The newly discovered meat-eating dinosaur is:

   F. closely related to Tyrannosaurus Rex
   G. not closely related to Tyrannosaurus Rex
   H. not closely related to Giganotosaurus
   J. closely related to the large cat family

5. The word dissect as used in this passage most nearly means:

   A. take apart
   B. swallow
   C. chew up
   D. escape from

Answers and Explanations

1. **B.** This answer is stated in the first sentence of the passage. The bones are the evidence. Choice **D** is incorrect because the passage states that the bones were discovered in a desert in South America.

2. **F.** Notice that all the other choices are statements that are made in the passage. But the question asks which is the most amazing fact about the find. In the passage, that the bones were found together is described as *astounding*, which means the same as the word *amazing* in the question.

3. **D.** In this question, choices **A** and **C** are contradicted by information in the passage. No information in the passage indicates whether or not it was believed that meat-eating dinosaurs lived in the Andes, so **B** cannot be a correct answer.

4. **G.** The correct answer is a paraphrase of the statement, "It is actually not of the same family as Tyrannosaurus Rex."

5. **A.** **D** clearly does not make sense because the sentence indicates that the jaws help the creatures. **C** seems possible, but teeth, not jaws, are used to chew on something. Similarly, while **B** might be an answer, according to the passage, the jaws make them able to *dissect* quickly and precisely. Swallowing is not an act that involves precision. Therefore, *take apart*, what the creature does to its prey with its jaws, is the best choice.

Verbal Reasoning Questions (Logic Questions)

The COOP exam has 20 questions in the Verbal Reasoning tests, and these sections are broken into two separate tests—Verbal Reasoning: Words and Verbal Reasoning: Context. Four types of questions are used. One type asks you to choose a word that names a necessary part of an underlined word. Another lists three words in a top row and asks you to add a third word to a bottom row of two words so that the words in the bottom row are related in the same way as the words in the top row. This is similar to but more complicated than an analogy question. The third type of question presents a short paragraph and asks which of the statements beneath it is true according to the information given in the paragraph. The last type of question involves words in an artificial language. It provides definitions of three words and then asks which of a list of four words in the artificial language means the same as a given English word.

On the HSPT, two types of questions involve logical reasoning. The Verbal Skills test includes 10 questions involving a series of three statements. You are asked to determine whether the third statement is true, false, or uncertain if the first two statements are true. Only three answer choices, **A, B,** and **C,** are given. The test also includes 16 questions asking which word in a group of four does not belong with the other three words. These are called verbal classification questions.

Answering COOP Verbal Reasoning Questions

The first type of logic question on the COOP Verbal Reasoning: Words test asks you to choose the word that names a necessary part of a given word.

For example:

---

1. Find the word that names a necessary part of a <u>house</u>?

   A. car
   B. barn
   C. roof
   D. apartment

The logical answer is the roof, choice **C.** It is a part of the house, itself. Remember, the questions are not asking you for a synonym.

Another form of this question asks you to find a word that is most like a series of underlined words. For example:

---

2. Find the word that is most like the underlined words.

<u>lake</u>, <u>ocean</u>, <u>bay</u>

   F. fish
   G. pond
   H. weeds
   J. boats

The correct answer is pond—choice **G.** While the other choices are somehow related, only a pond is a body of water, as are the underlined words.

A third type of question is similar to the preceding one, except that it requires you to select the word that *does not* belong.

3. Which of the following words does not belong?

    A. car

    B. truck

    C. bus

    D. submarine

Which one of these choices does not run on wheels, does not travel on roads—only the submarine. Choice **D** does not belong.

Next, you're given two rows of words that are related to each other in some pattern. The first row is complete, but the row beneath it is missing a word. That missing word should satisfy the pattern. For example:

4. big, bigger, biggest

    small, smaller, _____

    F. tiny

    G. smallest

    H. elfin

    J. microscopic

It should be obvious that the missing word is smallest. Try one more.

5. train, plane, car

    engineer, _____, driver

    A. horse

    B. airport

    C. passenger

    D. pilot

The correct answer is **D.** An engineer drives a train; a pilot flies a plane; and a driver drives a car.

The next type of question is a logic question and requires you to deduce information from a short paragraph and select the statement that is supported by the passage. This is a Verbal Reasoning: Context type of question. For example:

6. Emily always enjoys going to school. Her best subject is mathematics. She also enjoys social studies because she likes her teacher. She did not do so well in science, however. She always does better in subjects when she likes her teacher.

    F. Emily does not like her mathematics teacher.

    G. School is easy for Emily.

    H. Emily does not enjoy her science teacher.

    J. School is enjoyable for Emily because she like her teachers.

Let's analyze this. Choice **F** is not supported by the passage. It doesn't mention whether she likes her mathematics teacher or not, but because the passage says she does better in subjects when she likes her teacher and her best subject is mathematics, you can deduce that she probably likes her math teacher. Choice **G** is also not supported. No information is provided about how easy or difficult school is for Emily. Choice **J** is also not supported by the passage. While it is true she enjoys school and some of her teachers, it's possible that she enjoys school because she's with her friends.

Or she might enjoy school because she gets good grades. Perhaps she likes lunch. You can see that choice **H** is the only likely answer. Why? The last sentence is the clue: "She always does better in subjects when she likes her teacher." Because she does not do well in science, it's likely that she doesn't like her teacher.

These are not really difficult questions. You just need to check each choice step by step and make sure the concepts appear—and are supported—in the passage.

The final logic question involves artificial language. You are given three made-up words and their definitions. Although these are nonsense words, some things about them are similar—perhaps the sound, the stem, the root and so on. It's up to you to identify this similarity. Then, the question asks you to select a definition for a different word. To do so, you must use the similarity that you identified and apply it to the definition.

Let's try one.

Stigbotoma means prevent.

Starbotoba means precede.

Stambotolala means predict.

Which word means preview?

- **A.** *stilboomama*
- **B.** *steelbenlola*
- **C.** *stelbornora*
- **D.** *stewbotarca*

If you look at the given words, you see a common root—*bot*. The words given as the meaning for all the nonsense words contain a similar prefix—*pre*. Thus, if you look at the word preview, you see that it also contains the prefix *pre*. Of the four choices, the only word with the common root *bot* is choice **D.** Don't be mislead by all the letters in the given words. Some are just to distract you. Try to focus on repetitive letters, combinations of letters, similar roots, and so on.

Now try the following questions and check your answers.

Sample Questions

Directions: In the following questions, select that choice that best answers the question. There are several different types of questions and directions, so read each of them carefully before answering.

For questions 1–3, choose the word that names a necessary part of the underlined word.

1. squadron

- **A.** march
- **B.** train
- **C.** fly
- **D.** jet plane

2. yardstick

- **F.** inches
- **G.** meter
- **H.** measure
- **J.** length

3. orchard

- **A.** oranges
- **B.** leaves
- **C.** apples
- **D.** trees

For question 4, find the word that is most like the underlined words.

4. book, magazine, journal

    F. collections
    G. readings
    H. newspaper
    J. charts

5. Three of the following words belong together. Select the word that does not belong.

    A. lens
    B. album
    C. flash
    D. camera

In questions 6–10, the words in the top row are related in some way. The words in the bottom row are related in the same way. For each item, choose the word that completes the bottom row of words.

6. Coke, Pepsi, Sprite

    skier, snowboarder

    F. hockey
    G. toboggan
    H. bobsled
    J. speed skater

7. red, yellow, blue

    red, blue

    A. brown
    B. green
    C. orange
    D. purple

8. plane, boat, train

    plot, character

    F. setting
    G. detail
    H. main idea
    J. fact

9. Breyers, Edy's, Ben & Jerry's

    Twix, Snickers

    A. wintergreen
    B. spearmint
    C. M&Ms
    D. peppermint

10. Acadia, Grand Canyon, Zion

    Magic Kingdom, Epcot

    F. San Juan, Capistrano
    G. Seattle
    H. Disneyland
    J. San Francisco

For questions 11–15, choose the statement that is true according to the given information.

11. John's family got a computer so that his schoolwork would be easier and more pleasant. The computer had several games as well as word processing and graphic programs preloaded when they brought it home. John's teacher has taught her students how to use word processing to write stories and reports. She also showed them how to use a graphics program to draw or import pictures. In addition John is able to use the Internet for his research projects. His parents have placed the computer in the dining room so that they are able to monitor John's activities.

    A. John's grades on his reports have improved greatly because he spends more time on research and is more creative in his work.

    B. Even though he knows how to use the computer for homework, he prefers to play games on it.

    C. His parents don't want him using the computer so much.

    D. John spends most of the time on the computer in chat rooms and sending Instant Messages to his friends.

12. Sally went to college in a city far away from home. Her boyfriend went to college in a town approximately 150 miles away from her. Sally's parents gave her a telephone card and a credit card, to be used only in an emergency. The telephone card was used almost immediately to pay for calls to her boyfriend. When the bill for the credit card came, Sally's parents discovered that her idea of an emergency was not the same as theirs.

    F. Sally's parents think she should break up with her boyfriend.

    G. Sally's parents should just send another telephone card and pay the credit card bill.

    H. Sally should do her work and not spend money.

    J. Sally's parents should put a set amount of money on the credit card each month. When the money has been spent, the card can no longer be used until the next month.

13. Nicole is a school librarian. Because of financial changes in her district, a librarian's salary is no longer in the budget. She would like to continue working in some similar type of job. Instead of increasing services provided by the city libraries, the mayor has reduced them. It is not likely that she will be able to find a job with a city library.

    A. She should sue the city to make them change the budget.

    B. She might look for a job with a children's book publisher, giving book talks to promote sales.

    C. Nicole should try writing a book.

    D. She should retire and spend her time with friends and her hobbies.

14. Nearly every family on Betty's block has a dog. They bark at all times of the day, often in the early evening as well. When she comes out on her porch, the neighbor's dogs bark loud and long, as though they don't recognize her. The barking disturbs her when she goes to her backyard to work in her flowerbed. There seems to be no place where she can have peace and quiet.

    F. Betty should speak to her neighbors about the barking and try to make friends with the neighbor's dogs.

    G. She should move to another neighborhood.

    H. She should avoid going outside her house.

    J. Betty should speak to her councilman about passing a law against excess noise.

15. Dave has neighbors on both sides of his house. Each put up a fence surrounding his yard. They put gates on the fences so that neighborhood children can't get into their yard. Now all the neighborhood children play in Dave's driveway. He is afraid one of them will get hurt.

    A. Dave should ignore the children when they play in his driveway.

    B. Dave should complain to the parents of the children.

    C. Dave should increase his insurance in case someone gets hurt and they sue him.

    D. Dave should put a gate across his driveway to keep the children from playing there.

For questions 16–20, select the correct answer.

16. Here are some words translated from an artificial language:

    Mixplicker means cereals.

    Trixplorker means fruits.

    Stixplanker means eggs.

    Which word means breakfasts?

    F. rixpranker
    G. yinxlonker
    H. mankerlink
    J. conpraiko

17. Here are some words translated from an artificial language:

    Kgihyrab means flowers.

    Prhihyash means bush.

    Oerihytss means tree.

    Which word means plant?

    A. gnihysur
    B. sedgiklad
    C. wehrabti
    D. oerdokfo

18. Here are some words translated from an artificial language:

    Strgasaet means drive.

    Glnvartet means walk.

    Nvivgotet means run.

    Which word means ride?

    F. tienmrip
    G. dsehyan
    H. rrelctrav
    J. ninamsaet

19. Here are some words translated from an artificial language:

    Loknir means store.

    Stkalokneg means market.

    Hgriblokn means stand.

    Which word means shopping center?

    A. fublbre
    B. viart
    C. crklokten
    D. reslbrun

20. Here are some words translated from an artificial language:

    Ndurar means path.

    Vendur means road.

    Bldndrag means street.

    Which word means highway?

    F. ctsudrg
    G. shrndakg
    H. ycelbew
    J. storfpum

Answers and Explanations

1. **D.** A squadron is a collective noun for a group of planes, soldiers, or vessels. Pilot is singular. Fly is what planes or pilots do. Pilots also train. March is to move with a measured step.

2. **H.** A yardstick is a tool used to measure the length, width, height, or depth of something. Meter and inches are units of measurement.

3. **D.** An orchard is a group of trees, usually some type of fruit, not oranges, however. They grow in a grove.

4. **H.** Books, magazines, journals, and newspapers are publications to be read.

5. **B.** Lens, flash, and camera are all related. An album might be used to hold photographs, but might also be for a scrapbook.

6. **J.** The items in the top row are brands of soda. The items in the bottom row are athletes who participate in winter sports. Skiers and snowboarders, along with speed skaters all perform alone. The other answers are sports that require more than one person to participate. The bobsled can either be a team or a single person's sport.

7. **B.** The items in the top row are names of primary pigments of color. The items in the bottom row are primary colors of light.

8. **F.** The items in the top row all have to do with methods of transportation on air, water, and land. The items in the bottom row are elements in a story.

9. **C.** The items in the top row are brands of ice cream. The items in the bottom row are brand names of candy bars. The other three answers are flavors found in gum and/or candy.

10. **H.** The items in the top row are all national parks. The items in the bottom row are well-known theme parks. The remaining answers are names of cities.

11. **A.** John was able to make good use of the time spent on his computer. It paid off in improved grades. The other choices show the bad habits that might develop. The fact that John's parents are able to monitor his activities is very helpful as well.

12. **J.** Sally cannot be turned loose with a credit card in her hand. She has to understand how to budget her money. A credit card with a specific amount of money on it will help her.

13. **B.** It would be ridiculous as well as expensive for Nicole to sue the city. No indication is given as to whether or not Nicole would enjoy writing a book. That choice is out. Retirement is also not a choice. We do not know whether she can retire. She wants to continue working, so it seems a good idea to search for work in a related field.

14. **F.** To remain a prisoner insider her house or to move to another neighborhood seems extreme. The most sensible solution is to try to explain to the neighbors that the barking is a great annoyance. Perhaps if she makes friends with the dogs they will stop barking at her. To expect a councilman to do something about a barking dog problem is asking something outside his or her area of influence.

15. **D.** Dave needs to take preventive measures. He can do this by putting a gate across the driveway. To ignore the problem is dangerous because someone might get hurt. Complaints to parents work sometimes, but not all the time. Increasing his insurance might be a good idea, but it would be expensive.

16. **F.** All the words have the stem, *ixp,* that probably is an indication of food. In addition they all have the same suffix, *ker.* Some of the words have the stem and some the root, but not together.

17. **A.** All example words have the same stem, *ihy.* This is the only answer choice with the same stem.

18. **J.** All example words have the same suffix, *et.* Where an individual is active, the suffix is *tet.* In the activities that involve something else, a car, the suffix is *aet*; therefore, the suffix for *ride* matches the suffix for *drive.*

19. **C.** All example words have the same stem, *lok.* The answer choice is the only one with that same stem.

20. **G.** All example words have the same stem, *nd,* indicating a similarity. The answer word needs that same stem.

Answering HSPT Logic Questions

To answer the questions involving three statements, carefully consider the information in each statement. Think about how the statements are related to each other. The information in the first two statements might not provide enough information to be sure whether the third statement is true. In that case, the correct answer choice is **C**, uncertain. The information in the third statement might be contradicted either by one of the first two statements, or by the first two statements, taken together, contradicting the third statement. In that case, the correct answer is **B**, false. If the first two statements taken separately or together do not contradict the third statement, and if they provide enough information to confirm the statement, the correct answer is **A**, true.

When answering verbal classification questions, look for what three of the four items on the list might have in common or how they are related. They might be synonyms. They might all have the same use or function. Sometimes, three of the items are general terms, and the term that doesn't belong is a specific term. Sometimes this is reversed, with three specific terms and one general term. The items might share a characteristic, like color or size. Other possibilities also exist.

Sample Questions

Directions: Mark one answer—the answer you think is best—for each problem.

1. On state highways in California, the exit signs have white lettering on a green background. Mark is traveling on a state highway, and he sees an exit sign with white lettering on a green background. He is in California. If the first two statements are true, the third is:

   A. true
   B. false
   C. uncertain

2. Farmer Mac grows more apples than Farmer Jonathan. Farmer Jonathan grows more apples than Farmer Gala. Farmer Mac grows fewer apples than Farmer Gala. If the first two statements are true, the third is:

   A. true
   B. false
   C. uncertain

3. Which word does *not* belong with the others?

   A. knife
   B. fork
   C. plate
   D. spoon

4. Which word does *not* belong with the others?

   A. slim
   B. skinny
   C. thin
   D. chubby

5. Which word does *not* belong with the others?

   A. vegetable
   B. carrot
   C. beet
   D. cucumber

Answers and Explanations

1. **C.** Mark might be in California, but the information in the first two statements does not tell us whether any other state uses the same color scheme for its highway signs. Therefore, Mark might or might not be in California.

2. **B.** If Mac grows more than Jonathan, and Jonathan grows more than Gala, Mac must also grow more than Gala.

3. **C.** All the choices are things associated with eating food, but the first three are utensils used to eat food, and a plate is what food is served on.

4. **D.** The first three words are synonyms; the last word means the opposite of the other three.

5. **A.** The other choices are specific; the word vegetable is general.

Usage, Grammar, and Spelling

The COOP tests your ability to make and recognize correct sentences. The HSPT has 40 questions about grammar and usage and 10 spelling questions in the Language Skills test.

Answering Usage, Grammar, and Spelling Questions

Most of these questions ask you to choose the correctly written sentence from the possible answers or to choose the one sentence that contains an error. When answering these questions, if you immediately recognize one of the choices as the best answer, test that possibility by looking at the other choices. If you are uncertain about which choice is the best answer, first eliminate choices you think are least likely. Of the remaining choices, see if you can identify which parts of the answer choice are related to what the question is asking about. For example, some COOP questions ask about correct use of verbs. Therefore, focus on the verbs in the sentence. Similarly, HSPT questions about punctuation and capitalization should have you focusing on those areas. In HSPT spelling questions, each choice contains a word that is frequently misspelled. The correct answer contains the misspelled word. In the other answers, an often-misspelled word is spelled correctly. HSPT questions in this test always have "No mistakes" as choice **D**. Choose **D** if you find no errors in choices **A, B,** and **C.**

COOP Sample Questions

Directions: In the following questions, select the answer choice that best satisfies the question.

For questions 1–3, choose the word or phrase that best completes the sentence.

1. Nadia was the _____ of the five gymnasts on the team.

   A. talenteder
   B. more talented
   C. talentedest
   D. most talented

2. I didn't see the movie "Freddie and Jason" _____ I don't like horror films.

   F. being that
   G. because
   H. as if
   J. therefore

3. Last week Sarah _____ her horse in a jumping competition.

   A. rides
   B. ridden
   C. rided
   D. rode

For questions 4–7, choose the sentence that is correctly written.

4.
   F. The city having several ramps built a skateboard park.
   G. Having several ramps, the city built a skateboard park.
   H. The city built a skateboard park that had several ramps.
   J. The city it built a park that had skateboard ramps.

5.
   A. Reporters on television often appear at crime scenes.
   B. Appearing at crime scenes often, reporters on television.
   C. Often, reporters on television appear at crime scenes.
   D. At crime scenes reporters on television often appears.

6.

   F. My neighbor complained about my dog's barking because she is a writer who needs quiet to work.

   G. Because my neighbor is a writer who needs quiet to work, she complained about my dog's barking.

   H. Needing quiet to work because she is a writer, my dog barking caused my neighbor to complain.

   J. Because my neighbor needs quiet to work since she's a writer. She complained about my barking dog.

7.

   A. Tony enjoys the Harry Potter books, and he recommends them to his friends.

   B. Enjoying the Harry Potter books Tony recommends them to his friends.

   C. Tony enjoys the Harry Potter books and he recommends them to his friends.

   D. While Tony enjoys the Harry Potter books and recommends them to his friends.

For questions 8–10, choose the sentence that uses verbs correctly.

8.

   F. The meanings of words in foreign languages are not always clear to learners.

   G. The pronunciation of words that are unfamiliar are hard to learn.

   H. The idioms in American English creates difficulties for people learning to speak it.

   J. When Laura studied Russian, because it uses a different alphabet, it gives her problems.

9.

   A. After I finish this project, I was able to relax.

   B. Having worked on it for several weeks, I near the conclusion.

   C. I will feel a sense of accomplishment when it is complete.

   D. I expect that the money I earn for the work was spent on new clothes.

10.

   F. The candy was so good I could have eaten the whole box.

   G. Whenever Tod eats chocolate, he developed a rash.

   H. Both candy bars are made of nougat covered with caramel and coats with chocolate, but this one also contains peanuts.

   J. It was a well-known fact that President Reagan's favorite candy is jelly beans.

For questions 11–15, choose the underlined word that is the simple subject of the sentence.

11. Spending most of their time in <u>water</u>, <u>seals</u> are
                             [A]   [B]

    descended from <u>land</u> <u>animals.</u>
               [C]   [D]

12. The <u>breeding</u> <u>grounds</u> of <u>seals</u> are called <u>rookeries.</u>
        [F]   [G]   [H]   [J]

13. A <u>diving</u> <u>seal</u> can hold enough <u>air</u> in its lungs to
     [A]   [B]   [C]

    stay under <u>water</u> for several minutes.
           [D]

14. <u>Their</u> <u>flippers</u> help them to swim and are also used
    [F]   [G]

    like <u>legs</u> when they are on <u>land</u>.
        [H]   [J]

15. <u>There</u> are several <u>different</u> <u>species</u> of <u>seals</u>.
    [A]   [B]   [C]   [D]

For questions 16–20, choose the underlined word or group of words that is the simple predicate (verb) of the sentence.

16. Straining with effort, the little engine said,
[F]   [G]

"I think I can."
  [H] [J]

17. Because it was confident and persisted, the engine
[A]   [B]   [C]

succeeded.
[D]

18. Before replacing a lightbulb, you need to be sure
      [F]   [G]

you have turned the lamp off.
   [H]   [J]

19. Dorothy and her friends follow the yellow brick
                [A]

road while trying to reach Oz.
[B]   [C]   [D]

20. Wanting to return home safely, she asked the
[F]   [G]   [H]

wizard for help.
     [J]

For questions 21–23, choose the sentence that best combines the two given sentences into one.

21. Louis Chevrolet was a famous race-car driver in the early 1900s. The Chevrolet automobile was named for him.

  A. The Chevrolet automobile was named for Louis Chevrolet, a famous race-car driver in the early 1900s.
  B. Being that he was a famous race-car driver in the early 1900s, the Chevrolet automobile was named for Louis Chevrolet.
  C. Named after Louis Chevrolet, the Chevrolet automobile was a famous race-car driver in the early 1900s.
  D. In the early 1900s, the famous race-car driver and automobile were named Chevrolet.

22. Some chimney sweeps use dead trees for roosting and nesting. Most of these birds rely on chimneys to avoid predators.

  F. Although some chimney sweeps nest and roost in dead trees, most of these birds avoid predators by relying on chimneys as homes.
  G. Using dead trees for roosting and nesting, most chimney sweeps avoid predators in chimneys.
  H. Most chimney sweeps rely on chimneys to avoid predators, and they also roost and nest in dead trees.
  J. Avoiding predators, some chimney sweeps used dead trees to roost and nest and avoid predators and rely on chimneys.

23. Sherlock Holmes, the fictional detective, was created by Sir Arthur Conan-Doyle. He was a doctor and a writer.

  A. Sherlock Holmes, the fictional detective, created by Sir Arthur Conan-Doyle, a doctor and a writer.
  B. Sir Arthur Conan-Doyle was a doctor and a writer and he created the fictional detective Sherlock Holmes.
  C. Created by Sherlock Holmes, Sir Arthur Conan-Doyle was a doctor and a writer.
  D. Sherlock Holmes, the fictional detective, was created by Sir Arthur Conan-Doyle who was a doctor and a writer.

Answers and Explanations

1. **D.** Because more than two things are compared, the superlative form is needed. *Talented* is an adjective that uses *more* or *most* for comparative and superlative rather than adding *-er* or *-est*.

2. **G.** The sentence presents a reason in the second clause. *Being that*, **F,** is nonstandard usage to mean because.

3. **D.** Because the event occurred last week, the simple past tense is needed. The simple past tense of ride is rode.

4. **H.** In **F** and **G,** the city, not the park, has ramps. When a noun is the subject of the main verb, there is no need to use a pronoun to also refer to the subject, so the *it* in **J** is unnecessary.

5. **C.** This is the only choice with a clear meaning. In **A,** does *often* describe reporters who are on television or does it describe how frequently they appear at crime scenes? **B** is a sentence fragment. In **D,** the subject and verb do not agree.

6. **G.** **F** and **H** state that the dog is a writer. **J** begins with a sentence fragment.

7. **A.** **B** requires a comma after *books*. **C** requires a comma before *and*. **D** is a sentence fragment.

8. **F.** In **G** and **H,** the subject and verb do not agree. **J** shifts from past tense in the opening clause to present tense in the last clause.

9. **C.** Each of the other choices has a sequence of verb tenses that is not logical.

10. **F.** **G** shifts verb tenses. The verb *coats,* in **H,** has no subject; it should be *are coated.* **J** shifts from past to present tense, suggesting that the fact is no longer well known, when the meaning of the sentence is that when he was president, his favorite candy was jelly beans.

11. **B.** What is descended from land animals? Seals, not water.

12. **G.** The subject is never part of a prepositional phrase, so **H** is incorrect. **F,** *breeding,* is an adjective describing the subject.

13. **B.** **A** is an adjective describing the subject.

14. **G.** *Flippers* is the subject of both main verbs: *help* and *are used.*

15. **C.** In sentences starting with *there is* or *there are*, the subject follows the verb.

16. **G.** The main verb of a sentence cannot be in the object. *Think* and *can* are verbs in the clause that is the object of the verb *said.*

17. **D.** The main verb is in an independent clause, not in a subordinate or dependent clause.

18. **G.** A word ending in *-ing* cannot be a verb by itself, so **F** is incorrect. **H** is part of the object, and **J** is an adverb.

19. **A.** Because neither the *-ing* form nor the infinitive (*to* followed by the root verb) can be a verb by itself, **C** and **D** are incorrect.

20. **H.** In **J,** *help* is used as a noun, not a verb.

21. **A.** In choices **B** and **C,** the automobile is described as a race-car driver. In **D,** the relationship between the man and the name of the automobile is not explained.

22. **F.** **G** makes it appear that the predators live in the chimneys. **H** puts the most important idea first but does not explain its relationship to the second idea. **J** strings all the details together without explaining how they are related to each other.

23. **D.** **A** is a sentence fragment. **B** requires a comma after *writer*, but even if the comma was inserted, the sentence would merely put information in list form rather than explaining who did what. In **C,** The fictional detective created the writer, which obviously doesn't make sense.

HSPT Sample Questions

Directions: In the following questions, select the choice that best answers the question.

*In questions 1–5, look for errors in capitalization or punctuation. If you find no errors, mark **D** on your answer sheet.*

1.
   A. Why do the winners say "I'm going to Disneyland"?
   B. Do you think professional athletes really want to meet Mickey Mouse?
   C. Is winning a bigger thrill than a ride on the Matterhorn?
   D. No mistakes.

2.
   A. Lisa Simpson plays a saxophone.
   B. "Homer," Marge said, "what did you do with the box of doughnuts?"
   C. Bart the middle Simpson child is very mischievous.
   D. No mistakes.

3.
   A. Few people shop in the old section of town, and many of the stores have closed.
   B. "Isnt that your aunt I see across the street?"
   C. Believe it or not, the bakery was owned by Ms. Baker.
   D. No mistakes.

4.
   A. "What's for lunch" Simon asked?
   B. You'll find it hard to believe the story of that poorly done film.
   C. The three flavors in Neapolitan ice cream are vanilla, chocolate, and strawberry.
   D. No mistakes.

5.
   A. Why is the Notre Dame football team called The Fighting Irish?
   B. A college in California uses the banana slug as its mascot.
   C. Do the Boston Red Sox actually wear Red socks?
   D. No mistakes.

*In questions 6–10, look for errors in usage. If you find no errors, mark **D** on your answer sheet.*

6.
   A. Board games like Monopoly are fun to play.
   B. Think carefully before you give an opponent an opening for a triple word score when playing Scrabble.
   C. My friend and me learned to play video games more quickly by practicing.
   D. No mistakes.

7.
   A. The choice of brushes for painting are as important as the choice of paints.
   B. I haven't seen any of the films nominated for an Academy Award.
   C. Affected by a lack of rain, the crops dried up.
   D. No mistakes.

8.
   A. A flashing red light means the driver must stop.
   B. The boulder fell to the road as we rounded the curve with a crash.
   C. After I earned my driver's license, I was permitted to drive the car myself.
   D. No mistakes.

9.
   A. My friend did well on the math test.
   B. I should have studied Chapter 5, but I skipped over it.
   C. For me, history is the most interesting subject we study in school.
   D. No mistakes.

10.

    A. The final match at the U.S. Open Tennis Championship lasted for two hours.

    B. The title goes to the first player whom wins three sets.

    C. All the contestants practice for many hours before their matches.

    D. No mistakes.

*For questions 11–15, look for mistakes in spelling only. If you find no errors, mark **D** on your answer sheet.*

11.

    A. A driver was severely injured when his car ran into a telephone pole.

    B. Neither of the passengers was hurt.

    C. The class disgust how using the Internet helped with school assignments.

    D. No mistakes.

12.

    A. The bouncy rhythm of the song made me want to dance.

    B. Alex preferred hip-hop music.

    C. Jim cleaned his car thoroughly.

    D. No mistakes.

13.

    A. A new paint job improved the appearance of the old house.

    B. Ecru is the name of a color similar to beige.

    C. The player analysed the chess board before making a move.

    D. No mistakes.

14.

    A. All residents of the state over the age of 18 are eligible to vote.

    B. Encyclopedias are available on-line as well as in book form.

    C. Athletes use weights to develop their strength and endurance.

    D. No mistakes.

15.

    A. Helen wanted to major in mathematics when she went to college.

    B. I took my umbrella because the clouds suggested it would probaly rain today.

    C. Thunder and lightning meant the storm was approaching.

    D. No mistakes.

Answers and Explanations

1. **D.**

2. **C.** Commas are required around a parenthetical expression: *Bart, the middle Simpson child, is very mischievous.*

3. **B.** A contraction requires an apostrophe: *isn't.*

4. **A.** The question mark belongs in front of the closed quote, "What's for lunch?" rather than after the sentence, which is not a question.

5. **C.** The word *red* should not be capitalized in describing the color of the socks. It should be capitalized for the name of the team, Red Sox.

6. **C.** Use I as the subject of a verb even when the subject is a compound subject.

7. **A.** Singular subjects require singular verbs. The subject is *choice*, not *brushes* or *painting*. Those words are each part of a prepositional phrase. The subject is never part of a prepositional phrase.

8. **B.** Place describing words and phrases as close as possible to the words they describe. As the sentence is written, *with a crash* describes *we rounded the curve*, when it is meant to describe *the boulder fell to the road.*

9. **D.**

10. **B.** In the second clause in the sentence, the pronoun is the subject of the verb: *who wins three sets.*

11. **C.** Discussed

12. **D.**

13. **C.** Analyzed

14. **D.**

15. **B.** Probably

Composition

The HSPT has 10 questions under the heading Composition in the Language Skills test.

Answering Composition Questions

Composition questions involve the ability to see and recognize the main idea of a passage and to understand how the details of the passage support, prove, or describe the main idea. COOP and HSPT questions are similar. Some questions ask which sentence best represents the main idea or topic sentence of a paragraph, or ask what an appropriate title for the passage might be. Other questions ask which details best develop the topic sentence or which details least support a topic. One type of question asks which sentence does not belong in the paragraph. Still another type of question asks where in a paragraph a specific sentence should be placed or which sentence best fills a blank in a paragraph. Answering these questions requires good reading skills as well as an understanding of the principles of composition.

When answering questions that ask you to supply a topic sentence or title, look for a choice that covers all the details in the passage. But choose an answer that is as closely related as possible to the material. Choose a narrower rather than a broader answer. For example, if the paragraph is about events leading to the Boston Tea Party, a title like "The American Revolution" is too broad.

When answering questions that ask for the best details to develop the topic sentence, be careful not to choose answers that refer to the same subject in a general way. Look for answers that help to make the idea of the topic sentence clearer.

Look for clue words in the sentences and the answer choices to help you decide where in a paragraph a sentence belongs or to decide which sentence does not belong. If a sentence begins with a phrase like "as a result," it clearly has to follow a sentence stating a cause. If a sentence begins with the word "this," the previous sentence must contain something that "this" refers to.

Sample Questions

HSPT Directions: These questions deal with the subject of composition. Follow the directions for each question. (Note: The directions for each question are almost identical to the COOP directions in the following questions.)

COOP Directions: For questions 1–3, choose the topic sentence that best fits the paragraph.

1. Great Arab cities were places where new ideas circulated freely among scholars. Studies in medicine, astronomy, and science influenced European thought. Muslim, Christian, and Jewish scholars worked together in the royal courts.

   A. The Islamic religion has two major branches, Shia and Sunni.
   B. The fall of the Roman Empire led to a stagnant era in Europe.
   C. The city of Mecca is the most important religious site for Muslims.
   D. In the ninth century, the Islamic world was a center of knowledge and culture.

2. They create so much shade that few other trees grow near them. The tops of the trees are so high that they can't take up water from their roots. Instead, they absorb water from the heavy mists in the area.

   F. The ancient redwood trees in California coastal forests are extremely tall.
   G. California redwood trees can live for 2,000 years.
   H. The forest floor is covered with ferns and leaf mold.
   J. Some California redwood trees grow in Humboldt Redwoods State Park.

3. The press secretary to the president of the United States is a liaison between the president and reporters. A manufacturing engineer is a liaison between a product's designers and the workers who make the product. An interpreter could be called a liaison between two people who speak different languages.

   A. Liaison is a word that entered the English language from French.
   B. The word liaison can refer to a person who communicates information between two individuals or groups.
   C. The military services frequently use the word liaison to refer to a means of communicating between units.
   D. A liaison could also be called a connection.

For questions 4–6, choose the pair of sentences that best develops the topic sentence.

4. When our ancestors began to obtain food through farming, farmers in some areas had an advantage.

   F. Only a few species of wild plants and animals could be domesticated. These species were mostly natives of the Mideast, China, Mexico, the Andes, and Nigeria.
   G. People who were hunters and gatherers moved about frequently. Farming people began to settle in villages.
   H. Farmers chose to sow seeds from the wild plants that produced the best crops. They bred the animals with the strongest offspring.
   J. Because they were more successful at feeding their people, these societies became powerful. Because some of the people were not needed to produce food, they had time to invent new things.

5. Jackrabbits are not rabbits but members of the hare family.

   A. Some jackrabbits live in desert climates. The tiny blood vessels in their ears are so close to the skin that air blowing across them helps to cool the animal.
   B. The familiar figure of the Easter bunny is more like a rabbit than a hare. The Easter bunny is a gift giver, like Santa Claus.
   C. Rabbits were introduced to England in the twelfth century. They originally lived in western Mediterranean countries.
   D. Hares are larger than rabbits, and they have longer ears. Newborn rabbits are naked and helpless, but infant hares are covered with fur and are aware of their surroundings.

6. Chocolate is not only delicious; it can also be good for you.

   F. Chocolate was first used as a beverage by ancient people in Central America and Mexico. When the Spanish imported chocolate from those areas, they used it to treat heart disorders.

   G. Flavonoids are compounds found in red wine, grapes, apples, and tea. They are also found in chocolate.

   H. Recent studies have found that white chocolate and milk chocolate do not have the same health benefits as dark chocolate. So when you buy a candy bar, choose bittersweet or dark chocolate.

   J. Chocolate is rich in the minerals magnesium, copper, and manganese, all important in the human diet. Recent studies have shown that it contains flavonoids, compounds that lower blood pressure and protect the heart and arteries.

For questions 7–9, choose the sentence that does not belong in the paragraph.

7. (1) LEDs (light emitting diodes) are becoming common in flashlights and portable lamps. (2) These devices are more efficient than incandescent bulbs. (3) They produce light when an electric current is passed through a semiconductor crystal. (4) Because they last longer than incandescent bulbs, they save money. (5) Producing a strong steady beam of light, they use relatively small amounts of power.

   A. statement 2
   B. statement 3
   C. statement 4
   D. statement 5

8. (1) If you want to get close enough to wildlife to photograph animals in their natural habitat, you need to become as invisible to them as possible. (2) Everglades National Park, in Florida, is a unique habitat where wildlife can be photographed. (3) Rubbing dirt, ashes, or charcoal on your skin helps you blend into your surroundings. (4) Camouflage clothing, which mimics the random color patterns of foliage, also blends with the background. (5) Looking for animals in the afternoon or in predawn hours makes it possible to keep to the shadows, which makes it more difficult for the animals to see you.

   F. statement 1
   G. statement 2
   H. statement 4
   J. statement 5

9. (1) People often stereotype others, judging them based on their supposed association with a certain group. (2) For example, a person wearing glasses might immediately be assumed to be intelligent—or a nerd. (3) Stereotypes are reinforced by jokes, television, movies, and advertisements. (4) Unthinking comments by prejudiced people are another source of stereotypes. (5) One common stereotype of lawyers is that they are greedy and competitive.

    A. statement 1

    B. statement 2

    C. statement 4

    D. statement 5

Answers and Explanations

1. **D.** The sentences provide examples that show why the Islamic world at that time was a center of knowledge and culture.

2. **F.** The rest of the paragraph describes consequences arising from the trees' extreme height. While **J** looks like a possible choice, the content of the paragraph is about redwood trees generally. **J** suggests paragraph content related specifically to Humboldt Redwoods State Park.

3. **B.** The topic sentence defines the term, and the rest of the paragraph provides examples. **A** and **C** are true statements, but the content of the paragraph does not develop them. **D** defines the term, but it is not as clear as **B**.

4. **F.** These sentences explain what the advantage was and the areas in which it occurred. **G** describes a change that occurred when farming began, but does not give advantages. **H** explains what farmers did. **J** is about the effects of the advantage rather than explaining what the advantage was.

5. **D.** The topic sentence is a contrast. None of the other choices has information about the differences between hares and rabbits.

6. **J.** This is the only choice in which both sentences explain how chocolate can be good for your health.

7. **B.** The paragraph is about why LEDs are efficient. How they produce light is not necessary information.

8. **G.** The paragraph explains ways to become less visible. This choice gives an example of a place where wildlife can be photographed.

9. **D.** Although this is an example of stereotyping, it is not connected to the two sentences directly before it. They explain the sources of stereotypes.

Vocabulary

The HSPT has two types of vocabulary questions in the Verbal Skills test. There are 15 questions asking you to choose the best synonym for a word and 9 questions asking you to choose the best antonym for a word. In addition, the Reading—Vocabulary test has 22 questions asking you to select the word that means the same as a word given in the question.

Answering Vocabulary Questions

Before looking at the answer choices, think of your own definition of the word. If you can define the word, choosing the best answer should not be difficult. If you are uncertain about the meaning of a word, looking at the answer choices might remind you of a meaning that you didn't immediately think of. Or you might see answer choices that you know the meaning of and that do not seem to be related to the word in the question. If you have no idea of a word's meaning, you can at least eliminate answer choices that are a different part of speech than the word in the question. You might recognize that three of the answer choices are the same part of speech, and one of the answer choices is a different part of speech. It is probably safe to eliminate that as the best answer. Knowing common prefixes and suffixes is also helpful in trying to figure out the meaning of an unknown word.

Sample Questions

Directions: Select that choice that most nearly means the same as the selected word or phrase in the question.

1. Weird most nearly means:

   A. electric
   B. strange
   C. ordinary
   D. witch

2. A logical person is:

   A. thoughtful
   B. rational
   C. emotional
   D. thinking

3. Dawdle most nearly means:

   A. paint
   B. disgusting
   C. hurry up
   D. waste time

4. Habitat most nearly means:

   A. home
   B. natural
   C. repeated
   D. burrow

5. A pliable metal is:

   A. tool
   B. rigid
   C. flexible
   D. useful

6. Meandering is the *opposite* of:

   A. wandering
   B. measuring
   C. direct
   D. walking

7. Extinct is the *opposite* of:

   A. aroma
   B. frequent
   C. mortal
   D. living

8. Deplete is the *opposite* of:

   A. fold
   B. complete
   C. full
   D. increase

9. Agree is the *opposite* of:

   A. contradict
   B. predict
   C. discuss
   D. concur

10. Incredulous is the *opposite* of:

    A. skeptical
    B. believing
    C. terrible
    D. hoping

11. An envoy is an:

    A. assistant
    B. messenger
    C. planner
    D. expert

12. Being boorish is being:

    A. shy
    B. rude
    C. thieving
    D. cunning

13. To encompass is to:

    A. measure
    B. attempt
    C. include
    D. direct

14. To thwart is to:

    A. avoid
    B. accuse
    C. suffer
    D. block

15. To be wary is to be:

    A. sorrowful
    B. unfriendly
    C. lazy
    D. cautious

Answers and Explanations

1. B. Choice **A** means to trick you into misreading *weird* as *wired*. **C** is the opposite of *weird*. While a *witch,* **D,** might be weird, *witch* is a noun, and *weird* is an adjective.

2. B. **A** means considerate. **C** is the opposite of logical. **D** is the wrong part of speech.

3. D. Don't be confused by **C,** the opposite of *dawdle*.

4. A. A habitat is where something lives—its home. A *burrow,* **D,** is an example of a habitat. **C** tries to trick you into confusing *habitat* and *habit*.

5. C. Tools are made of metal, and metal is clearly useful, but neither of these defines the word. Something that is *pliable* can bend; it is *flexible*.

6. C. *Meandering* is an adjective meaning wandering aimlessly from place to place.

7. D. An *extinct* species no longer exists, so it is not alive.

8. D. To *deplete* means to use up something or to reduce the amount of it. To *increase,* to add to something, is the best opposite.

9. A. *Contradict* means to disagree, so it is the best opposite of *agree*.

10. B. *Incredulous* means unable to believe something. Do not confuse it with *incredible*, which means unbelievable, and is often incorrectly used to mean wonderful.

11. B. An envoy is a messenger.

12. B. To be boorish is to be rude.

13. C. To encompass is to include.

14. D. To thwart is to block.

15. D. To be wary is to be cautious.

COOP–HSPT Mathematics Review

The purpose of the math questions on both the COOP and the HSPT is to test your knowledge of the major topics and principles that you have been taught in school. Thus, the math topics that you are responsible for on these tests are, by and large, the same topics that you have been learning about in school: arithmetic, algebra, and geometry. Some of the problems test your knowledge of mathematical concepts, some test your computational skills, still others test your ability to solve mathematical word problems.

The section that follows contains a summary of the math that you need to know to answer the questions on the test. Solved problems are provided throughout so that you can test yourself on the required skills.

Review of Arithmetic

The Numbers of Arithmetic

Whole Numbers

The numbers 0, 1, 2, 3, 4, and so on are called *whole numbers*. The whole number system is a *place value* system; that is, the value of each digit in a whole number is determined by the place it occupies. For example, in the number 6,257, the 6 is in the thousands place, the 2 is in the hundreds place, the 5 is in the tens place, and the 7 is in the ones place.

The following table contains a summary of whole number place values:

Ones	1
Tens	10
Hundreds	100
Thousands	1,000
Ten-thousands	10,000
Hundred-thousands	100,000
Millions	1,000,000
Ten millions	10,000,000
Hundred millions	100,000,000
Billions	1,000,000,000

For example, the number 5,124,678 is read five million, one hundred twenty-four thousand, six hundred seventy-eight.

Example 1: Write the number thirty million, five hundred seven thousand, three hundred twelve.

30,507,312

Example 2: Write in words the number 34,521.

Thirty-four thousand, five hundred twenty-one

Rounding Whole Numbers

When you only need an approximate value of a whole number, the following procedure can be used to round off the number to a particular place:

Procedure for Rounding Whole Numbers:

1. Underline the digit in the place being rounded off.
2. If the digit to the right of the underlined digit is less than five, leave the underlined digit as it is. If the digit to the right of the underlined digit is equal to five or more, add one to the underlined digit.
3. Replace all digits to the right of the underlined digit with zeros.

Rounding whole numbers often helps you determine the correct answer to a multiple choice question more quickly.

Example 3: Round off the number 34,521 to the nearest hundred.

Because we are rounding to the nearest hundred, begin by underlining the digit in the hundreds place, which is a 5:

$$34,\underline{5}21$$

Now, look to the right of the underlined digit. Because the number to the right of the 5 is 2, leave the 5 as it is, and replace all digits to the right of the 5 with zeros.

$$34,500 \text{ is rounded to the nearest hundred.}$$

Example 4: Round off the number 236,789 to the nearest ten-thousand.

Because we are rounding to the nearest ten-thousand, begin by underlining the digit in the ten-thousands place, which is 3:

$$2\underline{3}6,789$$

Now, look to the right of the underlined digit. Because the number to the right of the 3 is 6, increase 3 by 1, obtaining 4, and replace all digits to the right of this 4 with zeros.

$$240,000 \text{ is rounded to the nearest ten-thousand.}$$

Fractions

A fraction is made up of two numbers, separated by a line that is known as a fraction bar. Typically, a fraction is used to represent a part of a whole. For example, in the following diagram, note that five out of eight pieces of the diagram are shaded:

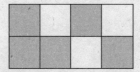

In this case, the fraction $\frac{5}{8}$ could be used to represent the fact that five of the eight equal pieces have been shaded. In the same way, the fraction $\frac{3}{8}$ could be used to represent the fact that three of the eight pieces have been left unshaded.

When the number on the top is *less than* the number on the bottom, fractions are said to be *proper*. Thus, the fractions $\frac{2}{9}$, $\frac{5}{8}$, and $\frac{3}{7}$ are proper fractions. The value of a proper fraction is always less than one.

When the number on the top is either *equal to* or *greater than* the number on the bottom, fractions are called *improper.* For example, the fractions $\frac{5}{2}$, $\frac{7}{4}$, and $\frac{11}{5}$ are improper. If the number on the top is greater than the number on the bottom, the value of the fraction is greater than one. If the number on the top and the number on the bottom are equal, such as in $\frac{8}{8}$, the value of the fraction is equal to one.

A *mixed number* is a whole number together with a fraction, such as $7\frac{1}{2}$ or $3\frac{5}{8}$. The mixed number $7\frac{1}{2}$ represents the number seven plus the fraction $\frac{1}{2}$. As we see later, every improper fraction can be written as a mixed number and vice versa.

Example 5: Classify the following numbers as proper fractions, improper fractions, or mixed numbers: $\frac{8}{9}$, $\frac{6}{6}$, $5\frac{2}{3}$, $\frac{6}{4}$, $\frac{112}{113}$.

The numbers $\frac{8}{9}$ and $\frac{112}{113}$ are proper fractions, the numbers $\frac{6}{6}$ and $\frac{6}{4}$ are improper fractions, and $5\frac{2}{3}$ is a mixed number.

Decimals

The numbers 10, 100, 1,000, 10,000, and so on, are called the *powers of 10.* Fractions like $\frac{7}{10}$, $\frac{59}{100}$, and $\frac{323}{1000}$, which have powers of 10 on the bottom, are called *decimal fractions* or *decimals.*

Decimals are typically written using a shorthand notation in which the number on the top of the fraction is written to the right of a dot, called a *decimal point.* The number on the bottom of the fraction is not written, but is indicated in the following way: If the number to the right of the decimal point contains one digit, the number on the bottom of the fraction is 10, if the number to the right of the decimal point contains two digits, the number on the bottom of the fraction is 100, and so on. Therefore, $\frac{7}{10} = .7$, $\frac{59}{100} = .59$, and $\frac{323}{1000} = .323$. The decimal .7 is read "point seven" or "seven tenths." In the same way, .59 is read "point fifty-nine" or "fifty-nine hundredths."

The following table contains a summary of decimal place values:

Tenths	0.1
Hundredths	0.01
Thousandths	0.001
Ten-thousandths	0.0001
Hundred-thousandths	0.00001
Millionths	0.000001

Thus, for example, the number 0.123 is read one hundred twenty-three thousandths.

Example 6: Write the number one hundred twelve millionths.

$$0.000112$$

Example 7: Write in words the number 0.5768

Five thousand, seven hundred sixty-eight ten-thousandths.

Example 8: Write the following fractions using decimal notation: $\frac{3}{10}$, $\frac{157}{1000}$, $\frac{7}{100}$.

$$\frac{3}{10} = .3, \frac{157}{1000} = .157, \text{ and } \frac{7}{100} = .07$$

Note that in the preceding example, a 0 must be placed between the decimal point and the 7 to indicate that the number on the bottom is 100.

Example 9: Write the following decimals as fractions: .7, .143, .079.

$$.7 = \frac{7}{10}, .143 = \frac{143}{1000}, \text{ and } .079 = \frac{79}{1000}$$

A number that consists of a whole number and a decimal is called a *mixed decimal*. The mixed decimal 354.56, for example, represents the mixed number $354\frac{56}{100}$.

Example 10: Write the following mixed decimals as mixed numbers: 76.3, 965.053.

$$76.3 = 76\frac{3}{10}, 965.053 = 965\frac{53}{1000}$$

Rounding Decimal Numbers

When you only need an approximate value of a decimal number, the following procedure can be used to round off the number to a particular place:

Procedure for Rounding Decimal Numbers:

1. Underline the digit in the place being rounded off.
2. If the digit to the right of the underlined digit is less than five, leave the underlined digit as it is. If the digit to the right of the underlined digit is equal to five or more, make the underlined digit one number bigger than it is.
3. Drop all digits to the right of the underlined digit.

As you can see, the procedure for rounding decimal numbers is very similar to the procedure for rounding whole numbers, except that digits to the right of the underlined digit can be dropped.

Example 11: Round off the number 0.18345 to the nearest hundredth.

Because we are rounding to the nearest hundredth, begin by underlining the digit in the hundredths place, which is an 8:

$$0.1\underline{8}345$$

Now, look to the right of the underlined digit. Because the number to the right of the 8 is 3, leave the 8 as it is, and drop all digits to the right of the 8.

$$0.18 \text{ is rounded to the nearest hundredth.}$$

Example 12: Round off the number 0.1437547 to the nearest thousandth.

Because we are rounding to the nearest thousandth, begin by underlining the digit in the thousandths place, which is a 3:

$$0.14\underline{3}7547$$

Now, look to the right of the underlined digit. Because the number to the right of the 3 is 7, increase the 3 by 1, obtaining 4, and remove all digits to the right of this 4.

$$0.144 \text{ is rounded to the nearest thousandth.}$$

Percents

A *percent* is a fraction whose bottom number is 100. Percents (the word percent means *per hundred*) are often written using a special symbol: %. For example, $\frac{67}{100}$ can be written 67%, and $\frac{3}{100}$ can be written 3%. Note that, just as every percent can be written as a fraction, every percent can also be written as a decimal. For example, $51\% = \frac{51}{100} = .51$, and $7\% = \frac{7}{100} = .07$.

A quick way to rewrite a percent as a decimal is to move the decimal point two places to the left and drop the percent sign. Thus, 35% = .35. In a similar way, to write a decimal as a percent, move the decimal point two places to the right and put in a percent sign. Thus, .23 = 23%.

Example 13: Write the following decimals as percents: .23, .08, 1.23.

$$.23 = 23\%, .08 = 8\%, 1.23 = 123\%$$

Example 14: Write the following percents as decimals: 17%, 2%, 224%.

$$17\% = .17, 2\% = .02, 224\% = 2.24$$

Arithmetic Operations

Addition, subtraction, multiplication, and division are called the Fundamental Operations of Arithmetic. In this section, the techniques for performing these operations on the numbers of arithmetic are reviewed.

Addition

Addition of Whole Numbers

When numbers are added, the result is called the *sum*. The first step in adding whole numbers is to line them up, placing ones under ones, tens under tens, hundreds under hundreds and so on. Then, add each column of numbers, beginning with the ones and moving to the tens, hundreds, thousands, and so on. If the sum of the digits in any column is 10 or more, write down the last figure of the sum as a part of the answer, and then "carry" the other figures into the next column.

For example, suppose you are asked to add 37, 64, and 151. Begin by lining up the numbers in columns as shown:

$$
\begin{array}{r}
37 \\
64 \\
+151 \\
\end{array}
$$

Now, add the digits in the ones column: 7 + 4 + 1 = 12. Because this number is more than 10, write the 2 below the units column in the answer, and carry the one over to the tens column.

$$
\begin{array}{r}
37 \\
64 \\
+151 \\
\hline
2 \\
\end{array}
$$

Now, add the 1 (that you carried over) to the other digits in the tens column: 1 + 3 + 6 + 5 = 15. Put the 5 below the tens column, and carry the remaining 1 to the hundreds column:

$$
\begin{array}{r}
37 \\
64 \\
+151 \\
\hline
52 \\
\end{array}
$$

Because 1 + 1 = 2, the final answer is 252:

$$
\begin{array}{r}
37 \\
64 \\
+151 \\
\hline
252 \\
\end{array}
$$

Example 15: Add 235, 654 and 12.

$$\begin{array}{r} 235 \\ 654 \\ +\ 12 \\ \hline 901 \end{array}$$

Addition of Decimals

Adding decimal numbers is also very straightforward. Simply line up the decimal points of the numbers involved, and add as you normally would. Suppose, for example, you wish to add 23.31, 19, and 3.125. Begin by writing the numbers in a column, lining up the decimal points:

$$\begin{array}{r} 23.31 \\ 19. \\ +\ 3.125 \end{array}$$

Note that the number 19 is a whole number, and, as such, the decimal point is to the right of the number; that is, 19 and 19.0 mean the same thing. If it helps you when you add these numbers, you can fill in the missing spaces to the right of the decimal points with 0's:

$$\begin{array}{r} 23.310 \\ 19.000 \\ +\ 3.125 \end{array}$$

Now, position a decimal point in the answer directly below the decimal points of the numbers in the problem:

$$\begin{array}{r} 23.310 \\ 19.000 \\ +\ 3.125 \\ \hline . \end{array}$$

Finish by adding as described previously:

$$\begin{array}{r} 23.310 \\ 19.000 \\ +\ 3.125 \\ \hline 45.435 \end{array}$$

Some problems on the test ask you to add money. Of course, to add money, just line up the decimal points, as shown previously, and add the money. For example, expenses of $23.25, $52.35 and $97.16 lead to a total expense of:

$$\begin{array}{r} \$\ 23.25 \\ \$\ 52.35 \\ +\$\ 97.16 \\ \hline \$172.76 \end{array}$$

Example 16: Add 23.56, 876.01, 34, and .007.

$$\begin{array}{r} 23.56 \\ 876.01 \\ 34 \\ +\quad .007 \end{array}$$

If you like, before doing the addition, you can put in some 0's so that all the numbers have the same number of digits:

$$\begin{array}{r} 23.560 \\ 876.010 \\ 34.000 \\ +\quad .007 \\ \hline 933.577 \end{array}$$

Example 17: If Brian buys three items priced at $3.45, $65.21, and $143.50, how much has he spent?

To find the answer to this problem, we need to add the three amounts spent:

$$\begin{array}{r} \$\ \ \ 3.45 \\ \$\ 65.21 \\ +\ \$143.50 \\ \hline \$212.16 \end{array}$$

Subtraction

Subtraction of Whole Numbers

When two numbers are subtracted, the result is called the *difference*. The first step in subtracting two whole numbers is to line them up, placing ones under ones, tens under tens, hundreds under hundreds, and so on. Then, subtract each column of numbers, beginning with the ones and moving to the tens, hundreds, thousands, and so on. If, in any step, the digit on the top is smaller than the digit on the bottom, add 10 to the digit on top by borrowing 1 from the figure directly to the left.

Let's take the following problem as an example:

$$\begin{array}{r} 567 \\ -382 \\ \hline \end{array}$$

The first step is, of course, to subtract two from seven. Because seven is bigger than two, no borrowing is necessary, so this step is easy:

$$\begin{array}{r} 567 \\ -382 \\ \hline 5 \end{array}$$

Now, we need to subtract the numbers in the tens column. Note that 6 is smaller than 8, so we need to borrow 1 from the 5 to the left of the 6. This makes the 6 into 16, and, by borrowing the 1 from the 5, it becomes 4, as shown:

$$\begin{array}{r} {\scriptstyle 4\ 1}\ \ \\ \cancel{5}67 \\ -382 \\ \hline 5 \end{array}$$

Next, we can subtract the 8 from the 16, which leaves us with 8. Finally, in the hundreds column, subtracting the 3 from the 4 leaves us with 1:

$$\begin{array}{r} {\scriptstyle 4\ 1}\ \ \\ \cancel{5}67 \\ -382 \\ \hline 185 \end{array}$$

Remember that if you want to check the answer to a subtraction problem, you can add the difference (that is, the answer) to the number you are subtracting, and see if you get the number you subtracted from. Because 185 + 382 = 567, we know we have the correct answer.

Example 18: Subtract 534 from 893.

$$\begin{array}{r} 893 \\ -534 \\ \hline 359 \end{array}$$

Subtraction of Decimals

Just as with addition of decimals, begin by lining up the decimal points of the two numbers involved. Then, place a decimal point for the answer directly below the decimal points of the two numbers. For example:

$$\begin{array}{r} 265.01 \\ -127.5 \\ \hline \end{array}$$

When performing a subtraction, it certainly helps to write in extra 0's so that both numbers have the same number of digits to the right of the decimal point.

$$\begin{array}{r} 265.01 \\ -127.50 \\ \hline 137.51 \end{array}$$

Of course, to subtract monetary amounts, line up the decimal points and subtract as usual. For example:

$$\begin{array}{r} \$324.56 \\ -\$34.07 \\ \hline \$290.49 \end{array}$$

Example 19: Jimmy pays a $14.51 dinner charge with a $20 bill. How much change does he receive?

Simply subtract $14.51 from $20.

$$\begin{array}{r} \$20.00 \\ -\$14.51 \\ \hline \$5.49 \end{array}$$

Multiplication

Multiplication of Whole Numbers

When two numbers are multiplied, the result is called the *product*. The first step in multiplying whole numbers is to line the numbers up, placing ones under ones, tens under tens, hundreds under hundreds, and so on. Now, consider two possible cases:

Case 1. If the number on the bottom of your multiplication contains a single digit, multiply every digit in the number on top by this digit. Start on the right, and move to the left. If, at any time, the result of a multiplication is a number that contains more than one digit, write down the ones digit of the number, and carry the tens digits over to the next column, to be added to the result of the multiplication in that column.

For example, suppose you need to multiply 542 by 3. Write the problem down as shown:

$$\begin{array}{r} 542 \\ \times3 \\ \hline \end{array}$$

Begin by multiplying 3 by 2, and write the result, which is 6, below the 3:

$$\begin{array}{r} 542 \\ \times3 \\ \hline 6 \end{array}$$

Next, multiply the 3 on the bottom by the 4 on the top. The result is 12. Write the ones digit from the 12 below the 4 in the problem, and carry the tens digit, which is 1, over to the next column:

$$\begin{array}{r} \overset{1}{5}42 \\ \times3 \\ \hline 26 \end{array}$$

Finally, multiply the 3 by the 5. The result of 15 should be added to the 1 that was carried from the previous column:

$$\begin{array}{r} \overset{1}{5}42 \\ \times\ \ \ 3 \\ \hline 1626 \end{array}$$

Case 2: If the number on the bottom contains more than one digit, begin as you did previously and multiply every digit on the top by the ones digit of the number on the bottom. Write the result in the usual spot. Then move over to the tens digit of the number on the bottom, and multiply each number on the top by this number. Write the result below your previous result, but position the ones digit of the result below the number you are multiplying by. Continue on to the hundreds digit, multiplying as usual, but positioning the ones digit of the result below the hundreds digit of the number on the bottom. Continue until you have multiplied the number on top by every digit on the bottom. Finish by adding together all the "partial products" you have written.

The following example illustrates the process discussed previously. To multiply 542 by 63, set up the problem as shown:

$$\begin{array}{r} 542 \\ \times\ 63 \\ \hline \end{array}$$

Begin exactly as you did in the preceding example, multiplying the 542 by 3. After doing this, you should have written:

$$\begin{array}{r} 542 \\ \times\ 63 \\ \hline 1626 \end{array}$$

Now, multiply the 542 by the 6 in the tens digit of the number on the bottom. Note that the result of this multiplication is 3,252. Also note how this number is positioned:

$$\begin{array}{r} 542 \\ \times\ 63 \\ \hline 1626 \\ 3252 \end{array}$$

Be very careful when multiplying to line up the numbers correctly. As the last step, add the 1,626 to the 3,252, as shown:

$$\begin{array}{r} 542 \\ \times\ 63 \\ \hline 1626 \\ 3252 \\ \hline 34,146 \end{array}$$

Example 20: Multiply 234 by 16.

$$\begin{array}{r} 234 \\ \times\ 16 \\ \hline 1404 \\ 234 \\ \hline 3744 \end{array}$$

Multiplication of Decimals

When we discussed addition and subtraction with decimals, we saw that the very first step in finding the answer is to correctly position the decimal point of the answer. When multiplying numbers with decimals, the procedure is almost exactly the opposite. Begin by ignoring the decimal points in the numbers you are multiplying, and figure out the answer as if the numbers involved were whole numbers. After you have done this, you can figure out where the decimal point in the answer goes.

To figure out where the decimal point in the answer goes, you need to do a little bit of counting. Begin by counting the total number of digits to the right of the decimal points in the two numbers you were multiplying. However many digits you count when you do this should also be the number of digits to the right of the decimal point in the answer.

A few examples make this procedure very clear. We previously solved the problem:

$$\begin{array}{r} 542 \\ \times\ \ 63 \\ \hline 1626 \\ 3252\ \ \\ \hline 34{,}146 \end{array}$$

Now, suppose that instead the problem had been:

$$\begin{array}{r} 5.42 \\ \times\ \ 6.3 \\ \hline \end{array}$$

Note that the number on the top contains two digits to the right of the decimal point and that the number on the bottom contains one digit to the right of the decimal point. To start, multiply as you normally would, ignoring the decimal points:

$$\begin{array}{r} 5.42 \\ \times\ \ 6.3 \\ \hline 1626 \\ 3252\ \ \\ \hline 34146 \end{array}$$

5.42   *Two digits to the right of the decimal point*
6.3   *One digit to the right of the decimal point*
34146   *Decimal point needs to be positioned*

Now, because we have a total of $2 + 1 = 3$ digits to the right of the decimal point in the two numbers we are multiplying, we need to have three digits to the right of the decimal point in the product:

$$\begin{array}{r} 5.42 \\ \times\ \ 6.3 \\ \hline 1626 \\ 3252\ \ \\ \hline 34.146 \end{array}$$

5.42   *Two digits to the right of the decimal point*
6.3   *One digit to the right of the decimal point*
34.146   *Three digits to the right of the decimal point in the answer*

That's all there is to it!

What if the problem had been instead:

$$\begin{array}{r} 5.42 \\ \times\ \ .63 \\ \hline \end{array}$$

In this case, we have a total of four digits to the right of the decimal point in the two numbers we are multiplying. Thus, the answer is not 34.146, but rather 3.4146.

Note that if you are multiplying an amount of money by a whole number, you can use the preceding process. Of course, when you do this, you have a total of two digits to the right of the decimal point in the two numbers you are multiplying, so the answer ends up looking like money—that is, it has two digits to the right of the decimal point.

Example 21: Multiply 23.4 by 1.6.

$$\begin{array}{r} 23.4 \\ \times\ \ 1.6 \\ \hline 1404 \\ 234\ \ \\ \hline 37.44 \end{array}$$

23.4   *One digit to the right of the decimal point*
1.6   *One digit to the right of the decimal point*
37.44   *Two digits to the right of the decimal point*

Example 22: John buys four calculators, each of which costs \$3.51. What is the total cost of the four calculators?

$$\begin{array}{r} \$3.51 \\ \times\ \ 4 \\ \hline \$14.04 \end{array}$$

\$3.51   *Two digits to the right of the decimal point*
4   *No digit to the right of the decimal point*
\$14.04   *Two digits to the right of the decimal point*

Division

Division of Whole Numbers

When one number is divided into another, the result is called the *quotient*. Division is probably the most complicated of the four fundamental arithmetic operations, but it becomes easier when you realize that the procedure for division consists of a series of four steps, repeated over and over again. The four steps are illustrated in the following sample problems.

Suppose, for example, you are asked to divide 7 into 245. Begin by writing the problem in the usual way:

$$7\overline{)245}$$

Now, for the first step, determine the number of times that 7 goes into 24. Because 7 goes into 24 three times (with something left over), begin by writing a 3 above the 4 in the division:

$$\begin{array}{r} 3 \\ 7\overline{)245} \end{array}$$

As a second step, multiply the 3 by the 7 to obtain 21 and write this product below the 24:

$$\begin{array}{r} 3 \\ 7\overline{)245} \\ 21 \end{array}$$

The third step is to subtract the 21 from the 24. When you do this, you get 3, of course. This should be written below the 21, as shown:

$$\begin{array}{r} 3 \\ 7\overline{)245} \\ -21 \\ \hline 3 \end{array}$$

The final step in the four-step process is to "bring down" the next digit from the number we are dividing into. This next (and last) digit is 5, so bring it down next to the 3:

$$\begin{array}{r} 3 \\ 7\overline{)245} \\ -21 \\ \hline 35 \end{array}$$

Now, the entire procedure starts over again. Divide 7 into 35. It goes in 5 times, so put a 5 next to the 3 in the solution.

$$\begin{array}{r} 35 \\ 7\overline{)245} \\ -21 \\ \hline 35 \end{array}$$

When you multiply and subtract, note that you end up with 0. This means that you have finished, and the quotient (answer) is 35:

$$\begin{array}{r} 35 \\ 7\overline{)245} \\ -21 \\ \hline 35 \\ -35 \\ \hline 0 \end{array}$$

The procedure for dividing by two digit numbers (or even larger numbers) is essentially the same, but involves a bit more computation. As an example, consider the following problem:

$$23\overline{)11408}$$

Note that 23 does not go into 11, so we have to start with 114. To determine how many times 23 goes into 114, you are going to have to estimate. Perhaps you might think that 23 is almost 25, and that it seems as if 25 goes into 114 four times. So, let's try 4. Write a 4 on top, and multiply, subtract, and bring down in the usual way:

$$
\begin{array}{r}
4 \\
23{\overline{\smash{)}11408}} \\
-92 \\
\hline
220
\end{array}
$$

Continue, as before, by trying to estimate the number of times 23 goes into 220. If you try 9, things continue rather nicely:

$$
\begin{array}{r}
49 \\
23{\overline{\smash{)}11408}} \\
-92 \\
\hline
220 \\
-207 \\
\hline
138
\end{array}
$$

As a final step, estimate that 23 goes into 138 six times:

$$
\begin{array}{r}
496 \\
23{\overline{\smash{)}11408}} \\
-92 \\
\hline
220 \\
-207 \\
\hline
138 \\
-138 \\
\hline
0
\end{array}
$$

If at any step you make the incorrect estimate, simply modify your estimate and start over. For example, suppose that in the last step of the preceding example, you had guessed that 23 goes into 138 seven times. Look what would have happened:

$$
\begin{array}{r}
497 \\
23{\overline{\smash{)}11408}} \\
-92 \\
\hline
220 \\
-207 \\
\hline
138 \\
-161 \\
\hline
\end{array}
$$

Because 161 is larger than 138, it means that you have over estimated. Try again, with a smaller number.

Example 23: Divide 12 into 540.

$$
\begin{array}{r}
45 \\
12{\overline{\smash{)}540}} \\
-48 \\
\hline
60 \\
-60 \\
\hline
0
\end{array}
$$

Remember that division problems can always be checked by multiplying. In this case, because $12 \times 45 = 540$, we know we have the right answer.

Division with Decimals

Recall that when we added and subtracted with decimals, we began by positioning the decimal point for the answer, and then added or subtracted as usual. When you are dividing a whole number into a decimal number, the idea is similar; begin by putting a decimal point for the quotient (answer) directly above the decimal point in the number you are dividing into. Then divide as normal. So, for example, if you need to divide 4 into 142.4, begin as shown:

$$4\overline{)142.4}$$ *Note the decimal point positioned*
above the decimal point in 142.4

Now, divide in the usual way:

$$
\begin{array}{r}
35.6 \\
4\overline{)142.4} \\
-12 \\
\hline
22 \\
-20 \\
\hline
24 \\
-24 \\
\hline
0 \\
\end{array}
$$

That's all that there is to it.

Example 24: A dinner bill of $92.80 is shared equally between four friends. How much does each friend pay?

To find the answer, we need to divide $92.80 by 4.

$$
\begin{array}{r}
23.20 \\
4\overline{)92.80} \\
-8 \\
\hline
12 \\
-12 \\
\hline
08 \\
-8 \\
\hline
00 \\
-0 \\
\hline
0 \\
\end{array}
$$

Number Theory

Factors

Remember that earlier we defined *whole numbers* as the set of numbers 0, 1, 2, 3, 4, 5, and so on. We are now going to look at some of the properties of whole numbers, and then of the set of numbers called the *integers*.

To begin, a *factor* of a given whole number is any number that can be used in a multiplication that results in the given whole number. For example, consider the whole number 24. Both 6 and 4 are factors of 24 because $6 \times 4 = 24$. Further, both 2 and 12 are factors of 24 because $2 \times 12 = 24$. Technically, both 1 and 24 are also factors of 24 because $1 \times 24 = 24$.

To determine whether a particular number is a factor of a given whole number, simply divide the number into the given whole number. If no remainder exists, the number is a factor.

Example 25: Is 8 a factor of 72?

To determine whether 8 is a factor of 72, divide 8 into 72. Because it goes in evenly (9 times), 8 is a factor of 72.

Example 26: If 13 is a factor of 91, determine another factor other than 1 and 91.

We are told that 13 is a factor of 91, so we know that if we divide 13 into 91 it goes in evenly. If we do this division, we get:

$$13\overline{)91} \quad 7$$

Thus, $13 \times 7 = 91$, so 7 is another factor of 91.

Common Factors

A number that is a factor of two different whole numbers is called a *common factor,* or a *common divisor,* of those numbers. As the following examples show, two given whole numbers might have no common factors (other than, of course, 1), or they might have one or more. If two numbers have several common factors, the largest one is called the *greatest common factor.*

Example 27: Find all the common factors and the greatest common factor of 36 and 48.

   The factors of 36 are 1, 2, 3, 4, 6, 9, 12, 18, and 36.
   The factors of 48 are 1, 2, 3, 4, 6, 8, 12, 16, 32, and 48.
   The common factors of 36 and 48 are 1, 2, 3, 4, 6, and 12.
   The greatest common factor is 12.

Example 28: Find all the common factors of 35 and 66.

   The factors of 35 are 1, 5, 7, and 35.
   The factors of 66 are 1, 2, 3, 6, 11, 22, 33, and 66.
   The only common factor is 1.

Prime Numbers

Obviously, every number has at least two factors: the number itself and 1. Some other numbers have additional factors as well. For example, the number 14 not only has 1 and 14 as factors, but also 2 and 7 because $2 \times 7 = 14$.

Numbers that have no additional factors other than themselves and 1, are known as *prime numbers.* An example of a prime number is 13. While 1 and 13 divide evenly into 13, no other whole numbers divide evenly into 13.

By definition, the smallest prime number is 2. The first 10 prime numbers are:

$$2, 3, 5, 7, 11, 13, 17, 19, 23, 29$$

To determine if a number is prime or not, you need to find out whether any whole numbers (other than the number itself and 1) divide evenly into the number.

Example 29: Which of the following numbers are prime: 33, 37, 39, 42, 43?

> 33 is not prime because $33 = 3 \times 11$.
>
> 37 is prime; it has no factors other than 1 and 37.
>
> 39 is not prime because $39 = 3 \times 13$.
>
> 42 is not prime because $42 = 2 \times 21$ or 6×7, and so on.
>
> 43 is prime; it has no factors other than 1 and 43.

A number that is not prime, is called a *composite* number. Any composite number can be *prime factored;* that is, it can be written as a product of prime numbers (excluding 1) in one and only one way. For example, 35 is a composite number, and can be prime factored as 5×7. The number 12 is also composite. Note that 2×6 is a factorization of 12, but is not the prime factorization because 6 is not prime. The prime factorization of 12 is $2 \times 2 \times 3$. The quickest way to prime factor a number is to break the number up as a product of two smaller numbers, and then to break these two numbers up, until you are left with only prime numbers. The following example illustrates this process.

Example 30: Prime factor the number 150.

By inspection, you can see that 150 can be factored as 15×10. This is not the prime factorization, however, as neither 15 nor 10 is prime. The number 15, however, can be further broken down as $15 = 3 \times 5$, and both 3 and 5 are prime. The number 10 can be further broken down as $10 = 2 \times 5$, and both 2 and 5 are prime. Therefore, the number 150 can be prime factored as $3 \times 5 \times 2 \times 5$. When prime factoring numbers, it is standard to rearrange the factors so that the numbers are in increasing order. Therefore, the prime factorization of 150 can best be expressed as $2 \times 3 \times 5 \times 5$.

Example 31: What are the prime factors of 54?

You can begin by writing 54 as, for example, 2×27. The number 2 is prime, but 27 is not, so it can be further factored. Because 27 is 3×9, we get $54 = 2 \times 3 \times 9$. Now, 3 is prime, but 9 is not, so we need to factor the 9. The only way to do this is $9 = 3 \times 3$, so the prime factorization of 54 is $2 \times 3 \times 3 \times 3$. Thus, the prime factors of 54 are 2 and 3.

Multiples

A multiple of a given whole number is a number that results from the multiplication of the given whole number by another whole number factor. For example, the multiples of 7 are 7, 14, 21, 28, 35, 42, 49 and so on because $7 = 7 \times 1$, $14 = 7 \times 2$, $21 = 7 \times 3$ and so on.

A *common multiple* of two numbers is a number that is a multiple of both of the numbers. For example, 32 is a common multiple of 8 and 16 because it is a multiple of both 8 and 16. Should you ever need to find a common multiple of two numbers, one quick way to find one is to multiply the two numbers together. For example, a common multiple of 4 and 10 is $4 \times 10 = 40$. Note, however, that 40 is not the smallest common multiple of 4 and 10 because 20 is also a common multiple.

The smallest common multiple of two numbers is called the *least common multiple,* abbreviated LCM. A quick way to find the LCM of two numbers is to write out the first several multiples of each number, and then find the smallest multiple that they have in common. The following examples show how to do this.

Example 32: Find the first 8 multiples of 11.

To answer this question, we simply need to compute 11×1, 11×2, 11×3 and so on. The first 8 multiples are 11, 22, 33, 44, 55, 66, 77 and 88.

Example 33: Find the least common multiple of 3 and 8.

The first several multiples of 3 are 3, 6, 9, 12, 15, 18, 21, 24 and 27.

The first several multiples of 8 are 8, 16, 24 and 32.

Clearly, the LCM is 24, which in this case is the same as the product of 3 and 8.

Example 34: Find the LCM of 6 and 9.

The first several multiples of 6 are 6, 12, 18, 24 and 30.

The first several multiples of 9 are 9, 18, 27 and 36.

Clearly, the LCM is 18, which in this case is less than $6 \times 9 = 54$.

Exponents

As we saw previously, the numbers used in multiplication are called factors. Whenever the same factor is repeated more than once, a special shorthand, called *exponential notation,* can be used to simplify the expression. In this notation, the repeated factor is written only once; above and to the right of this number is written another number that is called the *exponent,* or *power,* indicating the number of times the base is repeated.

For example, instead of writing 7×7, we can write 7^2. This expression is read "seven to the second power," or more simply, "seven squared," and it represents the fact that the seven is multiplied by itself two times. In the same way, $5 \times 5 \times 5 \times 5$ can be written as 5^4, which is read "five to the fourth power," or simply "five to the fourth."

Recall that previously, we prime factored the number 150 and obtained $2 \times 3 \times 5 \times 5$. It is more common (and a bit simpler) to write this prime factorization using exponential notation as $2 \times 3 \times 5^2$.

Example 35: What is the value of 3^5?

Based on the preceding definition, 3^5 represents $3 \times 3 \times 3 \times 3 \times 3 = 243$.

Example 36: Simplify the expression $a \times a \times a \times a \times b \times b \times b \times b \times b \times b \times b$ by using exponential notation.

Because we have four factors of a and seven factors of b, the expression is equal to $a^4 \times b^7$.

Example 37: Prime factor the number 72, and write the prime factorization using exponential notation.

Begin by prime factoring the number 72. One way to do this is as follows:

$72 = 2 \times 36 = 2 \times 6 \times 6 = 2 \times 2 \times 3 \times 2 \times 3 = 2 \times 2 \times 2 \times 3 \times 3$. Then, writing this using exponents, we get $2^3 \times 3^2$.

Square Roots

The *square root* of a given number is the number whose square is equal to the given number. For example, the square root of 25, is the number that yields 25 when multiplied by itself. Clearly, this number is 5 because $5 \times 5 = 25$. The square root of 25 is denoted by the symbol $\sqrt{25}$.

The square roots of most numbers turn out to be messy, infinite nonrepeating decimal numbers. For example, $\sqrt{2}$ is equal to 1.414213562. . . . When such numbers appear on the test, you are able to leave them in what is known as *radical form;* that is, if the answer to a problem is $\sqrt{2}$, you can express the answer as $\sqrt{2}$, without worrying about its value.

Certain numbers, however, have nice whole-number square roots. Such numbers are called *perfect squares*. You should certainly be familiar with the square roots of the first 10 or so perfect squares. They are shown in the following table:

Perfect Square	Square Root
1	$\sqrt{1} = 1$
4	$\sqrt{4} = 2$
9	$\sqrt{9} = 3$
16	$\sqrt{16} = 4$
25	$\sqrt{25} = 5$
36	$\sqrt{36} = 6$
49	$\sqrt{49} = 7$
64	$\sqrt{64} = 8$
81	$\sqrt{81} = 9$
100	$\sqrt{100} = 10$

From time to time, you might be asked to find the *cube root* of a number. The cube root is defined in a way similar to that of the square root. For example, the cube root of eight is the number that when multiplied by itself three times, is equal to eight. Clearly, the cube root of eight is two because $2 \times 2 \times 2 = 8$. A special notation also exists for the cube root. The cube root of eight is written as $\sqrt[3]{8}$. Therefore, $\sqrt[3]{8} = 2$.

Just as perfect squares have nice whole-number square roots, *perfect cubes* have whole-number cube roots. You don't really have to learn many of these, as they become large very quickly, but it is helpful to know the cube roots of the first five perfect cubes. The following table gives the values for the these numbers.

Perfect Cube	Cube Root
1	$\sqrt[3]{1} = 1$
8	$\sqrt[3]{8} = 2$
27	$\sqrt[3]{27} = 3$
64	$\sqrt[3]{64} = 4$
125	$\sqrt[3]{125} = 5$

Example 38: What is the value of $\sqrt{81} \times \sqrt{36}$?

Because $\sqrt{81} = 9$ and $\sqrt{36} = 6$, $\sqrt{81} \times \sqrt{36} = 9 \times 6 = 54$.

Example 39: What is the value of $12\sqrt{49}$?

To begin, you must know that $12\sqrt{49}$ is shorthand for $12 \times \sqrt{49}$. Because $\sqrt{49} = 7$, $12\sqrt{49} = 12 \times 7 = 84$.

The Order of Operations

Whenever a numerical expression contains more than one mathematical operation, the order in which the operations are performed can affect the answer. For example, consider the simple expression $2 + 3 \times 5$. On one hand, if the addition is performed first, the expression becomes $5 \times 5 = 25$. On the other hand, if the multiplication is performed first, the expression becomes $2 + 15 = 17$. To eliminate this ambiguity, mathematicians have established a procedure that makes the order in which the operations need to be performed specific. This procedure is called the *Order of Operations*, and is stated here:

The Order of Operations:

1. Perform all operations in parentheses or any other grouping symbol.
2. Evaluate all exponents and roots.
3. Perform all multiplications and divisions in the order they appear in the expression, from left to right.
4. Perform all additions and subtractions in the order they appear in the expression, from left to right.

Note that the Order of Operations consists of four steps. A common acronym to help you remember these steps is PEMDAS: parentheses, exponents, multiplication and division, addition and subtraction. If you choose to memorize this acronym, be careful. The expression PEMDAS might make it appear as if the Order of Operations has six steps, but it actually has only four. In the third step, all multiplications and divisions are done in the order they appear. In the fourth step, all additions and subtractions are done in the order they appear. The following examples make this clear.

Example 40: Evaluate the expression $18 - 6 \div 3 \times 7 + 4$.

Resist the temptation to begin by subtracting 6 from 18. Because this expression contains no parentheses and no roots, begin by starting on the left and performing all multiplications and divisions in the order they occur. This means that the division must be performed first. Because $6 \div 3 = 2$, we obtain:

$$18 - 6 \div 3 \times 7 + 4 = 18 - 2 \times 7 + 4$$

Next, we do the multiplication:

$$18 - 2 \times 7 + 4 = 18 - 14 + 4$$

Finally, we subtract, and then add:

$$18 - 14 + 4 = 4 + 4 = 8$$

Example 41: Evaluate $14 - 2(1 + 5)$.

To begin, the operation in parentheses must be performed. This makes the expression $14 - 2(6)$. Now, remember that a number written next to another number in parentheses, such as $2(6)$, is a way of indicating multiplication. Because multiplication comes before subtraction in the Order of Operations, we multiply $2(6)$ to get 12. Finally, $14 - 12 = 2$.

Example 42: Evaluate $5^3 - 3(8 - 2)^2$

The first operation to perform is the one in parentheses, which gives us $5^3 - 3(6)^2$.

Next, evaluate the two exponents: $125 - 3(36)$. We now multiply, and then finish by subtracting: $125 - 108 = 17$.

Operations with Integers

When we include the negatives of the whole numbers along with the whole numbers, we obtain the set of numbers called the *integers*. Therefore, the integers are the set of numbers:

$$\ldots -4, -3, -2, -1, 0, 1, 2, 3, 4, \ldots$$

The ellipses to the left and right indicate that the numbers continue forever in both directions.

Up to this point, when we have talked about adding, subtracting, multiplying and dividing, we have always been working with positive numbers. However, you are just as likely to have to compute with negative numbers as positive numbers. Therefore, let's take a look at how mathematical operations are performed on positive *and* negative numbers; that is, how mathematical operations are performed on *signed* numbers.

Adding Positive and Negative Numbers

Two different circumstances must be considered as we discuss how to add positive and negative numbers. The first circumstance is how to add two signed numbers with the same sign. If the numbers that you are adding have the same sign, simply add the numbers in the usual way. The sum, then, has the same sign as the numbers you have added. For example,

$$(+4) + (+7) = +11$$

This, of course, is the usual positive number addition you are used to.

$$(-5) + (-9) = -14$$

In this problem, because the signs of the two numbers we are adding are the same, simply add them ($5 + 9 = 14$). The result is negative because both numbers are negative. It might help to think of positive numbers as representing a gain, and negative numbers as representing a loss. In this case, $(-5) + (-9)$ represents a loss of 5 followed by a loss 9, which, of course, is a loss of 14.

Now, what if you have to add two numbers with different signs? Again, the rule is simple. Begin by ignoring the signs, and subtract the two numbers: the smaller from the larger. The sign of the answer is the same as the sign of the number with the larger size.

For example, to compute $(+9) + (-5)$, begin by computing $9 - 5 = 4$. Because 9 is bigger than 5, the answer is positive, or +4. You can think of the problem in this way: A gain of 9 followed by a loss of 5 is equivalent to a gain of 4.

On the other hand, to compute $(-9) + (+5)$, begin in the same way by computing $9 - 5 = 4$. This time, however, the larger number is negative, so the answer is –4. In other words, a loss of 9 followed by a gain of 5 is equivalent to a loss of 4.

Example 43: $(+6) + (-8) + (+12) + (-4)$

Two ways can be used to evaluate this expression. One way is to simply perform the additions in order from left to right. To begin, $(+6) + (-8) = -2$. Then, $(-2) + (+12) = +10$. Finally, $(+10) + (-4) = +6$.

The other way to solve the problem, which might be a bit faster, is to add the positive numbers, then add the negative numbers, and then combine the result. In this case, $(+6) + (+12) = +18$; $(-8) + (-4) = -12$, and finally, $(+18) + (-12) = +6$.

Subtracting Positive and Negative Numbers

The easiest way to perform a subtraction on two signed numbers is to change the problem to an equivalent addition problem, that is, an addition problem with the same answer. To do this, you simply need to change the sign of the second number and add instead of subtract. For example, suppose you need to compute $(+7) - (-2)$. This problem has the same solution as the addition problem $(+7) + (+2)$ and is therefore equal to +9. Take a look at the following samples that help clarify this procedure:

Determine the value of $(-7) - (+2)$.

To evaluate this, we make it into an equivalent addition problem by changing the sign of the second number. Therefore:

$$(-7) - (+2) = (-7) + (-2) = -9$$

In the same way, we see that $(-7) - (-2) = (-7) + (+2) = -5$.

Example 44: Find the value of $(-7) - (+4) - (-3) + (-1)$.

Begin by rewriting the problem with all subtractions expressed as additions:

$$(-7) - (+4) - (-3) + (-1) = (-7) + (-4) + (+3) + (-1)$$

Now, just add the four numbers in the usual way:

$$(-7) + (-4) + (+3) + (-1) = (-11) + (+3) + (-1) = -8 + (-1) = -9.$$

Multiplying and Dividing Positive and Negative Numbers

An easy way to multiply (or divide) signed numbers is to begin by ignoring the signs, and multiply (or divide) in the usual way. Then, to determine the sign of the answer, count up the number of negative signs in the original problem. If the number of negative signs is even, the answer is positive; if the number of negative signs is odd, the answer is negative. For example, $(-2) \times (+3) = -6$ because the original problem has one negative sign. However, $(-2) \times (-3) = +6$ because the original problem has two negative signs.

What about the problem $(-4) \times (-2) \times (-1) \times (+3)$? First of all, ignoring the signs and multiplying the four numbers, we get 24. Because the problem has a total of three negative signs, the answer must be negative. Therefore, the answer is -24.

Division works in exactly the same way. For example, $(-24) \div (+6) = -4$, but $(-24) \div (-6) = +4$.

Example 45: Find the value of $\dfrac{(-6)(+10)}{(-2)(-5)}$.

The easiest way to proceed with this problem is to evaluate the number on the top and the number on the bottom separately, and then divide them. Because $(-6)(+10) = -60$, and $(-2)(-5) = +10$, we have $\dfrac{(-6)(+10)}{(-2)(-5)} = \dfrac{-60}{+10} = -6$.

Example 46: $(-5)(-2)(+4) - 6(-3) =$

The multiplications in this problem must be done before the subtractions. Because:

$(-5)(-2)(+4) = 40$, and $6(-3) = -18$, we have:

$$(-5)(-2)(+4) - 6(-3) = 40 - (-18) = 40 + 18 = 58.$$

Negative Numbers and Exponents

Be a little bit careful when evaluating negative numbers raised to powers. For example, if you are asked to find the value of $(-2)^8$, the answer is positive because we are technically multiplying eight -2s. For a similar reason, the value of $(-2)^9$ is negative.

Also, you must be careful to distinguish between an expression like $(-3)^2$ and one like -3^2. The expression $(-3)^2$ means -3×-3 and is equal to $+9$, but -3^2 means $-(3^2)$, which is equal to -9.

Example 47: Evaluate $-2^4 - (-2)^2$.

Evaluating the exponents first, we get $-2^4 - (-2)^2 = -16 - (4) = -16 + -4 = -20$.

Example 48: Find the value of $\dfrac{(-3)^3 + (-2)(-6)}{-5^2 + (-19)(-1)}$.

Again, let's determine the values of the top and bottom separately, and then divide. To begin, $(-3)^3 = -27$, and $(-2)(-6) = +12$, so the value on the top is $-27 + 12 = -15$. On the bottom, we have $-25 + 19 = -6$. Therefore:

$$\frac{(-3)^3 + (-2)(-6)}{-5^2 + (-19)(-1)} = \frac{-15}{-6} = \frac{15}{6} = 2.5$$

Operations with Fractions

It is now time to review how to perform arithmetic operations on fractions.

Equivalent Fractions

You probably remember learning a procedure called *reducing* or *simplifying* fractions. Simplifying a fraction refers to rewriting it in an equivalent form, with smaller numbers. As an easy example, consider the fraction $\frac{5}{10}$. This fraction can be simplified by dividing the top and bottom by the number 5. If we do this division, we get $\frac{5}{10} = \frac{5 \div 5}{10 \div 5} = \frac{1}{2}$. Thus, $\frac{5}{10}$ and $\frac{1}{2}$ have the same value, but $\frac{1}{2}$ is in simpler form.

In general, to simplify a fraction, you need to find a number that divides evenly into both the top and bottom, and then do this division. Sometimes, after you divide by one number, you might notice another number you can further divide by. As an example, suppose you wish to simplify $\frac{12}{18}$. The first thing that you might notice is that the top and bottom can be divided by 2. If you do this division, you get the fraction $\frac{6}{9}$. Now, this fraction can be further divided by 3, and if you do this division, you get the fraction $\frac{2}{3}$. Because no other numbers (except 1, of course) can divide evenly into the top and bottom, we have reduced the fraction to its *lowest terms*. If a problem on one of the tests has a fractional answer, you should always reduce the answer to its lowest terms.

Just as you can reduce a fraction to lower terms by dividing the top and bottom by the same number, you can raise a fraction to *higher terms* by multiplying the top and bottom by the same number. For example, consider the fraction $\frac{3}{4}$. If we multiply the top and bottom by 2, we get $\frac{6}{8}$. If we instead multiply the top and bottom by 5, we get $\frac{15}{20}$. The fractions $\frac{6}{8}$ and $\frac{15}{20}$ are two different ways to write $\frac{3}{4}$ in higher terms. As we see in the next section, it is often necessary to raise fractions to higher terms to add and subtract them.

Example 49: Express the fraction $\frac{12}{15}$ in lowest terms.

It is easy to see that the number 3 can be divided evenly into both the numerator (the number on top of the fraction bar) and the denominator (the number on the bottom). Performing this division, we get $\frac{12}{15} = \frac{12 \div 3}{15 \div 3} = \frac{4}{5}$, which is in lowest terms.

Example 50: Rewrite the fraction $\frac{2}{3}$ as an equivalent fraction with a denominator of 21.

To change the denominator of 3 to 21, we need to multiply by 7. Because we need to perform the same operation to the numerator as well, we get $\frac{2}{3} = \frac{2 \times 7}{3 \times 7} = \frac{14}{21}$.

Adding and Subtracting Fractions

You probably recall that the number on the top of a fraction is called the *numerator* and the number on the bottom of a fraction is called the *denominator*. If two fractions have the same denominator, they are said to have *common denominators*.

Adding or subtracting two fractions with common denominators is easy. Simply add the numerators and retain the common denominator. For example,

$$\frac{2}{9} + \frac{5}{9} = \frac{7}{9} \text{ and } \frac{7}{8} - \frac{5}{8} = \frac{2}{8} = \frac{1}{4}$$

Note that, in the subtraction problem, we get a fraction that can be simplified, and we perform the simplification before finishing.

If you need to add or subtract two fractions that do not have the same denominator, you need to begin by raising them to higher terms so that they do have a common denominator. The first step in this process is determining a common denominator for the two fractions. For example, suppose that you are asked to add $\frac{3}{4} + \frac{1}{3}$. You need to find a common denominator for 4 and 3. Actually, an infinite number of common denominators exist for 4 and 3. Some of them are 24, 36, and 48. While you can work with any of these denominators, it is easiest to work with the smallest one, which in this case is 12. This number is called the *least common denominator* of 4 and 3, and it is actually the same number as the least common multiple (LCM), which has already been discussed. Thus, the least common denominator can be found by using the same process we used to find the LCM previously.

When we know the least common denominator (LCD), we simply need to multiply the top and bottom of each fraction by the appropriate number to raise the denominators to the LCD. For example:

$$\frac{3}{4} + \frac{1}{3} = \frac{3}{3} \times \frac{3}{4} + \frac{4}{4} \times \frac{1}{3} = \frac{9}{12} + \frac{4}{12} = \frac{13}{12}$$

Note that the answer, $\frac{13}{12}$, is an improper fraction. Any improper fraction can also be written as a mixed number by dividing the denominator into the numerator, and writing the remainder as the numerator of a fraction with the original denominator. In this case, 12 goes into 13 one time with a remainder of 1, so $\frac{13}{12} = 1\frac{1}{12}$, which is another way to write the answer to the question.

Note that this process can also be reversed. So, for example, the mixed number $2\frac{1}{5}$ can be written as an improper fraction. The denominator is the same, that is, 5, and the numerator is the denominator times the whole number plus the numerator; that is, $5 \times 2 + 1 = 11$. Therefore, $2\frac{1}{5} = \frac{11}{5}$. Often, when performing operations on mixed numbers, it is helpful to write them as improper fractions. The upcoming examples illustrate this.

Example 51: Add $2\frac{3}{5} + 3\frac{1}{7}$.

You can proceed in two ways. You can write both mixed numbers as improper fractions and add, but it is quicker to just add the whole number part ($2 + 3 = 5$) and the fractional part: $\frac{3}{5} + \frac{1}{7} = \frac{21}{35} + \frac{5}{35} = \frac{26}{35}$. The answer, then, is $5\frac{26}{35}$.

Example 52: Find the value of $\frac{3}{7} - \frac{1}{2}$.

The LCD is 14. Thus, $\frac{3}{7} - \frac{1}{2} = \frac{6}{14} - \frac{7}{14} = \frac{-1}{14}$.

Multiplying and Dividing Fractions

Multiplying fractions is actually a bit easier than adding or subtracting them. When multiplying, you don't need to worry about common denominators: Just multiply the numerators, then multiply the denominators, and then simplify if possible. For example, $\frac{2}{3} \times \frac{4}{5} = \frac{2 \times 4}{3 \times 5} = \frac{8}{15}$. That's all you need to do!

To understand the procedure for dividing fractions, we first need to define a term. The *reciprocal* of a number is the number that is obtained by switching the numerator and the denominator of the number. For example, the reciprocal of $\frac{3}{8}$ is simply $\frac{8}{3}$. To find the reciprocal of a whole number, such as 7, visualize the 7 as the fraction $\frac{7}{1}$. The reciprocal, then, is $\frac{1}{7}$.

Now, the easiest way to divide two fractions is to change the division to a multiplication with the same answer. In fact, if you change the second fraction to its reciprocal and multiply, you get the correct answer! For example, $\frac{4}{5} \div \frac{3}{4} = \frac{4}{5} \times \frac{4}{3} = \frac{16}{15} = 1\frac{1}{15}$.

Example 53: What is the value of $2\frac{2}{3} \times 1\frac{4}{5}$?

Before we can multiply these mixed numbers, we need to write them as improper fractions:

$$2\frac{2}{3} \times 1\frac{4}{5} = \frac{8}{3} \times \frac{9}{5} = \frac{72}{15} = 4\frac{12}{15} = 4\frac{4}{5}$$

Example 54: Evaluate $2\frac{2}{5} \div 6$.

Begin by writing the problem as $\frac{12}{5} \div \frac{6}{1}$. Then:

$$\frac{12}{5} \div \frac{6}{1} = \frac{12}{5} \times \frac{1}{6} = \frac{12}{30} = \frac{2}{5}$$

Arithmetic Word Problems

Basic One-Step and Two-Step Problems

Some of the word problems on your test involve only a single computation. Others are multiple-step problems in which several computations need to be performed. Following are examples of problems of both types.

Example 55: Brett earned $225.25 during his first week on a new job. During the second week, he earned $325.50, during the third week he earned $275.00 and during the fourth week he earned $285.75. How much did he earn over the course of the four weeks?

It should be obvious that, in this problem, all we need to do is add the weekly payments to find the total.

$$\begin{array}{r} \$225.25 \\ \$325.50 \\ \$275.00 \\ \$285.75 \\ \hline \$1,111.50 \end{array}$$

Example 56: Brett has a job that pays him $8.25 a hour. If, during the first week, he works 21 hours, and during the second, week he works 19 hours, how much money has he earned over the course of the two weeks?

This is an example of a two-step problem. One way to find the answer is to find how much he made each week by multiplying, and then add the two weekly totals:

$$\begin{array}{r} \$8.25 \\ \times \quad 21 \\ \hline \$173.25 \end{array} \qquad \begin{array}{r} \$8.25 \\ \times \quad 19 \\ \hline \$156.75 \end{array}$$

Then, because $173.25 + $156.75 = $330, he earned $330.

Perhaps you have noticed an easier way to solve the problem. If you begin by adding the number of hours he worked each week, you get $19 + 21 = 40$ as a total. Then, you only need to multiply $8.25 by 40 to get the answer.

Example 57: An office building is 540 feet high, including a 23-foot antenna tower on the roof. How tall is the building without the antenna tower?

It should be clear that, in this problem, we need to remove the 23-foot tower from the top of the building by subtracting. This is a one-step problem:

$$\begin{array}{r} 540 \\ - \quad 23 \\ \hline 517 \text{ feet} \end{array}$$

Example 58: At a restaurant, the bill for dinner is $137.50. Bill contributes $20 to the bill, and then leaves. The rest of the bill is split evenly between the remaining five people. How much does each person contribute?

Here is another two-step word problem. After Bill leaves, $137.50 − $20 = $117.50 remains to be paid. This has to be divided by the other five people.

$$
\begin{array}{r}
23.50 \\
5\overline{)117.50} \\
-\ 10 \\
\hline
17 \\
-\ 15 \\
\hline
25 \\
-\ 25 \\
\hline
0
\end{array}
$$

Clearly, each person needs to pay $23.50.

Some word problems are based on fractions. In such problems, always remember that, if a total is divided into a fractional part, the sum of all the fractional parts must add up to 1.

Example 59: Brian spends $\frac{2}{5}$ of his money on tuition, and $\frac{1}{6}$ of his money on books. What fraction of his money remains after these purchases?

Begin by adding together the two given fractions: $\frac{2}{5} + \frac{1}{6} = \frac{12}{30} + \frac{5}{30} = \frac{17}{30}$. Now, if he has spent $\frac{17}{30}$ of his money, he must have $1 - \frac{17}{30} = \frac{13}{30}$ of his money left.

Sometimes, such a problem is taken a step farther, by giving the amount of money at the beginning, and asking how much money is left at the end. For example, consider the following variation of the preceding problem.

Example 60: Brian has $300 available for school purchases. If he spends $\frac{2}{5}$ of his money on books, and $\frac{1}{6}$ of his money on supplies, how much of his money remains?

Recall that we have already found that Brian has $\frac{13}{30}$ of his money left. To answer the question, then, we need to compute $\frac{13}{30}$ of $300. To find a fraction of a total amount, you need to multiply:

$$
\frac{13}{30} \text{ of } \$300 = \frac{13}{30} \times \$300 = \frac{13 \times 300}{30} = 130. \text{ Therefore, Brian has } \$130 \text{ left.}
$$

Percent Problems

There are several varieties of percent problems that you might see on your test. All these percent problems can be solved using essentially the same procedure, which is outlined in the following paragraphs.

In every percent problem, there are three components involved. Generically speaking, these three components can be called the *whole,* the *part* and the *percent.* It is easy to identify which components you are given. The whole, for example, represents the total, entire value of quantity that is involved in the problem, the *part* is some of this quantity, and the *percent* is the percent of the whole that the part is equal to.

In every problem, you are given two of the three components, and asked to find the missing component. For example, you might be given the *whole* and the *part*, and be asked to find the *percent*.

The three components in a percent problem are related to each other by the percent product formula.

Percent Product Formula

percent × whole = part

This formula indicates that if you are given the percent and the whole, you multiply to find the part. If you are given the values of the either the part and the whole, or the part and the percent, you can use the following related versions of the percent product formula to find the value of the missing component.

$$
\text{Percent} = \frac{\text{Part}}{\text{Whole}} \qquad\qquad \text{Whole} = \frac{\text{Part}}{\text{Percent}}
$$

When solving percent problems, it is often easier to write the percent as a decimal or a fraction before performing the computation. Following are several examples of this type of problem.

Example 61: A family spends 26% of its monthly income on its mortgage. If the family's monthly income is $2,400, how much do they spend on their mortgage each month?

In this problem, the *whole* is $2,400, which is the total monthly income. The *percent* is 26%. We need to find the part of the monthly income that is spent on the mortgage, which is 26% of $2,400. To do this, write 26% as .26, and then multiply, as indicated by the percent product formula.

$$\text{percent} \times \text{whole} = \text{part}$$
$$26\% \times \$2,400 = \text{part}$$
$$0.26 \times \$2,400 = \text{part}$$

$2,400	*No digits to the right of the decimal point*
× .26	*Two digits to the right of the decimal point*
14400	
4800	
$624.00	*Two digits to the right of the decimal point*

Thus, the monthly expenditure is $624.00.

Example 62: Bob invests $5,500 in an account that pays 9% annual interest. How much interest does he earn in one year?

In this problem, we are again given the whole, the total investment of $5,500, and the percent, 9%. We need to find the part; the amount of interest he earns in a year. Begin by writing 9% as a decimal, which is .09. *(Note carefully that 9% is equal to .09, not .9.)* Then multiply to finish the problem: percent × whole = part.

$ 5,500	*No digits to the right of the decimal point*
× .09	*Two digits to the right of the decimal point*
$495.00	*Two digits to the right of the decimal point*

He earns $495 in interest in one year.

Example 63: In a particular math class, 24 out of 30 student passed a test. What percent of the students passed the test?

We have the whole, the 30 students in the class, and the part, the 24 students who passed the test. We need to find the percent.

$$\text{Percent} = \frac{\text{Part}}{\text{Whole}}$$

$$\text{Percent} = \frac{24}{30} = 0.80$$

Writing the decimal 0.80 as 80%, we see that 80% of the students passed the test.

Example 64: Michael earns $80 in interest on a savings bond over the course of a year. If the bond paid 8% in interest, what was the amount of the bond?

In this problem, we have the part, the $80 in interest, and the percent, 8%. We need to find the whole, the total amount of the bond.

$$\text{Whole} = \frac{\text{Part}}{\text{Percent}}$$

$$\text{Whole} = \frac{\$80}{8\%} = \frac{\$80}{0.08} = \$1,000$$

The amount of the bond is $1,000.

One common variation of the basic percent problem described previously is the *percent of change* problem. These problems center around a quantity that has a particular starting value, called the *original value*. The original value changes by a certain amount, called the *change,* or, more specifically, the *increase* or the *decrease*. This leads to a different value, called the *new value*.

In the most common type of percent of change problem, you are given the original value and the new value, and asked to determine the percent of change. This can be computed using a variation of the formula for finding the percent that we have already been using:

$$\text{Percent} = \frac{\text{Part}}{\text{Whole}}$$

In a percent of change problem, the original value is the whole, and the change is the part, so we have the formula:

$$\text{Percent of Change} = \frac{\text{Change}}{\text{Original}}$$

Example 65: John earns $50 a week at a part time job. After getting a raise, his weekly salary becomes $60 a week. What is the percent of increase in his weekly salary?

In this problem, the original value is $50, and the change is $60 − $50 = $10. Thus,

$$\text{Percent of Change} = \frac{\text{Change}}{\text{Original}} = \frac{\$10}{\$50} = 0.20 = 20\%$$

Thus, John's salary increased by 20%.

Example 66: Bob invests $5,500 in an account that pays 9% in annual interest. How much money is in the account at the end of one year?

In this problem, we are given the original value and the percent of increase, and asked to find the new value. To begin, you need to find the amount of increase, which is $5,500 × 9% = $495. *(Note that we have already determined this in a pervious problem.)* After determining how much interest is in the account at the end of the year, this amount needs to be added to the $5,500 to obtain $5,500 + $495 = $5,995.

Example 67: After 5% sales tax is added, the final selling price of a CD player is $210. What is the price of the CD player before the tax?

In this problem, you have the new value and the percent of increase, and are asked to find the original value. Thus, we are looking for the *"original value before a percent of increase."* The formula for this is similar to those we have used before:

To Find the Original Value Before a Percent of Increase:

$$\text{Original Value} = \frac{\text{New Value}}{100\% + \text{Percent of Increase}}$$

Using this formula, we get

$$\text{Original Value} = \frac{\text{New Value}}{100\% + \text{Percent of Increase}} = \frac{\$210}{100\% + 5\%} = \frac{\$210}{105\%} = \frac{\$210}{1.05}.$$

Performing the division, we obtain an original value of $200.

Note that, if you are asked to find the original value before a percent of *decrease,* you need to use a slightly different version of this formula.

To Find the Original Value Before a Percent of Decrease:

$$\text{Original Value} = \frac{\text{New Value}}{100\% - \text{Percent of Increase}}$$

Ratio and Proportion

Another variety of word problem that might appear on the test involves ratios and proportions.

A ratio is a comparison of two numbers. For example, a school might say that its student-teacher ratio is 8 to 1. This means that, for every 8 students at the school, there is 1 teacher. Another way to look at this ratio is that, for every 1 teacher, there are 8 students.

You might have seen a ratio written with a colon between the two numbers, like 8:1. A ratio can also be written as a fraction, like $\frac{8}{1}$. When it comes to solving word problems involving ratios, it is usually best to write the ratio as a fraction so that you can perform computations on it.

In the preceding ratio, we are comparing a number of people (students) to a number of people (teachers). When a ratio is used to compare two different kinds of quantities, it is called a *rate*. As an example, suppose that a car drives 300 miles in 5 hours. Then we can write the rate of the car as $\frac{300\ miles}{5\ hours}$. If we divide the number on the bottom into the number on the top, we get the number 60, and can then say that the rate of the car is $\frac{60\ miles}{1\ hour}$, or simply 60 *miles per hour*. Sixty miles per hour is also known as the *speed* of the car.

When we divide the number on the bottom of a ratio or a rate into the number on the top, the result is what is known as a *unit ratio* or a *unit rate*. Often, solving ratio problems hinges on computing a unit ratio or rate. The techniques of working with ratios and rates are illustrated in the following problems.

Example 68: A supermarket customer bought a 15-ounce box of oatmeal for $3.45. What was the cost per ounce of oatmeal?

The rate of cost to ounces is given in the problem as $\frac{\$3.45}{15\ oz}$. To find the *unit cost*, we divide $3.45 by 15 ounces.

$$
\begin{array}{r}
.23 \\
15\overline{)3.45} \\
-30 \\
\hline
45 \\
-45 \\
\hline
0
\end{array}
$$

Therefore, the cost is 23 cents per ounce.

Example 69: A supermarket sells a 15-ounce box of oatmeal for $3.45. At the same rate, what would be the cost of a 26-ounce box of oatmeal?

This type of problem is what is known as a proportion problem. In a proportion problem, you are given the rate at which two quantities vary, and asked to find the value of one of the quantities given the value of the other. A good way to approach a problem of this type is by first finding the unit rate and then multiplying. Note that in the preceding problem we found the unit rate of the oatmeal; it was 23 cents per ounce. The cost of 26 ounces, then, is 23 cents × 26:

$$
\begin{array}{r}
.23 \\
\times\ 26 \\
\hline
138 \\
46 \\
\hline
5.98
\end{array}
$$

Thus, 26 ounces costs $5.98.

Example 70: A bus travels at a constant speed of 45 miles per hour. How far can the bus go in $5\frac{1}{2}$ hours?

Previously, we saw that the rate (speed) of a vehicle is equal to its distance divided by its time. In the same way, the distance that the vehicle travels is equal to its rate multiplied by its time. You might remember from previous math classes that this formula is written $d = r \times t$, meaning distance equals rate × time.

It is easier to solve this problem if we write $5\frac{1}{2}$ as its decimal equivalent 5.5. Then, we simply need to multiply 45 by 5.5 to find the distance:

$$\begin{array}{r} 45 \\ \times\ 5.5 \\ \hline 225 \\ 225 \\ \hline 247.5 \end{array}$$

Thus, the car goes 247.5 miles in $5\frac{1}{2}$ hours.

Another, extremely common, type of problem asks you to *find the missing term in a proportion*. In such problems, you are told the rate at which two quantities vary, and then asked to find a value for one of the quantities, given the value of the other quantity. As an example, consider the following problem:

If 4 tomatoes cost 80 cents, what do 13 tomatoes cost at the same rate?

To solve this problem, begin by noting that the two units being compared are tomatoes and cents. To avoid getting units confused at this point, it is helpful to write down the comparison of units as a fraction: $\frac{tomatoes}{cents}$.

A *proportion* is simply a statement that two pairs of numbers have the same ratio. For example, because the ratio of 2 to 4 is the same as the ratio of 3 to 6, we say that the numbers 2 and 4, and the numbers 3 and 6 are proportional to each other. This proportion can be written as $\frac{2}{4} = \frac{3}{6}$. In words, this statement is sometimes read, "2 is to 4 as 3 is to 6."

In the preceding proportion, we have all four numbers. In the tomatoes problem, however, you are only given three of the numbers in the proportion, and are asked to find the missing number that completes the proportion. We now need to write the proportion. Begin by writing a blank proportion next to the $\frac{tomatoes}{cents}$ we already wrote.

$$\frac{tomatoes}{cents} \qquad \underline{\quad} = \underline{\quad}$$

The three numbers given in the problem, as well as the missing number (which we will call *N*) are going to be placed in this blank proportion. The crucial thing to remember is that, because we have written tomatoes on the top of our comparison, any numbers that we write on the top of the proportion must represent numbers of tomatoes. In the same way, any numbers we write on the bottom of the proportion should represent cents. The following diagram indicates that numbers of tomatoes should go on the top and numbers of cents should go on the bottom:

$$\frac{tomatoes}{cents} \quad \begin{array}{c}\rightarrow\\\rightarrow\end{array} \quad \underline{\quad} = \underline{\quad}$$

Now, the first number given in the problem is 4, and this represents a number of tomatoes, so we write this number on top of the first ratio:

$$\frac{tomatoes}{cents} \quad \begin{array}{c}\rightarrow\\\rightarrow\end{array} \quad \frac{4}{\underline{\quad}} = \underline{\quad}$$

Continuing, the next number is 80 cents, which goes on the bottom:

$$\frac{tomatoes}{cents} \quad \begin{array}{c}\rightarrow\\\rightarrow\end{array} \quad \frac{4}{80} = \underline{\quad}$$

Now, the third number is 13, and because that represents a number of tomatoes, it goes on top of the second fraction:

$$\frac{tomatoes}{cents} \quad \begin{array}{c}\rightarrow\\\rightarrow\end{array} \quad \frac{4}{80} = \frac{13}{}$$

We do not know how many cents the 13 tomatoes cost, so we write N on the bottom:

$$\frac{\text{tomatoes}}{\text{cents}} \; \begin{array}{c} \rightarrow \\ \rightarrow \end{array} \; \frac{4}{80} = \frac{13}{N}$$

This is the proportion that is needed to solve the problem. To find the value of N, begin by *cross-multiplying*, that is, multiplying the numbers along the diagonals in the proportion.

Multiply 80 by 13.

$$80 \times 13 = 4 \times N$$
$$1{,}040 = 4 \times N$$

Find the value for N by dividing 1,040 by 4.

$$N = \frac{1{,}040}{4} = 260$$

Thus, the 13 tomatoes costs 260 cents, which is, of course, $2.60.

Example 71: If a distance of 2 inches on a map represents 5 miles, how far apart are two cities that are 7 inches apart on the map?

In this problem, we are comparing miles to inches. Thus, the proportion we need to solve can be written as follows:

$$\frac{miles}{inches} \; \begin{array}{c} \rightarrow \\ \rightarrow \end{array} \; \frac{5}{2} = \frac{N}{7}$$

Cross-multiply.

$$7 \times 5 = 2 \times N$$
$$35 = 2 \times N$$

Divide 35 by 2.

$$N = 35 \div 2 = 17.5$$

Thus, the two cities are $17\frac{1}{2}$ miles apart.

Algebraic Operations and Equations

Numerical Evaluation

Algebra is a generalization of arithmetic. In arithmetic, you learned how to perform mathematical operations (such as addition, subtraction, multiplication and division) on different types of numbers, such as whole numbers, decimals, percents and fractions. Algebra extends these concepts by considering how to perform mathematical operations on symbols standing for numbers and how to use these techniques to solve a variety of practical word problems.

In algebra, we refer to numbers that have a definite value as *constants*. For example, the numbers 17, -3, $\frac{2}{3}$, $\sqrt{41}$, 5.123, and 12% are constants. Symbols standing for numbers are called *variables* because, until we specify further, they can take on any value. For example, in the expression $3x + 13y + 29$, the numbers 3, 13 and 29 are constants, and the symbols x and y are variables. As the following examples show, when we are given the values of all variables in an expression, we can find the value of the expression.

Example 72: If $a = 4$ and $b = -3$, find the value of the expression $a^3 - b$.

When evaluating numerical expressions, it is crucial to remember the Order of Operations, and to pay careful attention to plus and minus signs. Begin by substituting the values of a and b in the given expression, and then carefully evaluate as in the previous section:

$$a^3 - b = (4)^3 - (-3) = 64 + 3 = 67$$

Example 73: If $x = 3$ and $y = 2$, find the value of $\dfrac{24 - 2x}{-6y}$.

$$\frac{24 - 2x}{-6y} = \frac{24 - 2(3)}{-6(2)} = \frac{24 - 6}{-12} = \frac{18}{-12} = -\frac{3}{2}$$

Example 74: The formula for the perimeter of a rectangle is $P = 2l + 2w$, where l represents the length of the rectangle and w represents the width. What is the perimeter of a rectangle with length 21 and width 15?

$$P = 2l + 2w = 2(21) + 2(15) = 42 + 30 = 72$$

Solving Equations

An *equation* is simply a mathematical expression that contains an equal sign. For example, $10 = 4 + 6$ is an equation, and is always true. Alternately, $10 = 5 + 4$ is also an equation, but it is always false.

An equation that contains a variable, such as $2x + 1 = 7$, might or might not be true depending on the value of x. *Solving an equation* refers to finding the value of the unknown that makes both sides of the equation equal. Note that the number three makes both sides of the equation equal. We therefore say that three *solves* the equation, or that three is the *solution* of the equation.

Some equations, like the preceding one, are easy to solve by just looking at them. Others are so complicated that we need an organized series of steps to solve them. In this section, we examine how to do this.

The principle for solving equations is, essentially, to rewrite the equation in simpler and simpler forms (without, of course, changing the solution), until the solution becomes obvious. The simplest equation of all, of course, is an equation of the form $x = a$, where x is the variable and a is some number. Whenever you are given an equation that is more complicated than $x = a$, the idea is to change the equation so that it eventually looks like $x = a$, and you can read the answer right off.

Now, what can you do to change an equation? The answer is simple: almost anything you want as long as you do the same thing to both sides. To start, you can add or subtract the same number to or from both sides, multiply both sides by the same number, or divide both sides by the same number (as long as that number isn't zero). The following examples demonstrate this procedure with some very simple equations; after this, we will look at some more complicated ones.

Example 75: Solve for x: $x + 7 = 20$.

Even though you can easily solve this equation in your head, pay attention to the procedure, as it will help you when we get to more complicated equations. Remember that the easiest possible type of equation is one of the form $x = a$. The equation that we have isn't quite like that; it has a +7 on the left side that we want to get rid of. Now, how can we get rid of an addition of 7? Easy; we just subtract 7 from both sides:

$$\begin{aligned} x + 7 &= 20 \\ -7 & -7 \\ \hline x &= 13 \end{aligned}$$

So, the solution to this equation is $x = 13$.

Example 76: Solve for y: $9y = 72$.

In this equation, we have a 9 multiplying the y that we want to get rid of. Now, how can we undo a multiplication by 9? Clearly, we need to divide both sides by 9:

$$\frac{9y}{9} = \frac{72}{9}$$

$y = 8$ is the solution.

The equations in the two preceding examples are called one-step equations because they can be solved in one step. Some examples of equations that require more than one step to solve follow. The procedure is the same; keep doing the same thing to both sides of the equation until it looks like $x = a$.

Example 77: Solve for t: $4t - 3 = 9$.

In this equation, we have a few things on the left hand side that we want to get rid of. First of all, let's undo the subtraction of 3 by adding 3 to both sides.

$$\begin{aligned} 4t - 3 &= 9 \\ +3 & +3 \\ \hline 4t &= 12 \end{aligned}$$

Now, we need to undo the multiplication by 4, which can be done by dividing both sides by 4:

$$\frac{4t}{4} = \frac{12}{4}, \text{ or } t = 3.$$

Note that you can check your answer to any equation by substituting the answer back into the equation and making certain that both sides are equal. For example, we know that we did the preceding problem correctly because:

$$4(3) - 3 = 9$$
$$12 - 3 = 9$$
$$9 = 9$$

Example 78: Solve for p: $15p = 3p + 24$.

This problem puts us in a situation that we have yet to encounter. The variable p appears on both sides of the equation, but we only want it on one side. To get this into the form we want, let's subtract $3p$ from both sides:

$$\begin{aligned} 15p &= 3p + 24 \\ -3p & -3p \\ \hline 12p &= 24 \end{aligned}$$

Now, we have an equation that looks a bit better. It is easy to see that if we divide both sides by 12, we end up with the answer $p = 2$.

A few more examples for you to practice with follow. Before we get to them, it will be helpful if you refamiliarize yourself with a very important mathematical property called the *Distributive Property*.

Consider, for example, the expression 7(2 + 3). According to the Order of Operations, we should do the work in parentheses first, and therefore 7(2 + 3) = 7(5) = 35. However, note that we get the same answer if we "distribute" the 7 to the 2 and the 3, and add afterward:

$$7(2 + 3) = 7(2) + 7(3) = 14 + 21 = 35$$

The Distributive Property tells us that we can always use this distribution as a way of evaluating an expression. Algebraically, the Distributive Property tells us that $a(b + c) = ab + ac$. The following examples incorporate the Distributive Property into the solving of equations.

Example 79: Solve for c: $3(c - 5) = 9$.

Before we can get the c by itself on the left, we need to get it out of the parentheses, so let's distribute:

$$3c - 15 = 9$$

The rest is similar to what we have already done. Add 15 to both sides to get:

$$3c = 24$$

Now divide by 3 to get:

$$c = 8$$

Example 80: Solve for q: $5q - 64 = -2(3q - 1)$.

As in the preceding example, we must begin by eliminating the parentheses, using the Distributive Property:

$$5q - 64 = -6q + 2$$

Now, add $6q$ to both sides:

$$11q - 64 = +2$$

Next, add 64 to both sides:

$$11q = 66.$$

Finally, dividing both sides by 11 gives us the answer: $q = 6$.

Solving Word Problems

Many problems that deal with practical applications of mathematics are expressed in words. To solve such problems, it is necessary to translate the words into an equation that can then be solved. The following table lists some common words and the mathematical symbols that they represent:

Words	Mathematical Representation
a equals 9, a is 9, a is the same as 9	a = 9
a plus 9, the sum of a and 9, a added to 9, a increased by 9, a more than 9	a + 9
9 less than a, a minus 9, a decreased by 9, the difference of a and 9, a less 9	a − 9

Words	Mathematical Representation
9 times a, the product of 9 and a, 9 multiplied by a	$9a$ (or $9 \times a$)
The quotient of a and 9, a divided by 9, 9 divided into a	$\frac{a}{9}$
$\frac{1}{2}$ of a	50% of a
$\frac{1}{2} \times a$	$50\% \times a$

Now, when you are given a word problem to solve, begin by translating the words into an equation, and then solve the equation to find the solution.

Example 81: If 6 increased by 3 times a number is 21, what is the number?

Let's call the number x. Then, the problem statement tells us that:

$$6 + 3x = 21$$

Subtract 6 from both sides:

$$3x = 15$$

Divide by 3:

$$x = 5$$

Thus, the number is 5.

Example 82: Brian needs $54 more to buy new hockey gloves. If the gloves cost $115, how much money does he already have to spend on the gloves?

Let m represent the amount of money that Brian has to spend on the gloves. Then, we have an easy equation: $m + 54 = 115$.

If we subtract 54 from both sides, we get $m = 61$.

Brian already has $61 to spend on the gloves.

Example 83: Edgar bought a portable compact disc player for $69 and a number of discs for $14 each. If the total cost of his purchases (before tax) was $167, how many compact discs did he buy?

Let's start by letting d represent the number of discs he bought. Then, the cost of the player plus d discs at $14 each must add up to $167. Therefore:

$$14d + 69 = 167$$

Subtract 69 from both sides:

$$14d = 98$$

Divide both sides by 14:

$$d = 7$$

Therefore, he bought 7 discs.

Geometry and Measurement

Perimeter and Area

The perimeter of a figure is the distance around it, that is, the sum of the lengths of its sides. Perimeter is measured in units of length, such as inches, feet, or meters. The area of a figure is the amount of surface contained within its boundaries. Area is measured in square units, such as square inches, square feet, or square meters.

Two important geometric figures that you should know how to find the perimeter and area of are the rectangle and the square.

A rectangle is a figure with four sides. The opposite sides are the same length. For example, the following figure depicts a rectangle with measurement of 4 inches by 3 inches:

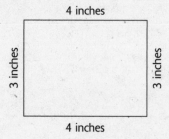

The perimeter of a rectangle is given by the formula $P = 2l + 2w$, which means that, to find the perimeter of a rectangle, you need to add together two lengths and two widths. If the rectangle is 4 inches by 3 inches, then its perimeter is $P = 4 + 4 + 3 + 3 = 14$ inches.

The area of a rectangle is given by the formula $A = l \times w$, which means that the area is the length multiplied by the width. In this case, the area would be 4 inches $\times$ 3 inches = 12 square inches. By the way, a square inch is simply a square that is an inch long on all four sides. If you look again at the preceding picture of the rectangle, you can see that it can be thought of as consisting of 12 squares that are each an inch on all sides. That is what is meant when we say that the area is 12 square inches.

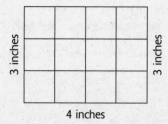

A square is a rectangle with 4 equal sides. In the case of a square, the formulas for the perimeter and the area of a rectangle take a simpler form. The perimeter of a square is $P = 4s$, where s is the length of the side, and the area is $A = s \times s$.

It will also help you to know some common measurement conversions, such as the facts that there are 12 inches in a foot, 3 feet in a yard and 36 inches in a yard.

The following examples are based on the concepts discussed in the preceding paragraphs.

Example 84: A small bag of fertilizer covers 20 square feet of lawn. How many bags are needed to cover a lawn that is 4 yards by 3 yards?

The most direct way to handle this problem is to change the measurement of the lawn to feet because that is how the capacity of the bag of fertilizer is measured. A lawn that is 4 yards by 3 yards is 12 feet by 9 feet. Thus, its area is 12×9 = 108 square feet. Now, to determine the number of bags needed, we need to divide 20 into 108. When we do this division, we get 5.4. Because, obviously, you cannot purchase 5.4 bags, you need 6 bags to cover the lawn.

Example 85: A lot of land measures 50 meters by 40 meters. A house 24 meters by 18 meters is built on the land. How much area is left over?

Begin by finding the area of the lot and the house:

$$\begin{array}{r} 50 \\ \times\ 40 \\ \hline 2000 \end{array} \qquad \begin{array}{r} 24 \\ \times\ 18 \\ \hline 432 \end{array}$$

Thus, the area of the lot is 2,000 square meters, and the area of the house is 432 square meters. To determine how much area is left, we need to subtract 432 square meters from 2,000 square meters: $2,000 - 432 = 1,568$ square meters left over.

Angle Measurement

You measure angles in degrees, which you indicate with the symbol °. By definition, the amount of rotation needed to go completely around a circle one time is 360°.

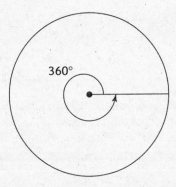

You can measure every angle by determining what fraction of a complete rotation around a circle it represents. For example, an angle that represents $\frac{1}{4}$ of a rotation around a circle has a measurement of $\frac{1}{4}$ of 360° = 90°. The following diagram depicts a 90° angle. $\overrightarrow{AB}$ and $\overrightarrow{AC}$ are the sides of the angle, and the point A is the vertex (which is marked with the symbol ⌐ to indicate that it is a 90° angle).

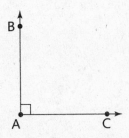

Angles that measure less than 90° are called *acute* angles, and angles that measure more than 90° are called *obtuse* angles. The following diagram depicts an acute angle of 60° as well as an obtuse angle of 120°.

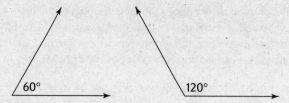

Note that an angle with the size of $\frac{1}{2}$ a revolution around the circle has a measure of 180°. In other words, a straight line can be thought of as an angle of 180°.

Two angles whose measures add up to 90° are called *complementary* angles, and two angles whose measures add up to 180° are called *supplementary* angles. In the following diagram, angles 1 and 2 are complementary, and angles 3 and 4 are supplementary. As the diagram shows, whenever a straight angle is partitioned into two angles, the angles are supplementary.

Another very important fact about angles relates to what are known as *vertical* angles. As the following diagram shows, when two lines intersect, four angles are formed. In this situation, the angles that are across from each other are called *vertical* angles. All vertical angles are equal, so $a° = b°$, and $c° = d°$.

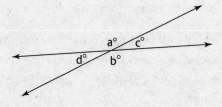

Example 86: In the following diagram, what is the value of a?

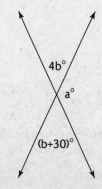

Begin by noting that the angles labeled $4b$ and $b + 30$ are vertical angles, and therefore have the same measure. In this case, we can set the two angles equal and solve the resulting equation for b:

$$4b = b + 30$$
$$3b = 30$$
$$b = 10$$

Now, if $b = 10$, then $4b = 40$. Because the angle labeled $a°$ is supplementary to this angle, a must be equal to $140°$.

Example 87: In the following diagram, what is the value of x?

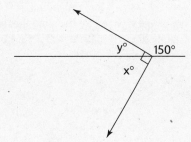

Begin by noting that the angle labeled y is supplementary to the angle labeled $150°$, and is therefore equal to $30°$. Next, note that the angle labeled x is complementary to that $30°$ angle, and is therefore equal to $60°$.

Properties of Triangles

A triangle is a geometric figure having three straight sides. One of the most important facts about a triangle is that, regardless of its shape, the sum of the measures of the three angles it contains is always $180°$. Of course, then, if you know the measures of two of the angles of a triangle, you can determine the measure of the third angle by adding the two angles you are given, and subtracting from 180.

Some triangles have special properties that you should know about. To begin, an *isosceles* triangle is a triangle that has two sides of the same length. In an isosceles triangle, the two angles opposite the equal sides have the same measurement. For example, in the following figure, $AB = BC$, and therefore the two angles opposite these sides, labeled $x°$, have the same measure.

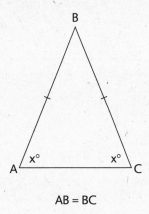

AB = BC

A triangle that has all three sides the same length is called an *equilateral* triangle. In an equilateral triangle, all three angles also have the same measure. Because the sum of the three angles must be $180°$, each angle in an equilateral triangle must measure $180° \div 3 = 60°$. Therefore, in the following equilateral triangle, all three angles are $60°$.

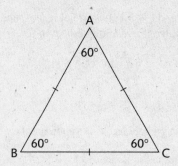

Another extremely important triangle property relates to what are known as *right* triangles, that is, triangles containing a right angle. In such triangles, the side opposite the right angle is called the *hypotenuse,* and must be the longest side of the triangle. The other two sides of the triangle are called its legs. Therefore, in the following right triangle, the side labeled c is the hypotenuse, and sides a and b are the legs.

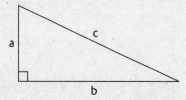

The three sides of a right triangle are related by a formula known as the Pythagorean theorem. The Pythagorean theorem states that the square of the hypotenuse is equal to the sum of the squares of the legs of the triangle, or, using the notation in the preceding diagram, $a^2 + b^2 = c^2$.

The importance of this result is that it enables you, given the lengths of two of the sides of a right triangle, to find the length of the third side, as is illustrated in Example 89.

Example 88: In triangle XYZ, angle X is twice as big as angle Y, and angle Z is equal to angle Y. What is the measure of angle X?

Because the measure of angle X is twice as big as angle Y, we can say that the measure of angle X is equal to $2Y$. Because it must be true that $X + Y + Z = 180$, we can write:

$$2Y + Y + Y = 180$$
$$4Y = 180$$
$$Y = 45$$

If the measure of angle Y is 45°, the measure of angle X, which is twice as big, must be 90°.

Example 89: In the following triangle, what is the length of a?

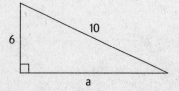

The triangle is a right triangle, so we can use the Pythagorean theorem to find the length of the missing side. Note that the hypotenuse is 10, one of the legs is 6, and we are looking for the length of the other leg. Therefore:

$$a^2 + 6^2 = 10^2$$
$$a^2 + 36 = 100$$
$$a^2 = 64$$
$$a = 8$$

Properties of Circles

A circle is a closed figure, consisting of all the points that are the same distance from a fixed point called the *center* of the circle. A line segment from the center of the circle to any point on the circle is called a *radius* of the circle. A line segment from one point on a circle, through the center of the circle, to another point on the circle is called a *diameter* of the circle. As you can see in the following diagram, the length of a diameter of a circle is always twice the length of a radius of a circle.

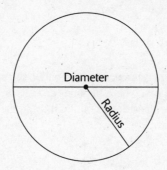

Perimeter and Area

To find the perimeter of a triangle, you simply need to add together the lengths of the three sides. The area of a triangle is given by the formula Area $= \frac{1}{2} bh,$ where b represents the length of the base of the triangle, and h represents the height of the triangle. The height of a triangle is defined as the length of a line segment drawn from a *vertex* (corner) of the triangle to the base, so that it hits the base at a right angle.

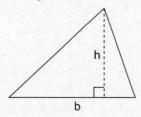

Formulas for the perimeter (which is more commonly known as the *circumference)* and the area of circles are based on the length of the radius, and include the symbol π, which represents a number that is approximately equal to 3.14.

The circumference of a circle is given by the formula $C = 2\pi r,$ where r is the radius of the circle. The area of the circle is given by the formula $A = \pi r^2$. Unless you are told otherwise, when answering problems involving the circumference or area of a circle, you can leave the answer in terms of π, as in the following problem.

Example 90: What is the circumference of a circle whose area is 36π?

The area of a circle is πr^2, so you have $\pi r^2 = 36\pi$. This means that $r^2 = 36$, so $r = 6$.

Now, the circumference of a circle is $2\pi r$, so the circumference in this case is $2\pi 6) = 12\pi$

Example 91: What is the area of the shaded part of the following rectangle?

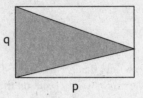

The shaded area is a triangle, so we can use the formula $A = \frac{1}{2} bh$ to find its area. The width of the rectangle, labeled q, is also the base of the triangle. You can see that the length of the rectangle, labeled p, is equal to the height of the triangle. Therefore, the area of the shaded region is $\frac{1}{2} pq$.

Coordinates and Slope

Points in a plane can be located by means of a reference system called the coordinate system. Two number lines are drawn at right angles to each other, and the point where the lines cross is considered to have a value of zero for both lines. Then, positive and negative numbers are positioned on the lines in the usual way:

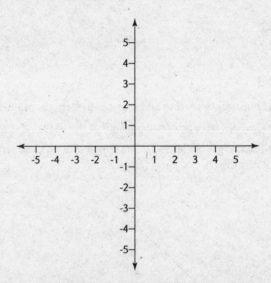

The horizontal line is called the *x-axis*, and the points on this axis are called *x-coordinates*. The vertical line is called the *y-axis*, and the points on this axis are called *y-coordinates*. Points on the plane are identified by first writing a number that represents where they lie in reference to the *x*-axis, and then writing a number that expresses where they lie in reference to the *y*-axis. These numbers are called the coordinates of the point. The coordinates of a variety of points are shown in the following diagram:

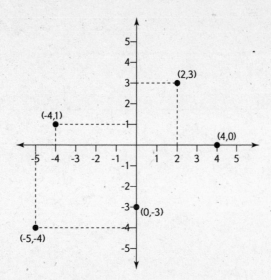

Any two points on a plane determine a line. One of the important characteristics of a line is its steepness, or *slope*. The slope of a line can be determined from the coordinates of the two points that determine the line. If the coordinates of the two points are (x_1, y_1) and (x_2, y_2), the formula for the slope is $\frac{y_2 - y_1}{x_2 - x_1}$. In other words, to find the slope of a line, find two points on the line and divide the difference of the *y*-coordinates by the difference of the *x*-coordinates.

Example 92: Find the slope of the line that goes through the points (9, 5) and (3, −2).

The slope of the line can be computed as $\frac{y_2 - y_1}{x_2 - x_1} = \frac{5 - (-2)}{9 - 3} = \frac{5 + 2}{6} = \frac{7}{6}$.

Quantitative Reasoning Review

The Quantitative Reasoning section of the COOP assesses your ability to recognize patterns and relationships within diagrams and numbers. Although some of the questions do involve numbers, this section cannot really be considered a math section. The math that you need to use is nothing more complicated than basic arithmetic computations using addition, subtraction, multiplication and division. Furthermore, many of the Quantitative Reasoning questions do not involve numbers at all.

This section contains several different question formats. While the structure of these question formats varies substantially, fundamentally all formats test the same skill—your ability to look at some type of diagram, identify a pattern or relationship, and either state what the pattern is or use the pattern to make a further deduction.

The best way to prepare for this section, of course, is to practice with the various types of questions that appear. In the practice tests that follow, you have plenty of opportunity to work your way through many sample problems. To help you prepare for these sample problems, the following section discusses how to approach the types of questions that appear the most frequently on the test.

Number Relationships

This type of question is actually rather similar to the sequence questions that appear elsewhere on the test. Consider the sample Number Relationship problem that follows.

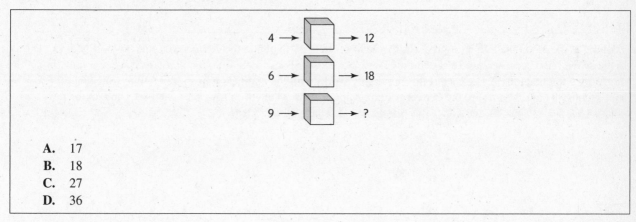

A. 17
B. 18
C. 27
D. 36

Notice that the diagram contains three lines. The first two lines are intended to establish a relationship between certain numbers. Your job is to determine the relationship by examining the first two lines, and then to apply the relationship to the third line, and thus determine the value of the missing number, which is indicated by a question mark.

Let's start by looking at the first line, and try to understand what it is telling us. The first line begins with the number 4, which, essentially, is put into a box, and then comes out equal to 12. Your job is to determine what has been done mathematically inside the box to the number 4 to turn it into a 12. You likely realize right away that more than one possibility exists. For example, the number 4 might have been added to the number 8 to result in the number 12. Or, the number 4 might have been multiplied by the number 3 to result in the number 12. How can you tell what actually happened to the number 4? Well, whatever was done to the 4 in the first line to turn it into a 12 was also done to the 6 in the second line to turn it into an 18. Thus, you need to begin by thinking up a possible mathematical operation that changes the 4 into a 12, and then see if the same operation changes the 6 into an 18. If your first guess doesn't work, try again until you find something that does work.

Suppose, for example, you guess that the box that the 4 was put into added 8 to it to obtain a total of 12. If this is correct, we ought to be able to add 8 to the number 6 on the second line and end up with 18. However, 6 + 8 = 14, so this cannot be right. Another possibility, as we have seen, is that the box that the 4 was put into multiplied it by 3 to obtain 12.

Trying this possibility out on the numbers in the second line, we see that $6 \times 3 = 18$! This means we have discovered the correct pattern. In the first and second lines, the numbers on the left were multiplied by 3 to obtain the numbers on the right.

To finish up the problem, all we need to do is take the number on the third line, and predict what it becomes when it is put into the box. Because we have already determined that the box multiplies numbers by 3, it is clear that when the 9 is put into the box, it becomes $9 \times 3 = 27$. Thus, the answer is **C.**

Typically, the best way to approach these problems is to start with the first number on the left and determine a way to either add something to it, subtract something from it, multiply something by it or divide it by something to obtain the first number on the right. When you come up with a possibility, see if the possibility also works for the numbers in the second row. If it does work, apply it to the third row to find the answer. If it doesn't, start over again and look for another option.

Let's consider another example.

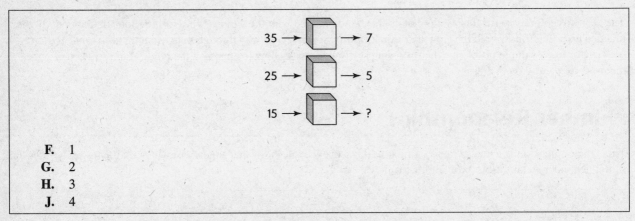

  F. 1
  G. 2
  H. 3
  J. 4

Looking at the 35 on the left, it might occur to you to subtract 28 to obtain the 7. However, this possibility doesn't work in the second line because $25 - 28$ is certainly not 5. So, let's go back to the first line. Perhaps instead you might divide the 35 by 5 to obtain the 7. Let's see if this possibility works with the numbers in the second line. Note that $25 \div 5 = 5$, so it seems we have determined the correct pattern. Applying this to the third row, we take the 15 and divide it by 5 to obtain $15 \div 5 = 3$. Thus, the answer to this question is **H.** That's all there is to it.

Visual Problems

The questions in this category are fairly straightforward. You are typically given a diagram that consists of a number of squares, some of which are shaded. You simply need to express the portion of the diagram that is shaded as a fraction. Consider, for example, the following problem.

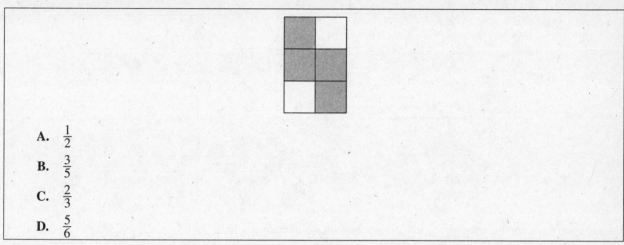

    A. $\frac{1}{2}$

    B. $\frac{3}{5}$

    C. $\frac{2}{3}$

    D. $\frac{5}{6}$

Begin by noting that the diagram consists of a total of 6 squares and that 4 of them are shaded. Overall, then, we can say that $\frac{4}{6}$ of the figure is shaded. Taking a look at the possible solutions, however, reveals that $\frac{4}{6}$ is not a choice. However, the fraction $\frac{4}{6}$ can be simplified by dividing the top and bottom by 2, to obtain $\frac{4}{6} = \frac{4 \div 2}{6 \div 2} = \frac{2}{3}$. The answer is **C.**

In some slightly trickier problems, you might find squares that are only half shaded. Consider the following problem.

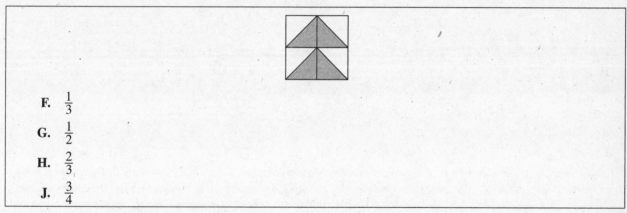

    F. $\frac{1}{3}$

    G. $\frac{1}{2}$

    H. $\frac{2}{3}$

    J. $\frac{3}{4}$

To solve this problem, simply note that the diagram contains 4 squares and that half of each one is shaded. Thus, overall, $\frac{1}{2}$ of the figure is shaded. Therefore, the answer is **G.**

Symbol Relationships

This third type of question in the Quantitative Reasoning section of the COOP might be the trickiest, at least until you learn the best way to approach the questions. Each Symbol Relationship question begins with a picture of a scale showing two sets of shapes of equal weight. Your job is to examine these two sets of shapes that balance the scale, and then to select another two sets of shapes that also balance the scale. Consider the following problem for an easy example of how these questions are to be answered.

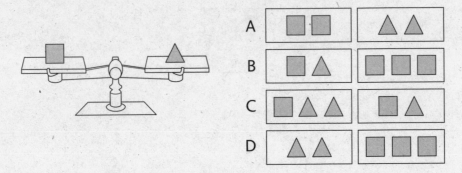

According to the scale, the cube on the left weighs the same as the cone on the right. Overall, then, we can conclude that one cube = one cone. If this is the case, then by doubling the weight on both sides, we can conclude that two cubes are equal to two cones. Thus, the answer is **A.**

Many of the questions, however, are not quite as straightforward as the preceding example and hinge on your ability to move shapes on and off the scale, while still maintaining the balance. Consider, for example, this problem:

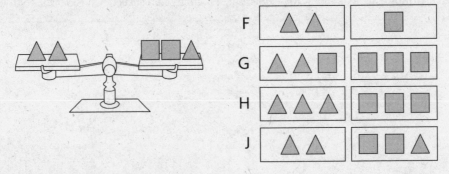

Begin by noting that the scale tells us that two cones are equal to two cubes and a cone. To simply this relationship, we begin by removing one cone from each side. Because we are taking the same weight from each side, the scale still balances, and we can see that one cone is equal to two cubes. In general, it is always a good idea to begin by removing any common shapes from both sides so as to simplify the relationship.

Now, we need to manipulate our fundamental relationship of *one cone is equal to two cubes* to determine which other set of shapes balance the scale. To do this, it is often a good idea to put equal weights back on each side of the scale until you come up with a combination that matches one of the answer choices. Here, if we add a cone to each side of the fundamental relationship *one cone is equal to two cubes*, we get the new relationship, *two cones are equal to two cubes and a cone.* This relationship is depicted in choice **J,** so that is the answer.

The key to approaching this section, then, is to begin by removing equal weights from both sides, and then to add equal weights back to both sides until you end up with a combination that matches one of the answer choices. With a little practice, this can be done quite quickly.

The following questions give you some additional practice. First answer the questions, and then check the answers that follow.

Practice Questions

Directions: There are three different sets of questions in this section designed to measure your aptitude with numbers. Try the following questions.

For questions 1–4, find the relationship of the numbers in one column to the numbers in the other column. Then find the missing number.

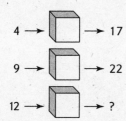

4 → → 17

9 → → 22

12 → → ?

1.

   A. 25
   B. 26
   C. 27
   D. 28

2 → → 10

7 → → 35

11 → → ?

2.

   F. 39
   G. 40
   H. 50
   J. 55

64 → → 8

40 → → 5

24 → → ?

3.

   A. 4
   B. 3
   C. 2
   D. 1

20 → → 11

15 → → 6

10 → → ?

4.

   F. 5
   G. 3
   H. 1
   J. 0

For questions 5–7, find the fraction of the grid that is shaded.

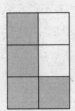

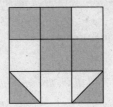

5.

  A. $\frac{1}{3}$

  B. $\frac{1}{2}$

  C. $\frac{2}{3}$

  D. $\frac{5}{6}$

7.

  A. $\frac{5}{9}$

  B. $\frac{2}{3}$

  C. $\frac{7}{9}$

  D. $\frac{8}{9}$

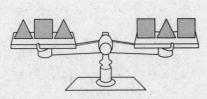

6.

  F. $\frac{1}{2}$

  G. $\frac{2}{3}$

  H. $\frac{3}{4}$

  J. $\frac{5}{6}$

For questions 8–10, look at the scale showing sets of shapes of equal weight. Find an equivalent set that also balances the scale.

8.

9.

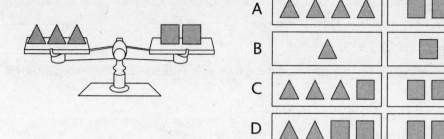

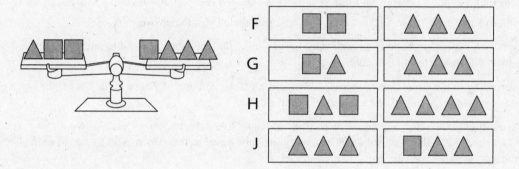

10.

Answers and Explanations

1. **A.** The pattern is $4 + 13 = 17$, and $9 + 13 = 22$. Therefore, $12 + 13 = 25$.

2. **J.** Note that $2 \times 5 = 10$, and $7 \times 5 = 35$. Therefore, $11 \times 5 = 55$.

3. **B.** In this problem, note that the first number, 64, divided by 8, is 8. Then, the second number, 40, divided by 8, is 5. Finally, 24 divided by 8 is 3.

4. **H.** In this case, $20 - 9 = 11$, and $15 - 9 = 6$. Thus, $10 - 9 = 1$.

5. **B.** Here, $\frac{1}{2}$ of each square is shaded, so, overall, $\frac{1}{2}$ of the figure is shaded.

6. **G.** Here, 4 squares out of 6 are shaded. Thus, the answer is $\frac{4}{6} = \frac{2}{3}$.

7. **A.** This diagram has 9 squares. Of these, 4 squares are shaded completely, and two half squares are shaded. Overall, this is equivalent to 5 squares out of 9 being shaded. Thus, the answer is $\frac{5}{9}$.

8. **J.** Remove a cone and a cube from both sides to determine that one cone is equal to one cube. If this is the case, then, two cones are equal to two cubes.

9. **C.** According to the scale, three cones equal two cubes. If we add an extra cube to each side, the scale is still in balance with three cones and one cube equal to three cubes.

10. **G.** According to the scale, a cone and two cubes are equal to a cube and three cones. If we remove a cone and a cube from each side, the scale still balances, with one cube equal to two cones. Add a cone to each side, and we see that a cube and a cone are equal to three cones.

PART II

PRACTICE EXAMS

Practice COOP Exam 1

Practice COOP Exam 2

Practice COOP Exam 3

Practice HSPT Exam 1

Practice HSPT Exam 2

Practice HSPT Exam 3

Answer Sheet for Practice COOP Exam 1

TEST 1 Sequences

1 Ⓐ Ⓑ Ⓒ Ⓓ	5 Ⓐ Ⓑ Ⓒ Ⓓ	9 Ⓐ Ⓑ Ⓒ Ⓓ	13 Ⓐ Ⓑ Ⓒ Ⓓ	17 Ⓐ Ⓑ Ⓒ Ⓓ
2 Ⓕ Ⓖ Ⓗ Ⓙ	6 Ⓕ Ⓖ Ⓗ Ⓙ	10 Ⓕ Ⓖ Ⓗ Ⓙ	14 Ⓕ Ⓖ Ⓗ Ⓙ	18 Ⓕ Ⓖ Ⓗ Ⓙ
3 Ⓐ Ⓑ Ⓒ Ⓓ	7 Ⓐ Ⓑ Ⓒ Ⓓ	11 Ⓐ Ⓑ Ⓒ Ⓓ	15 Ⓐ Ⓑ Ⓒ Ⓓ	19 Ⓐ Ⓑ Ⓒ Ⓓ
4 Ⓕ Ⓖ Ⓗ Ⓙ	8 Ⓕ Ⓖ Ⓗ Ⓙ	12 Ⓕ Ⓖ Ⓗ Ⓙ	16 Ⓕ Ⓖ Ⓗ Ⓙ	20 Ⓕ Ⓖ Ⓗ Ⓙ

TEST 2 Analogies

1 Ⓐ Ⓑ Ⓒ Ⓓ	5 Ⓐ Ⓑ Ⓒ Ⓓ	9 Ⓐ Ⓑ Ⓒ Ⓓ	13 Ⓐ Ⓑ Ⓒ Ⓓ	17 Ⓐ Ⓑ Ⓒ Ⓓ
2 Ⓕ Ⓖ Ⓗ Ⓙ	6 Ⓕ Ⓖ Ⓗ Ⓙ	10 Ⓕ Ⓖ Ⓗ Ⓙ	14 Ⓕ Ⓖ Ⓗ Ⓙ	18 Ⓕ Ⓖ Ⓗ Ⓙ
3 Ⓐ Ⓑ Ⓒ Ⓓ	7 Ⓐ Ⓑ Ⓒ Ⓓ	11 Ⓐ Ⓑ Ⓒ Ⓓ	15 Ⓐ Ⓑ Ⓒ Ⓓ	19 Ⓐ Ⓑ Ⓒ Ⓓ
4 Ⓕ Ⓖ Ⓗ Ⓙ	8 Ⓕ Ⓖ Ⓗ Ⓙ	12 Ⓕ Ⓖ Ⓗ Ⓙ	16 Ⓕ Ⓖ Ⓗ Ⓙ	20 Ⓕ Ⓖ Ⓗ Ⓙ

TEST 3 Quantitative Reasoning

1 Ⓐ Ⓑ Ⓒ Ⓓ	5 Ⓐ Ⓑ Ⓒ Ⓓ	9 Ⓐ Ⓑ Ⓒ Ⓓ	13 Ⓐ Ⓑ Ⓒ Ⓓ	17 Ⓐ Ⓑ Ⓒ Ⓓ
2 Ⓕ Ⓖ Ⓗ Ⓙ	6 Ⓕ Ⓖ Ⓗ Ⓙ	10 Ⓕ Ⓖ Ⓗ Ⓙ	14 Ⓕ Ⓖ Ⓗ Ⓙ	18 Ⓕ Ⓖ Ⓗ Ⓙ
3 Ⓐ Ⓑ Ⓒ Ⓓ	7 Ⓐ Ⓑ Ⓒ Ⓓ	11 Ⓐ Ⓑ Ⓒ Ⓓ	15 Ⓐ Ⓑ Ⓒ Ⓓ	19 Ⓐ Ⓑ Ⓒ Ⓓ
4 Ⓕ Ⓖ Ⓗ Ⓙ	8 Ⓕ Ⓖ Ⓗ Ⓙ	12 Ⓕ Ⓖ Ⓗ Ⓙ	16 Ⓕ Ⓖ Ⓗ Ⓙ	20 Ⓕ Ⓖ Ⓗ Ⓙ

TEST 4 Verbal Reasoning - Words

1 Ⓐ Ⓑ Ⓒ Ⓓ	5 Ⓐ Ⓑ Ⓒ Ⓓ	9 Ⓐ Ⓑ Ⓒ Ⓓ
2 Ⓕ Ⓖ Ⓗ Ⓙ	6 Ⓕ Ⓖ Ⓗ Ⓙ	10 Ⓕ Ⓖ Ⓗ Ⓙ
3 Ⓐ Ⓑ Ⓒ Ⓓ	7 Ⓐ Ⓑ Ⓒ Ⓓ	11 Ⓐ Ⓑ Ⓒ Ⓓ
4 Ⓕ Ⓖ Ⓗ Ⓙ	8 Ⓕ Ⓖ Ⓗ Ⓙ	12 Ⓕ Ⓖ Ⓗ Ⓙ

TEST 5 Verbal Reasoning - Context

1 Ⓐ Ⓑ Ⓒ Ⓓ	5 Ⓐ Ⓑ Ⓒ Ⓓ
2 Ⓕ Ⓖ Ⓗ Ⓙ	6 Ⓕ Ⓖ Ⓗ Ⓙ
3 Ⓐ Ⓑ Ⓒ Ⓓ	7 Ⓐ Ⓑ Ⓒ Ⓓ
4 Ⓕ Ⓖ Ⓗ Ⓙ	8 Ⓕ Ⓖ Ⓗ Ⓙ

TEST 6 Reading and Language Arts

1 Ⓐ Ⓑ Ⓒ Ⓓ	9 Ⓐ Ⓑ Ⓒ Ⓓ	17 Ⓐ Ⓑ Ⓒ Ⓓ	25 Ⓐ Ⓑ Ⓒ Ⓓ	33 Ⓐ Ⓑ Ⓒ Ⓓ
2 Ⓕ Ⓖ Ⓗ Ⓙ	10 Ⓕ Ⓖ Ⓗ Ⓙ	18 Ⓕ Ⓖ Ⓗ Ⓙ	26 Ⓕ Ⓖ Ⓗ Ⓙ	34 Ⓕ Ⓖ Ⓗ Ⓙ
3 Ⓐ Ⓑ Ⓒ Ⓓ	11 Ⓐ Ⓑ Ⓒ Ⓓ	19 Ⓐ Ⓑ Ⓒ Ⓓ	27 Ⓐ Ⓑ Ⓒ Ⓓ	35 Ⓐ Ⓑ Ⓒ Ⓓ
4 Ⓕ Ⓖ Ⓗ Ⓙ	12 Ⓕ Ⓖ Ⓗ Ⓙ	20 Ⓕ Ⓖ Ⓗ Ⓙ	28 Ⓕ Ⓖ Ⓗ Ⓙ	36 Ⓕ Ⓖ Ⓗ Ⓙ
5 Ⓐ Ⓑ Ⓒ Ⓓ	13 Ⓐ Ⓑ Ⓒ Ⓓ	21 Ⓐ Ⓑ Ⓒ Ⓓ	29 Ⓐ Ⓑ Ⓒ Ⓓ	37 Ⓐ Ⓑ Ⓒ Ⓓ
6 Ⓕ Ⓖ Ⓗ Ⓙ	14 Ⓕ Ⓖ Ⓗ Ⓙ	22 Ⓕ Ⓖ Ⓗ Ⓙ	30 Ⓕ Ⓖ Ⓗ Ⓙ	38 Ⓕ Ⓖ Ⓗ Ⓙ
7 Ⓐ Ⓑ Ⓒ Ⓓ	15 Ⓐ Ⓑ Ⓒ Ⓓ	23 Ⓐ Ⓑ Ⓒ Ⓓ	31 Ⓐ Ⓑ Ⓒ Ⓓ	39 Ⓐ Ⓑ Ⓒ Ⓓ
8 Ⓕ Ⓖ Ⓗ Ⓙ	16 Ⓕ Ⓖ Ⓗ Ⓙ	24 Ⓕ Ⓖ Ⓗ Ⓙ	32 Ⓕ Ⓖ Ⓗ Ⓙ	40 Ⓕ Ⓖ Ⓗ Ⓙ

TEST 7 Mathematics

1 Ⓐ Ⓑ Ⓒ Ⓓ	9 Ⓐ Ⓑ Ⓒ Ⓓ	17 Ⓐ Ⓑ Ⓒ Ⓓ	25 Ⓐ Ⓑ Ⓒ Ⓓ	33 Ⓐ Ⓑ Ⓒ Ⓓ
2 Ⓕ Ⓖ Ⓗ Ⓙ	10 Ⓕ Ⓖ Ⓗ Ⓙ	18 Ⓕ Ⓖ Ⓗ Ⓙ	26 Ⓕ Ⓖ Ⓗ Ⓙ	34 Ⓕ Ⓖ Ⓗ Ⓙ
3 Ⓐ Ⓑ Ⓒ Ⓓ	11 Ⓐ Ⓑ Ⓒ Ⓓ	19 Ⓐ Ⓑ Ⓒ Ⓓ	27 Ⓐ Ⓑ Ⓒ Ⓓ	35 Ⓐ Ⓑ Ⓒ Ⓓ
4 Ⓕ Ⓖ Ⓗ Ⓙ	12 Ⓕ Ⓖ Ⓗ Ⓙ	20 Ⓕ Ⓖ Ⓗ Ⓙ	28 Ⓕ Ⓖ Ⓗ Ⓙ	36 Ⓕ Ⓖ Ⓗ Ⓙ
5 Ⓐ Ⓑ Ⓒ Ⓓ	13 Ⓐ Ⓑ Ⓒ Ⓓ	21 Ⓐ Ⓑ Ⓒ Ⓓ	29 Ⓐ Ⓑ Ⓒ Ⓓ	37 Ⓐ Ⓑ Ⓒ Ⓓ
6 Ⓕ Ⓖ Ⓗ Ⓙ	14 Ⓕ Ⓖ Ⓗ Ⓙ	22 Ⓕ Ⓖ Ⓗ Ⓙ	30 Ⓕ Ⓖ Ⓗ Ⓙ	38 Ⓕ Ⓖ Ⓗ Ⓙ
7 Ⓐ Ⓑ Ⓒ Ⓓ	15 Ⓐ Ⓑ Ⓒ Ⓓ	23 Ⓐ Ⓑ Ⓒ Ⓓ	31 Ⓐ Ⓑ Ⓒ Ⓓ	39 Ⓐ Ⓑ Ⓒ Ⓓ
8 Ⓕ Ⓖ Ⓗ Ⓙ	16 Ⓕ Ⓖ Ⓗ Ⓙ	24 Ⓕ Ⓖ Ⓗ Ⓙ	32 Ⓕ Ⓖ Ⓗ Ⓙ	40 Ⓕ Ⓖ Ⓗ Ⓙ

CUT HERE

CUT HERE

Practice COOP Exam 1

Test 1: Sequences

Time: 15 Minutes

Directions: For questions 1 through 20, select the answer that best continues the pattern or sequence given.

1.

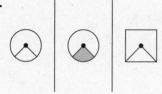

A.

B.

C.

D.

2.

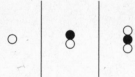

F.

G.

H.

J.

3.

A●B | B●A | Y●Z

A. Y●Z

B. A●B

C. B●A

D. Z●Y

4.

F.

G.

H.

J.

GO ON TO THE NEXT PAGE

5.

A. ⬤ ⬤

B. ◯ ⬤

C. ◯ ◯

D. △ △

6. ◁ | ▷ | ⊐

F. ⊐

G. ⊓

H. ⊐

J. ⊔

7. 7 10 13 | 19 22 25 | 31 34 ___

    A. 35
    B. 36
    C. 37
    D. 38

8. 16 8 4 | 20 10 5 | 28 ___ 7

    F. 10
    G. 12
    H. 13
    J. 14

9. 10 8 24 | 8 6 18 | 4 2 ___

    A. 4
    B. 6
    C. 8
    D. 10

10. 1 1 1 | 2 4 16 | 3 9 ___

    F. 27
    G. 54
    H. 81
    J. 243

11. 36 41 37 | 43 48 44 | 51 ___ 52

    A. 56
    B. 57
    C. 58
    D. 59

12. 16 4 2 | 28 16 8 | 36 24 ___

    F. 6
    G. 12
    H. 16
    J. 18

13. 5 10 30 | 7 14 42 | 12 ___ 72

    A. 15
    B. 18
    C. 20
    D. 24

14. B D F | E G I | H J L | K M O | ___

    F. N O P
    G. P R T
    H. Q S U
    J. N P R

15. J I K | P O Q | F E G | K J L | ___

    A. R Q S
    B. R S Q
    C. R T S
    D. R P Q

16. A C F | K M P | Q S V | L N Q | _____

    F. G H J

    G. G I L

    H. G I K

    J. G J K

17. Z W T | Y V S | X U R | _____ | V S P

    A. W U Q

    B. W T S

    C. W T Q

    D. X T G

18. F 5 G | J 4 K | M 3 N | Q 2 S | _____

    F. U 2 V

    G. U 1 V

    H. U 1 W

    J. U 1 X

19. A 4 E | C 5 G | E 6 I | J 7 N | _____

    A. P 8 T

    B. P 7 T

    C. M 8 P

    D. S 8 U

20. A C 8 E | B D 6 F | C E 4 G | D F 2 H | _____

    F. E F 1 I

    G. E F 0 I

    H. E G 1 L

    J. E G 0 I

IF YOU FINISH BEFORE TIME IS CALLED, CHECK YOUR WORK ON THIS SECTION ONLY. DO NOT WORK ON ANY OTHER SECTION IN THE TEST.

Test 2: Analogies

Time: 7 Minutes

Directions: For the questions in this test, choose the picture that should go in the empty box so that the bottom two pictures are related in the same way that the top two are related.

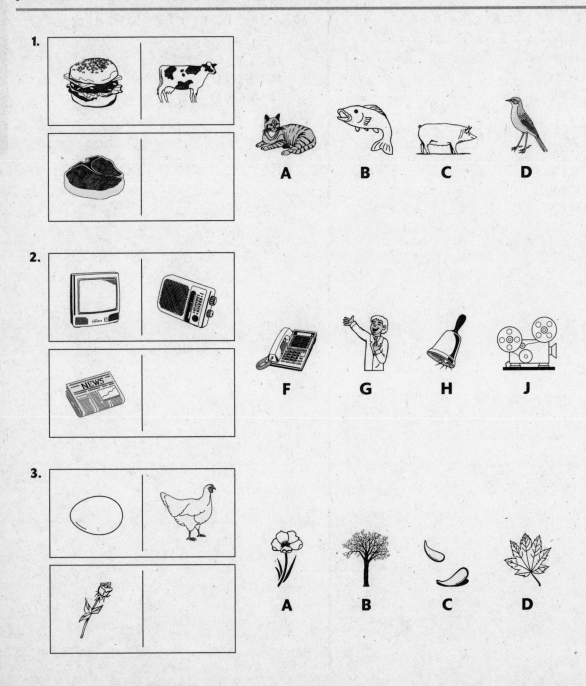

4.

F   G   H   J

5.

A   B   C   D

6.

F   G   H   J

7.

A   B   C   D

GO ON TO THE NEXT PAGE

93

12.

F G H J

13.

A B C D

14.

F G H J

15.

A B C D

GO ON TO THE NEXT PAGE

16.

17.

18.

19.

F   G   H   J

A   B   C   D

F   G   H   J

A   B   C   D

20.

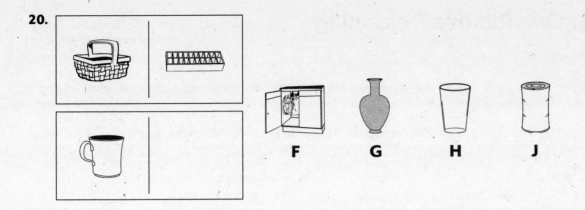

F   G   H   J

IF YOU FINISH BEFORE TIME IS CALLED, CHECK YOUR WORK ON THIS SECTION ONLY. DO NOT WORK ON ANY OTHER SECTION IN THE TEST.

Test 3: Quantitative Reasoning

Time: 20 Minutes

Directions: For each of the three types of questions in this section, select the choice that best answers each question.

For questions 1–7, find the relationship of the numbers in one column to the numbers in the other column. Then find the missing number.

1.

6 → ☐ → 18

9 → ☐ → 21

15 → ☐ → ?

A. 25
B. 27
C. 29
D. 31

2.

4 → ☐ → 20

1 → ☐ → 5

8 → ☐ → ?

F. 25
G. 30
H. 35
J. 40

3.

2 → ☐ → 4

4 → ☐ → 16

6 → ☐ → ?

A. 24
B. 30
C. 36
D. 42

4.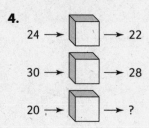

24 → ☐ → 22

30 → ☐ → 28

20 → ☐ → ?

F. 19
G. 18
H. 17
J. 16

5.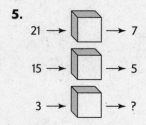

21 → ☐ → 7

15 → ☐ → 5

3 → ☐ → ?

A. 0
B. 1
C. 2
D. 3

6.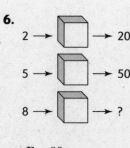

2 → ☐ → 20

5 → ☐ → 50

8 → ☐ → ?

F. 80
G. 88
H. 90
J. 95

7.

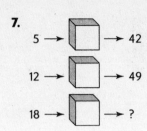

$5 \rightarrow \boxed{} \rightarrow 42$

$12 \rightarrow \boxed{} \rightarrow 49$

$18 \rightarrow \boxed{} \rightarrow ?$

A. 55
B. 58
C. 62
D. 65

For questions 8–13, find the fraction of the grid that is shaded.

8.

F. $\frac{1}{4}$

G. $\frac{1}{3}$

H. $\frac{1}{2}$

J. $\frac{3}{4}$

9.

A. $\frac{1}{4}$

B. $\frac{1}{3}$

C. $\frac{1}{2}$

D. $\frac{2}{3}$

10.

F. $\frac{1}{6}$

G. $\frac{1}{4}$

H. $\frac{1}{3}$

J. $\frac{1}{2}$

11.

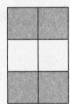

A. $\frac{2}{5}$

B. $\frac{1}{2}$

C. $\frac{3}{5}$

D. $\frac{2}{3}$

GO ON TO THE NEXT PAGE

12.

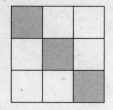

F. $\frac{1}{4}$

G. $\frac{1}{3}$

H. $\frac{1}{2}$

J. $\frac{2}{3}$

13.

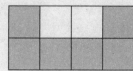

A. $\frac{1}{2}$

B. $\frac{3}{5}$

C. $\frac{3}{4}$

D. $\frac{5}{6}$

For questions 14–20, look at the scale showing sets of shapes of equal weight. Find an equivalent pair of sets that also balances the scale.

14.

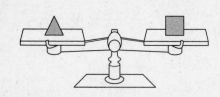

15.

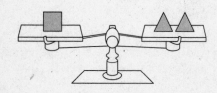

16.

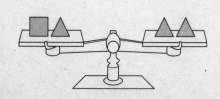

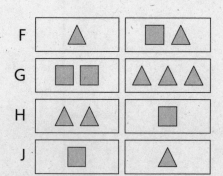

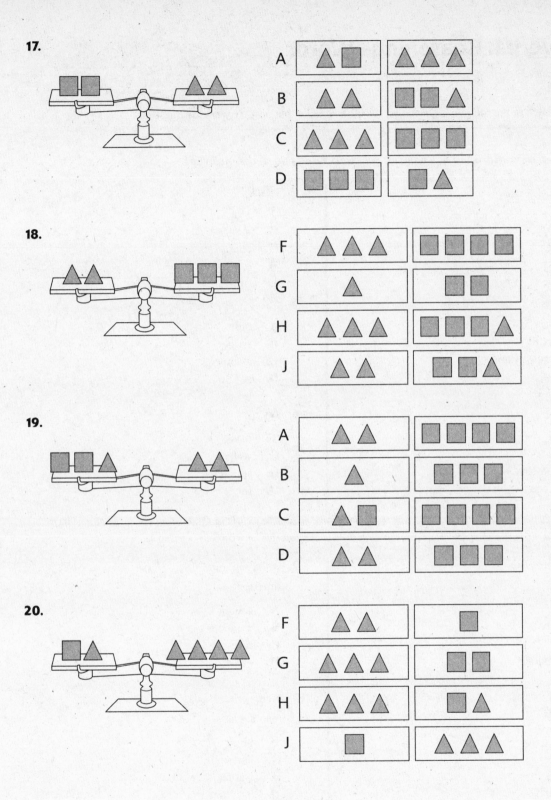

17.

A △ ■ | △ △ △

B △ △ | ■ ■ △

C △ △ △ | ■ ■ ■

D ■ ■ ■ | ■ △

18.

F △ △ △ | ■ ■ ■ ■

G △ | ■ ■

H △ △ △ | ■ ■ ■ △

J △ △ | ■ ■ △

19.

A △ △ | ■ ■ ■ ■

B △ | ■ ■ ■

C △ ■ | ■ ■ ■ ■

D △ △ | ■ ■ ■

20.

F △ △ | ■

G △ △ △ | ■ ■

H △ △ △ | ■ △

J ■ | △ △ △

IF YOU FINISH BEFORE TIME IS CALLED, CHECK YOUR WORK ON THIS
SECTION ONLY. DO NOT WORK ON ANY OTHER SECTION IN THE TEST.

Test 4: Verbal Reasoning—Words

Time: 15 Minutes

Directions: For each of the following questions, select the choice that best answers the questions.

For questions 1–6, choose the word that names a necessary part of the underlined word.

1. <u>cello</u>

   A. bow
   B. notes
   C. strings
   D. melody

2. <u>computer</u>

   F. mouse
   G. keyboard
   H. operating system
   J. e-mail

3. <u>sing</u>

   A. music
   B. vocal cords
   C. instruments
   D. audience

4. <u>novel</u>

   F. plot
   G. author
   H. characters
   J. setting

5. <u>sail</u>

   A. hull
   B. rudder
   C. anchor
   D. wind

6. <u>swim</u>

   F. mask
   G. water
   H. snorkel
   J. fins

In questions 7–12, the words in the top row are related in some way. The words in the bottom row are related in the same way. For each item, choose the word that completes the bottom row of words.

7. knife, hatchet, axe

   son, father

   A. family
   B. brother
   C. aunt
   D. grandfather

8. grain, flour, bread

   sheep, wool

   F. spin
   G. yarn
   H. coat
   J. sweater

9. walk, jog, run

   run, trot

   A. canter
   B. compete
   C. race
   D. gait

10. pine, spruce, cedar

    maple, oak

    F. birch
    G. butternut
    H. walnut
    J. hazelnut

11. walnut, pecan, almond

Memorial Day, Fourth of July

    A. Christmas
    B. Easter
    C. Lent
    D. Labor Day

12. spring, summer, fall

England, United States

    F. Asia
    G. Denmark
    H. South America
    J. Africa

IF YOU FINISH BEFORE TIME IS CALLED, CHECK YOUR WORK ON THIS SECTION ONLY. DO NOT WORK ON ANY OTHER SECTION IN THE TEST.

Test 5: Verbal Reasoning—Context

Time: 15 Minutes

Directions: There are two types of questions in this section. For each of the questions, select the choice that best answers the question.

For questions 1–5, choose the statement that is true according to the given information.

1. Julio smoked for 45 years. He had lung cancer when he was 65.

   A. Julio's smoking caused his lung cancer.
   B. Julio's smoking might have contributed to his lung cancer.
   C. Julio's lung cancer had nothing to do with his smoking.
   D. Julio would have gotten lung cancer whether or not he smoked.

2. Nguyen has a Honda, which he has driven 100,000 miles and has had only small mechanical problems to correct. Kanishiro has a Honda, which is 15 years old. He has had it serviced routinely and has had only minor repairs made. Shaniqua has a Honda, which he has driven across the country and back three times. He, too, has had no major repairs.

   F. All Hondas are well built and reliable.
   G. Because Shaniqua, Nguyen, and Kanishiro took care of their cars, the Hondas were very dependable and lasted a long time.
   H. Hondas are good cars.
   J. Hondas are never reliable.

3. Paul puts peanuts, almonds, and raisins on the lawn to feed the squirrels. In the morning, the peanuts and almonds are gone.

   A. Peanuts are good for squirrels.
   B. Squirrels prefer almonds to peanuts.
   C. Squirrels do not eat raisins.
   D. Paul shouldn't feed wild creatures.

4. Tomorrow is the first day of school. Most of the children in the community ride to school on a school bus. Some children who live near their school are able to walk. Other children are able to take public transportation. The town has very few sidewalks. The drivers of the school bus company have announced that they are going on strike tomorrow.

   F. Children who ride the bus will not be able to attend school tomorrow.
   G. Parents of children who usually take the school bus will have to provide transportation to school.
   H. Very few children will be in school tomorrow.
   J. Students who walk or take public transportation will stay home from school.

5. Linda collects porcelain dolls as a hobby and to sell for a profit. She has 12 dolls that belong in a set. The complete set has 15 dolls. Each represents a character from a well-known fairy tale. A complete set of dolls is more valuable than a partial set. The 3 dolls needed to complete the set are very difficult to find. Linda saw them for sale on E-Bay, but they were much more expensive than the price she paid for the other dolls. The complete set of dolls was also available.

   A. Linda ordered the remaining three dolls even though they were expensive.
   B. Linda wrote E-Bay a letter complaining about the cost of the dolls.
   C. Linda ordered a complete set of the dolls from E-Bay.
   D. Linda decided not to buy any more of the dolls.

For questions 6–8, choose the correct answer.

6. Here are some words translated from an artificial language.

Kiowabossifls means ocean.

Roaluwabostirs means lake.

Roaluwabosloo means pond.

Which word means river?

- **F.** *hsfruatuk*
- **G.** *asloowaboschaka*
- **H.** *siflsstirroalwobos*
- **J.** *yenquaoirsh*

7. Here are some words translated from an artificial language.

Oexrawifhg means running.

Fluxwarifhg means jumping.

Rsxarwifhg means skipping.

Which word means sleeping?

- **A.** *rwifhg*
- **B.** *xulfoerifhg*
- **C.** *rawrawifhg*
- **D.** *worrowifhg*

8. Here are some words translated from an artificial language.

Rilneffo means train.

Albineffo means bus.

Fonisnefforl means car.

Which word means bicycle?

- **F.** *fonibal*
- **G.** *ghfiwoffl*
- **H.** *wanibefforl*
- **J.** *tepudeds*

IF YOU FINISH BEFORE TIME IS CALLED, CHECK YOUR WORK ON THIS SECTION ONLY. DO NOT WORK ON ANY OTHER SECTION IN THE TEST.

Test 6: Reading and Language Arts

Time: 40 Minutes

Directions: For the questions in this test, read the passage and questions that follow. Choose the best possible answer.

Passage for questions 1–4:

When Levi Strauss immigrated to New York from Germany in 1848, he found work with his brothers as a peddler, selling small items like needles and thread by going from door to door. When his sister, who lived in San Francisco, offered to pay his way west, he was happy to go. He took bolts of cloth with him. He hoped to sell the cloth to people who would use it to make tents. While talking with a miner who had come from the gold country, he learned that the miners could not find sturdy pants that would stand up to the rough work of gold mining. So he decided to turn his cloth into pants for the miners. When he ran out of canvas, he wrote to his brothers in New York asking them to send more. Instead, they sent him a tough brown cotton cloth called *serge de Nimes*, which means a kind of fabric made in the French city of Nimes. The fabric's name was shortened to denim, and Strauss dyed it blue. He took the idea of using rivets to hold the pants together from a tailor named Davis. Eventually, Strauss patented the idea of the rivets and hired Davis as a manager in his company.

1. This selection is primarily about:

    A. Levi Strauss

    B. the California gold rush

    C. the invention of blue jeans

    D. immigration in the nineteenth century

Passage for questions 5–9:

It was the first time a grave had opened in my road of life, and the gap that it made in the smooth ground was wonderful. The figure of my sister in her chain by the kitchen fire haunted me night and day. That the place could possibly be, without her, was something my mind seemed unable to compass; and whereas she had seldom or never been in my thoughts of late, I had now the strangest idea that she was coming towards me in the street, or that she would presently knock at the door.

Whatever my fortunes might have been, I could scarcely have recalled my sister with much tenderness. But I suppose there is a shock of regret which may exist without much tenderness. Under its influence (and perhaps to make up for the want of the softer feeling) I was seized with a violent indignation against the assailant from

2. Strauss turned his cloth into pants because:

    F. he wanted to make money

    G. he learned the miners needed pants

    H. denim is a tough cotton fabric

    J. rivets hold the pants together

3. Blue jeans were made from a fabric that originated in:

    A. France

    B. New York

    C. California

    D. Germany

4. Why do you suppose Strauss hired Davis?

    F. He liked him.

    G. Davis supplied the idea for using rivets on the pants.

    H. The miners had been buying their pants from Davis.

    J. Strauss's sister suggested that he do so.

whom she had suffered so much; and I felt on sufficient proof I could have revengefully pursued Orlick, or anyone else, to the last extremity.

From *Great Expectations* by Charles Dickens

5. The first sentence means that:

    A. the speaker saw a hole in the road on which he was walking

    B. this was the first time someone the speaker knew had died

    C. the gap in his life was a pleasant surprise

    D. he had not seen his sister for a long period of time

6. The speaker's sister died:

   F. of natural causes
   G. because she missed the speaker
   H. as a result of a crime
   J. from overwork

7. From the passage, the reader can infer that the speaker:

   A. hated his sister
   B. did not have kind feelings toward his sister
   C. loved his sister very much
   D. was indifferent to his sister's death

Passage for questions 10–14:

Most penguins breed during the brief Antarctic summer. Fighting noisily over territory, each pair builds its nest in a small hole it has scooped out and lined with rocks and pebbles. The female lays two eggs. The male incubates them, while the female goes to sea to feed. When the eggs hatch, the male and female take turns finding food and feeding the chicks. By the end of the summer, the chicks are capable of swimming and feeding themselves.

But emperor penguin chicks, because emperor penguins are so large, take longer than the brief summer to reach maturity. So the emperors have reversed the normal breeding time table. The emperor breeding process starts at the beginning of winter. By the end of summer, when they spend all their time feeding, the emperors are fat. They come ashore on the sea ice. They do not nest. The female lays one egg, which she removes from the ice before it freezes by lifting it toward her toes with the underside of her belly. It rests on top of her feet. There, it is covered by a fold of skin hanging down from the belly. Then the male transfers the egg to his own feet. The female immediately leaves to go to sea to feed.

For two months the male, without eating, moving only to protect the egg from winds and cold, broods over the egg. The egg hatches in 60 days. Unable to keep warm by itself, the chick stays huddled beneath the male. Amazingly, just at this point, the female reappears and gives the chick a meal of regurgitated fish. Now the male goes to feed, and he returns weeks later with a meal for the chick. The pair take turns fishing and feeding the chick until the beginning of spring when the sea ice begins to crack. At that point, the chicks are ready to swim, and they and the parents dive into the water to begin their summer feeding to supply them with energy for the next breeding season.

8. The word *indignation* probably means:

   F. joy
   G. sadness
   H. calm
   J. anger

9. From the context of the passage, the reader can infer that Orlick:

   A. was suspected of the murder
   B. knew who committed the crime
   C. married the speaker's sister
   D. was acquainted with the speaker

10. The chicks of most species of penguins:

   F. are hatched in the spring
   G. mature by the end of summer
   H. learn to feed themselves by imitating their parents
   J. fight noisily

11. After the female emperor penguin lays her egg, she:

   A. spends two months feeding at sea
   B. rebuilds the nest
   C. transfers the egg to the male
   D. lays a second egg

12. Emperors take longer than other penguins to reach maturity because:

   F. they have folds of skin hanging from their bellies
   G. they breed at a different time
   H. sea ice is very cold
   J. they are larger than other penguins

13. The word *amazingly* suggests the following question:

   A. How do the chicks keep warm?
   B. Why does the female go to sea to feed?
   C. Which emperor penguin parent works harder?
   D. How does the female know exactly when to return?

GO ON TO THE NEXT PAGE

14. To allow time for their chicks to mature, emperor penguins:

    F. have reversed the seasons of the usual penguin breeding cycle

    G. take turns finding food for the chicks

    H. do not make nests

    J. all of the above

Passage for questions 15–18:

The story of Benjamin Franklin's experiment with a kite during a lightning storm has lead some people to believe that he discovered electricity. But this is not true. The phenomenon of electricity had been known for some time. By 1745, two scientists at the University of Leyden, in Holland, had created the earliest form of a capacitor. Their Leyden jar is still used for demonstrations and experiments.

Franklin sent reports to the Royal Academy in London, the English-speaking world's collector of scientific information, about many of his experiments, including experiments with electricity. Humorist that he was, he could not resist an occasional joke in those letters. In one letter, he wrote "a turkey is to be killed for our dinners by the electrical shock, and roasted by the electrical jack [spit], before a fire kindled by the electrical battery."

15. Benjamin Franklin's famous experiment with a kite demonstrated:

    A. the existence of electricity

    B. the existence of lightning

    C. how a Leyden jar works

    D. none of the above

Passage for questions 19–22:

Argument is the technical name for speech or writing with the purpose of causing someone to agree with a point of view. The classical form of argument tries to prove the opponent is wrong. It uses evidence and logic to show why the arguer is correct and the opponent is wrong. Its tone is hostile. As a result, the opponents might feel threatened and defend their own ideas rather than hearing what is said to them.

But a modern form of argument tries to reduce the threat to opponents. While its content also comes from evidence and logic, it admits to the possibility of some truth in opponents' views. It treats opponents' ideas respectfully and tries to find common grounds for agreement. Its tone is friendly. As a result, opponents might be more open to listening to what the arguer says.

16. Franklin sent his reports to London because:

    F. he had a good sense of humor

    G. no comparable organization existed in the United States

    H. electricity was a phenomenon that had been known for some time

    J. the Leyden jar had been invented there

17. According to this passage, Franklin:

    A. did not discover electricity

    B. experimented in scientific fields other than electricity

    C. enjoyed jokes

    D. all of the above

18. Franklin's joking letter describes:

    F. actual events at the time

    G. what the people in the past believed to be true

    H. something that could occur today

    J. science fiction possibilities

19. The best title for this passage is:

    A. The Content of Arguments

    B. How to Win Arguments

    C. Two Kinds of Arguments

    D. Threat and Respect

20. The word *hostile* most probably means:

    F. homelike

    G. unfriendly

    H. definite

    J. nervous

21. The classical and modern forms of argument described:

   A. have no similarities
   B. stress the arguer's point of view
   C. differ in tone
   D. respect other points of view

22. The author of this passage probably thinks that:

   F. classical arguments are more effective than modern ones
   G. a friendly approach is move convincing than an unfriendly one
   H. the form of modern argument is weak
   J. opponents of arguers do not listen to logic and evidence

Passage for questions 23–26:

Having little kids running around and over you, maybe even hitting you and kicking you, doesn't sound like much fun. But it's part of my job. I work at an old warehouse that has been made into a kids party house. Parents arrange to have their children's parties here. There is equipment kids jump on, run on, crawl under, and climb up. Birthday cake and other treats are eaten in the kitchen, which has a long table and child-sized chairs. My job is to make sure that everyone has a good time and no one gets hurt. This requires playing with the children and acting like a child. That's where the kicking comes in. But I don't mind the body contact. I enjoy walking into the huge space filled with bouncers and balls, taking off my shoes, and jumping up and down with the children. The warehouse becomes a fun house.

I'm proud to be trusted with taking care of the children. I like to see the parents relaxing and even playing with the children without having to worry about preparing for the party and cleaning up afterward. My most gratifying moments come at the end of the day. The parents often thank me. The children hug me and say they want to come back for their next birthday party. The place looks wrecked, and part of my job is cleaning up. But I don't mind this chore because I was partly responsible for the messy remains of happiness.

23. The tone of this passage could best be described as:

   A. responsible
   B. enthusiastic
   C. helpful
   D. pained

24. The responsibilities of the author of this passage include:

   F. baking the birthday cake
   G. hugging the children
   H. sweeping the floor
   J. selling the services of the kids party house

25. The parents like using the services of the kids party house because:

   A. someone takes care of their responsibilities
   B. they can act like children
   C. the cost of the services is reasonable
   D. the author of the passage appeals to them when they meet her

26. *Gratifying* most probably means:

   F. thankful
   G. annoying
   H. confusing
   J. satisfying

Passage for questions 27–30:

Lacrosse is a game in which the object is to score points by sending the ball through the goal of the opposing team. Each goal counts as one point. Players use a stick that is hooked on top with woven strings forming a basketlike network across the hooked portion. The stick is known as a crosse. The ball is made of hard rubber.

The ball cannot be touched by the players. It can be thrown, caught or carried with the crosse in any direction. The crosse can be used to try to force the ball out of the net of an opponent's crosse. In men's lacrosse, players can also try to keep their opponents from moving the ball toward the goal or keep them from catching the ball by body checking. They are permitted to shove their bodies against an opponent, but they must keep one foot on the ground and cannot check from behind. In women's lacrosse, no physical contact is permitted.

GO ON TO THE NEXT PAGE

Men's lacrosse is played on a field 60 yards wide and 110 yards long. The women's field measures 120 yards by 70 yards. There are 10 players on men's teams and 12 players on women's teams. The men's game lasts 60 minutes divided into four quarters, with two timeouts per team per half. The women's game is played in two 25-minute halves. The men play four-minute sudden-death overtimes if the game is tied at the end of regulation. The women play two three-minute overtimes.

Originally used by Native Americans to train for warfare, the game was taken up by French Canadians. It is very popular in Canada, which has professional lacrosse leagues. In the United States, the game is played most frequently in intercollegiate athletic programs.

27. The playing field for women's lacrosse is:

    A. limited to 12 players
    B. protected by a goal
    C. narrower and longer than the men's field
    D. wider and shorter than the men's field

28. From the description given in the passage, lacrosse is most similar to:

    F. basketball
    G. soccer
    H. hockey
    J. tennis

29. From the information in the preceding passage, you could conclude:

    A. lacrosse is more popular in Canada than in the United States
    B. the United States has no professional lacrosse players
    C. most lacrosse players are French Canadians
    D. college athletes in the United States prefer other sports to lacrosse

30. The purpose of body checking is:

    F. defense
    G. to advance the ball
    H. keeping one foot on the ground
    J. to prevent injury to women players

Passage for questions 31–35:

North American brown bats eat insects. Bats find their prey by a kind of sonar. The bats emit high-pitched sounds that echo against insects or other solid objects. The echoes return to the bats' ears, and the bats interpret them to determine the location of the objects.

Night-flying moths are a common insect in the bat's diet. The moth, however, has developed a defense that gives it a chance to avoid these predators. I was surprised to learn that moths have ears. Some night-flying moths can hear the noises made by bats. This ability warns them of approaching bats that they can then try to avoid.

Even stranger than the idea that moths have ears is the relation between the moths and the mites that infest their ears. The mites lay their eggs in the moth's ear, a safe and protected spot. But while laying their eggs, they damage the delicate structure of the moth's ear. Because many mites lay their eggs on a single moth, the moth might become deaf if mites lay their eggs in both ears. In a manner that remains a mystery, the first mite on a moth leaves some kind of trail, and other mites follow the trail to lay their eggs in the same ear, leaving the opposite ear undamaged. The amazing ways of nature permit the moth to continue to hear, improving its chances of escaping from bats, and increasing the mites chances of finding safe places to lay their eggs.

31. The sounds that bats hear:

    A. are made by insects
    B. determine the size of their prey
    C. echo off insects
    D. vary from low to high pitch

32. The word *emit* most probably means:

    F. send out
    G. throw away
    H. listen to
    J. consist of

33. It is not good for mites to lay eggs in both ears of a moth because:

    A. the mite wouldn't remember where the eggs were
    B. deaf moths find it hard to escape from bats
    C. mites leave a trail to one ear only
    D. bats prey on mites as well as moths

34. The writer's attitude toward the relationship of bats, moths, and mites is best described as:

    F. amazement
    G. admiration
    H. disgust
    J. concern

35. The word *infest* most probably means:

    A. invade
    B. return to
    C. affect
    D. instruct

Passage for questions 36–40:

Henry Adams, a nineteenth-century American author, described the United States during the administration of Thomas Jefferson as it would appear to a visitor from Europe. Such a person would find a few flourishing towns on the east coast supported by business. Beyond them were thousands of miles of forests where no one lived, interrupted only by a few settlements. Arts and culture scarcely existed. Slavery was a disease infecting the small nation. Every area had its own political theory designed to protect itself. The visitor would foresee nothing but the possibility of conflict and violence. Yet, Adams goes on to write, the visitor would be wrong, for he had misjudged the American character. Cheerful and self-confident, optimistic if partly because of ignorance of the difficulties of building a complex society, Americans would not fulfill the European vision. Except for slavery, Adams wrote, American society was "sound and healthy in every part. Stripped for the hardest work, every muscle firm and elastic, every ounce of brain ready for use, and not a trace of superfluous flesh on his nervous and supple body, the American stood in the world as a new order of man."

36. Henry Adams:

    F. thought America under Thomas Jefferson was a desperate land
    G. did not agree with the European's vision of Jefferson's America
    H. criticized Europeans for their errors
    J. believed Thomas Jefferson was a great president

37. *Foresee* most probably means:

    A. find
    B. consider
    C. remember
    D. predict

38. The purpose of the quotation at the end of the passage is to:

    F. describe the healthy bodies of Americans
    G. compare American society to a healthy person
    H. compare Americans and Europeans
    J. criticize slavery

39. At the time Adams describes, the interior of the United States:

    A. had many flourishing settlements
    B. consisted largely of wilderness
    C. did not need arts and culture
    D. permitted the existence of slavery

40. Henry Adams wrote:

    F. during the administration of Thomas Jefferson
    G. when Jefferson's era was history
    H. arguments for the European point of view
    J. to predict the future of America

IF YOU FINISH BEFORE TIME IS CALLED, CHECK YOUR WORK ON THIS SECTION ONLY. DO NOT WORK ON ANY OTHER SECTION IN THE TEST.

Test 7: Mathematics

Time: 40 Minutes

Directions: For questions 1 through 40, solve the problems and select the best answer for each question.

1. Rounded to the nearest tenth, 52.98 is equal to:

   A. 52.0
   B. 52.9
   C. 53.0
   D. 53.1

2. $3^2 + 5^3 =$

   F. 21
   G. 24
   H. 131
   J. 134

3. If $4x - 6 = 3x + 4$, then $x^2 =$

   A. 10
   B. 20
   C. 50
   D. 100

4. Last year, 420 students attended Brian's school. This year, the number of students decreased by 5%. How many students are at Brian's school this year?

   F. 20
   G. 395
   H. 399
   J. 400

5. What is the value of 0.03 expressed as a percent?

   A. 0.03%
   B. 0.3%
   C. 3%
   D. 30%

6. What is the median of the numbers 2, 5, 7, 9, 12, 14, 16, and 18?

   F. 9

   G. 10

   H. $10\frac{1}{2}$

   J. 12

7. Which of the following numbers is *not* a perfect square?

   A. 16
   B. 48
   C. 49
   D. 64

8.

   What percent of the square in the preceding figure is shaded?

   F. $\frac{1}{4}$%

   G. 25%

   H. 40%

   J. 50%

9. The scale of a map is $\frac{1}{2}$ inch equals 6 miles. If the distance between the airport and the city is 3 inches on the map, what is the actual distance between the airport and the city?

   A. 12 miles
   B. 24 miles
   C. 36 miles
   D. 48 miles

10. If ABC is a three-digit number that is divisible by both 2 and 5, what is the value of C?

    F. 0
    G. 2
    H. 5
    J. It cannot be determined.

11. Which of the following is equal to $\frac{x^6 y^6}{x^2 y^3}$?

    A. $x^4 y^3$
    B. $x^3 y^2$
    C. $x^4 y^2$
    D. $x^3 y^3$

12. Which of the following ratios is the same as the ratio of 12 to 16?

    F.   2 to 5
    G.   3 to 4
    H.   8 to 15
    J.   4 to 3

13. An office supply store is having a sale during which, for every package of pens purchased for $2.10, another package of pens can be purchased for $0.90. How many packages of pens did Peter buy if he spent $11.10 on packages of pens?

    A.   5
    B.   6
    C.   7
    D.   8

14. If $a = 2$ and $b = 10$, what is the value of $\frac{a+b}{2a}$?

    F. $\frac{1}{5}$

    G. $\frac{1}{3}$

    H.   3

    J.   5

15. A three-digit number is formed by using the digits 2, 3, and 4 one time each. This number must be:

    A.   prime
    B.   odd
    C.   even
    D.   divisible by 3

16.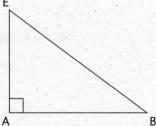

If the measure of ∠ABE is 40°, what is the measure of ∠BEA?

    F.   40°
    G.   45°
    H.   50°
    J.   90°

17. What percent of 4 is $\sqrt{4}$?

    A.   10%
    B.   25%
    C.   40%
    D.   50%

18. In the formula $a = bc$, if b is multiplied by 6 and c is divided by 6, then the value of a is:

    F.   multiplied by 6
    G.   multiplied by 36
    H.   divided by 36
    J.   left unchanged

19. Jimmy has 4 shirts, 3 pairs of shoes, and 5 pairs of pants. If an outfit consists of a shirt, a pair of shoes, and a pair of pants, how many different outfits can Jimmy select?

    A.   12
    B.   24
    C.   30
    D.   60

20. If $4a - 6 = 10$, then $a =$

    F.   −4

    G. $-\frac{2}{3}$

    H. $\frac{2}{3}$

    J.   4

21. Which of the following fractions is larger than $\frac{2}{5}$?

    A. $\frac{41}{100}$

    B. $\frac{3}{10}$

    C. $\frac{9}{25}$

    D. $\frac{19}{50}$

GO ON TO THE NEXT PAGE

22. Five boys have the following amounts of money in their banks: $13.31, $12.66, $0.36, $9.32, and $0.00. What is the average amount of money that these boys have in their banks?

    F. $7.13
    G. $8.91
    H. $9.22
    J. $35.65

23. The difference between two supplementary angles is 40°. How many degrees are in the measure of the smaller angle?

    A. 60°
    B. 65°
    C. 70°
    D. 75°

24. Fidel jogs $\frac{2}{3}$ of a mile, rests, and then jogs $\frac{1}{6}$ of a mile. What fractional part of a mile must she still jog to have jogged 1 mile?

    F. $\frac{1}{12}$

    G. $\frac{1}{9}$

    H. $\frac{1}{6}$

    J. $\frac{5}{6}$

25. $(-3)^3 - 2(-4) =$

    A. −33
    B. −19
    C. 19
    D. 35

26. If $a > b$, and $b > c$, which of the following statements *must* be true?

    F. $c > b$
    G. $a - b = c$
    H. $a > c$
    J. $c > a$

27. An investment of $63,000 is divided among three sisters in a ratio of 2 : 3 : 4. How much is the smallest share?

    A. $7,000
    B. $14,000
    C. $21,000
    D. $28,000

28. If the price of a computer doubles, the increase is what percent of the new price?

    F. 20%
    G. 50%
    H. 100%
    J. 200%

29.

In the preceding figure, AB is parallel to CD. If $\angle AEF = a°$, then $\angle CFE$ expressed in terms of a is equal to:

    A. $a°$
    B. $(180 - a)°$
    C. $(180 + a)°$
    D. $(90 + a)°$

30. Find the value of $-5D^2E$ if $D = -3$, and $E = -4$.

    F. −180
    G. −120
    H. 120
    J. 180

31. On Tuesday, 18 students are absent from Peter's school. If this represents 9% of the students at the school, how many students attend Peter's school?

    A. 162
    B. 182
    C. 200
    D. 218

32. The expression $3(1 + x) - (1 + 3x)$ is equal to:

    F. −2
    G. 0
    H. 2
    J. $6x$

33. What is the perimeter of a rectangle whose length is 9 centimeters and whose width is 4 centimeters?

    A. 13 centimeters
    B. 26 centimeters
    C. 36 centimeters
    D. 72 centimeters

34. $3\frac{1}{3} + (-8) =$

    F. $\quad -11\frac{1}{3}$

    G. $\quad -4\frac{2}{3}$

    H. $\quad 4\frac{2}{3}$

    J. $\quad 11\frac{1}{3}$

35. The sum of $\dfrac{x+y}{4}$ and $\dfrac{2x-y}{4}$ is:

    A. $\quad \dfrac{3x-2y}{4}$

    B. $\quad \dfrac{3x-2y}{16}$

    C. $\quad \dfrac{3x}{16}$

    D. $\quad \dfrac{3x}{4}$

36. The circumference of a circle whose diameter is 9 feet is approximately:

    F.   14 feet
    G.   28 feet
    H.   34 feet
    J.   61 feet

37. The solution set of the inequality $6x - 12 > 12$ is:

    A. $x > 2$
    B. $x < 2$
    C. $x > 4$
    D. $x < 4$

38. If 45% of a number is 90, what is the number?

    F.   40.5
    G.   50
    H.   185
    J.   200

39. $37\frac{1}{2}\%$

    A. $\quad \dfrac{3}{8}$

    B. $\quad \dfrac{4}{9}$

    C. $\quad \dfrac{8}{5}$

    D.   37.5

40. If a $1,000 investment earns $60 in interest over 1 year, the annual interest rate is:

    F.   0.6%
    G.   6%
    H.   30%
    J.   60%

IF YOU FINISH BEFORE TIME IS CALLED, CHECK YOUR WORK ON THIS SECTION ONLY. DO NOT WORK ON ANY OTHER SECTION IN THE TEST.

Answer Key

Test 1: Sequences

1. A	6. F	11. A	16. G
2. J	7. C	12. G	17. C
3. D	8. J	13. D	18. G
4. G	9. B	14. J	19. A
5. B	10. H	15. A	20. J

Test 2: Analogies

1. C	6. J	11. C	16. F
2. G	7. C	12. J	17. B
3. A	8. F	13. A	18. F
4. F	9. C	14. J	19. C
5. A	10. J	15. D	20. H

Test 3: Quantitative Reasoning

1. B	6. F	11. D	16. J
2. J	7. A	12. G	17. C
3. C	8. J	13. C	18. H
4. G	9. C	14. G	19. A
5. B	10. H	15. A	20. J

Test 4: Verbal Reasoning—Words

1. C	4. G	7. D	10. F
2. H	5. D	8. G	11. D
3. B	6. G	9. A	12. G

Test 5: Verbal Reasoning—Context

1. B	3. C	5. A	7. C
2. G	4. G	6. G	8. H

Test 6: Reading and Language Arts

1. C	11. A	21. C	31. C
2. G	12. J	22. G	32. F
3. A	13. D	23. B	33. B
4. G	14. J	24. H	34. F
5. B	15. D	25. A	35. A
6. H	16. G	26. J	36. G
7. B	17. D	27. D	37. D
8. J	18. H	28. H	38. G
9. A	19. C	29. A	39. B
10. G	20. G	30. F	40. G

Test 7: Mathematics

1. C	11. A	21. A	31. C
2. J	12. G	22. F	32. H
3. D	13. C	23. C	33. B
4. H	14. H	24. H	34. G
5. C	15. D	25. B	35. D
6. H	16. H	26. H	36. G
7. B	17. D	27. B	37. C
8. G	18. J	28. G	38. J
9. C	19. D	29. B	39. A
10. F	20. J	30. J	40. G

Answers and Explanations

Test 1: Sequences

1. **A.** From the first to the second diagram, the unshaded sector inside the circle becomes a shaded sector. The third diagram is a square with an unshaded sector; therefore, the missing diagram should be a square with a shaded sector in the same position as the unshaded sector.

2. **J.** The first diagram is an unshaded circle. In the second diagram, a *shaded* circle has been placed on top of the first diagram. In the third diagram, an *unshaded* circle has been placed on the second diagram. The fourth diagram, therefore, should consist of a *shaded* circle placed on top of the third diagram.

3. **D.** From the first diagram to the second, the letters on either side of the shaded circle are reversed. Therefore, from the third diagram to the fourth, the letters on either side of the shaded circle should also be reversed.

4. **G.** The second diagram is obtained by turning the first diagram upside down. The fourth diagram, therefore, is obtained by turning the third diagram upside down.

5. **B.** The first two diagrams consist of a pair of triangles, one on top of the other. In the first diagram, the top triangle is shaded, and in the second diagram, the bottom triangle is shaded. Because the third diagram consists of a pair of circles, one on top of the other with the one on the top shaded, the fourth diagram should consist of a pair of circles, one on top of the other, with the bottom circle shaded.

6. **F.** The first diagram is rotated $180°$ to obtain the second diagram. The third diagram should be rotated $180°$ to obtain the fourth diagram.

7. **C.** The pattern is $7 + 3 = 10 + 3 = 13 \,|\, 19 + 3 = 22 + 3 = 25$. Therefore, $31 + 3 = 34 + 3 = \mathbf{37}$.

8. **J.** The pattern is $16 \div 2 = 8 \div 2 = 4 \,|\, 20 \div 2 = 10 \div 2 = 5$. Therefore, $28 \div 2 = \mathbf{14} \div 2 = 7$.

9. **B.** The pattern is $10 - 2 = 8 \times 3 = 24 \,|\, 8 - 2 = 6 \times 3 = 18 \,|\, 4 - 2 = 2 \times 3 = \mathbf{6}$.

10. **H.** Each number is obtained by squaring the previous number. That is, $1^2 = 1$, and $1^2 = 1$. Similarly, $2^2 = 4$, and $4^2 = 16$. Finally, $3^2 = 9$, and $9^2 = 81$.

11. **A.** The pattern is $36 + 5 = 41 - 4 = 37 \,|\, 43 + 5 = 48 - 4 = 44$. Therefore, $51 + 5 = \mathbf{56} - 4 = 52$.

12. **G.** The pattern is $16 - 12 = 4 \div 2 = 2 \,|\, 28 - 12 = 16 \div 2 = 8$. Thus, $36 - 12 = 24 \div 2 = \mathbf{12}$.

13. **D.** The pattern is $5 \times 2 = 10 \times 3 = 30 \,|\, 7 \times 2 = 14 \times 3 = 42$. So, $12 \times 2 = \mathbf{24} \times 3 = 72$.

14. **J.** The letters follow the pattern $B + 2 = D + 2 = F \,|\, E + 2 = G + 2 = I \,|\, H + 2 = J + 2 = L \,|\, K + 2 = M + 2 = O$. The correct sequence must follow this pattern. Also, note that the first letter of each sequence is alphabetically one letter *before* the last letter of the previous sequence. For example, the E that begins the second sequence is the letter before the F that ends the first sequence. Therefore, the missing sequence must begin with the letter before O, which is N. Then, $N + 2 = P$, and $P + 2 = R$.

15. **A.** Look at the letter in the middle of each sequence. In every case, the letter to the left is the next letter in the alphabet, and the letter to the right is the letter after that. For example, J comes after I, and K comes after J. The only answer choice that has this same pattern is R Q S because R comes after Q, and S comes after R.

16. **G.** The letters follow the pattern $A + 2 = C + 3 = F \,|\, K + 2 = M + 3 = P \,|\, Q + 2 = S + 3 = V \,|\, L + 2 = N + 3 = Q$. The only choice that follows this pattern is $G + 2 = I + 3 = L$.

17. **C.** The pattern is $Z - 3 = W - 3 = T \,|\, Y - 3 = V - 3 = S \,|\, X - 3 = U - 3 = R \,|\, V - 3 = S - 3 = P$. Also, note that the first letters of each sequence are in reverse alphabetical order. Therefore, the first letter of the missing sequence must be W, and the sequence must be $W - 3 = T - 3 = Q$.

18. **G.** The numbers are arranged in descending order, so the missing number must be 1. In each sequence, the letters are consecutive. Note that U 1 V is the only choice with these two characteristics.

19. **A.** The numbers are arranged in ascending order, so the missing number must be 8. In each sequence, the two letters differ by 4. The only choice with both of these characteristics is P 8 T.

20. **J.** The numbers in these sequences descend by 2, so the missing number must be 0. In each sequence, each letter differs from the previous one by 2. The only choice with both of these characteristics is E G 0 I.

Test 2: Analogies

1. **C.** Hamburger is made of beef, which comes from cattle, and pork chops come from pigs.

2. **G.** The relationship is of opposites: new and old. Just as television is a newer way to communicate information than radio is, a newspaper is a newer way to communicate information than a town crier.

3. **A.** An egg becomes a chicken as a bud becomes a flower.

4. **F.** The relationship is one of degree, large to small.

5. **A.** The relationship is one of function. A wrench is used by a mechanic; a hose is used by a firefighter.

6. **J.** The relationship is of opposites: old and new ways to cool and to heat.

7. **C.** Apples and pears are parts of the whole category fruit; corn and carrots are part of the whole category vegetables.

8. **F.** Both hats and caps are worn on the head; both gloves and rings are worn on the hand.

9. **C.** The relationship is the characteristic place of work for a specific job.

10. **J.** The relationship is that of a part to a whole.

11. **C.** The relationship is of degrees. A crying person is sadder than a frowning one, and a laughing person is happier than a smiling one.

12. **J.** The relationship is of degree. A dinner is a larger meal than a sandwich; a house is a larger dwelling than a cabin.

13. **A.** Jack o'lanterns and skeletons are associated with Halloween; a decorated tree and Santa Claus are associated with Christmas.

14. **J.** The relationship is about function. A spoon is used to eat soup; a match is used to light a fire.

15. **D.** This is a little tricky. It is a part-to-whole relationship about what an object is made of. A desk is made of wood (from a tree) as a skyscraper is made of steel beams.

16. **F.** The pictures show a cause-effect relationship. A yawning person is tired, which causes sleep; the sun creates heat, which makes a person hot.

17. **B.** The relationship can be interpreted as either old to new or small to large.

18. **F.** The relationship is a sequence. A caterpillar becomes a butterfly as a child becomes an adult.

19. **C.** The relationship is location. A dog lives in a kennel; a goldfish lives in an aquarium bowl.

20. **H.** Both baskets and cartons are used to store solid things; both cups and glasses are used to hold liquids.

Test 3: Quantitative Reasoning

1. **B.** The pattern is $6 + 12 = 18$, and $9 + 12 = 21$. Therefore, $15 + 12 = 27$.

2. **J.** Note that $4 \times 5 = 20$, and $1 \times 5 = 5$. Therefore, $8 \times 5 = 40$.

3. **C.** In this problem, note that the first number, 2, times itself, is 4. Then, the second number, 4, times itself is 16. Finally, 6 times itself is 36.

4. **G.** In this case, $24 - 2 = 22$, and $30 - 2 = 28$. Thus, $20 - 2 = 18$.

5. **B.** The pattern here is to divide each term by 3. Thus, $21 \div 3 = 7$, $15 \div 3 = 5$, and, finally, $3 \div 3 = 1$.

6. **F.** The pattern is $2 \times 10 = 20$, and $5 \times 10 = 50$. Thus, $8 \times 10 = 80$.

7. **A.** Note that $5 + 37 = 42$, and $12 + 37 = 49$. It follows that $18 + 37 = 55$.

8. **J.** In this diagram, 3 of the 4 squares are shaded. Thus, $\frac{3}{4}$ of the diagram is shaded.

9. **C.** Here, 1 full square and 2 half squares are shaded. Because 2 halves make a whole, overall, 2 squares out of 4 are shaded. Therefore, $\frac{2}{4} = \frac{1}{2}$ of the figure is shaded.

10. **H.** Here, 2 squares out of 6 are shaded. Thus, the answer is $\frac{2}{6} = \frac{1}{3}$.

11. **D.** In this diagram, 4 of the 6 squares are shaded. Now, note that $\frac{4}{6} = \frac{2}{3}$.

12. **G.** Of the 9 squares, 3 are shaded. The answer is $\frac{3}{9} = \frac{1}{3}$.

13. **C.** In this diagram, 6 out of 8 squares are shaded. The answer is $\frac{6}{8} = \frac{3}{4}$.

14. **G.** According to the scale, one cube = one cone. Thus, two cubes are equal to two cones.

15. **A.** According to the scale, one cube = two cones. If we added an extra cube to each side, the scale is in balance with two cubes = two cones and one cube.

16. **J.** According to the scale, a cube and a cone are equal to two cones. If we remove a cone from each side, the scale still balances, with one cube = one cone.

17. **C.** According to the scale, two cubes equal two cones, which can only be true if one cube equals one cone. If this is true, then, it follows that three cones must equal three cubes.

18. **H.** According to the scale, two cones equal three cubes. If a cone is added to each side, the scale still balances, with three cones equal to three cubes and a cone.

19. **A.** If we remove a cone from each side, we see that two cubes are equal to one cone. By doubling the amount on each side, we see that four cubes must equal two cones.

20. **J.** According to the scale, four cones are equal to a cube and a cone. Removing a cone from each side shows us that three cones are equal to a cube.

Test 4: Verbal Reasoning—Words

1. **C.** Music cannot be made without the strings. Plucking the strings as well as bowing can make music. Notes and melody are part of the music, not the instrument.

2. **H.** The operating system is the heart of the computer. The computer does not exist if it is missing. It controls the mouse and keyboard operations. E-mail is a process that can be used with a computer.

3. **B.** Vocal cords produce sound, therefore singing. Music is what is sung; instruments produce music to accompany the singing, and an audience listens to the singing.

4. **G.** The novel cannot exist without the author. Plot, characters, and setting are the three elements of a novel.

5. **D.** Wind is needed to sail. Hull and rudder are parts of a boat. An anchor is an accessory.

6. **G.** Water is needed to swim. A mask, snorkel, and fins are equipment one might use while in the water.

7. **D.** The items in the top row are all cutting instruments that start small and get progressively larger. The people named in the bottom row start young and get progressively older, from one generation to the next.

8. **G.** The items in the top row start with raw materials and end with a product. The items in the bottom row repeat that pattern.

9. **A.** The items in the top row start slow and increase in speed. They describe the movement of people. The items in the bottom row repeat the pattern and describe the gaits of a horse.

10. F. The items in the top row are coniferous trees. The items in the bottom row are deciduous trees. Their woods are used to make furniture or in building houses. The remaining choices are all deciduous trees that produce edible nuts.

11. D. The items in the top row are all edible nuts, often used in cooking. The items in the bottom row are all holidays progressing through the year, Memorial Day in May, Fourth of July in July, and Labor Day in September. The remaining holidays listed have to do with religion.

12. G. The items in the top row are seasons of the year. The items in the bottom row are countries. The remaining answers are continents.

Test 5: Verbal Reasoning—Context

1. B. Given this situation, the most we can say is that Julio's smoking might have contributed to the cancer. We can't say it caused his cancer, nor can we say smoking had nothing to do with it. No information is offered to show whether he would have gotten cancer if he hadn't smoked.

2. G. Answers **F, H,** and **J** are all opinions and cannot be applied to every single Honda. Obviously, if care is given to a car, repairs and breakdowns can be avoided and a great deal of use can be had.

3. C. If the two kinds of nuts have disappeared by the next morning, the raisins still remain. The squirrels ate the nuts, but did not eat the raisins.

4. G. The children need to get to school one way or another. Parents must see to it that their child gets to school because the buses are not available.

5. A. Linda ordered the remaining three dolls because they were hard to find, but were available on E-Bay. They would complete her set. Now if she wished to sell them she could get more money than she would with an incomplete set.

6. G. The stem *wabos* is found in all the example words. Because all these formations have to do with water in various sizes, the answer must also contain that stem.

7. C. All example words have the same stem letters *w-a-r* arranged in a variety of ways. The answer word needs those same stem letters in the center of the word. All the words in the question and the answer choices have the same four-letter suffix, indicating *-ing*.

8. H. The letters *neff* near the end of the word indicate a commonality. All the items are forms of transportation. The difference lies in how many people/things can be carried. Trains, buses and cars are able to carry one or more than one passenger. Cars and bicycles carry far fewer passengers than trains or buses, so the suffixes for car and bicycle are similar.

Test 6: Reading and Language Arts

1. C. Although the paragraph tells what Strauss did, its focus is on his invention, not his life.

2. G. While it is true that he was selling cloth to earn money (choice **F**), **G** is a better answer. It is explicitly stated in sentence 5.

3. A. While the other places are also mentioned in the paragraph, they are not where the cloth originated.

4. G. This is the only choice that comes from information in the paragraph. The other choices are guesses with no support in the passage.

5. B. The words *the grave* and the content of the first paragraph of the passage indicate someone had died. Do not be confused by **C**. *Wonderful* in the paragraph means filled with wonder; it does not describe a positive reaction.

6. H. The word *assailant* in the next to last sentence of the passage explains this answer.

7. B. Because he could not recall his sister with *much tenderness*, **C** is clearly incorrect. But nothing indicates he had very negative feelings toward her, so **A** is not a good choice. Because the last sentence says he felt he might seek revenge, he was not *indifferent*, **D**, to her death.

8. **J.** The other choices do not make sense if inserted in the sentence in place of *indignation*.

9. **A.** This is the only choice that explains why the speaker would pursue Orlick seeking revenge.

10. **G.** The answer is stated in the last sentence of the first paragraph.

11. **A.** The passage states that she goes to sea to feed, and returns after 60 days, the equivalent of two months. **C** is not correct because the passage states that the male transfers the egg to his own feet, not that the female moves it to his feet.

12. **J.** The answer is stated in the first sentence of the second paragraph.

13. **D.** *Amazingly* is used to describe the female's return exactly when the chick hatches.

14. **J.** The second paragraph states that the "emperors have reversed the normal breeding time table." It also says that "they do not nest." The next to the last sentence says that "the pair take turns fishing and feeding the chick."

15. **D.** While electricity, lightning, and the Leyden jar are mentioned, none of these was demonstrated by Franklin's experiment according to the paragraph.

16. **G.** Because the Royal Academy collected scientific information for the English-speaking world, a reader can infer that no such collection point existed in the United States. Choices **F** and **H** are true according to the passage, but they don't explain why Franklin sent his reports to London. **J** is contradicted by information in the passage.

17. **D.** All of the choices are true. Paragraph one states that it was not true that Franklin discovered electricity, but rather two scientists in Holland were responsible. In paragraph two, the phrase "many of his experiments, including experiments with electricity" indicates that he experimented in many fields. Finally, the paragraph also says that "he could not resist an occasional joke."

18. **H.** Because the letter is a joke, choices **F** and **G** can be eliminated. A joke is not the same as science fiction, so **J** cannot be correct. Franklin's description could easily occur today. We have electric spits; although we might call them rotisseries, and of course we have electric batteries.

19. **C.** Although **B** is a possible answer, **C** is a better choice because it describes both paragraphs in the passage.

20. **G.** If you don't know the word, the clue is in the second paragraph, where modern arguments are described as having a *friendly* tone. Because the passage is a contrast, the word in the first paragraph should mean the opposite of *friendly*.

21. **C.** **A** is incorrect because both forms of argument seek agreement. **B** is only true of classical arguments, and **D** is only true of modern arguments.

22. **G.** **F** is contradicted by the content of the passage. When you combine the last sentence in both paragraphs, you can infer that the author thinks modern arguments can be more effective than classical ones.

23. **B.** Although the author is both responsible, **A,** and helpful, **C,** her evident joy in her job makes **B** the best answer.

24. **H.** The passage does not mention who bakes the cake, **F,** nor who sells the company's services **J.** It states that the children hug her, not that she hugs the children (although it's possible she hugs them back), so **G** is not correct. Because part of her job is cleaning up after the party, **H** is the best choice.

25. **A.** The answer is explicitly stated in the second paragraph.

26. **J.** Because the author likes her job, *satisfying* is the best choice. **F** is wrong because it confuses *gratifying* with a word meaning to be thankful, *gratitude*.

27. **D.** **A** is about the number of players on a team, not the field. **B** is true of both men's and women's lacrosse. To choose between **C** and **D**, read the description carefully. The dimensions of the men's field state the width, then the length. Thus the dimensions of the women's field should be in the same order, and in spite of having a larger number before the smaller number, the women's field is wider than the men's.

28. **H.** **F, G,** and **H,** like lacrosse, are all games in which the object is to score a goal. But basketball players use their hands to move the ball. Soccer players do not use their hands, but they do not use equipment. Because hockey players do not use their hands and do use sticks, it is closest to lacrosse.

29. A. Although the paragraph does not mention professional lacrosse in the United States, that does not prove it does not exist, so **B** is incorrect. **C** cannot be inferred from the information that French Canadians adopted the game; others might also now play it. No information is given in the passage to support **D.**

30. F. The passage states that body checking is used to keep opponents from advancing the ball—in other words, for defense.

31. C. The answer is stated in the third sentence of the passage.

32. F. Because the bats make the sounds, this is the correct choice. **G** is not a good choice because the bats need to hear echoes of the sounds; therefore, they are not discarding them.

33. B. According to the passage, moths use the noises they hear bats make to avoid the bats, so this is the correct answer.

34. F. The words *surprised, stranger,* and *astonishing* establish the writer's attitude. The last sentence of the passage mentions "the amazing ways" but the use of the phrases "I was surprised," and "even stranger," indicate that the writer's attitude was one of amazement. The other choices are not relevant.

35. A. Because the mites can damage the ears of the moths, *invade* is the best choice.

36. G. According to the passage, the European visitor *would be wrong.*

37. D. The verb tenses of the passage indicate the visitor would be looking into the future.

38. G. **F** is not correct because the description is not literally of a body, but of American society.

39. B. The answer is known by combining the information in the second and third sentences of the passage.

40. G. Because Adams lived in the nineteenth century, clearly Jefferson's era was in the past. **J** is incorrect because Adams knew what the future of America after Jefferson was. He is describing it, not predicting it.

Test 7: Mathematics

1. C. Because the hundredths digit is 8, the tenths digit needs to be rounded up. The tenths digit is 9, and, when rounded up, becomes 10. The 0 is placed in the tenths spot, and the units spot becomes one larger, or 3. Thus, the rounded number is 53.

2. J. To begin, $3^2 = 3 \times 3 = 9$, and $5^3 = 5 \times 5 \times 5 = 125$. Finally, $9 + 125 = 134$.

3. D. Begin by solving the equation for x:

$4x - 6 = 3x + 4$. Add 6 to both sides.

$4x = 3x + 10$. Subtract $3x$ from both sides.

$x = 10$.

Because $x = 10$, $x^2 = 100$.

4. H. Five percent of 420 is equal to $5\% \times 420 = 0.05 \times 420 = 21$. Therefore, the number of students this year is $420 - 21 = 399$.

5. C. To express a decimal as a percent, move the decimal point two places to the right. Therefore, $0.03 = 3\%$.

6. H. To find the median of a series of numbers, write the numbers in numerical order, and find the number in the middle. Because there are an even number of numbers in this case, two numbers are in the middle, 9 and 12. The median is the average (arithmetic mean) of these two numbers.

$$\frac{9 + 12}{2} = \frac{21}{2} = 10\frac{1}{2}$$

7. B. Note that $4 \times 4 = 16$, $7 \times 7 = 49$, and $8 \times 8 = 64$. The number that is not a perfect square is 48.

8. G. The figure consists of four triangles of equal size. One of the triangles is shaded, which is to say that $\frac{1}{4}$ of the figure is shaded. This is the same as saying that 25% of the figure is shaded.

9. C. The quickest way to solve this problem is to note that, if $\frac{1}{2}$ of an inch is 6 miles, then 1 inch is 12 miles, and 3 inches is $12 + 12 + 12 = 36$ miles.

10. F. A number is divisible by 2 if it is even. A number is divisible by 5 if it ends in either 0 or 5. For a number to be divisible by 10, which is equal to 2×5, it must be divisible by 2 and 5. Thus, the number must be even and must end in either 5 or 0. The only way that this can happen is if it ends with 0.

11. A. Following the rules for division of exponents, we have $\frac{x^6 y^6}{x^2 y^3} = x^{6-2} y^{6-3} = x^4 y^3$.

12. G. Writing the ratio as a fraction and simplifying gives $\frac{12}{6} = \frac{3}{4}$, which represents a ratio of 3 to 4.

13. C. Two packages of pens can be purchased for $2.10 + $0.90 = $3.00. From this, it can be seen that six packages of pens cost $9.00. One more package makes the total cost $9.00 + $2.10 = $11.10.

14. H. Substituting values, we obtain $\frac{a+b}{2a} = \frac{2+10}{2(2)} = \frac{12}{4} = 3$.

15. D. First, note that the number 234 is neither prime nor odd. In addition, the number 243 is not even. The only choice left is "divisible by 3," so this must be the answer. In fact, recall that if the sum of the digits of a number are divisible by 3, then the number must be divisible by 3. Because $2 + 3 + 4 = 9$, which is divisible by 3, the answer **D** follows.

16. H. The number of degrees in the angles of a triangle must total 180°. We are told that the triangle has a 40° angle, and the picture shows that another angle is 90°. The missing angle, thus, must be $180° - 90° - 40° = 50°$.

17. D. Because $\sqrt{4} = 2$, the question is actually asking what percent 2 is of 4. Because 2 is half of 4, the answer is 50%.

18. J. Note that multiplying one number by 6 and dividing the other by 6 leaves the product unchanged:

$$a = (6b)\left(\frac{c}{6}\right) = \frac{6bc}{6} = bc.$$

19. D. By the Fundamental Counting Principal, Jimmy can select $4 \times 3 \times 5 = 60$ outfits.

20. J.

$4a - 6 = 10$. Add 6 to both sides.

$4a = 16$. Divide both sides by 4.

$a = 4$.

21. A. One easy way to solve this problem is to write all the fractions with a common denominator of 100. Note that $\frac{2}{5} = \frac{40}{100}$. In the same way, $\frac{3}{10} = \frac{30}{100}$, $\frac{9}{25} = \frac{36}{100}$, and $\frac{19}{50} = \frac{38}{100}$. Therefore, all these fractions are less than $\frac{2}{5}$. The only fraction that is bigger is $\frac{41}{100}$.

22. F. Begin by adding the five dollar amounts to get $35.65. To get the average, this number must be divided by five because there are five boys: $35.65 \div 5 = $7.13.

23. C. Supplementary angles are angles whose measures add up to 180°. If we call the measure of one of the angles x, then the other angle must have a measure of $180 - x$. Because the two measures differ by 40, we have the equation:

$x - (180 - x) = 40$.

$x - 180 + x = 40$. Combine like terms.

$2x - 180 = 40$. Add 180 to both sides.

$2x = 220$. Divide both sides by 2.

$x = 110$.

The larger angle has a measure of 110°, and the measure of the smaller angle is $180° - 110° = 70°$.

24. H. She has already jogged $\frac{2}{3} + \frac{1}{6} = \frac{4}{6} + \frac{1}{6} = \frac{5}{6}$, of a mile. Therefore, she has $\frac{1}{6}$ of a mile left to jog.

25. B. $(-3)^3 - 2(-4) = -27 - (-8) = -27 + 8 = -19$.

26. H. The only conclusion that can be made from the fact that a is bigger than b, and b is bigger than c is that a is bigger than c.

27. B. Picture the investment as consisting of $2 + 3 + 4 = 9$ parts. The smallest share consists of 2 of the 9 parts, or $\frac{2}{9}$, of the total investment.

$$\frac{2}{9} \times \$63,000 = 2 \times \$7,000 = \$14,000 \times \$63,000 = 2 \times \$7,000 = \$14,000$$

28. G. This problem can easily be solved by picking a price for the computer. Let's say the computer originally costs $100 and doubles to $200. Therefore, the increase is $100, and the new price is $200. It is easy to see that the increase is half, or 50%, of the new price.

29. B. The two angles are interior angles on the same side of a transversal, and are therefore supplementary. The supplement of $a°$ is $(180 - a)°$.

30. J. $-5D^2E = -5(-3)^2(-4) = -5(9)(-4) = 180$.

31. C. The number of students in Peter's school is $\frac{18}{9\%} = \frac{18}{0.09} = 200$.

32. H. $3(1 + x) - (1 + 3x) = 3 + 3x - 1 - 3x = 2$.

33. B. $P = 2L + 2W = 2(9) + 2(4) = 18 + 8 = 26$ centimeters.

34. G. $3\frac{1}{3} + (-8) = 3\frac{1}{3} - \frac{24}{3} = \frac{10}{3} - \frac{24}{3} = -\frac{14}{3} = -4\frac{2}{3}$

35. D. $\frac{x+y}{4} + \frac{2x-y}{4} = \frac{x+y+2x-y}{4} = \frac{3x}{4}$

36. G. The formula for the circumference of a circle is $C = \pi d$, where d is the diameter, and π is approximately 3.14. Therefore, the circumference is about $3.14 \times 9 = 28.26$, which is closest to 28 feet.

37. C.

$6x - 12 > 12$. Divide both sides by 6.

$x - 2 > 2$. Add 2 to both sides.

$x > 4$.

38. J. The number is $\frac{90}{45\%} = \frac{90}{0.45} = 200$.

39. A. $37\frac{1}{2}\% = \frac{75}{2}\% = \frac{\frac{75}{2}}{100} = \frac{75}{2} \times \frac{1}{100} = \frac{75}{200} = \frac{3}{8}$.

40. G. 60 percent of $1,000 is $600.

Answer Sheet for Practice COOP Exam 2

TEST 1 Sequences

1 Ⓐ Ⓑ Ⓒ Ⓓ	5 Ⓐ Ⓑ Ⓒ Ⓓ	9 Ⓐ Ⓑ Ⓒ Ⓓ	13 Ⓐ Ⓑ Ⓒ Ⓓ	17 Ⓐ Ⓑ Ⓒ Ⓓ
2 Ⓕ Ⓖ Ⓗ Ⓙ	6 Ⓕ Ⓖ Ⓗ Ⓙ	10 Ⓕ Ⓖ Ⓗ Ⓙ	14 Ⓕ Ⓖ Ⓗ Ⓙ	18 Ⓕ Ⓖ Ⓗ Ⓙ
3 Ⓐ Ⓑ Ⓒ Ⓓ	7 Ⓐ Ⓑ Ⓒ Ⓓ	11 Ⓐ Ⓑ Ⓒ Ⓓ	15 Ⓐ Ⓑ Ⓒ Ⓓ	19 Ⓐ Ⓑ Ⓒ Ⓓ
4 Ⓕ Ⓖ Ⓗ Ⓙ	8 Ⓕ Ⓖ Ⓗ Ⓙ	12 Ⓕ Ⓖ Ⓗ Ⓙ	16 Ⓕ Ⓖ Ⓗ Ⓙ	20 Ⓕ Ⓖ Ⓗ Ⓙ

TEST 2 Analogies

1 Ⓐ Ⓑ Ⓒ Ⓓ	5 Ⓐ Ⓑ Ⓒ Ⓓ	9 Ⓐ Ⓑ Ⓒ Ⓓ	13 Ⓐ Ⓑ Ⓒ Ⓓ	17 Ⓐ Ⓑ Ⓒ Ⓓ
2 Ⓕ Ⓖ Ⓗ Ⓙ	6 Ⓕ Ⓖ Ⓗ Ⓙ	10 Ⓕ Ⓖ Ⓗ Ⓙ	14 Ⓕ Ⓖ Ⓗ Ⓙ	18 Ⓕ Ⓖ Ⓗ Ⓙ
3 Ⓐ Ⓑ Ⓒ Ⓓ	7 Ⓐ Ⓑ Ⓒ Ⓓ	11 Ⓐ Ⓑ Ⓒ Ⓓ	15 Ⓐ Ⓑ Ⓒ Ⓓ	19 Ⓐ Ⓑ Ⓒ Ⓓ
4 Ⓕ Ⓖ Ⓗ Ⓙ	8 Ⓕ Ⓖ Ⓗ Ⓙ	12 Ⓕ Ⓖ Ⓗ Ⓙ	16 Ⓕ Ⓖ Ⓗ Ⓙ	20 Ⓕ Ⓖ Ⓗ Ⓙ

TEST 3 Quantitative Reasoning

1 Ⓐ Ⓑ Ⓒ Ⓓ	5 Ⓐ Ⓑ Ⓒ Ⓓ	9 Ⓐ Ⓑ Ⓒ Ⓓ	13 Ⓐ Ⓑ Ⓒ Ⓓ	17 Ⓐ Ⓑ Ⓒ Ⓓ
2 Ⓕ Ⓖ Ⓗ Ⓙ	6 Ⓕ Ⓖ Ⓗ Ⓙ	10 Ⓕ Ⓖ Ⓗ Ⓙ	14 Ⓕ Ⓖ Ⓗ Ⓙ	18 Ⓕ Ⓖ Ⓗ Ⓙ
3 Ⓐ Ⓑ Ⓒ Ⓓ	7 Ⓐ Ⓑ Ⓒ Ⓓ	11 Ⓐ Ⓑ Ⓒ Ⓓ	15 Ⓐ Ⓑ Ⓒ Ⓓ	19 Ⓐ Ⓑ Ⓒ Ⓓ
4 Ⓕ Ⓖ Ⓗ Ⓙ	8 Ⓕ Ⓖ Ⓗ Ⓙ	12 Ⓕ Ⓖ Ⓗ Ⓙ	16 Ⓕ Ⓖ Ⓗ Ⓙ	20 Ⓕ Ⓖ Ⓗ Ⓙ

TEST 4 Verbal Reasoning - Words

1 Ⓐ Ⓑ Ⓒ Ⓓ	5 Ⓐ Ⓑ Ⓒ Ⓓ	9 Ⓐ Ⓑ Ⓒ Ⓓ
2 Ⓕ Ⓖ Ⓗ Ⓙ	6 Ⓕ Ⓖ Ⓗ Ⓙ	10 Ⓕ Ⓖ Ⓗ Ⓙ
3 Ⓐ Ⓑ Ⓒ Ⓓ	7 Ⓐ Ⓑ Ⓒ Ⓓ	11 Ⓐ Ⓑ Ⓒ Ⓓ
4 Ⓕ Ⓖ Ⓗ Ⓙ	8 Ⓕ Ⓖ Ⓗ Ⓙ	12 Ⓕ Ⓖ Ⓗ Ⓙ

TEST 5 Verbal Reasoning - Context

1 Ⓐ Ⓑ Ⓒ Ⓓ	5 Ⓐ Ⓑ Ⓒ Ⓓ
2 Ⓕ Ⓖ Ⓗ Ⓙ	6 Ⓕ Ⓖ Ⓗ Ⓙ
3 Ⓐ Ⓑ Ⓒ Ⓓ	7 Ⓐ Ⓑ Ⓒ Ⓓ
4 Ⓕ Ⓖ Ⓗ Ⓙ	8 Ⓕ Ⓖ Ⓗ Ⓙ

TEST 6 Reading and Language Arts

1 Ⓐ Ⓑ Ⓒ Ⓓ	9 Ⓐ Ⓑ Ⓒ Ⓓ	17 Ⓐ Ⓑ Ⓒ Ⓓ	25 Ⓐ Ⓑ Ⓒ Ⓓ	33 Ⓐ Ⓑ Ⓒ Ⓓ
2 Ⓕ Ⓖ Ⓗ Ⓙ	10 Ⓕ Ⓖ Ⓗ Ⓙ	18 Ⓕ Ⓖ Ⓗ Ⓙ	26 Ⓕ Ⓖ Ⓗ Ⓙ	34 Ⓕ Ⓖ Ⓗ Ⓙ
3 Ⓐ Ⓑ Ⓒ Ⓓ	11 Ⓐ Ⓑ Ⓒ Ⓓ	19 Ⓐ Ⓑ Ⓒ Ⓓ	27 Ⓐ Ⓑ Ⓒ Ⓓ	35 Ⓐ Ⓑ Ⓒ Ⓓ
4 Ⓕ Ⓖ Ⓗ Ⓙ	12 Ⓕ Ⓖ Ⓗ Ⓙ	20 Ⓕ Ⓖ Ⓗ Ⓙ	28 Ⓕ Ⓖ Ⓗ Ⓙ	36 Ⓕ Ⓖ Ⓗ Ⓙ
5 Ⓐ Ⓑ Ⓒ Ⓓ	13 Ⓐ Ⓑ Ⓒ Ⓓ	21 Ⓐ Ⓑ Ⓒ Ⓓ	29 Ⓐ Ⓑ Ⓒ Ⓓ	37 Ⓐ Ⓑ Ⓒ Ⓓ
6 Ⓕ Ⓖ Ⓗ Ⓙ	14 Ⓕ Ⓖ Ⓗ Ⓙ	22 Ⓕ Ⓖ Ⓗ Ⓙ	30 Ⓕ Ⓖ Ⓗ Ⓙ	38 Ⓕ Ⓖ Ⓗ Ⓙ
7 Ⓐ Ⓑ Ⓒ Ⓓ	15 Ⓐ Ⓑ Ⓒ Ⓓ	23 Ⓐ Ⓑ Ⓒ Ⓓ	31 Ⓐ Ⓑ Ⓒ Ⓓ	39 Ⓐ Ⓑ Ⓒ Ⓓ
8 Ⓕ Ⓖ Ⓗ Ⓙ	16 Ⓕ Ⓖ Ⓗ Ⓙ	24 Ⓕ Ⓖ Ⓗ Ⓙ	32 Ⓕ Ⓖ Ⓗ Ⓙ	40 Ⓕ Ⓖ Ⓗ Ⓙ

TEST 7 Mathematics

1 Ⓐ Ⓑ Ⓒ Ⓓ	9 Ⓐ Ⓑ Ⓒ Ⓓ	17 Ⓐ Ⓑ Ⓒ Ⓓ	25 Ⓐ Ⓑ Ⓒ Ⓓ	33 Ⓐ Ⓑ Ⓒ Ⓓ
2 Ⓕ Ⓖ Ⓗ Ⓙ	10 Ⓕ Ⓖ Ⓗ Ⓙ	18 Ⓕ Ⓖ Ⓗ Ⓙ	26 Ⓕ Ⓖ Ⓗ Ⓙ	34 Ⓕ Ⓖ Ⓗ Ⓙ
3 Ⓐ Ⓑ Ⓒ Ⓓ	11 Ⓐ Ⓑ Ⓒ Ⓓ	19 Ⓐ Ⓑ Ⓒ Ⓓ	27 Ⓐ Ⓑ Ⓒ Ⓓ	35 Ⓐ Ⓑ Ⓒ Ⓓ
4 Ⓕ Ⓖ Ⓗ Ⓙ	12 Ⓕ Ⓖ Ⓗ Ⓙ	20 Ⓕ Ⓖ Ⓗ Ⓙ	28 Ⓕ Ⓖ Ⓗ Ⓙ	36 Ⓕ Ⓖ Ⓗ Ⓙ
5 Ⓐ Ⓑ Ⓒ Ⓓ	13 Ⓐ Ⓑ Ⓒ Ⓓ	21 Ⓐ Ⓑ Ⓒ Ⓓ	29 Ⓐ Ⓑ Ⓒ Ⓓ	37 Ⓐ Ⓑ Ⓒ Ⓓ
6 Ⓕ Ⓖ Ⓗ Ⓙ	14 Ⓕ Ⓖ Ⓗ Ⓙ	22 Ⓕ Ⓖ Ⓗ Ⓙ	30 Ⓕ Ⓖ Ⓗ Ⓙ	38 Ⓕ Ⓖ Ⓗ Ⓙ
7 Ⓐ Ⓑ Ⓒ Ⓓ	15 Ⓐ Ⓑ Ⓒ Ⓓ	23 Ⓐ Ⓑ Ⓒ Ⓓ	31 Ⓐ Ⓑ Ⓒ Ⓓ	39 Ⓐ Ⓑ Ⓒ Ⓓ
8 Ⓕ Ⓖ Ⓗ Ⓙ	16 Ⓕ Ⓖ Ⓗ Ⓙ	24 Ⓕ Ⓖ Ⓗ Ⓙ	32 Ⓕ Ⓖ Ⓗ Ⓙ	40 Ⓕ Ⓖ Ⓗ Ⓙ

CUT HERE

CUT HERE

Test 1: Sequences

Time: 15 Minutes

Directions: For the questions in this test, select the answer that best continues the pattern or sequences given.

1.

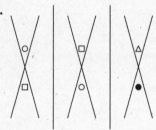

A.
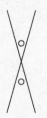

B.

C.

D.

2.

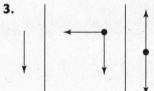

F. PQR**S**

G. P**Q**RS

H. PQ**RS**

J. PQR**S**

3.

A.

B.

C.

D.

GO ON TO THE NEXT PAGE

4.

F. ▽

G. ◁

H. ⬡

J. ⯃

5.

A. ▭▯▭▮

B. ▯▯▭▮

C. ▭▯▭▯

D. ▯▯▭▮

6.

F. ◁

G. ▽

H. ◁

J. △

7. 27 9 3 | 36 12 4 | 45 15 ___
A. 5
B. 7
C. 10
D. 12

8. 10 15 20 | 12 17 22 | 19 ___ 29
F. 22
G. 24
H. 26
J. 28

9. 13 8 64 | 8 3 9 | 7 2 ___
A. 4
B. 6
C. 8
D. 12

10. 50 10 20 | 60 20 40 | 70 30 ___
F. 60
G. 80
H. 90
J. 100

11. 9 12 4 | 15 18 6 | 21 24 ___
A. 6
B. 8
C. 10
D. 12

12. 12 18 15 | 24 30 27 | 38 ___ 41
F. 44
G. 45
H. 46
J. 47

13. 9 27 9 | 10 30 10 | 11 ___ 11
A. 31
B. 32
C. 33
D. 34

14. Z X V | W U S | T R P | ____ | N L J
F. Q P O
G. Q O M
H. O M K
J. N L J

15. B C A | J K I | N O M | G H F | _____

   A. U V T
   B. V W X
   C. X W Y
   D. T U V

16. A E I | B F J | C G K | _____ | E I M

   F. D G J
   G. D G L
   H. D H L
   J. D H K

17. X W V | V U T | T S R | _____ | P O N

   A. R S T
   B. R P O
   C. P Q O
   D. R Q P

18. B 5 A | F 6 E | J 7 I | M 8 L | _____

   F. P 8 O
   G. P 9 Q
   H. P 9 O
   J. P 9 N

19. A B 1 C | E F 3 G | H I 5 J | K L 7 M | _____

   A. M N 9 P
   B. N P 9 Q
   C. N O 8 P
   D. N O 9 P

20. Z Y 9 W | V U 8 S | R Q 7 O | _____ | J I 5 G

   F. N M 6 K
   G. M N 6 K
   H. N M 5 K
   J. M L 5 J

IF YOU FINISH BEFORE TIME IS CALLED, CHECK YOUR WORK ON THIS
SECTION ONLY. DO NOT WORK ON ANY OTHER SECTION IN THE TEST.

Test 2: Analogies

Time: 7 Minutes

Directions: For the questions in this test, choose the picture that should go in the empty box so that the bottom two pictures are related in the same way that the top two are related.

1.

A   B   C   D

2.

F   G   H   J

3.

A   B   C   D

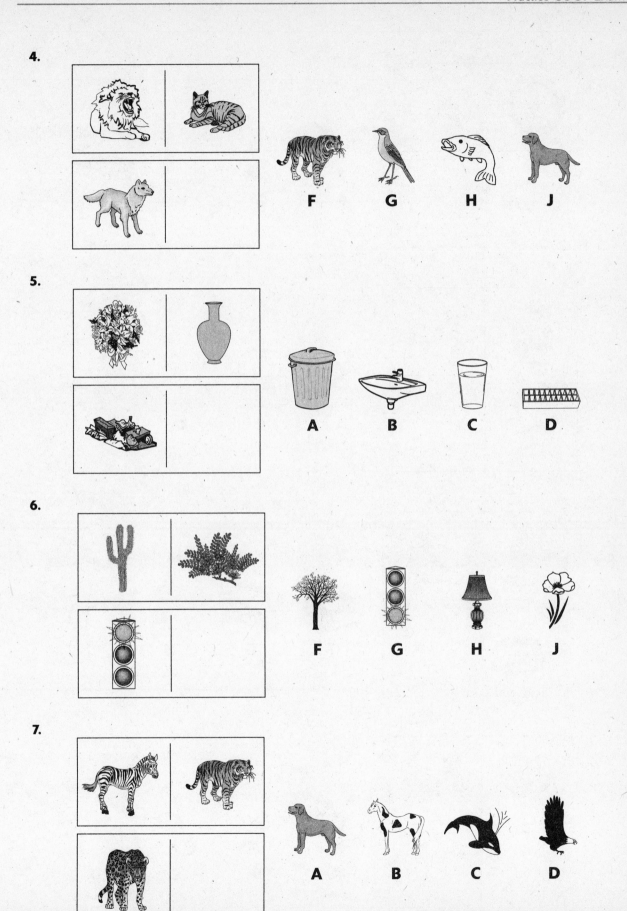

4.

F   G   H   J

5.

A   B   C   D

6.

F   G   H   J

7.

A   B   C   D

GO ON TO THE NEXT PAGE

8.

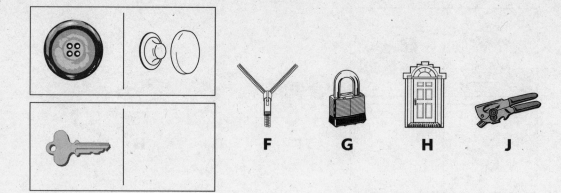

F   G   H   J

9.

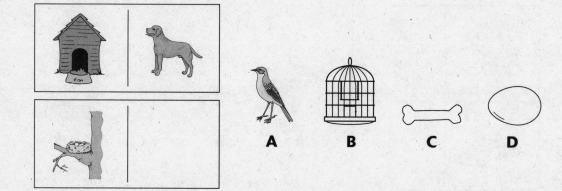

A   B   C   D

10.

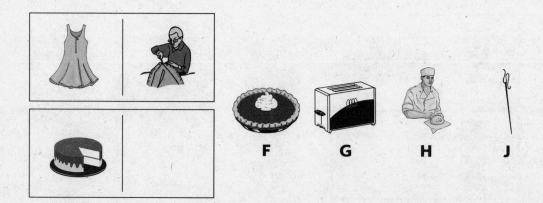

F   G   H   J

11.

A   B   C   D

12.

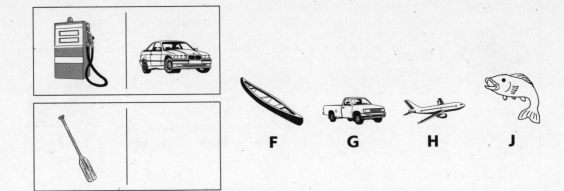

F   G   H   J

13.

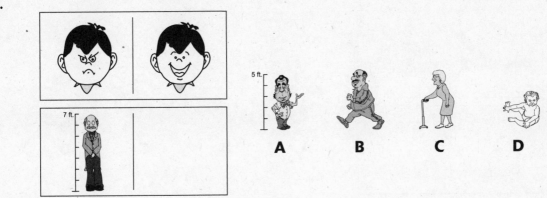

5 ft.

A   B   C   D

7 ft.

14.

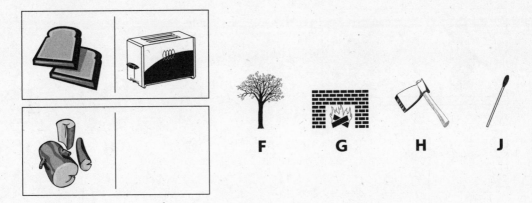

F   G   H   J

15.

A   B   C   D

GO ON TO THE NEXT PAGE

135

Practice COOP Exam 2

16.

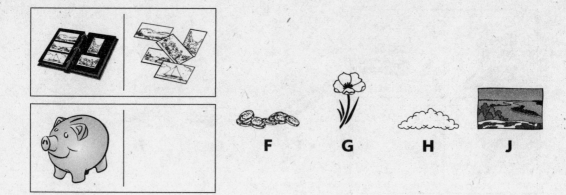

17.

18.

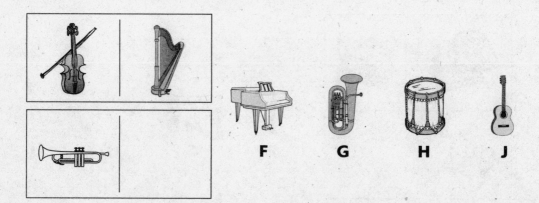

19.

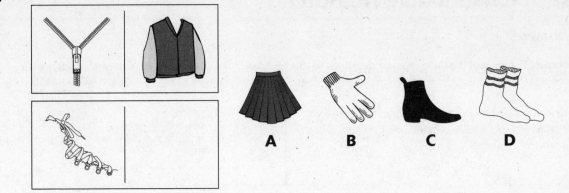

A   B   C   D

20.

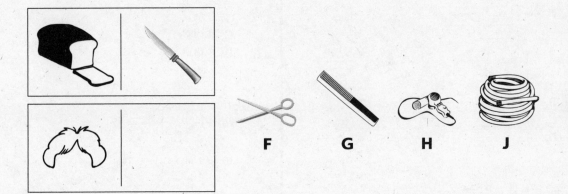

F   G   H   J

IF YOU FINISH BEFORE TIME IS CALLED, CHECK YOUR WORK ON THIS SECTION ONLY. DO NOT WORK ON ANY OTHER SECTION IN THE TEST.

Test 3: Quantitative Reasoning

Time: 20 Minutes

Directions: For each of the three types of questions in this test, select the choice that best answers each question.

For questions 1–7, find the relationship of the numbers in one column to the numbers in the other column. Then find the missing number.

1.

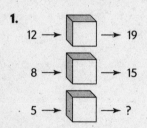

12 → ▢ → 19
8 → ▢ → 15
5 → ▢ → ?

A. 10
B. 11
C. 12
D. 13

2.

8 → ▢ → 2
20 → ▢ → 5
16 → ▢ → ?

F. 2
G. 4
H. 8
J. 12

3.

20 → ▢ → 10
17 → ▢ → 7
25 → ▢ → ?

A. 5
B. 10
C. 15
D. 20

4.

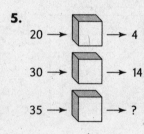

2 → ▢ → 12
5 → ▢ → 30
7 → ▢ → ?

F. 35
G. 42
H. 44
J. 49

5.

20 → ▢ → 4
30 → ▢ → 14
35 → ▢ → ?

A. 19
B. 20
C. 21
D. 22

6.

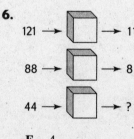

121 → ▢ → 11
88 → ▢ → 8
44 → ▢ → ?

F. 4
G. 5
H. 6
J. 7

7.

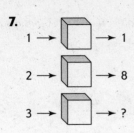

1 → → 1

2 → → 8

3 → → ?

A. 9
B. 18
C. 21
D. 27

For questions 8–13, find the fraction of the grid that is shaded.

8.

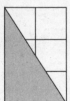

F. $\frac{1}{4}$

G. $\frac{1}{3}$

H. $\frac{1}{2}$

J. $\frac{3}{4}$

9.

A. $\frac{1}{6}$

B. $\frac{1}{3}$

C. $\frac{1}{2}$

D. $\frac{2}{3}$

10.

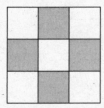

F. $\frac{2}{9}$

G. $\frac{1}{3}$

H. $\frac{4}{9}$

J. $\frac{2}{3}$

11.

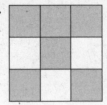

A. $\frac{4}{9}$

B. $\frac{1}{2}$

C. $\frac{2}{3}$

D. $\frac{6}{7}$

12.

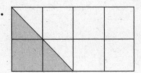

F. $\frac{1}{8}$

G. $\frac{1}{6}$

H. $\frac{1}{4}$

J. $\frac{1}{3}$

13.

A. $\frac{1}{3}$

B. $\frac{1}{2}$

C. $\frac{2}{3}$

D. $\frac{3}{4}$

GO ON TO THE NEXT PAGE

Practice COOP Exam 2

For questions 14–20, look at the scale showing sets of shapes of equal weight. Find an equivalent pair of sets that also balances the scale.

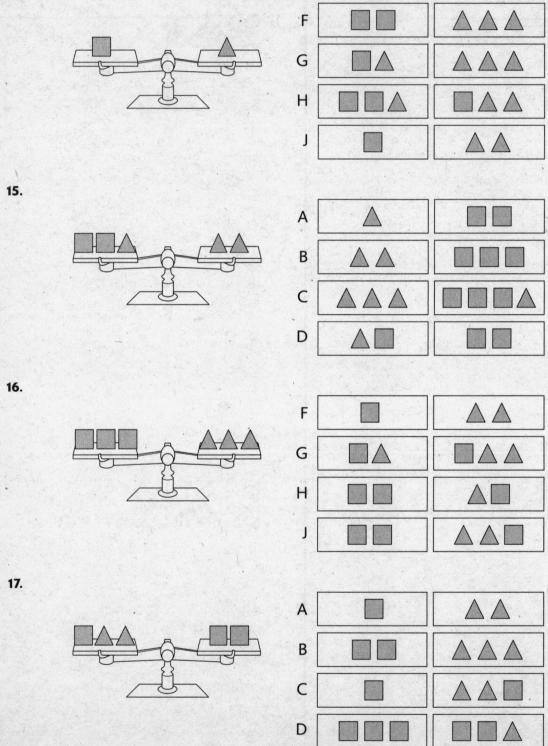

14.

F

G

H

J

15.

A

B

C

D

16.

F

G

H

J

17.

A

B

C

D

18.

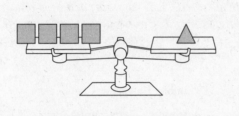

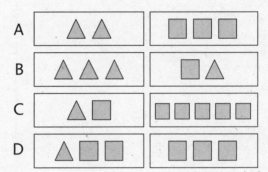

19.

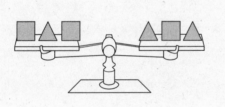

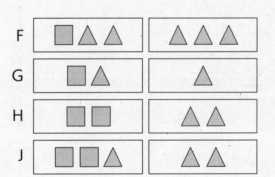

20.

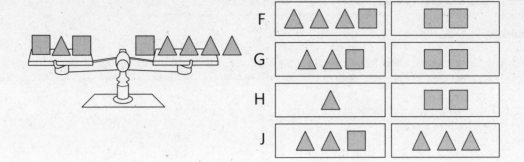

IF YOU FINISH BEFORE TIME IS CALLED, CHECK YOUR WORK ON THIS SECTION ONLY. DO NOT WORK ON ANY OTHER SECTION IN THE TEST.

Test 4: Verbal Reasoning—Words

Time: 15 Minutes

Directions: For the questions in this test, select the answer choice that best satisfies the question.

For questions 1–6, choose the word that names a necessary part of the underlined word.

1. skeleton
   A. finger
   B. toes
   C. bones
   D. eyes

2. insects
   F. wings
   G. six legs
   H. flies
   J. larynx

3. clarinet
   A. reed
   B. notes
   C. sheet music
   D. chair

4. house
   F. car
   G. shrubbery
   H. flowers
   J. door

5. ice cream
   A. milk
   B. freezer
   C. taste
   D. ice

6. football
   F. globe
   G. circle
   H. cylinder
   J. laces

In questions 7–12, the words in the top row are related in some way. The words in the bottom row are related in the same way. For each item, choose the word that completes the bottom row of words.

7. Columbia, Endeavor, Challenger

   Constitution, Gettysburg Address
   A. Sputnik
   B. Huang Ho
   C. Mohandas Gandhi
   D. Declaration of Independence

8. ocean, lake, pool

   Sun, Earth
   F. Saturn
   G. moon
   H. Jupiter
   J. Neptune

9. Andes, Himalayas, Rocky Mountains

   nitrogen, oxygen
   A. carbon dioxide
   B. sodium
   C. silicon
   D. iron

10. pets, pollen, dust

flood, earthquake

    F. small pox
    G. cholera
    H. forest fire
    J. bubonic plague

11. vulture, condor, eagle

tarantula, brown recluse

    A. owl
    B. black widow
    C. hummingbird
    D. garden spider

12. cheetah, antelope, gazelle

honeybee, firefly

    F. bluebird
    G. lady bug
    H. cactus wren
    J. hermit thrush

IF YOU FINISH BEFORE TIME IS CALLED, CHECK YOUR WORK ON THIS
SECTION ONLY. DO NOT WORK ON ANY OTHER SECTION IN THE TEST.

Test 5: Verbal Reasoning—Context

Time: 15 Minutes

Directions: Select the answer choice that best satisfies the question.

For questions 1–5, choose the statement that is true according to the given information.

1. Susie is 12 years old. She does well in school and spends a great deal of time working on her computer. She dreams of having a pet of her own, especially a kitten or puppy. However, when she is near a cat or dog her eyes begin to itch. They become red, swollen, and tear. She begins to sneeze and sometimes has trouble breathing.

    A. Susie's mother said she could not have a pet.
    B. She needs to take allergy shots.
    C. She adopts a kitten anyway.
    D. Susie uses her computer to research about allergies and pets.

2. It is Kira's birthday. She will be 30 years old. She used to think that was a very old age. Lately her attitude has changed. Which statement does NOT fit with her changed attitude?

    F. She says, "You're only as old as you feel."
    G. She plans her own party, rents a boat, and invites all her friends and family to help her celebrate.
    H. She doesn't mention this birthday to anyone.
    J. She hopes the weather will be perfect for her party.

3. George is not happy in his job as an auto mechanic. He has worked at the same shop for 10 years and has had a few raises. Some of his coworkers have had more raises than he. He thinks he should get a higher salary, equal to those coworkers. What should he do about his problem?

    A. George should speak to his boss and demand a raise.
    B. He should quit his job and look for work in another auto body shop.
    C. He should complain to his coworkers.
    D. He should take extra training to make himself more qualified for a higher-paying job.

4. Daniel is 16 years old. He lives in a large metropolitan city. He took driver's education in school and passed the class. He also passed the test for a junior driver's license. He wants to take the family car and drive some of his friends to the movies some evening. His parents don't approve of this idea.

    F. They don't want him driving at night.
    G. They trust his driving, but not that of other drivers.
    H. They are afraid he will show off for his friends and get into trouble.
    J. In the state where Daniel lives, it is illegal for a person with a junior license to be driving without an adult in the car.

5. Sharon is a teacher. During summer vacation she goes to the gym six mornings a week, spending several hours there. On Monday, Wednesday, and Friday she works to strengthen her lungs and heart using the treadmill and other cardio machines. Tuesday, Thursday, and Saturday she swims, working on endurance and general fitness.

    A. When school begins, she will have to arrange her schedule to find time to teach and work out.
    B. Sharon will have to stop working out.
    C. Sharon will be too tired to go to the gym after school.
    D. Sharon should retire so that she won't have to give up her workouts at the gym.

For questions 6–8, choose the correct answer.

6. Here are some words translated from an artificial language.

Ionabossifls means elephant.

Ionluostir means lion.

Ionluwasloo means giraffe.

Which word means tiger?

   F. *fruolctme*
   G. *wolasbosaka*
   H. *ionsfirstir*
   J. *sierotpf*

7. Here are some words translated from an artificial language.

Xetrobgasalamos means Tyrannosaurus Rex.

Eleturahsalamos means Brontosaurus.

Sshmatosalamos means Stegosaurus.

Which word means Diplodocus?

   A. *Salamossaerion*
   B. *Ttlefraugour*
   C. *Sadnhdisia*
   D. *Uislcjets*

8. Here are some words translated from an artificial language.

Rilyofo means eating.

Rialbinyofo means sleeping.

Rifonisnefyofo means reading.

Which word means walking?

   F. *rflabinofl*
   G. *peretnho*
   H. *rinewbefyofo*
   J. *rqirtysoln*

IF YOU FINISH BEFORE TIME IS CALLED, CHECK YOUR WORK ON THIS SECTION ONLY. DO NOT WORK ON ANY OTHER SECTION IN THE TEST.

Test 6: Reading and Language Arts

Time: 40 Minutes

Directions: For each question in this test, read the passages and questions that follow. Choose the best possible answer.

Passage for questions 1–5:

Fat and skinny black lines with mysterious numbers under the lines appear on many packages of items we buy. They are called bar codes, or UPCs (universal pricing codes), and they are scanned at a computer station to enter the price of an item when it's purchased. But the codes themselves don't contain price information. The mysterious lines and numbers identify the product. The lines are representations of the digits that can be scanned by a computer. The first 6 digits of the number identify the manufacturer. The next 5 digits represent the item. For example, the first 6 digits might mean that a specific candy company was the manufacturer, and the next 5 digits might indicate whether the product is a chocolate bar or a package of hard candy. The last digit is called a check digit. Using a complicated formula involving the other 11 digits, a number for the check digit is calculated. When an item is scanned, the scanner performs the calculation, and if the check digits don't match, an error has occurred. The scanner sends the correct information to the store's central computer to look up the UPC number, and that computer relays it back to the checkout station where the purchase is being made to enter the price.

1. The number of digits making up a UPC is:

    A. 5
    B. 6
    C. 11
    D. 12

2. According to the passage, the purpose of the UPC is to:

    F. identify the item
    G. list the item's price
    H. provide a checking system
    J. avoid mistakes by sales personnel

3. A check digit is produced by:

    A. scanning the item
    B. a mathematical formula
    C. the bars on the label
    D. a computer

4. Which of the following is an example of information that might be found in one UPC?

    F. Andy Cookie Company and Carlos Cookie Company
    G. orange soda and cola
    H. Queens Pudding Company and chocolate
    J. ice cream and vanilla

5. The prices of items are stored in the:

    A. bar codes
    B. product price list
    C. central computer
    D. checkout station

Passage for questions 6–9:

Her nose was rather short than otherwise; and her cheeks a great deal too round and red for a heroine; but her face blushed with rosy health, and her lips with the freshest of smiles, and she had a pair of eyes which sparkled with the brightest and most honest good humor, except indeed when they filled with tears, and that was a great deal too often; for the silly thing would cry over a dead canary bird; or over a mouse, that the cat had seized upon, or over the end of a novel were it ever so stupid; and as for saying an unkind word to her, were any persons hardhearted enough to do so—why so much the worse for them.

From *Vanity Fair* by William Makepeace Thackeray

6. The best word to describe the young lady described in this passage is:

    F. beautiful
    G. sensitive
    H. sad
    J. comical

7. The author describes persons being unkind to the young lady as hardhearted because:

    A. they were worse than the young lady was
    B. there was no reason to do so
    C. doing this makes her cry
    D. she would scold them in return

8. The author implies that a heroine usually:

    F. has a thin pale face

    G. blushes easily

    H. has a fresh smile

    J. doesn't have sparkling eyes

9. The author's attitude toward the young lady is one of:

    A. dislike

    B. fear

    C. admiration

    D. love

Passage for questions 10–13:

If you are a coin collector, you probably would like to know which of your coins has the most value. Usually, coins that are popular or rare are valuable. But the coin's grade also plays a very important role in its value. A coin that is popular and scarce would normally be valuable, but it might be worth little if it has a low grade. Therefore, learning to grade coins becomes a necessary skill for a collector.

Grading is standardized, and one can buy books and take courses to learn how to do it.

Grades are given with letter designations followed by numbers. The letters represent general levels of the grade, while the numbers are more detailed. For example, 11 number grades exist within the letter grade for a mint state coin. A mint state coin is uncirculated, which means it has never been used in commerce. It is in the condition that it left the mint, the place where a coin is created. The mint state letter designation is MS, and the numbers range from 60 through 70. Other letter designations are for coins that are About Uncirculated (AU), Fine (EF or VF), and Good (VG or G). In general, coin collectors dislike cleaned coins, so artificial cleaning by adding any chemical decreases a coin's value. A true coin collector says that the dirt in the creases of a coin is a positive feature and much prefers it to a cleaned coin.

Books and magazines about the coin market appear regularly. They describe a coin's type, date, and grade, assigning a price to every coin.

10. The best title for this passage is:

    F. The Financial Benefits of Coin Collecting

    G. How Popularity Affects Coin Value

    H. Coin Grading—An Important Skill

    J. How to Grade Coins—A Detailed Study

11. The passage suggests that the most important feature of a coin is its:

    A. cleanliness

    B. rarity

    C. grade

    D. popularity

12. The letter designations for coins:

    F. always have one letter

    G. can have one or two letters

    H. include a number

    J. are known only to experts

13. According to the passage, which of the following statements is true?

    A. A mint state coin has never been spent.

    B. A scarce coin is always valuable.

    C. Cleaning a coin can increase its value.

    D. You must be a professional to obtain information on coin value.

Passage for questions 14–18:

It was previously thought that dinosaurs were cold-blooded creatures, like reptiles. However, a recent discovery has led researchers to believe they might have been warm-blooded. The fossilized remains of a 66-million-year-old dinosaur's heart were discovered and examined by x-ray.

Reptiles are cold-blooded, meaning that they depend on the environment to heat their bodies. Most reptiles have three chambers in their hearts, although some do have four. Those that have four chambers have two arteries to mix the oxygen-rich blood with oxygen-lean blood. But the fossilized heart had four chambers in the heart and only one artery. The single artery means that the oxygen-rich blood was completely separated from the oxygen-poor blood, as it is in mammals.

Mammals are warm-blooded, meaning that they generate their own body heat and are thus more tolerant of temperature extremes. Mammals, because they are warm-blooded, move more swiftly and have greater physical endurance than reptiles.

Scientists believe that the evidence now points to the idea that all dinosaurs were actually warm-blooded. Ironically, the particular dinosaur in which the discovery was made was a Tescelosaurus, which translates to "marvelous lizard." A lizard, of course, is a reptile.

14. According to the passage, what previously held theory is now questioned?

    F. Dinosaurs were warm-blooded.

    G. Dinosaurs had four-chambered hearts.

    H. Dinosaurs were swifter and stronger than reptiles.

    J. Dinosaurs were cold-blooded.

GO ON TO THE NEXT PAGE

15. According to the passage, all reptiles:

 A. have four-chambered hearts
 B. are cold-blooded
 C. have one artery
 D. have hearts that mix different kinds of blood

16. The word *generate* in paragraph three most probably means:

 F. produce
 G. lose
 H. use
 J. tolerate

17. From the passage, a reader can conclude that mammals move:

 A. faster and have more endurance than reptiles
 B. slower and have less endurance than reptiles
 C. faster and have more endurance than dinosaurs
 D. slower and have less endurance than dinosaurs

18. The author calls the name of the dinosaur in the discovery ironic because:

 F. it is surprising that a fossil heart was discovered
 G. scientists should have known dinosaurs were warm-blooded
 H. the dinosaur was a marvelous animal
 J. the "marvelous lizard" turned out not to be a reptile

Passage for questions 19–22:

Mickey Mouse first appeared on screen in 1928. He appeared in the cartoon "Steamboat Willie." Walt Disney drew the character and supplied the voice. In the 1930s alone, Mickey appeared in about 90 cartoons. The exact number is unknown because some early films might have been lost. In 1940, he starred in the Disney film "Fantasia." His section of that film was the only part of the original used when the film was remade in 2000.

Just as other stars have had their faces and images used to sell products, so has Mickey. In the 1930s, Mickey Mouse dolls were popular. The Mickey Mouse watch was introduced in 1933. In her autobiography, author Maya Angelou writes about her delight in receiving one for a present when she graduated from elementary school. The watch was so successful it kept the company that made it from going out of business. Mickey Mouse has appeared on T-shirts, lunchboxes, toy trains, and many other products.

He had a fan club as early as 1932. In 1955, the first television edition of the Mickey Mouse Club was broadcast. New versions of that show were created in 1977 and 1989. In 2001, Walt Disney Television created "House of Mickey," a show that appeared on the Disney Channel.

19. According to the passage, Mickey has been on movie screens:

 A. 3 times
 B. more than 90 times
 C. since 1940
 D. since 1955

20. The Mickey Mouse Club began in:

 F. 1932
 G. 1957
 H. 1977
 J. 1989

21. The author includes the information about Maya Angelou to:

 A. give an example of the watch's popularity
 B. praise Maya Angelou
 C. explain the watch company's problem
 D. contrast it with other watches

22. According to the passage, images of stars appear on products to:

 F. advertise the stars
 G. make money for the stars
 H. increase sales of the product
 J. create a beautiful product

Passage for questions 23–27:

In a trial, the jury has the job of deciding the facts in question, while the judge decides questions of law. A fair and impartial trial depends on the efforts of the jury, the judge, and the attorneys who act as representatives for each side.

When the trial starts, the attorneys each make an opening statement telling the jury what they expect the evidence will show. These introductions are not evidence. But they give the jury a framework to understand the evidence.

Evidence is anything presented to the jurors by an attorney that they can hear, see, or touch. It can be testimony by a witness, a photograph, a piece of clothing, a fingerprint, or anything physical. Jurors can use their common sense in considering evidence, but they are not permitted to guess about things that have not been presented.

After both sides have presented their evidence, the judge instructs jurors on the law they must apply to the case. Then the attorneys present their arguments. These arguments are not evidence. They are attempts by the attorneys to summarize what the evidence has shown. After these arguments, the jury discusses the case and tries to reach a decision.

23. The word *impartial* most probably means:

A. complete
B. important
C. unprejudiced
D. uninterested

24. Which of the following is not an example of evidence?

F. a picture of a person
G. a jacket with a torn sleeve
H. an orange crayon
J. an open window in the courtroom

25. The word *testimony* most probably means:

A. statements
B. facial expressions
C. falsehoods
D. questions to the attorney

26. The purpose of the attorneys' opening statements is to provide:

F. witnesses
G. background
H. evidence
J. proof

27. The judge explains the law to the jury:

A. before opening statements
B. before evidence is presented
C. after one side presents evidence
D. after all evidence has been presented

Passage for questions 28–31:

It has long been believed that the first humans to enter the Americas crossed a land bridge from Asia. But scientists have discovered that settlements in the area of Asia where the people lived existed at about the same time as the settlement in Clovis, New Mexico, one of the early sites of settlement in the Americas. Previously, they thought the Asian settlements were much older. Because the Asian settlements are younger, there could not have been a long span of years during which people could travel from Asia to North America.

The scientists' discoveries were made using radiocarbon dating. This is a process comparing the amounts of regular carbon and radioactive carbon in a sample. The amount of time it takes for radioactive carbon to decay is known. So the age of a sample can be determined by comparing the amounts of each type of carbon remaining in it.

If the land bridge was not humans' path to the Americas, how did they get here?

One theory guesses that they might have used boats, crossing the Atlantic from ice floe to ice floe. Another theory suggests that humans from the area of Japan followed whales and other marine food sources across the Pacific Ocean.

28. Scientists now think the earliest humans did not enter the Americas by a land bridge because:

F. Clovis, New Mexico, is not on the coast of the American continent
G. no one lived in Asia when this migration supposedly occurred
H. the time of the settlements in Asia and North America is too close together
J. radioactive carbon and carbon are found in all organisms

29. The scientists discovered the age of the settlements by:

A. dating samples from the settlements
B. retracing the route the people might have taken
C. having new theories about how humans arrived in the Americas
D. finding out how long it takes radioactive carbon to decay

30. The best title for this passage is:

F. The Radiocarbon Dating Process
G. Clovis, New Mexico
H. Asia and the Americas
J. Human Settlement in the Americas

31. Both new theories about human settlement in the Americas:

A. have humans migrating from the same place
B. suggest the Americas were reached by boats
C. prove that no land bridge to the Americas existed
D. are a result of radioactive carbon dating

GO ON TO THE NEXT PAGE

Passage for questions 32–36:

The strangler fig tree, home to many birds and animals that eat the figs, is found in the rain forests of Indonesia and a national park on the island of Borneo.

The trees are referred to as stranglers because of the way they envelop other trees. Yet, the expression strangler is not exactly accurate because the fig trees do not squeeze the trees around which they grow, nor do they actually take any nutrients from the host tree. But they might stifle the host tree's growth as the fig tree's roots meet and fuse together, forming stiff rings around the host's trunk and restricting further growth of the supporting tree.

The most interesting aspect of the strangler fig is that it grows from the sky down to the ground. Birds eat the fruit and drop the seeds contained in them. Most seeds that are dropped to the ground do not grow. But those that drop into moist masses of decayed leaves and mosses that have collected in branches of trees have a chance of survival. They are more likely to receive sunlight than those that drop all the way to the ground.

32. According to the passage, fig trees are referred to as stranglers because they:

    F. are found in the tropics
    G. kill the host tree
    H. wrap themselves around other trees
    J. kill wildlife

33. The passage states that the term strangler is not accurate because:

    A. while the fig trees might damage the host tree, they do not actually squeeze it
    B. the host tree actually strangles the fig
    C. the fig tree does not harm animals
    D. the fig tree provides nutrition to the host tree

34. The word *stifle* in the second paragraph most probably means:

    F. assist
    G. nourish
    H. suffocate
    J. live on

35. According to the passage, the fig trees:

    A. grow from seeds dropped to the ground
    B. grow from the top of a tree down to the ground
    C. grow from the ground up
    D. receive nutrients from the host tree

36. Seeds that fall into the host tree are more likely to survive than seeds on the ground because they:

    F. receive more moisture
    G. were deposited by birds
    H. are nourished by the tree
    J. might get more sunshine

Passage for questions 37–40:

I Wandered Lonely As a Cloud

I wandered lonely as a cloud
That floats on high o'er vales and hills,
When all at once I saw a crowd
A host of golden daffodils;
Beside the lake beneath the trees,
Fluttering and dancing in the breeze.

Continuous as the stars that shine
And twinkle on the Milky Way
They stretched in never-ending line
Along the margin of a bay:
Ten thousand saw I at a glance,
Tossing their heads in sprightly dance.

The waves beside them danced; but they
Outdid the sparkling waves in glee;
A poet could not but be gay,
In such a jocund company;
I gazed—and gazed—but little thought
What wealth to me the show had brought.

From "I Wandered Lonely As a Cloud" by William Wordsworth

37. In the second stanza, the quality of the daffodils that the poet emphasizes is their:

   A. color
   B. growth
   C. movement
   D. quantity

38. The word *jocund* most probably means:

   F. happy
   G. silly
   H. athletic
   J. stubborn

39. The poet was delighted to see the daffodils because he:

   A. liked flowers
   B. had been lonely
   C. knew they meant spring had arrived
   D. had few thoughts

40. In the last line of the passage, by *wealth* the poet is referring to:

   F. money
   G. pleasure
   H. sadness
   J. flowers

Practice COOP Exam 2

IF YOU FINISH BEFORE TIME IS CALLED, CHECK YOUR WORK ON THIS SECTION ONLY. DO NOT WORK ON ANY OTHER SECTION IN THE TEST.

Test 7: Mathematics

Time: 35 Minutes

Directions: Read each of the following problems, and select the best answer.

1. The number 210 is divisible by how many different prime numbers?

   A. 3
   B. 4
   C. 5
   D. 6

2. If $a = 2$, then $(a^2)^3 =$

   F. 12
   G. 28
   H. 32
   J. 64

3. $\dfrac{a+b}{a} - \dfrac{a-b}{a} =$

   A. 0

   B. 2

   C. $\dfrac{2b}{a}$

   D. $\dfrac{2a+2b}{a}$

4. If N is a number between 0 and 1, which of the following is the biggest?

   F. N
   G. N^2
   H. N^3
   J. N^4

5. If $2x = 7 - 2y$, what is the value of $x + y$?

   A. $\dfrac{7}{2}$

   B. 7

   C. 14

   D. It cannot be determined.

6. What is the area of the triangle with vertices (0, 0), (4, 0) and (0, 5)?

   F. 10
   G. 15
   H. 20
   J. 40

7. $6.3 + (6.3 \times 10) + (6.3 \times 10^2) =$

   A. 18.9
   B. 63
   C. 630
   D. 699.3

8. If $P = 5$, what is the value of $(5 - 5P)(5P + 5)$?

   F. −600
   G. 0
   H. 10
   J. 600

9.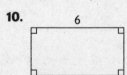

   The five cards in the preceding figure have numbers written on them. If two of the cards are chosen at random, what is the probability that the sum of the numbers on the two cards is less than 10?

   A. $\dfrac{3}{10}$

   B. $\dfrac{2}{5}$

   C. $\dfrac{1}{2}$

   D. $\dfrac{3}{5}$

10.

   If the area of the rectangle shown in the preceding figure is 24, what is the perimeter of the rectangle?

   F. 10
   G. 12
   H. 18
   J. 20

11.

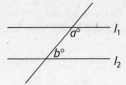

In the preceding figure, l_1 is parallel to l_2. What is the value of $a + b$?

A. 90°
B. 180°
C. 270°
D. 360°

12. If $x = 4y + 7$, what is the value of y in terms of x?

F. $\dfrac{x - 7}{4}$

G. $\dfrac{x + 7}{4}$

H. $4(x + 7)$

J. $4(x - 7)$

13. $\dfrac{10^2 \left(10^6 + 10^6\right)}{10^4} =$

A. 10^2
B. 2×10^2
C. 10^4
D. 2×10^4

14. If q^3 is odd, which of the following statements is *not* true?

F. $2q$ is even
G. q^2 is even
H. q^5 is odd
J. $3q$ is odd

15.

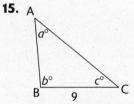

In the triangle shown in the preceding figure, $b > 90$. Which of the following could possibly be the length of side AC?

A. 7
B. 8
C. 9
D. 10

16. The average of x, y, and z is 10. If $z = 0$, what is the value of $x + y$?

F. 10
G. 20
H. 25
J. 30

17.

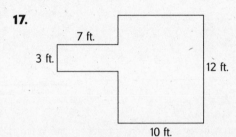

The preceding diagram shows the dimensions of a hall and a bedroom. All angles in the figure are right angles. What is the area of the bedroom and hall in square feet?

A. 58
B. 61
C. 141
D. 153

18.

If the average of a and b in the preceding triangle is 60, what is the value of c?

F. 40
G. 50
H. 60
J. 70

19. The sum of two prime numbers is 10. Which of the following could *not* be one of the prime numbers?

A. 2
B. 3
C. 5
D. 7

GO ON TO THE NEXT PAGE

20. The base of a triangle is equal to 4. What is the height of the triangle if the area is 28?

    F. 7

    G. 14

    H. 16

    J. 20

21. $(-4)^2 - 3(-4) =$

    A. −28

    B. 30

    C. 4

    D. 28

22. The sum of two consecutive integers is 39. What is the larger of the integers?

    F. 7

    G. 19

    H. 20

    J. 21

23. If $\frac{4}{c}$ is subtracted from $\frac{6}{c}$, the result is:

    A. 2

    B. $\frac{2}{c}$

    C. $-\frac{2}{c}$

    D. $\frac{10}{c}$

24. What is the largest of five consecutive integers whose sum is 0?

    F. −5

    G. 0

    H. 2

    J. 5

25. What is 0.05% expressed as a decimal?

    A. 0.0005

    B. 0.005

    C. 0.05

    D. 5

26. If $10x - 4 = 4x + 20$, what is the value of x?

    F. 1

    G. 2

    H. 4

    J. 6

27. The recipe for a loaf of bread requires $\frac{3}{4}$ of a cup of flour. How many loaves did Hazel bake if she used 6 cups of flour?

    A. 4

    B. 6

    C. 8

    D. 10

28. Which of the following represents a whole number?

    F. $\sqrt{79}$

    G. $\sqrt{80}$

    H. $\sqrt{81}$

    J. $\sqrt{82}$

29. Which of the following is the closest to 35.69?

    A. 35.6

    B. 35.65

    C. 35.7

    D. 36

30. Brian's test scores are 97, 80, and 87. What is his average test score?

    F. 88

    G. 89

    H. 90

    J. 91

31. The scale on a map is such that each inch represents 55 miles. What actual distance corresponds to 4.2 inches on the map?

    A. 76

    B. 131

    C. 220

    D. 231

32. What is the sum of $2a + 7$, $4a - 3$, and $a - 2$?

    F. $7a + 2$

    G. $7a - 12$

    H. $7a - 2$

    J. $6a^3 + 2$

33. The area of a square is Q^2 square meters. What is the perimeter of the square?

    A. $2Q$

    B. $4Q$

    C. $2Q^2$

    D. $4Q^2$

34. Dan's weekly allowance increases from $15 to $20. By what percent does his allowance increase?

    F. 20%

    G. 25%

    H. $33\frac{1}{3}$%

    J. 75%

35. If $a = -2$, find the value of $\frac{-12}{4-a}$.

    A. -6

    B. -2

    C. 2

    D. 6

36. Which of the following represents 54 expressed as a product of prime factors?

    F. $(2)(3)$

    G. $(2)(3)(9)$

    H. $(9)(6)$

    J. $(2)(3)(3)(3)$

37.

The preceding figure shows three congruent squares arranged in a row. If the perimeter of *WZYX* is 40, what is the area of *WXYZ*?

    A. 55

    B. 75

    C. 80

    D. 150

38. If $8x - 6 = 34$, then x is equal to:

    F. -5

    G. $-\frac{7}{2}$

    H. $\frac{7}{2}$

    J. 5

39. Solve the proportion for a: $\frac{40}{24} = \frac{5}{a}$

    A. 3

    B. 8

    C. $10\frac{1}{3}$

    D. 15

40. What percent of 64 is $\sqrt{64}$?

    F. 8%

    G. 12.5%

    H. 25%

    J. 100%

IF YOU FINISH BEFORE TIME IS CALLED, CHECK YOUR WORK ON THIS SECTION ONLY. DO NOT WORK ON ANY OTHER SECTION IN THE TEST.

STOP

Answer Key

Test 1: Sequences

1. C	**6.** H	**11.** B	**16.** H
2. F	**7.** A	**12.** F	**17.** D
3. D	**8.** G	**13.** C	**18.** H
4. H	**9.** A	**14.** G	**19.** D
5. B	**10.** F	**15.** A	**20.** F

Test 2: Analogies

1. C	**6.** G	**11.** B	**16.** F
2. G	**7.** B	**12.** F	**17.** D
3. C	**8.** J	**13.** A	**18.** G
4. J	**9.** A	**14.** G	**19.** C
5. A	**10.** H	**15.** C	**20.** F

Test 3: Quantitative Reasoning

1. C	**6.** F	**11.** C	**16.** H
2. G	**7.** D	**12.** H	**17.** A
3. C	**8.** H	**13.** B	**18.** F
4. G	**9.** C	**14.** H	**19.** C
5. A	**10.** H	**15.** A	**20.** H

Test 4: Verbal Reasoning—Words

1. C	**4.** J	**7.** D	**10.** H
2. G	**5.** A	**8.** G	**11.** B
3. A	**6.** J	**9.** A	**12.** G

Test 5: Verbal Reasoning—Context

1. D	**3.** D	**5.** A	**7.** A
2. H	**4.** J	**6.** H	**8.** H

Test 6: Reading and Language Arts

1. D	11. C	21. A	31. B
2. F	12. G	22. H	32. H
3. B	13. A	23. C	33. A
4. H	14. J	24. J	34. H
5. C	15. B	25. A	35. B
6. G	16. F	26. G	36. J
7. C	17. A	27. D	37. D
8. F	18. J	28. H	38. F
9. C	19. B	29. A	39. B
10. H	20. F	30. J	40. G

Test 7: Mathematics

1. B	11. B	21. D	31. D
2. J	12. F	22. H	32. F
3. C	13. D	23. B	33. B
4. F	14. G	24. H	34. H
5. A	15. D	25. A	35. B
6. F	16. J	26. H	36. J
7. D	17. C	27. C	37. B
8. F	18. H	28. H	38. J
9. B	19. A	29. C	39. A
10. J	20. G	30. F	40. G

Answers and Explanations

Test 1: Sequences

1. C. From the first diagram to the second, the positions of the circle and square switch. Therefore, from the third to the fourth diagram, the positions of the triangle and the shaded circle should switch.

2. F. In the first diagram, the first letter is larger than the others. In the second diagram, the second letter is larger than the others, and, in the third diagram, the third letter is larger than the others. Therefore, in the fourth diagram, the fourth letter should be larger than the others.

3. D. Visualize the first diagram as the two hands of a clock at 6:30, with both hands pointing straight down. As one hand remains in the same location, the other hand rotates 45° clockwise from the second to the third to the fourth picture.

4. H. The first diagram contains a three-sided figure, the second diagram contains a four-sided figure, and the third diagram contains a five-sided figure. Therefore, the fourth diagram should contain a six-sided figure.

5. B. In the first diagram, the first and third figures are shaded; this reverses for the second diagram. In the third diagram, because the first and third figures are shaded, this should reverse in the fourth figure.

6. H. The first figure consists of four triangles. Then, moving from figure to figure, the triangles are removed, one at a time, in a clockwise direction.

7. A. The pattern is $27 \div 3 = 9 \div 3 = 3 \mid 36 \div 3 = 12 \div 3 = 4$. Therefore, $45 \div 3 = 15 \div 3 = \mathbf{5}$.

8. G. The pattern is $10 + 5 = 15 + 5 = 20 \mid 12 + 5 = 17 + 5 = 22$. Therefore, $19 + 5 = \mathbf{24} + 5 = 29$.

9. A. The pattern is $13 - 5 = 8$, and $8^2 = 64 \mid 8 - 5 = 3$, and $3^2 = 9$. Thus, $7 - 5 = 2$ and $2^2 = \mathbf{4}$.

10. F. The pattern is $50 - \mathbf{40} = 10 \times 2 = 20 \mid 60 - \mathbf{40} = 20 \times 2 = 40$. So, $70 - \mathbf{40} = 30 \times 2 = \mathbf{60}$.

11. B. The pattern is $9 + 3 = 12 \div 3 = 4 \mid 15 + 3 = 18 \div 3 = 6 \mid 21 + 3 = 24 \div 3 = \mathbf{8}$.

12. F. The pattern is $12 + 6 = 18 - 3 = 15 \mid 24 + 6 = 30 - 3 = 27 \mid 38 + 6 = \mathbf{44} - 3 = 41$.

13. C. The pattern is $9 \times 3 = 27 \div 3 = 9 \mid 10 \times 3 = 30 \div 3 = 10 \mid 11 \times 3 = \mathbf{33} \div 3 = 11$.

14. G. The pattern is $Z - 2 = X - 2 = V \mid W - 2 = U - 2 = S \mid T - 2 = R - 2 = P \mid N - 2 = L - 2 = J$. In addition, the first letter of each sequence directly follows the last letter of the previous sequence. For example, the V at the end of the first sequence is followed by the W at the start of the second sequence. Because the third sequence ends with P, the missing sequence must begin with Q, and follow the pattern $Q - 2 = O - 2 = M$.

15. A. The first letter of each sequence is followed by the letter directly after it, and then by the letter directly before it. Thus, for example, C comes after B, and A comes before B. The sequence U V T also has this pattern.

16. H. The pattern is $A + 4 = E + 4 = I \mid B + 4 = F + 4 = J \mid C + 4 = G + 4 = K \mid E + 4 = I + 4 = M$. Also, the first letters of each sequence are in alphabetical order, starting with A. Therefore, the correct answer choice must begin with D and proceed $D + 4 = H + 4 = L$.

17. D. The pattern is $X - 1 = W - 1 = V \mid V - 1 = U - 1 = T \mid T - 1 = S - 1 = R \mid P - 1 = O - 1 = N$. In addition, each sequence begins with the letter that ended the previous sequence. Thus, the missing sequence must begin with R, and proceed $R - 1 = Q - 1 = P$.

18. H. The numbers in each sequence are ascending, so the missing sequence must contain 9. The letters follow the pattern $B - 1 = A \mid F - 1 = E \mid J - 1 = I \mid M - 1 = L$, so the missing sequence is P 9 O.

19. D. The numbers ascend by 2, while the letters follow the pattern $A + 1 = B + 1 = C$, and so on. In addition, the first letter of each sequence follows the letter that ended the previous sequence. Thus, the missing sequence must be N O 9 P.

20. **F.** The numbers descend, so the missing number must be 6. The letters follow the pattern Z − 1 = Y − 2 = W, and so on. Finally, note that the first letter in each sequence is the letter that alphabetically precedes the letter that ended the previous sequence. Because N comes before O, which ends the previous sequence, the missing sequence is N M 6 K.

Test 2: Analogies

1. **C.** The arm is located between the wrist and the hand as the ankle is located between the leg and the foot.

2. **G.** The relationship is what a person in this job usually wears.

3. **C.** The relationship is location. Eyes are above a nose; a roof is above a house.

4. **J.** The relationship is that they are part of the same family of animals. Lions and cats are felines; wolves and dogs are canines.

5. **A.** Location explains the answer. What is the appropriate place to put the object?

6. **G.** The relationship is opposites. A cactus grows in a dry place; a fern grows in a wet place. The top traffic light is red, meaning stop; the bottom light is green, meaning go.

7. **B.** The relationship is similar characteristics: having stripes and having spots.

8. **J.** Buttons and snaps close things; keys and can openers open things.

9. **A.** A dog house is a place for a dog to live; a nest is a place for a bird to live.

10. **H.** The relationship is that of the object to the person who creates the object.

11. **B.** Cats have claws; birds have beaks.

12. **F.** The relationship is function. Gasoline makes an automobile move; a paddle makes a canoe move.

13. **A.** The relationship is opposites.

14. **G.** Toast is made in a toaster; logs are burned in a fireplace.

15. **C.** The relationship is function. A trunk is used to store objects in a car; a locker is used to store objects in a gymnasium.

16. **F.** An album is a place to keep photos; a piggy bank is a place to keep money.

17. **D.** Seat belts protect people in cars; life vests protect people on boats.

18. **G.** The relationship is members of a group. Both a violin and harp are instruments with strings; a tuba and a trumpet are instruments to blow into.

19. **C.** A zipper is used to close a jacket; shoelaces are used to close shoes.

20. **F.** Bread is cut by a knife; hair is but by scissors.

Test 3: Quantitative Reasoning

1. **C.** The pattern is 12 + 7 = 19, and 8 + 7 = 15. Thus, we have 5 + 7 = 12.

2. **G.** Here, 8 ÷ 4 = 2, and 20 ÷ 4 = 5. Therefore, 16 ÷ 4 = 4.

3. **C.** Notice that 20 − 10 = 10, and 17 − 10 = 7. Then, 25 − 10 = 15.

4. **G.** The pattern is 2 × 6 = 12, and 5 × 6 = 30. It follows that 7 × 6 = 42.

5. **A.** Note that 20 − 16 = 4, and 30 − 16 = 14. Thus, 35 − 16 = 19.

6. **F.** The pattern is 121 ÷ 11 = 11, and 88 ÷ 11 = 8. Therefore, 44 ÷ 11 = 4.

7. **D.** Note that three 1's multiplied together are 1, and three 2's multiplied together are 8. Therefore, three 3's multiplied together are 27.

8. **H.** Half of each of the four squares is shaded. Because four halves are equal to 2, the equivalent of 2 squares out of 4 are shaded. Then, note that $\frac{2}{4} = \frac{1}{2}$.

9. **C.** The diagonal divides the total figure into two equal halves. Therefore, $\frac{1}{2}$ of the figure is shaded.

10. **H.** The total figure contains 9 squares, of which 4 are shaded. Therefore, $\frac{4}{9}$ of the figure is shaded.

11. **C.** The figure contains 9 squares, of which 6 are shaded. Therefore, $\frac{6}{9} = \frac{2}{3}$ of the figure is shaded.

12. **H.** The total figure contains 8 squares. One whole square and two half squares are shaded, which is equivalent to 2 squares shaded. Thus, overall, $\frac{2}{8} = \frac{1}{4}$ of the figure is shaded.

13. **B.** Here, half of each square in the figure is shaded, thus, overall, $\frac{1}{2}$ of the figure is shaded.

14. **H.** According to the scale, one cube = one cone. Add a cube and a cone to both sides, and we see that two cubes and a cone are equal to a cube and two cones.

15. **A.** According to the scale, two cubes and a cone are equal to two cones. If we remove a cone from each side, the scale still balances, and we can conclude that two cubes are equal to one cone.

16. **H.** If three cubes are equal to three cones, then one cube must be equal to one cone. Therefore, one cube and one cone balance, and if we add a cube to each side, we see that two cubes balance a cube and a cone.

17. **A.** We are shown that a cube and two cones are equal to two cubes. Removing a cube from each side shows us that two cones are equal to one cube.

18. **F.** According to the scale, two cubes and a cone are equal to one cube and four cones. Removing a cube and a cone from each side, we see that one cube is equal to three cones. If we add a new cube to each side, we determine that two cubes are equal to three cones and a cube.

19. **C.** We are told that four cubes equal one cone. If we place a cube on each side, we determine that five cubes are equal to a cube and a cone.

20. **H.** Because two cubes and a cone are equal to two cones and a cube, we can see, by removing a cube and a cone from each side, that one cube equals one cone. This being the case, two cubes are equal to two cones.

Test 4: Verbal Reasoning—Words

1. **C.** A skeleton cannot exist without bones. All the other answer choices are parts of the body, as is the skeleton.

2. **G.** The identifying feature of an insect is that it has six legs. Other creatures, like birds, have wings and can fly. A human has a larynx.

3. **A.** A reed produces sound in a clarinet. Notes are written on and played from sheet music while sitting on a chair.

4. **J.** It is impossible to properly enter a house without a door. Shrubbery and flowers decorate the exterior of the house. A car has nothing to do with a house.

5. **A.** Ice cream is made from milk. You need a freezer or ice to keep it frozen, and ice cream has a variety of tastes (flavors), but only milk is a necessary ingredient.

6. **J.** A football has laces. A cylinder is a three-dimensional object, however, it does not relate to a football. A curve is part of a circle. Both are one-dimensional shapes, but none of these choices is a necessary part of the football.

7. **D.** The items in the first row are names of United States space shuttles. The items in the second row are political documents. The Declaration of Independence can be included with them. Sputnik was the first artificial satellite, launched by Russia. Huang Ho is a river in China. Mohandas Gandhi was an Indian leader who advocated for peace.

8. **G.** The items in the first row all have to do with bodies of water. The ocean is the largest. A lake is smaller, and the pool is smallest of all. The items in the second row repeat that pattern, ending with the moon. Saturn, Jupiter, and Neptune are all larger than the Earth.

9. **A.** The items in the first row are all mountain ranges of the world. Carbon dioxide is one of the components of air.

10. **H.** The items in the first row are items to which people are commonly allergic. The items in the second row are disasters occurring in nature. A forest fire fits that category. While small pox, cholera, and bubonic plague could also be considered disasters, they are diseases that have been eradicated except in remote parts of the world.

11. **B.** The items in the first row are large raptors. The items in the second row are poisonous spiders. While an owl is a predator, it isn't poisonous; neither are garden spiders or hummingbirds.

12. **G.** The items in the first row are creatures that are fast runners. The items in the second row are insects.

Test 5: Verbal Reasoning—Context

1. **D.** Given this situation, the most we can assume is that Susie, being a modern girl, knows how to use her computer to access information she needs. She might be able to get information on a type of pet she could have. It seems as though allergy shots would help her, but we don't know. It would not be a good idea to adopt a kitten; given her reactions to them and the fact that her mother said she couldn't have pets.

2. **H.** The line about Kira's attitude changing is the key. Instead of ignoring her birthday she is celebrating it, making it a very memorable event.

3. **D.** It only makes sense to upgrade skills to advance in a profession. Demanding a raise or complaining to coworkers only angers the boss. George's coworkers are then put in an embarrassing position. To quit a job before securing another is a very dangerous idea. He might not find work easily and then realize he wasn't so bad off at his former job.

4. **J.** While answers **F, G,** and **H** might be quite true, they are overruled by the fact that Daniel's junior license doesn't allow him to drive without an adult in the car.

5. **A.** Sharon doesn't need to stop working out completely, nor should she retire for that reason alone. Many factors need to be considered in regard to retirement, least of all is time at the gym. Initially, she might be tired after school. Perhaps she will have to cut back on the gym time. Answer **A** is a good compromise.

6. **H.** The prefix *ion* is found in all the example words. Because all these animals live in the jungle, the prefix might indicate that commonality. The answer must also contain that prefix. In addition, the answer has the same suffix, *stir*, indicating a relationship, that of the cat family.

7. **A.** All example words have the same suffix, *salamos*, indicating a similarity. The answer word needs those same letters somewhere in the word. The only word having those letters uses them as a prefix. None of the other choices correspond.

8. **H.** All these words have the same prefix, *ri*, possibly indicating the type of creature that is doing this, and the same suffix, *yofo*, indicating the ending "ing". The answer requires the same prefix and suffix.

Test 6: Reading and Language Arts

1. **D.** The UPC is made up of six digits that identify the manufacturer, five that identify the item, and a check digit.

2. **F.** The passage states that the codes do not contain price information.

3. **B.** The passage states that the check digit is calculated.

4. **H.** This is the only choice that names both a manufacturer and an item.

5. **C.** The other choices are contradicted by information in the passage.

6. **G.** She cries easily, so she is sensitive.

7. **C.** The mention of hardhearted persons saying unkind words is part of the list of things that make the young lady cry.

8. **F.** Because this person has cheeks that are too round and red for a heroine, a heroine must look the opposite: thin and pale.

9. **C.** Although some of the language of the passage appears critical, the criticism is immediately taken back or changed. She might not look like a heroine, but she looks healthy. She might cry too often and at silly things, but persons who make her cry are hardhearted, implying that her sensitiveness is a valued quality.

10. **H.** This is the subject of most of the passage. **D** is not a good choice because the information about grading is general, not detailed.

11. **C.** The first paragraph states that even a rare or popular coin could be worth less if it was not of a high grade.

12. **G.** The information is in paragraph two of the passage. **C** is not correct because it is the grade that includes both a letter and a number.

13. **A.** In the third paragraph it states that "a mint state coin is uncirculated." **B** is contradicted by paragraph one ("it might be worth little if it has a low grade"); **C** by paragraph 3 ("dirt in the creases of a coin is a positive feature"); and **D** by the last paragraph ("Books and magazines about the coin market appear regularly").

14. **J.** The correct answer is in the passage's first two sentences.

15. **B.** Do not be confused by **D**; the blood is mixed in the arteries, not the heart.

16. **F.** This is a contrast with reptiles who need to get their heat from the environment as stated in paragraph two.

17. **A.** This is stated in paragraph three. Don't be fooled by choices **C** and **D**. According to the passage, dinosaurs are now thought to be more similar to mammals than to reptiles.

18. **J.** The last sentence of the passage reveals the irony. The "marvelous lizard," according to the new theory, wasn't a reptile.

19. **B.** The passage mentions 3 films and at least 90 cartoons in the 1930s alone.

20. **F.** The first sentence of the third paragraph gives this information. Note that the question does not ask when the Mickey Mouse Club first appeared on television.

21. **A.** There is no basis in the passage for choosing any of the other answers.

22. **H.** The passage states that the images are used *to sell products*.

23. **C.** The word *fair* in the sentence is the clue to the meaning of *impartial*.

24. **J.** Things that are part of the courtroom are not part of the subject matter of a trial.

25. **A.** Because pieces of evidence are things that tend to prove something, *testimony* is *statements* about the facts of the case.

26. **G.** *Background* means approximately the same thing as *framework*.

27. **D.** The passage states that the judge instructs the jurors *after both sides* have presented evidence.

28. **H.** This is explained in the first paragraph of the passage.

29. **A.** The second paragraph explains how the settlements were dated.

30. **J.** Although the other possible choices relate to information in the passage, only this choice is appropriate for the whole passage.

31. **B.** Choice **A** is contradicted by the content of the passage. The new discovery is that humans did not cross the land bridge, not that the land bridge did not exist, so **C** is not correct. **D** is incorrect because the passage does not state whether these new theories have been tested.

32. **H.** The word *envelop* means to *wrap around*. Choice **B** reverses the relationship of the fig and its host.

33. **A.** This is explained in the second paragraph of the passage.

34. **H.** To *stifle* means to suffocate or cut off, to *choke*.

35. **B.** This information begins the passage's third paragraph.

36. **J.** The last two sentences of the passage explain this choice.

37. D. He describes them as *continuous*, *never-ending*, and says that he saw 10,000, which is clearly an exaggeration as he could not have counted them, but it emphasizes the great number of flowers.

38. F. The words *glee* and *gay* describe the emotions of the flowers, which are communicated to the poet.

39. B. This is stated in the first line of the poem.

40. G. Choice **F** doesn't make sense because looking at the flowers does not earn money for the poet. **H** is contradictory because wealth is something desirable; *sadness* is not. The *show* in the last line is the flowers, so **J** is incorrect. Choice **F** tells what the show brought to him—*pleasure*.

Test 7: Mathematics

1. B. Begin by prime factoring the number 210. One way to do this is to note that $210 = 21 \times 10 = 2 \times 3 \times 5 \times 7$. Therefore, 210 is divisible by 4 different prime numbers.

2. J. $(a^2)^3 = (2^2)^3 = (4)^3 = 64$

3. C. $\dfrac{a+b}{a} - \dfrac{a-b}{a} = \dfrac{a+b-a+b}{a} = \dfrac{2b}{a}$

4. F. When a number between 0 and 1 is raised to a power, the result is a smaller number. For example, note that if $\frac{1}{2}$ is squared, the result is $\frac{1}{4}$, which is a smaller number.

5. A.

$$2x = 7 - 2y \text{ (Add } 2y \text{ to both sides.)}$$

$$2x + 2y = 7 \text{ (Divide both sides by 2.)}$$

$$\frac{2x + 2y}{2} = x + y = \frac{7}{2}$$

6. F. Begin by making a sketch of the triangle.

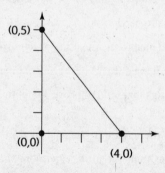

The picture shows that the base of the triangle has length 4, while the height is 5. The area, then, is $A = \frac{1}{2}bh = \frac{1}{2}(4)(5) = 10.$

7. D. $6.3 + (6.3 \times 10) + (6.3 \times 10^2) = 6.3 + 63 + 630 = 699.3$

8. F. $(5 - 5P)(5P + 5) = (5 - 5(5))(5(5) + 5) = (5 - 25)(25 + 5) = (-20)(30) = -600$

9. B. Ten possible combinations can be selected, but only four of them give totals less than 10. The four pairs that have this property are 2 and 3, 2 and 5, 2 and 7, and 3 and 5. Thus, the probability is $\frac{4}{10} = \frac{2}{5}.$

10. J. The figure shows that one side of the rectangle is 6, so the other side must be 4 to have an area of $4 \times 6 = 24$. The perimeter, thus, is $6 + 6 + 4 + 4 = 20.$

11. B. The two angles indicated are interior angles on the same side of a transversal, and therefore are supplementary.

12. F.

$$x = 4y + 7 \text{ (Subtract 7 from both sides.)}$$

$$x - 7 = 4y \text{ (Divide both sides by 4.)}$$

$$\frac{x - 7}{4} = y$$

13. D. $\dfrac{10^2\left(10^6 + 10^6\right)}{10^4} = \dfrac{10^2\left(2 \times 10^6\right)}{10^4} = \dfrac{2 \times 10^8}{10^4} = 2 \times 10^4$

14. G. The only way that q^3 can be odd is if q is odd. Now, $2q$ must be even because it contains a factor of 2. In addition, q^5 and $3q$ are odd because they are products of odd numbers. However, q^2 must be odd because q is odd, so **G** is not true.

15. D. Because $b > 90$, the angle labeled b must be the biggest angle of the triangle. Because the longest side is opposite the biggest angle, the side opposite the angle labeled b must be the longest side. Because another side of the triangle is labeled 9, the side opposite the angle labeled b must be bigger than 9.

16. J. The fact that the average of x, y, and z is 10 can be written as $\dfrac{x + y + z}{3} = 10$. Because we are told that $z = 0$, we know that $\dfrac{x + y}{3} = 10$. If both sides of this equation are multiplied by 3, we get $x + y = 30$.

17. C. The hall is 3×7, and so has an area of 21 square feet. The bedroom is 10×12, and so has an area of 120 square feet. The overall area is $120 + 21 = 141$ square feet.

18. H. The fact that the average of a and b is 60 can be expressed as $\dfrac{a + b}{2} = 60$. If we multiply both sides of this equation by 2, we obtain $a + b = 120$. Because the sum of the angles in a triangle add up to 180, the missing angle must be 60°.

19. A. The number 2 cannot be one of the prime numbers because the number that adds together with 2 to give a sum of 10 is 8, and 8 is not prime.

20. G. The formula for the area of a triangle is $A = \frac{1}{2}bh$, so, in this problem, we have $28 = \frac{1}{2}(4)h$. This can be rewritten as $28 = 2h$. This means that h has to be 14.

21. D. $(-4)^2 - 3(-4) = 16 - (-12) = 16 + 12 = 28$

22. H. Note that $19 + 20 = 39$. Therefore, the larger integer is 20.

23. B. $\dfrac{6}{c} - \dfrac{4}{c} = \dfrac{6 - 4}{c} = \dfrac{2}{c}$

24. H. The five consecutive integers that add up to 0 are -2, -1, 0, 1, and 2. The largest of these integers is 2.

25. A. To express a percent as a decimal, move the decimal point two places to the left. Thus, $0.05\% = 0.0005$.

26. H.

$$10x - 4 = 4x + 20 \text{ (Subtract } 4x \text{ from both sides.)}$$

$$6x - 4 = 20 \text{ (Add 4 to both sides.)}$$

$$6x = 24 \text{ (Divide both sides by 6.)}$$

$$x = 4$$

27. C. Begin by writing $\frac{3}{4}$ as 0.75. Now, write a proportion that expresses the situation in the problem:

$$\frac{flour}{loaves} \rightarrow \frac{0.75}{1} = \frac{6}{N}$$

Cross multiply to get the equation $0.75N = 6$. Then, divide both sides by 0.75 to get $N = 8$.

28. H. $\sqrt{81} = 9$, so $\sqrt{81}$ represents a whole number. All the other square roots are not the square roots of perfect squares, and so do not represent whole numbers.

29. C. The number 35.7 differs from 35.69 by $35.7 - 35.69 = 0.01$, which makes it the closest number to 35.69.

30. F. To find his average test score, begin by adding the three scores: $97 + 80 + 87 = 264$. Next, divide 264 by 3: $264 \div 3 = 88$.

31. D. If each inch is 55 miles, then 4.2 inches represent $55 \times 4.2 = 231$ miles.

32. F. $(2a + 7) + (4a - 3) + (a - 2) = (2a + 4a + a) + (7 - 3 - 2) = 7a + 2$

33. B. If the area is Q^2, then each side must be of length Q because $Q \times Q = Q^2$. The perimeter is $Q + Q + Q + Q = 4Q$.

34. H. To find the percent of increase, divide the amount of the increase, which is \$5, by the original allowance, \$15.

$$\frac{5}{15} = \frac{1}{3} = 33\frac{1}{3}\%$$

35. B. $\dfrac{-12}{4-a} = \dfrac{-12}{4-(-2)} = \dfrac{-12}{4+2} = \dfrac{-12}{6} = -2$

36. J. The answer cannot be **G** or **H** because 9 is not prime. Choice **F** is also incorrect because $2 \times 3 = 6$, not 54. However, note that $2 \times 3 \times 3 \times 3 = 54$.

37. B. The perimeter of the figure consists of 8 sides of the square. If the perimeter of the entire figure is 40, then the length of each side of the square must be $40 \div 8 = 5$. Each square, then, must have an area of $5 \times 5 = 25$, and, because there are three squares, the overall area is $3 \times 25 = 75$.

38. J.

$8x - 6 = 34$ (Add 6 to both sides.)

$\quad 8x = 40$ (Divide both sides by 8.)

$\quad\quad x = 5$

39. A.

$\dfrac{40}{24} = \dfrac{5}{a}$ (Cross multiply.)

$40a = 5 \times 24$

$40a = 120$ (Divide both sides by 40.)

$\quad a = 3$

40. G. Because $\sqrt{64} = 8$, the question is asking what percent 8 is of 64. To find this, we need to express $\dfrac{8}{64}$ as a percent. Because $\dfrac{8}{64} = \dfrac{1}{8} = 0.125$, the percent is 12.5%.

Answer Sheet for Practice COOP Exam 3

TEST 1 Sequences

1 Ⓐ Ⓑ Ⓒ Ⓓ	5 Ⓐ Ⓑ Ⓒ Ⓓ	9 Ⓐ Ⓑ Ⓒ Ⓓ	13 Ⓐ Ⓑ Ⓒ Ⓓ	17 Ⓐ Ⓑ Ⓒ Ⓓ
2 Ⓕ Ⓖ Ⓗ Ⓙ	6 Ⓕ Ⓖ Ⓗ Ⓙ	10 Ⓕ Ⓖ Ⓗ Ⓙ	14 Ⓕ Ⓖ Ⓗ Ⓙ	18 Ⓕ Ⓖ Ⓗ Ⓙ
3 Ⓐ Ⓑ Ⓒ Ⓓ	7 Ⓐ Ⓑ Ⓒ Ⓓ	11 Ⓐ Ⓑ Ⓒ Ⓓ	15 Ⓐ Ⓑ Ⓒ Ⓓ	19 Ⓐ Ⓑ Ⓒ Ⓓ
4 Ⓕ Ⓖ Ⓗ Ⓙ	8 Ⓕ Ⓖ Ⓗ Ⓙ	12 Ⓕ Ⓖ Ⓗ Ⓙ	16 Ⓕ Ⓖ Ⓗ Ⓙ	20 Ⓕ Ⓖ Ⓗ Ⓙ

TEST 2 Analogies

1 Ⓐ Ⓑ Ⓒ Ⓓ	5 Ⓐ Ⓑ Ⓒ Ⓓ	9 Ⓐ Ⓑ Ⓒ Ⓓ	13 Ⓐ Ⓑ Ⓒ Ⓓ	17 Ⓐ Ⓑ Ⓒ Ⓓ
2 Ⓕ Ⓖ Ⓗ Ⓙ	6 Ⓕ Ⓖ Ⓗ Ⓙ	10 Ⓕ Ⓖ Ⓗ Ⓙ	14 Ⓕ Ⓖ Ⓗ Ⓙ	18 Ⓕ Ⓖ Ⓗ Ⓙ
3 Ⓐ Ⓑ Ⓒ Ⓓ	7 Ⓐ Ⓑ Ⓒ Ⓓ	11 Ⓐ Ⓑ Ⓒ Ⓓ	15 Ⓐ Ⓑ Ⓒ Ⓓ	19 Ⓐ Ⓑ Ⓒ Ⓓ
4 Ⓕ Ⓖ Ⓗ Ⓙ	8 Ⓕ Ⓖ Ⓗ Ⓙ	12 Ⓕ Ⓖ Ⓗ Ⓙ	16 Ⓕ Ⓖ Ⓗ Ⓙ	20 Ⓕ Ⓖ Ⓗ Ⓙ

TEST 3 Quantitative Reasoning

1 Ⓐ Ⓑ Ⓒ Ⓓ	5 Ⓐ Ⓑ Ⓒ Ⓓ	9 Ⓐ Ⓑ Ⓒ Ⓓ	13 Ⓐ Ⓑ Ⓒ Ⓓ	17 Ⓐ Ⓑ Ⓒ Ⓓ
2 Ⓕ Ⓖ Ⓗ Ⓙ	6 Ⓕ Ⓖ Ⓗ Ⓙ	10 Ⓕ Ⓖ Ⓗ Ⓙ	14 Ⓕ Ⓖ Ⓗ Ⓙ	18 Ⓕ Ⓖ Ⓗ Ⓙ
3 Ⓐ Ⓑ Ⓒ Ⓓ	7 Ⓐ Ⓑ Ⓒ Ⓓ	11 Ⓐ Ⓑ Ⓒ Ⓓ	15 Ⓐ Ⓑ Ⓒ Ⓓ	19 Ⓐ Ⓑ Ⓒ Ⓓ
4 Ⓕ Ⓖ Ⓗ Ⓙ	8 Ⓕ Ⓖ Ⓗ Ⓙ	12 Ⓕ Ⓖ Ⓗ Ⓙ	16 Ⓕ Ⓖ Ⓗ Ⓙ	20 Ⓕ Ⓖ Ⓗ Ⓙ

TEST 4 Verbal Reasoning - Words

1 Ⓐ Ⓑ Ⓒ Ⓓ	5 Ⓐ Ⓑ Ⓒ Ⓓ	9 Ⓐ Ⓑ Ⓒ Ⓓ
2 Ⓕ Ⓖ Ⓗ Ⓙ	6 Ⓕ Ⓖ Ⓗ Ⓙ	10 Ⓕ Ⓖ Ⓗ Ⓙ
3 Ⓐ Ⓑ Ⓒ Ⓓ	7 Ⓐ Ⓑ Ⓒ Ⓓ	11 Ⓐ Ⓑ Ⓒ Ⓓ
4 Ⓕ Ⓖ Ⓗ Ⓙ	8 Ⓕ Ⓖ Ⓗ Ⓙ	12 Ⓕ Ⓖ Ⓗ Ⓙ

TEST 5 Verbal Reasoning - Context

1 Ⓐ Ⓑ Ⓒ Ⓓ	5 Ⓐ Ⓑ Ⓒ Ⓓ
2 Ⓕ Ⓖ Ⓗ Ⓙ	6 Ⓕ Ⓖ Ⓗ Ⓙ
3 Ⓐ Ⓑ Ⓒ Ⓓ	7 Ⓐ Ⓑ Ⓒ Ⓓ
4 Ⓕ Ⓖ Ⓗ Ⓙ	8 Ⓕ Ⓖ Ⓗ Ⓙ

TEST 6 Reading and Language Arts

1 Ⓐ Ⓑ Ⓒ Ⓓ	9 Ⓐ Ⓑ Ⓒ Ⓓ	17 Ⓐ Ⓑ Ⓒ Ⓓ	25 Ⓐ Ⓑ Ⓒ Ⓓ	33 Ⓐ Ⓑ Ⓒ Ⓓ
2 Ⓕ Ⓖ Ⓗ Ⓙ	10 Ⓕ Ⓖ Ⓗ Ⓙ	18 Ⓕ Ⓖ Ⓗ Ⓙ	26 Ⓕ Ⓖ Ⓗ Ⓙ	34 Ⓕ Ⓖ Ⓗ Ⓙ
3 Ⓐ Ⓑ Ⓒ Ⓓ	11 Ⓐ Ⓑ Ⓒ Ⓓ	19 Ⓐ Ⓑ Ⓒ Ⓓ	27 Ⓐ Ⓑ Ⓒ Ⓓ	35 Ⓐ Ⓑ Ⓒ Ⓓ
4 Ⓕ Ⓖ Ⓗ Ⓙ	12 Ⓕ Ⓖ Ⓗ Ⓙ	20 Ⓕ Ⓖ Ⓗ Ⓙ	28 Ⓕ Ⓖ Ⓗ Ⓙ	36 Ⓕ Ⓖ Ⓗ Ⓙ
5 Ⓐ Ⓑ Ⓒ Ⓓ	13 Ⓐ Ⓑ Ⓒ Ⓓ	21 Ⓐ Ⓑ Ⓒ Ⓓ	29 Ⓐ Ⓑ Ⓒ Ⓓ	37 Ⓐ Ⓑ Ⓒ Ⓓ
6 Ⓕ Ⓖ Ⓗ Ⓙ	14 Ⓕ Ⓖ Ⓗ Ⓙ	22 Ⓕ Ⓖ Ⓗ Ⓙ	30 Ⓕ Ⓖ Ⓗ Ⓙ	38 Ⓕ Ⓖ Ⓗ Ⓙ
7 Ⓐ Ⓑ Ⓒ Ⓓ	15 Ⓐ Ⓑ Ⓒ Ⓓ	23 Ⓐ Ⓑ Ⓒ Ⓓ	31 Ⓐ Ⓑ Ⓒ Ⓓ	39 Ⓐ Ⓑ Ⓒ Ⓓ
8 Ⓕ Ⓖ Ⓗ Ⓙ	16 Ⓕ Ⓖ Ⓗ Ⓙ	24 Ⓕ Ⓖ Ⓗ Ⓙ	32 Ⓕ Ⓖ Ⓗ Ⓙ	40 Ⓕ Ⓖ Ⓗ Ⓙ

TEST 7 Mathematics

1 Ⓐ Ⓑ Ⓒ Ⓓ	9 Ⓐ Ⓑ Ⓒ Ⓓ	17 Ⓐ Ⓑ Ⓒ Ⓓ	25 Ⓐ Ⓑ Ⓒ Ⓓ	33 Ⓐ Ⓑ Ⓒ Ⓓ
2 Ⓕ Ⓖ Ⓗ Ⓙ	10 Ⓕ Ⓖ Ⓗ Ⓙ	18 Ⓕ Ⓖ Ⓗ Ⓙ	26 Ⓕ Ⓖ Ⓗ Ⓙ	34 Ⓕ Ⓖ Ⓗ Ⓙ
3 Ⓐ Ⓑ Ⓒ Ⓓ	11 Ⓐ Ⓑ Ⓒ Ⓓ	19 Ⓐ Ⓑ Ⓒ Ⓓ	27 Ⓐ Ⓑ Ⓒ Ⓓ	35 Ⓐ Ⓑ Ⓒ Ⓓ
4 Ⓕ Ⓖ Ⓗ Ⓙ	12 Ⓕ Ⓖ Ⓗ Ⓙ	20 Ⓕ Ⓖ Ⓗ Ⓙ	28 Ⓕ Ⓖ Ⓗ Ⓙ	36 Ⓕ Ⓖ Ⓗ Ⓙ
5 Ⓐ Ⓑ Ⓒ Ⓓ	13 Ⓐ Ⓑ Ⓒ Ⓓ	21 Ⓐ Ⓑ Ⓒ Ⓓ	29 Ⓐ Ⓑ Ⓒ Ⓓ	37 Ⓐ Ⓑ Ⓒ Ⓓ
6 Ⓕ Ⓖ Ⓗ Ⓙ	14 Ⓕ Ⓖ Ⓗ Ⓙ	22 Ⓕ Ⓖ Ⓗ Ⓙ	30 Ⓕ Ⓖ Ⓗ Ⓙ	38 Ⓕ Ⓖ Ⓗ Ⓙ
7 Ⓐ Ⓑ Ⓒ Ⓓ	15 Ⓐ Ⓑ Ⓒ Ⓓ	23 Ⓐ Ⓑ Ⓒ Ⓓ	31 Ⓐ Ⓑ Ⓒ Ⓓ	39 Ⓐ Ⓑ Ⓒ Ⓓ
8 Ⓕ Ⓖ Ⓗ Ⓙ	16 Ⓕ Ⓖ Ⓗ Ⓙ	24 Ⓕ Ⓖ Ⓗ Ⓙ	32 Ⓕ Ⓖ Ⓗ Ⓙ	40 Ⓕ Ⓖ Ⓗ Ⓙ

CUT HERE

Practice COOP Exam 3

Test 1: Sequences

Time: 15 Minutes

Directions: For questions in this test, select the answer that best continues the pattern or sequences given.

1.

A.

B.

C.

D.

2.

F.

G.

H.

J.

3.

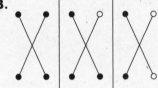

A.

B.

C.

D.

GO ON TO THE NEXT PAGE

4.

F. ▱ △
  ● ▭

G. ▱ △
  ● ▬

H. ▱ △
  ○ ▬

J. ▱ △
  ○ ▭

5.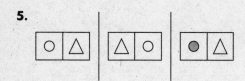

A. △ ●

B. △ ●

C. △ ○

D. ● △

6.

F.

G.

H.

J.

7. 4 8 12 | 10 14 18 | 17 21 ___
  A. 25
  B. 26
  C. 27
  D. 28

8. 75 15 3 | 50 10 2 | 100 ___ 4
  F. 8
  G. 10
  H. 20
  J. 25

9. 9 4 12 | 7 2 6 | 5 ___ 0

A. 0
B. 2
C. 3
D. 4

10. 15 23 20 | 22 30 27 | 35 43 ___

F. 39
G. 40
H. 41
J. 42

11. 5 1 1 | 7 3 9 | 9 5 ___

A. 10
B. 15
C. 20
D. 25

12. 7 21 16 | 5 15 10 | 9 ___ 22

F. 27
G. 29
H. 31
J. 33

13. 49 54 18 | 58 63 21 | 67 ___ 24

A. 68
B. 72
C. 75
D. 78

14. A C D | E G H | I K L | _____ | Q S T

F. MNO
G. NPQ
H. MOP
J. MNP

15. Y X W | D C B | L K J | P O N | _____

A. TRS
B. TSR
C. TRP
D. TRQ

16. K M J | B D A | H J G | O Q N | _____

F. PQO
G. MNL
H. GHF
J. SUR

17. E J O | G L Q | I N S | _____ | M R W

A. JOT
B. KPU
C. LQV
D. MSX

18. A 7 Z | B 6 Y | C 5 X | D 4 W | _____

F. E 3 V
G. E 4 V
H. F 3 U
J. E 3 U

19. Z 1 X | W 2 U | T 4 R | _____ | N 16 L

A. R 8 Q
B. R 6 Q
C. Q 8 O
D. Q 6 O

20. A F K | B G L | C H M | D I N | _____

F. FJO
G. EJO
H. EJP
J. EJN

IF YOU FINISH BEFORE TIME IS CALLED, CHECK YOUR WORK ON THIS
SECTION ONLY. DO NOT WORK ON ANY OTHER SECTION IN THE TEST.

STOP

Test 2: Analogies

Time: 7 Minutes

Directions: For the questions in this test, choose the picture that should go in the empty box so that the bottom two pictures are related in the same way that the top two are related.

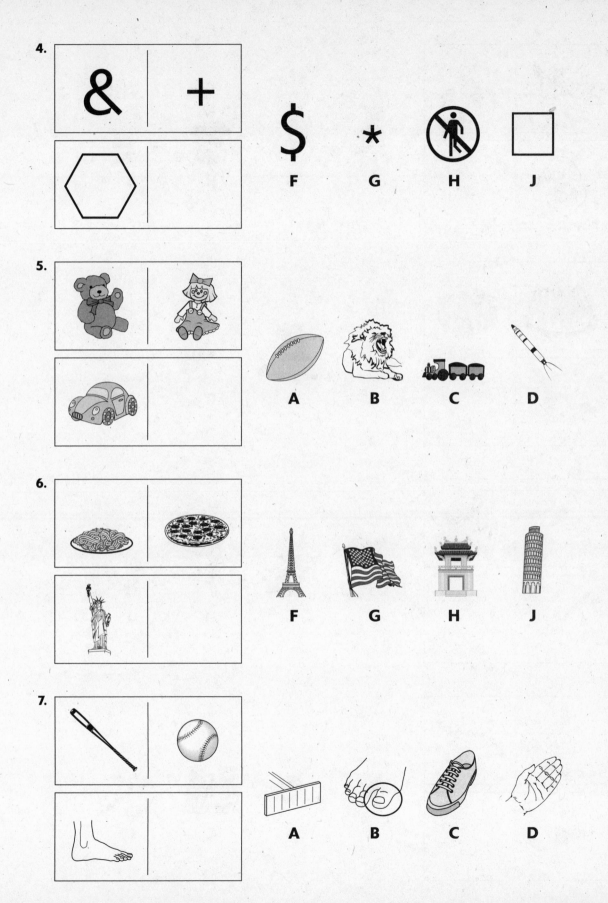

4.

5.

6.

7.

GO ON TO THE NEXT PAGE

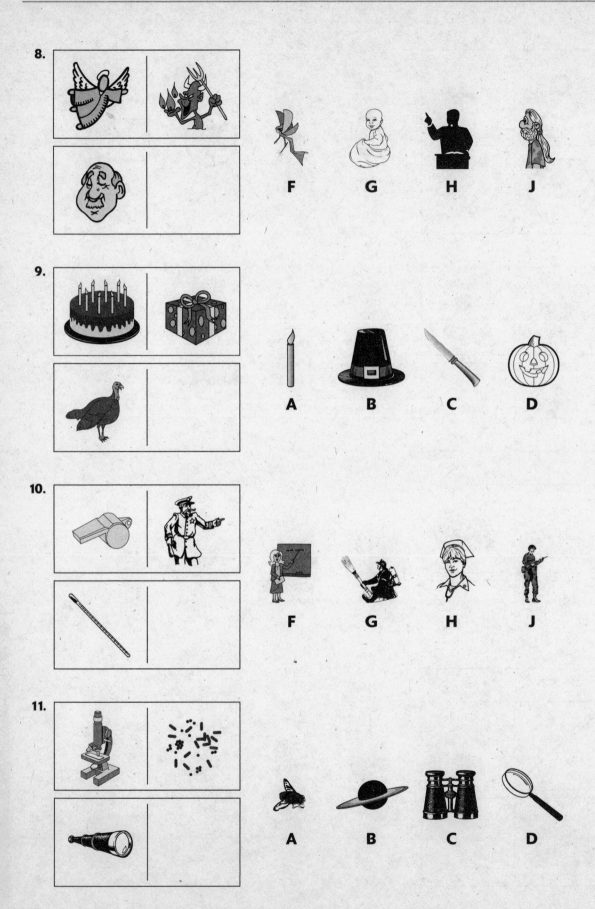

8.

F G H J

9.

A B C D

10.

F G H J

11.

A B C D

12.

F G H J

13.

A B C D

14.

F G H J

15.

A B C D

GO ON TO THE NEXT PAGE

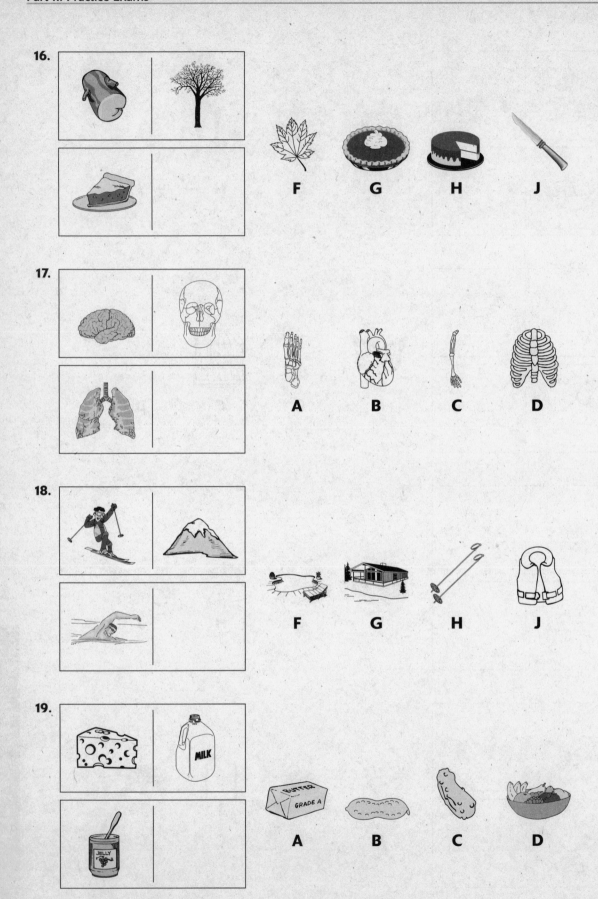

20.

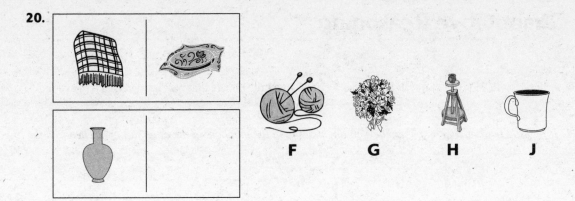

F   G   H   J

IF YOU FINISH BEFORE TIME IS CALLED, CHECK YOUR WORK ON THIS SECTION ONLY. DO NOT WORK ON ANY OTHER SECTION IN THE TEST.

Test 3: Quantitative Reasoning

Time: 20 Minutes

Directions: For each of the three types of questions in this section, select the choice that best answers each question.

For questions 1–7, find the relationship of the numbers in one column to the numbers in the other column. Then find the missing number.

1.

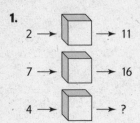

2 → 11
7 → 16
4 → ?

A. 10
B. 11
C. 12
D. 13

2.

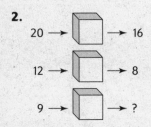

20 → 16
12 → 8
9 → ?

F. 5
G. 6
H. 7
J. 8

3.

3 → 9
5 → 15
8 → ?

A. 18
B. 21
C. 24
D. 27

4.

4 → 25
7 → 28
12 → ?

F. 33
G. 35
H. 36
J. 38

5.

28 → 13
35 → 20
42 → ?

A. 23
B. 27
C. 29
D. 33

6.

14 → 2
35 → 5
56 → ?

F. 6
G. 8
H. 10
J. 12

7.

8 → ▢ → 88

5 → ▢ → 55

1 → ▢ → ?

- **A.** 1
- **B.** 5
- **C.** 8
- **D.** 11

For questions 8–13, find the fraction of the grid that is shaded.

8.

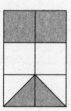

- **F.** $\frac{1}{6}$
- **G.** $\frac{1}{4}$
- **H.** $\frac{1}{3}$
- **J.** $\frac{1}{2}$

9.

- **A.** $\frac{1}{4}$
- **B.** $\frac{1}{3}$
- **C.** $\frac{1}{2}$
- **D.** $\frac{2}{3}$

10.

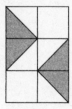

- **F.** $\frac{1}{6}$
- **G.** $\frac{1}{4}$
- **H.** $\frac{1}{3}$
- **J.** $\frac{1}{2}$

11.

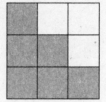

- **A.** $\frac{4}{9}$
- **B.** $\frac{5}{9}$
- **C.** $\frac{2}{3}$
- **D.** $\frac{7}{9}$

12.

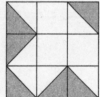

- **F.** $\frac{1}{4}$
- **G.** $\frac{1}{3}$
- **H.** $\frac{1}{2}$
- **J.** $\frac{2}{3}$

13.

- **A.** $\frac{5}{8}$
- **B.** $\frac{3}{4}$
- **C.** $\frac{7}{8}$
- **D.** $\frac{8}{9}$

GO ON TO THE NEXT PAGE

For questions 14–20, look at the scale showing sets of shapes of equal weight. Find an equivalent pair of sets that also balance the scale.

14.

15.

16.

17.

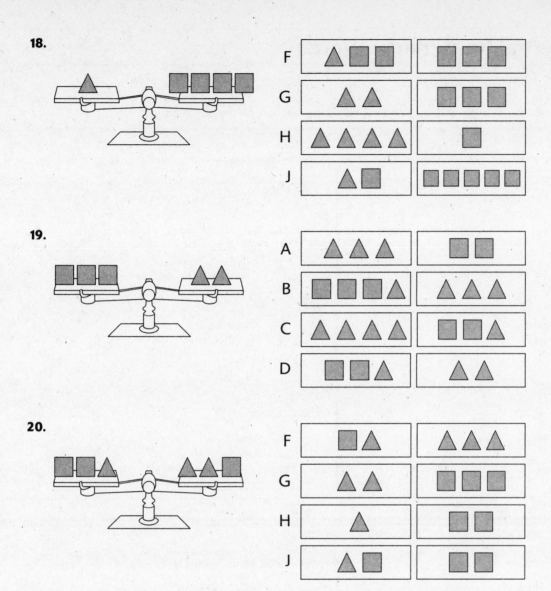

18.

19.

20.

IF YOU FINISH BEFORE TIME IS CALLED, CHECK YOUR WORK ON THIS
SECTION ONLY. DO NOT WORK ON ANY OTHER SECTION IN THE TEST.

Test 4: Verbal Reasoning—Words

Time: 15 Minutes

Directions: For the questions in this test, select the answer choice that best satisfies the question.

For questions 1–6, choose the word that names a necessary part of the underlined word.

1. cogwheel

   A. gear
   B. mechanic
   C. motor
   D. teeth

2. orchestra

   F. music stand
   G. musicians
   H. conductor
   J. notes

3. thermometer

   A. fahrenheit
   B. mercury
   C. centigrade
   D. celadon

4. muse

   F. thought
   G. fly
   H. run
   J. walk

5. hot dog

   A. mustard
   B. bun
   C. meat
   D. ball park

6. sailboat

   F. wind
   G. bow
   H. pitch
   J. yaw

In questions 7–12, the words in the top row are related in some way. The words in the bottom row are related in the same way. For each item, choose the word that completes the bottom row of words.

7. Kix, Cheerios, Life

   Tow Sawyer, Huck Finn

   A. Samuel Clemens
   B. Bilbo Baggins
   C. Jim
   D. Mark Twain

8. brook, stream, river

   United States, United Kingdom

   F. China
   G. Canada
   H. Mexico
   J. Italy

9. cattle, chickens, swine

   Taco Bell, McDonald's

   A. Siam Orchid
   B. Burger King
   C. Red Lobster
   D. Olive Garden

10. poodle, spaniel, schnauzer

   basil, parsley

   F. rose
   G. sunflower
   H. zinnia
   J. thyme

11. pelican, vulture, stork

koala, sloth

    A. donkey
    B. opossum
    C. turkey
    D. antelope

12. Venus, Pluto, Mars

Mercury, Ford

    F. Subaru
    G. Audi
    H. Dodge
    J. Kia

IF YOU FINISH BEFORE TIME IS CALLED, CHECK YOUR WORK ON THIS
SECTION ONLY. DO NOT WORK ON ANY OTHER SECTION IN THE TEST.

Test 5: Verbal Reasoning—Context

Time: 15 Minutes

Directions: For the questions in this test, select the answer choice that best satisfies the question.

For questions 1–5, choose the statement that is true according to the given information.

1. It was Thanksgiving Day. Three-year-old Brian fell and hit his face on the toy chest, causing a wound near the corner of his eye. He needed to be seen by a doctor. Luckily, one of Brian's pediatricians was in the office on emergency duty. After examining the injury, the doctor said the wound needed to be closed with a stitch. His parents would have to hold him down for the procedure because no nurse was in the office that day. Instead of a stitch, the parents requested that the doctor use a special Band-Aid. The doctor argued that Brian would have a scar. The parents said he would have a scar with the stitch, too. The doctor agreed, but said the scar from a stitch would be smaller, less noticeable.

   A. The parents should complain to the other doctors in the group about the argument.
   B. The parents should insist on using the Band-Aid to avoid further hysteria.
   C. The parents should allow the doctor to put in the stitch.
   D. The parents should change to a different doctor.

2. Jane is 16 years old. She has a younger brother and sister. Her first priority is spending time with her friends. She no longer wants to take vacations with her family. She feels as though she is expected to take care of her siblings with no remuneration of any kind. While she loves her brother and sister, she becomes resentful and sullen. Her parents are reluctant to leave her at home for an extended period of time. Jane and her parents are constantly arguing over this matter. No one in the family is happy.

   F. Jane's parents might offer to take a friend along on the vacation.
   G. If any type of baby-sitting is asked of Jane, she should be paid for her time and efforts.
   H. Jane should be allowed input on the vacation plans.
   J. All of the above.

3. Georgette loves to bake cookies, cakes, and pies. She is a gourmet baker who loves to experiment, inventing many new delicious and delectable creations. She has been asked to provide desserts for several parties and is seriously considering opening a catering business. The trouble is she also likes to sample what she makes, especially when she has tried a recipe for the first time. This habit has resulted in a significant weight gain.

   A. Georgette should ask someone else to sample her creations.
   B. Georgette should make only low-calorie desserts.
   C. Georgette should limit her sampling to new recipes and take only a very small taste.
   D. She should stop baking.

4. Donald is a finicky eater. For lunch, he is not tempted by tuna fish or cold cuts in a sandwich with fruit. He will not even try any of the food served in the school cafeteria. The only thing he will eat for lunch is a peanut butter and grape jelly sandwich with apple juice. Other food his mother might put in his lunch bag gets thrown away.

   F. His mother should ignore his eating habits, knowing that he will outgrow them as he gets older.
   G. Donald should pack his own lunch or go without.
   H. His mother should give up and pack a peanut butter and jelly sandwich with apple juice.
   J. His mother should let him snack on chips and pretzels.

5. Frederick chose to go to school in his hometown. He lives with his parents because he plans to save his money for graduate school. He has just discovered that he can use a credit card to buy things with his computer. He loves to participate in the on-line auctions held on E-Bay, an Internet shopping service. Many packages arrive in the mail, addressed to Frederick. He also plays games on the Internet with friends. His grades at college go from poor to failing.

    A. Instead of saving his money for graduate school, Frederick is accumulating very large credit card bills.

    B. Mom thought Frederick was spending his time on the computer doing his homework.

    C. Frederick's credit card should be surrendered to his parents.

    D. The computer should be taken away.

For questions 6–8, select the correct answer.

6. Here are some words translated from an artificial language:

Tauraleutio means started.

Cenleutio means stopped.

Mextralaleu means go.

Which word means move?

    F. *arhtral*

    G. *prahlabitio*

    H. *traleu*

    J. *tibalhar*

7. Here are some words translated from an artificial language:

Pregrhep means climbing.

Pregmanep means falling.

Pregronep means creeping.

Which word means moving?

    A. *regharti*

    B. *pregvirothep*

    C. *egrepatre*

    D. *prantiep*

8. Here are some words translated from an artificial language:

Brionit means painting.

Yashionitz means collage.

Dasionit means photograph.

Which word means picture?

    F. *tinoitrab*

    G. *dasribnitz*

    H. *rabionar*

    J. *vorshdasionit*

IF YOU FINISH BEFORE TIME IS CALLED, CHECK YOUR WORK ON THIS SECTION ONLY. DO NOT WORK ON ANY OTHER SECTION IN THE TEST.

Test 6: Reading and Language Arts

Time: 40 Minutes

Directions: For the questions in this test, read the passage and questions that follow. Choose the best possible answer.

Passage for questions 1–4

When someone is choking on something they swallowed, whether it is food or a foreign object, the most common way to remove the object is the Heimlich maneuver. This method was developed by Dr. Henry Heimlich. Heimlich was a chest surgeon who, during his career, invented several important surgical procedures. He developed an operation to replace the esophagus, which was the first total organ replacement. He invented a valve used in chest surgeries that was used by the military to help save the lives of soldiers. His procedure for improving the delivery of oxygen to patients undergoing surgery has benefited many.

Before the use of the Heimlich maneuver, people who were choking were slapped on their backs in an attempt to dislodge the blocking object. But this often drove whatever they were choking on further down into the windpipe, making the situation worse. Many people choked to death every year.

Because of his experience with the chest and lungs as a surgeon, Heimlich knew that pressing sharply on the diaphragm would force air from the lungs up through the windpipe. To perform the maneuver, standing behind the victim, the rescuer places both arms around the victim's waist. One fist is slightly above the navel and below the rib cage, with the thumb against the victim's body. The other hand holds the fist and applies pressure. The abdomen is pressed inward and upward, which produces a blast of air from the lungs, forcing the object up through the throat, and it is expelled through the mouth. With proper instruction, the Heimlich maneuver is easy for anyone to learn and to use. It has helped save many peoples' lives.

Passage for questions 5–9

Humming birds are tiny and swift, darting from flower to flower, eating constantly to maintain their energy. They have compact bodies and strong muscles. Their wings are shaped like blades. Unlike the wings of other birds, hummingbird wings connect to the body only at the shoulder joint. This allows them to fly not only forward but also straight up and down, sideways, and backward. Because of their unusual wings, hummingbirds can also hover in front of flowers so that they can suck nectar and find insects. The hummingbird's bill, adapted

1. The development of a method to help choking patients was needed because:

   A. Dr. Heimlich was a chest surgeon
   B. people eat too quickly and swallow foreign objects
   C. air is forced from the lungs
   D. an earlier procedure could be dangerous

2. To perform the Heimlich maneuver, a person:

   F. presses in and up
   G. stands behind the victim
   H. places both hands around the victim's waist
   J. all of the above

3. The word *expelled* means:

   A. swallowed
   B. controlled
   C. thrown out
   D. corrected

4. Dr. Heimlich is an important figure because he:

   F. developed several new medical techniques
   G. has helped to save the lives of people who are choking
   H. improved military surgery
   J. made the Heimlich maneuver easy to learn

for sipping nectar from certain types of flowers, is usually rather long and always slender, and it is curved slightly downward in many species.

The birds have a unique look and color. The body feathers are thinly spaced and more like scales than feathers. The structure of these feathers produces brilliant and iridescent colors, resulting from the refraction of light. The color of other feathers also contributes to the unique color and look. Males of most species are extremely colorful, although in some species the males and females look alike.

Most hummingbirds, especially the smaller species, make scratchy, twittering, or squeaky songs. The humming sound that gives them their name is produced by the wings, and sometimes the tail feathers. These songs seem to serve the same function as the songs of other birds.

5. A hummingbird's wings are different from those of other birds because:

    A. they attach to the body at one point only

    B. they attach to the body at more points than other birds

    C. they attach and detach from the body

    D. they are controlled by a different section of the brain

6. The passage suggests that the hummingbird's wing structure makes it able to fly like a:

    F. seaplane

    G. helicopter

    H. jet airplane

    J. rocket

Passage for questions 10–14

The nearer he approached the house, the more absolutely unequal Paul felt to the sight of it all; his ugly sleeping chamber; the cold bathroom with the grimy zinc tub, the cracked mirror, the dripping faucets; his father, at the top of the stairs, his hairy legs sticking out from his night-shirt, his feet thrust into carpet slippers. He was so much later than usual that there would certainly be questions and reproaches. Paul stopped short before the door. He felt that he could not be accosted by his father tonight. He would not go in. He would tell his father that he had no car fare, and it was raining so hard he had gone home with one of the boys and stayed all night.

Meanwhile, he was wet and cold. He went around to the back of the house and tried one of the basement windows, found it open, raised it cautiously, and scrambled down the cellar wall to the floor. There he stood, holding his breath, terrified by the noise he had made, but the floor above him was silent, and there was no creak on the stairs. He found a soap-box, and carried it over to the soft ring of light that streamed from the furnace door, and sat down. He was horribly afraid of rats, so he did not try to sleep, but sat looking distrustfully at the dark, still terrified lest he might have awakened his father.

From "Paul's Case" by Willa Cather

7. The word bill in the first paragraph means:

    A. beak

    B. body

    C. tail

    D. wing

8. The unique color and look of hummingbirds are caused by the:

    F. color of the feathers

    G. structure of the feathers as well as the color

    H. rapidity of flight

    J. pigmentation of the body

9. According to the passage, hummingbirds make sounds through their:

    A. wing and sometimes tail movement

    B. unique vocal chords

    C. throats only

    D. tail movements only

10. Paul plans to lie to his father because he:

    F. does not like him

    G. spent the night with one of his friends

    H. does not want him to know he came home late

    J. wanted to spend the night in the basement

11. The word accosted means:

    A. stopped

    B. ignored

    C. excused

    D. confronted

12. Paul did not try to fall asleep because:

    F. he was afraid he would awaken his father

    G. rats terrified him

    H. the light from the furnace kept him awake

    J. there was nothing for him to lie down on

GO ON TO THE NEXT PAGE

13. The description of Paul's home suggests that Paul feels it is:

 A. frightening

 B. comfortable

 C. disgusting

 D. harmonious

Passage for questions 15–18

On a hot day, washing a car can almost be fun. Getting splashed by the soap and water can make you feel cooler, but you have to do the work of rubbing the suds with a rag or sponge to make sure all the dirt is removed, rinsing the soap completely, and drying the car thoroughly to avoid water spots on the finish. It's much easier to take the car to an automated car wash.

In an automatic car wash, the vehicle moves through a tunnel on a conveyor belt, and it is pushed forward by a system of small rollers that pop up behind the wheels of the car. Most car washes begin by spraying a special solution over the car from an arch that contains several small nozzles. The solution begins the process of loosening the dirt on the car while wetting it. In many car washes, a series of long strips of cloth hanging from a frame near the top of the tunnel are used to rub back and forth across the car to spread the special solution.

Next, a foam applicator sprays a detergent on the car that becomes a deep-cleaning foam when it comes in contact with the car. Then the scrubbers, large vertical cylinders with hundreds of small cloth strips attached to them, clean the car by rotating rapidly. As the car moves past the scrubbers, the cloth strips clean the car. Although the cloth is soft, the scrubbers move so rapidly that they feel like a whip if they touch you. Rinsing is the next step. Although car washes often recycle their water, the water for the final rinse must be clean. It is sprayed from a series of nozzles mounted on an arch. Most carwashes have a wax arch following the rinse arch, but not every customer has the car waxed as there is an extra charge for this service. The final device in the process is the dryer. It blows large amounts of air through a series of nozzles to dry the car. At some car washes, that completes the process, but at other establishments, after the car comes out of the tunnel, attendants hand dry it with towels to make sure no spots remain.

14. According to the passage, all the following are true except:

 F. it had been raining

 G. the time was after dark

 H. Paul's father was a kind man

 J. Paul had no money for car fare

15. The author's purpose in this passage was most probably to:

 A. explain how an automatic car wash works

 B. describe the benefits to the environment of automatic car washes

 C. encourage people to use automatic car washes

 D. tell why washing your car can be fun

16. The scrubbers are:

 F. horizontal brushes

 G. long strips of cloth

 H. cylinders covered with cloth strips

 J. nozzles in an overhead arch

17. The price of a car wash:

 A. depends on whether or not the water is recycled

 B. is always the same

 C. is based on the services the customer chooses

 D. can vary at different times of year

18. The author uses the word *almost* when writing about washing a car by yourself because:

 F. getting cooler on a hot day is pleasant

 G. taking the car to an automatic car wash is easier than washing it yourself

 H. if it rains the next day, all your work is wasted

 J. doing the job properly requires careful work

Passage for questions 19–23

Count Dracula, the vampire, is a well-known character. Created by Bram Stoker, a nineteenth-century English novelist, he was portrayed by Bela Lugosi in the 1931 film based on the novel. And Hollywood didn't leave him to sleep quietly in his coffin after that. Many films, serious and comic, have been based on the story of the sinister count.

A man named Dracula really existed, but scholars say Stoker knew little about him, and he was not the inspiration for the novel. Vlad Dracula lived in Romania in the fifteenth century. He was the ruler of an area that now includes the city of Bucharest. He was a cruel despot. Some historians say his strong rule was needed to insure the independence of his country. But his measures were so extreme that he was nicknamed Vlad the Impaler. To punish his enemies, he had them impaled upon wooden stakes, and they died agonizing deaths. An enemy wrote a pamphlet about him titled "The Frightening and Truly Extraordinary Story of a Blood-Drinking Tyrant called Prince Dracula," although there is no evidence that he drank blood.

A proposal has been made to build a Dracula theme park in Romania, but the Dracula who would be honored is the fictional character, not the historical figure. One scholar said that such a place would not really be frightening because the character is so familiar. She described the possibility as Disneyland with fangs.

19. The fictional character, Dracula, first appeared in:

A. the fifteenth century
B. the nineteenth century
C. a movie
D. Romania

Passage for questions 24–27

The element chlorine is a greenish-yellow gas. It is easy and cheap to produce. Running an electrical current through salt water, which is a solution of sodium chloride in water, causes the sodium and chlorine ions to separate, and the gas can be collected.

Used to keep the water clean, chlorine's odor lingers in the hair and on the skin after a day at a swimming pool. It can bleach and clean because it bonds with and destroys the outer surfaces of bacteria and viruses. But this quality also makes it dangerous to human tissues. It was

20. The best title for this passage is:

F. A History of Vampires
G. A Romanian Legend
H. Bela Lugosi's Most Famous Role
J. Who Was Dracula?

21. The word *despot* means:

A. tyrant
B. vampire
C. garbage
D. commander

22. According to the passage, Vlad Dracula's cruelty might have been justified by:

F. his thirst for blood
G. the need to defend his country
H. the people of Bucharest
J. the painful deaths his enemies suffered

23. If a Dracula theme park is built, according to the passage it would not be truly frightening because:

A. it would not be based on the historical Dracula
B. as at Disneyland, visitors would know the effects were make believe
C. the story of the fictional Dracula is so well known
D. all of the above

used in the poison gas weapons of World War I, and it can cause cancer.

But in compounds, chlorine is an extremely useful chemical. Compounds of chlorine are used in perfumes, PVC water pipes, toothbrush bristles, and guitar strings. It is used to bleach paper and purify the silicon used to make computer chips. Natural compounds containing chlorine are common. It is part of the hydrochloric acid in the human stomach and the methyl chloride in volcanic ash.

GO ON TO THE NEXT PAGE

24. According to the passage, chlorine is produced by:

    F. dissolving salt in water

    G. swimming in a pool

    H. electrifying a salt solution

    J. collecting the gas

25. The word *lingers* means:

    A. sleeps

    B. colors

    C. combs

    D. remains

26. Chlorine can be described as:

    F. useful and dangerous

    G. natural and artificial

    H. smelly and wet

    J. gaseous and salty

27. Chlorine purifies liquids by:

    A. changing them to gases

    B. altering the way they smell

    C. destroying the outer surface of harmful organisms

    D. combining with them to form new compounds

Passage for questions 28–31

The Death of Lincoln

Oh slow to smite and swift to spare,
Gentle and merciful and just!
Who, in the fear of God, didst bear
The sword of power, a nation's trust.

In sorrow by thy bier we stand,
Amid the awe that hushes all,
And speak the anguish of a land
That shook with horror at thy fall.

Thy task is one; the bond are free;
We bear thee to an honored grave,
Whose proudest monument shall be
The broken fetters of the slave.

Pure was thy life; its bloody close
Hath placed thee with the sons of light.
Among the noble host of those
Who perished in the cause of Right.

"The Death of Lincoln" by William Cullen Bryant

28. When the poet writes that Lincoln "didst bear/The sword of power, a nation's trust," he is referring to:

    F. Lincoln's role as president of the United States

    G. the Civil War

    H. the United States' motto "In God we trust."

    J. Lincoln's simple life when he was young

29. According to the poem, Lincoln's greatest achievement was:

    A. leading the Union to victory in the Civil War

    B. ending legal slavery in the United States

    C. giving savings bonds to veterans of the Civil War

    D. becoming one of the sons of light

30. The poet's emotions in the poem can best be described as:

    F. fear of God and love of country

    G. relief that the slaves were freed and awe at Lincoln's power

    H. pride in his country and delight in righteousness

    J. admiration of Lincoln and grief at his death

31. The poet uses the word *we* because:

    A. others are standing by Lincoln's bier with him

    B. he believes that he speaks for all Americans

    C. Lincoln was part of "the noble host"

    D. the Confederate Army was defeated

Passage for questions 32–36

Sinkholes can occur slowly and be completely harmless or can quickly cause devastating damage. It is interesting that sinkholes can be caused by two opposite conditions—extreme drought or too much rain.

In some places where the surface soil is sandy, a layer of clay and then a layer of limestone lie beneath the soil. Sinkholes generally occur only in areas where the earth has this composition. Within the limestone areas are pockets of water and air. When the underground water supply is full of groundwater, the pockets are generally filled with water and perhaps air above the water. But when it rains too much or not enough, the caverns can become unstable. When it rains too much, the cavern walls can be broken through because of excess pressure, and when it doesn't rain enough, the cavern walls can collapse because the internal pressure is not enough to withstand the weight from above. When that occurs, the cavern collapses, and the sandy soil close to the surface seeps or pours into the cavern. The speed of the collapse and amount of damage depends on the size of the collapsing cavern.

Sinkholes can harmlessly appear in a lawn and then stop. Sometimes, small sinkholes recur or continue to eat soil for years without causing any damage. But at other times they open in the middle of streets, surprising drivers and swallowing cars, or in residential areas, swallowing houses. Sinkholes have also swallowed lakes. In Florida, many homes had been built around a beautiful lake. One day, the entire lake disappeared because the cavern beneath the ground opened. Instead of sand being above the cavern, there was water, which flowed into the cavern, leaving behind dead and dying fish and plants, and docks that led nowhere. It is very rare for people to be hurt when a sinkhole is created because the process usually occurs over some length of time and is noisy as the ground becomes unstable.

Passage for questions 37–40

The 5th of May, Cinco de Mayo in Spanish, is a Mexican national holiday. Many people in the United States, including people who are not of Mexican descent, celebrate on that day with parties, fireworks, and Mexican foods. Americans often think they are honoring Mexican Independence Day, a holiday parallel to our own 4th of July. But Mexican Independence Day is September 16, the day in 1810 when Mexico's independence from Spain was declared. Cinco de Mayo commemorates a military victory.

32. The word devastating in the first sentence means:

   F. overwhelming
   G. quick
   H. slow
   J. unpleasant

33. A good title for this passage is:

   A. Where Did the Water Go? How Lakes Disappear.
   B. The Causes and Effects of Sinkholes
   C. The Dangers of Living Above Limestone
   D. How to Avoid Sinkhole Damage

34. Sinkholes can be caused by:

   F. too much rain or not enough rain
   G. too little rain or unstable sandy soil
   H. too much rain or certain types of limestone
   J. water filling limestone caverns or air filling limestone caverns

35. According to the passage, sinkholes:

   A. can occur anywhere
   B. can be prevented
   C. only occur where there are limestone caverns
   D. occur very rapidly and without notice

36. An example of a harmless sinkhole is one that:

   F. eliminates a lake, leaving the lake's contents on dry land
   G. opens in a city street but does not cause injuries or deaths
   H. one that opens under a house
   J. opens in a yard and never expands

In 1861, Benito Juarez was president of Mexico. Because the country was facing economic difficulties, he declared that the country would no longer repay its loans from other countries. Angered by this refusal, Emperor Napoleon III of France decided that his country would indirectly rule Mexico by installing an Austrian archduke, Maximilian, as emperor of Mexico. In 1862, a huge French army invaded Mexico, expecting an easy victory. A Mexican general, Ignacio Zaragoza, took his troops to the city of Puebla, east of Mexico City, in an

GO ON TO THE NEXT PAGE

attempt to stop the advancing French. On May 5, 1862, after two hours of fierce fighting, the smaller Mexican Army forced the French to retreat. This is the event celebrated as Cinco de Mayo.

37. Cinco de Mayo in Mexico is a celebration of:

    A. political independence

    B. friendship between the United States and Mexico

    C. winning a battle

    D. the French invasion of Mexico

38. The word *commemorates* means:

    F. comments

    G. buries

    H. honors

    J. distinguishes

39. The passage suggests that in 1861, France:

    A. was not owed any money

    B. did not have a large army

    C. had made Mexico a colony

    D. controlled Austria

40. President Juarez angered Napoleon III by:

    F. sending troops into battle

    G. announcing that loans would not be repaid

    H. appointing Ignacio Zaragoza as a general

    J. starting a battle at Puebla

IF YOU FINISH BEFORE TIME IS CALLED, CHECK YOUR WORK ON THIS SECTION ONLY. DO NOT WORK ON ANY OTHER SECTION IN THE TEST.

Test 7: Mathematics

Time: 35 Minutes

Directions: Read each of the following questions, and select the best answer.

1. If $\frac{x}{y} = 7$, what is the value of $\frac{x+y}{y}$?

    A. 1
    B. 7
    C. 8
    D. 10

2. $(4.01 \times 10) + (4.01 \times 10^2) + (4.01 \times 10^4) =$

    F. 445.11
    G. 4,415.01
    H. 4,451.1
    J. 40,541.1

3. Which of the following is the same as the ratio of $1\frac{1}{2}$ to $2\frac{3}{4}$?

    A. 2:4
    B. 3:5
    C. 3:11
    D. 5:12

4. What is the maximum number of cubes with a side of length $\frac{1}{3}$ that can fit inside a cube with a side of length 1?

    F. 3
    G. 9
    H. 18
    J. 27

5. If r boxes of rubber bands cost d dollars, how much do 7 boxes cost at the same rate?

    A. $7dr$

    B. $\frac{7d}{r}$

    C. $\frac{d}{7r}$

    D. $\frac{r}{7d}$

6. Which of the following is equal to $\frac{64a^{12}b^6}{4a^4b^2}$?

    F. $16a^8b^4$
    G. $16a^3b^3$
    H. $60a^33\ b^3$
    J. $60a^8b^4$

7. Roger got scores of 88, 89, 93, and 81 on his first four math tests. What score does he need to get on his fifth test to have an overall average of 90?

    A. 97
    B. 98
    C. 99
    D. 100

8. $(9) + (-9) + (-5 + 3) =$

    F. -2
    G. 16
    H. 20
    J. 26

9.

    What is the perimeter of pentagon *FGHJK* shown in the preceding figure?

    A. 29
    B. 32
    C. 34
    D. 35

10. In the formula $Q = P - (R - 1)T$, if $R = 7$, $P = 4$, and $T = -2$, what is the value of Q?

    F. -8
    G. -4
    H. 4
    J. 16

11. If a is odd and $a + b$ is even, which of the following is *not* true?

   A. $a - b$ is even.

   B. b^2 is odd.

   C. b^3 is odd.

   D. $(a + b)^2$ is odd.

12.

In the preceding circle, FG is a diameter. If the length of FG is 9, what is the area of the circle?

   F. $\dfrac{9}{2}\pi$

   G. 9π

   H. 18π

   J. $\dfrac{81}{4}\pi$

13. If $a - b = 0$, what is the value of $(2a - b)^2 - a^2$?

   A. 0

   B. a^2

   C. $2a^2$

   D. $3a^2$

14. A square has an area of 100. If the length of one side of the square decreases by 10%, and the length of the adjacent side increases by 10%, what is the area of the new rectangle?

   F. 99

   G. 100

   H. 102

   J. 120

15. The ratio of $\left(\dfrac{1}{7}\right)^3$ to $\left(\dfrac{1}{7}\right)^4$ is:

   A. 7 to 1

   B. 1 to 7

   C. 49 to 1

   D. 4 to 3

16. If $a = (b - 1)^{(b-1)^{(b-1)}}$ and $b = 3$, what is the value of a?

   F. 8

   G. 16

   H. 32

   J. 64

17. If $\dfrac{4}{y} + \dfrac{3}{y} = \dfrac{1}{5}$, then $y =$

   A. $\dfrac{1}{35}$

   B. $\dfrac{5}{7}$

   C. $\dfrac{7}{5}$

   D. 35

18.

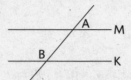

In the preceding figure, lines K and M are parallel. Which of the following statements describes the relationship between angle A and angle B?

   F. The two angles are vertical angles.

   G. The two angles are congruent.

   H. The two angles are supplementary.

   J. The two angles are complementary.

19. Mike bought 8 videotapes. The total cost for the tapes was $\dfrac{D}{2}$ dollars. What was the average price per videotape?

   A. $\dfrac{D}{16}$

   B. $\dfrac{D}{8}$

   C. $2D$

   D. $4D$

20. If $2x - y = 7$, and $3x + y = 3$, what is the value of x?

   F. 2

   G. 3

   H. 4

   J. 5

21. What is the area of a rectangle if the coordinates of three of its vertices are (0, 0), (5, 0), and (0, 8)?

   A. 20

   B. 30

   C. 35

   D. 40

22. How many positive integers less than 10 are equal to the sum of two different prime numbers?

    F. 3
    G. 4
    H. 5
    J. 6

23. If $\frac{1}{8}$ of a is 18, what is the value of $\frac{1}{4}$ of a?

    A. $4\frac{1}{2}$

    B. 9

    C. 36

    D. 72

24. In the following rectangle, what is the area of the shaded region?

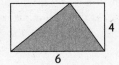

    F. 12
    G. 18
    H. 20
    J. 24

25. In the expression $\dfrac{\frac{a}{b}}{\frac{c}{d}}$, if the value of d is tripled, then the overall value of the expression is:

    A. multiplied by 9
    B. tripled
    C. divided by 3
    D. divided by 9

26. Jimmy is saving money for college. He currently has saved $240, which is 20% of the amount of money he hopes to save by the time college starts. How much money does he hope to save?

    F. $1,200
    G. $1,800
    H. $2,400
    J. $4,800

27. If $x = -4$, what is the value of $x^2 - 4^2$?

    A. −32
    B. −16
    C. 0
    D. 32

28. How many positive integers are both multiples of 6 and divisors of 54?

    F. 1
    G. 2
    H. 3
    J. 4

29. If $x = 20\%$ of 30% of 250, what is the value of x?

    A. 15
    B. 30
    C. 125
    D. 150

30. Three candidates are running for mayor of Union. The following table shows the outcome of the election.

Name	Number of Votes
Jean	276
Brenda	535
Mark	489

If Union has 2,000 residents, and no one voted more than once, what percent of the residents did not vote?

    F. 35%
    G. 45%
    H. 55%
    J. 65%

31. If a and b are odd numbers, which of the following is *not* true?

    A. ab is odd.
    B. a^2b^2 is odd.
    C. $2ab$ is odd.
    D. $a - b$ is even.

32. If $z = -3$, what is the value of $(z^2)^3 - z^3$?

    F. −756
    G. −702
    H. 702
    J. 756

GO ON TO THE NEXT PAGE

33.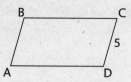

If the preceding parallelogram has an area of 40, what is the length of *AD*?

A. 4
B. 8
C. 12
D. It cannot be determined.

34. The radius of circle *A* is *x*, and the radius of circle *B* is 2*x*, what is the ratio of the area of circle *B* to the area of circle *A*?

F. 2 to 1
G. 4 to 1
H. 1 to 2
J. 1 to 4

35. Janet worked $\frac{1}{2}$ of an hour on day 1, $\frac{3}{4}$ of an hour on day 2, $\frac{5}{8}$ of an hour on day 3 and $\frac{7}{16}$ of an hour on day 4. How much time, in total, did she spend working on these days?

A. $1\frac{5}{16}$

B. $2\frac{1}{4}$

C. $2\frac{5}{16}$

D. $2\frac{3}{8}$

36. Which of the following lines illustrates the correct graph of $-3 < x < 4$?

F.
G.
H.
J.

37. If $M = 5$, $N = -3$, $C = -3$ and $D = -1$, what is the value of $\frac{M - N}{C + D}$?

A. −2

B. $-\frac{1}{2}$

C. $\frac{1}{2}$

D. 2

38. What is the value of $2 + 3(12 \div 4) - 4$?

F. 7
G. 9
H. 10
J. 11

39. Peter is taking a multiple-choice test with four questions, each of which has three possible answers. What is the total number of different ways that Peter could answer the questions?

A. 12
B. 16
C. 27
D. 81

40. Lauren is four years younger than twice Kimberly's age. If *K* is used to represent Kimberly's age, which of the following represents Lauren's age?

F. $2K + 4$
G. $2K - 4$
H. $4 - 2K$
J. $2(K - 4)$

IF YOU FINISH BEFORE TIME IS CALLED, CHECK YOUR WORK ON THIS SECTION ONLY. DO NOT WORK ON ANY OTHER SECTION IN THE TEST.

Answer Key

Test 1: Sequences

1. C	6. F	11. D	16. J
2. J	7. A	12. F	17. B
3. B	8. H	13. B	18. F
4. G	9. A	14. H	19. C
5. A	10. G	15. B	20. G

Test 2: Analogies

1. C	6. G	11. B	16. G
2. F	7. A	12. J	17. D
3. C	8. J	13. A	18. F
4. H	9. B	14. H	19. D
5. C	10. H	15. D	20. H

Test 3: Quantitative Reasoning

1. D	6. G	11. C	16. H
2. F	7. D	12. G	17. A
3. C	8. G	13. B	18. J
4. F	9. C	14. H	19. B
5. B	10. H	15. B	20. J

Test 4: Verbal Reasoning—Words

1. D	4. F	7. C	10. J
2. G	5. C	8. G	11. B
3. B	6. F	9. B	12. H

Test 5: Verbal Reasoning—Context

1. B	3. C	5. C	7. B
2. J	4. H	6. H	8. J

Test 6: Reading and Language Arts

1. D	11. D	21. A	31. B
2. J	12. G	22. G	32. F
3. C	13. C	23. D	33. B
4. F	14. H	24. H	34. F
5. A	15. A	25. D	35. C
6. G	16. H	26. F	36. J
7. A	17. C	27. C	37. C
8. G	18. G	28. F	38. H
9. A	19. B	29. B	39. D
10. H	20. J	30. J	40. G

Test 7: Mathematics

1. C	11. D	21. D	31. C
2. J	12. J	22. G	32. J
3. C	13. A	23. C	33. D
4. J	14. F	24. F	34. G
5. B	15. A	25. B	35. C
6. F	16. G	26. F	36. H
7. C	17. D	27. C	37. A
8. F	18. H	28. G	38. F
9. C	19. A	29. A	39. D
10. J	20. F	30. F	40. G

Answers and Explanations

Test 1: Sequences

1. **C.** Each diagram consists of a circle followed by a triangle followed by a circle. In the first diagram, none of the figures are shaded, and then, one at a time, figures are shaded from left to right. If the pattern continues, in the final figure, all the figures will be shaded.

2. **J.** From one diagram to the next, triangles are turned upside down and placed on top of the previous diagram.

3. **B.** In the first figure, all four circles on the tips of the "X" are shaded. One by one, the shading disappears in a clockwise direction. If the pattern continues, the final figure will only have the circle in the upper left shaded.

4. **G.** Each diagram contains identical figures. From the first diagram to the second, the pattern of shading is reversed. Therefore, from the third diagram to the fourth, the shading should also be reversed.

5. **A.** The positions of the unshaded circle and shaded triangle are reversed from the first diagram to the second. In the same way, the positions of the shaded circle and unshaded triangle should be reversed from the third figure to the fourth.

6. **F.** From one diagram to the next, a diagonal line has been added to the *bottom* of the figure. Continuing the pattern, the fourth diagram should look like the third with a diagonal line, slanting from right to left, added to the bottom.

7. **A.** The pattern is $4 + 4 = 8 + 4 = 12 \,|\, 10 + 4 = 14 + 4 = 18$. Therefore, $17 + 4 = 21 + 4 = \mathbf{25}$.

8. **H.** The pattern is $75 \div 5 = 15 \div 5 = 3 \,|\, 50 \div 5 = 10 \div 5 = 2$. Therefore, $100 \div 5 = 20 \div 5 = 4$.

9. **A.** The pattern is $9 - 5 = 4 \times 3 = 12 \,|\, 7 - 5 = 2 \times 3 = 6$. Therefore, $5 - 5 = \mathbf{0} \times 3 = 0$.

10. **G.** The pattern is $15 + 8 = 23 - 3 = 20 \,|\, 22 + 8 = 30 - 3 = 27$. Therefore, $35 + 8 = 43 - 3 = \mathbf{40}$.

11. **D.** The pattern is $5 - 4 = 1$, and $\mathbf{1^2} = 1 \,|\, 7 - 4 = 3$, and $3^2 = 9$. Therefore, $9 - 4 = 5$, and $\mathbf{5^2 = 25}$.

12. **F.** The pattern is $7 \times 3 = 21 - 5 = 16 \,|\, 5 \times 3 = 15 - 5 = 10 \,|\, 9 \times 3 = 27 - 5 = 22$.

13. **B.** The pattern is $49 + 5 = 54 \div 3 = 18 \,|\, 58 + 5 = 63 \div 3 = 21$. Therefore, $67 + 5 = \mathbf{72} \div 3 = 24$.

14. **H.** The pattern is $A + 2 = C + 1 = D \,|\, E + 2 = G + 1 = H \,|\, I + 2 = K + 1 = L \,|\, Q + 2 = S + 1 = T$. In addition, the first letter of each sequence alphabetically follows the last letter of the previous sequence. Because the sequence before the missing one ends in L, the missing sequence must begin with M. Then, note that $M + 2 = O + 1 = P$.

15. **B.** The letters in each of these sequences are in reverse alphabetical order. The only answer choice with this property is T S R.

16. **J.** The pattern is $K + 2 = M - 3 = J \,|\, B + 2 = D - 3 = A \,|\, H + 2 = J - 3 = G \,|\, O + 2 = Q - 3 = N$. The only sequence with this pattern is S U R.

17. **B.** The pattern is $E + 5 = J + 5 = O \,|\, G + 5 = L + 5 = Q \,|\, I + 5 = N + 5 = S \,|\, M + 5 = R + 5 = W$. Also, the first letter of each sequence comes two letters after the first letter of the previous sequence. For example, the G in the second sequence is two letters after the E in the first sequence. Thus, the first letter of the missing sequence must be $I + 2 = K$. From this point on, the sequence is $K + 5 = P + 5 = U$.

18. **F.** The numbers are in descending order, so the missing number must be 3. The first letters of each sequence are in alphabetical order, and the last letters of each sequence are in reverse alphabetical order.

19. **C.** The numbers double as we move through the sequences, so the missing number must be 8. The pattern for the letters is $Z - 2 = X \,|\, W - 2 = U \,|\, T - 2 = R \,|\, N - 2 = L$. Finally, each sequence begins with the letter that is alphabetically before the letter that ended the previous sequence. Thus, the missing sequence begins with Q and ends with O.

20. G. The first letters of each sequence are in alphabetical order: A, B, C, D, so the first letter of the missing sequence should be E. The middle letters of each sequence are also alphabetical: F, G, H, I, so the middle letter of the missing sequence must be J. The last letters of each sequence are in alphabetical order too: K, L, M, N, so the last letter of the missing sequence is O.

Test 2: Analogies

1. C. A needle uses thread for sewing; a pen uses ink for writing.

2. F. Combs and brushes are used to groom hair; mops and brooms are used to clean floors.

3. C. The relationship is between a thing and where it belongs or where it is usually kept.

4. H. The relationship is that of synonyms. The first two pictures mean *and*. The second two pictures mean *stop* or *don't walk*.

5. C. The relationship is between similar kinds of toys. Teddy bears and rag dolls are stuffed toys; cars and trains have wheels and are toys made of wood or metal.

6. G. Spaghetti and pizza are associated with Italy; the Statue of Liberty and the flag are associated with the United States.

7. A. The relationship is between an object and its function. A bat is used to hit a baseball; a foot is used to press on a pedal.

8. J. Opposites explain this relationship.

9. B. These are associations. The cake and gift are associated with birthdays. Turkey and pilgrims are associated with Thankgiving.

10. H. A police officer uses a whistle, and a nurse uses a thermometer.

11. B. This is another relationship between an object and its function. Microscopes are used to see things too small for the naked eye to see clearly. Telescopes are used to see things (like the planet Saturn) that are too far away for the naked eye to see.

12. J. Hands play the piano, and a mouth blows into the musical instrument.

13. A. A net is used to catch butterflies.

14. H. The relationship is between similar characteristics. Both snails and crabs have shells. Both horses and mice have tails.

15. D. The analogy is based on a protective function. Goggles protect eyes; a helmet protects the head.

16. G. The relationship is between a part and the whole. A log is made from part of a tree; a slice of pie is part of a whole pie.

17. D. This is a relationship based on place. The brain is inside the skull, and the lungs are inside the rib cage.

18. F. This is a slightly different kind relationship based on place. People ski in the mountains and swim in pools.

19. D. What is the first item made from? Cheese is made from milk. Jelly is made from fruit.

20. H. What is the item made on? A blanket is made on a loom; a clay vase is made on a potter's wheel.

Test 3: Quantitative Reasoning

1. D. The pattern is $2 + 9 = 11$, and $7 + 9 = 16$. Therefore, $4 + 9 = 13$.

2. F. Here, the pattern is $20 - 4 = 16$, and $12 - 4 = 8$. Thus, $9 - 4 = 5$.

3. C. Note that $3 \times 3 = 9$, and $5 \times 3 = 15$. Thus, $8 \times 3 = 24$.

4. **F.** Because $4 + 21 = 25$ and $7 + 21 = 28$, we have $12 + 21 = 33$.

5. **B.** The pattern is $28 - 15 = 13$, and $35 - 15 = 20$. Thus, $42 - 15 = 27$.

6. **G.** Note that $14 \div 7 = 2$, and $35 \div 7 = 5$. It follows that $56 \div 7 = 8$.

7. **D.** Because $8 \times 11 = 88$ and $5 \times 11 = 55$, we have $1 \times 11 = 11$.

8. **G.** The figure contains 4 squares, and 2 half squares are shaded. Because 2 half squares are equal to 1 whole square, the figure is $\frac{1}{4}$ shaded.

9. **C.** This figure contains 6 squares. Two whole squares and 2 half squares are shaded, and, because 2 halves make a whole, this is equivalent to 3 whole squares being shaded. Overall, then, $\frac{3}{6} = \frac{1}{2}$ of the figure is shaded.

10. **H.** In this figure, 4 half squares are shaded, which is equivalent to 2 whole squares. Because the total figure contains 6 squares, overall $\frac{2}{6} = \frac{1}{3}$ of the figure is shaded.

11. **C.** Here, 6 out of 9 squares are shaded. Thus, $\frac{6}{9} = \frac{2}{3}$ of the figure is shaded.

12. **G.** In this figure, 6 half squares, which is equivalent to 3 whole squares, are shaded. Overall, then $\frac{3}{9} = \frac{1}{3}$ of the figure is shaded.

13. **B.** This figure consists of 8 squares. Of these, 5 squares are totally shaded, and 2 squares are half shaded. This is equivalent to 6 shaded squares. Thus $\frac{6}{8} = \frac{3}{4}$ of the figure is shaded.

14. **H.** According to the scale, 1 cone is equal to 2 cubes. If a cube is added to each side, it can be seen that 1 cone and 1 cube are equal to 3 cubes.

15. **B.** The scale shows that 1 cone and 1 cube are equal to 2 cubes. Remove a cube from each side, and you see that 1 cube is equal to 1 cone. If this is true, then 2 cones are equal to 2 cubes.

16. **H.** According to the scale, 3 cones are equal to 1 cone and 1 cube. By removing 1 cone from each side, we see that 2 cones are equal to 1 cube. Doubling the weight on both sides shows us that 4 cones are equal to 2 cubes.

17. **A.** Remove 1 cube from each side of the scale, and we see that 1 cone is equal to 3 cubes. Add a cone to each side, and you see that 2 cones are equal to 3 cubes and a cone.

18. **J.** According to the scale, 1 cone is equal to 4 cubes. Add a cube to both sides, and we obtain the result that 1 cone and 1 cube are equal to 5 cubes.

19. **B.** Here, the scale shows that 3 cubes are equal to 2 cones. By adding a cone to each side, we see that 3 cubes and a cone are equal to 3 cones.

20. **J.** By removing a cone from each side, we see that 2 cubes are equal to a cube and a cone.

Test 4: Verbal Reasoning—Words

1. **D.** A cogwheel cannot exist without teeth. A cogwheel is part of a gear. A motor can be employed to turn a cogwheel or gear. A mechanic might or might not have something to do with cogwheels, gears, or motors; however, a mechanic is often employed to perform repairs on machinery.

2. **G.** Because musicians are needed to create music, without them no music could be performed. Musicians read notes from the music placed on a music stand. Concerts are usually performed in a concert hall, but can be staged elsewhere.

3. **B.** A thermometer measures temperature using markings and the rise or fall of mercury within a tube. Without mercury, there is no way to measure. Fahrenheit and centigrade are scales of measurement on a thermometer. An equation can be used to change from one scale to the other. Celadon is a very pale green color.

4. **F.** To muse is to reflect, meditate, or think deeply. All other answers are self-explanatory.

5. **C.** Hot dogs are made of a variety of kinds of meat. Mustard, a bun, and a ball park are not necessary parts of a hot dog.

6. F. To use a sailboat properly, one must have wind. Sailboats can get to open water either by paddling or using a small motor. When there, the wind propels a sailboat. The bow is the front end of a ship or boat. Pitch and yaw refer to movement of a boat caused by waves in the water.

7. C. The items in the first row are names of cereals. The items in the second row are characters in novels created by Samuel Clemens whose pen name was Mark Twain. Bilbo Baggins is a character in several books by Tolkein.

8. G. The items in the first row all have to do with bodies of water. A brook is the smallest. A stream is larger, and a river is largest of all. The items in the second row are countries where the most English speakers are found. When you realize the common factor, the answer is obvious.

9. B. The items in the first row are all animals that are raised for the meat they provide. The items in the second row are fast-food restaurants. Red Lobster, Siam Orchid, and Olive Garden are not categorized as fast-food restaurants.

10. J. The items in the first row are breeds of dogs. The items in the second row are examples of common herbs. All the other answer choices are flowers.

11. B. The items in the first row are large birds. The items in the second row are slow-moving, sleepy animals. Donkeys, turkeys, and antelope do not fall into this category.

12. H. The items in the first row are planets in our solar system. The items in the second row are cars produced in the United States.

Test 5: Verbal Reasoning—Context

1. B. This is a stressful situation. Accidents always seem to happen on holidays when a full staff of doctors and nurses is not on duty. When a child is injured, both the parents and the child are upset. The doctor needs to be sympathetic to everyone, not argumentative. The parents reasoned that if a scar was going to result from both methods of treatment, the least traumatic method (the use of a Band-Aid rather than a stitch) should be used. They could complain about the doctor's attitude to the other doctors the next day, but not at the time of the visit. Changing to a different doctor does not change the doctor's attitude toward a patient or the parents.

2. J. All these suggestions help make Jane feel more adult and give the parents a relaxing, stress-free vacation. While Jane wants to become more independent, her parents are not willing to give her the freedom to do so, especially when vacations are involved. Perhaps being allowed input on the vacation would make it more desirable. Jane wouldn't feel tied to her family all the time if a friend were along. In addition, payment for any needed baby-sitting services places a value on her skills.

3. C. It makes sense to limit the sampling to untried recipes. A smaller portion, too, will help her keep weight off. Georgette doesn't have to eat a serving-sized portion to know whether the flavors meld well together. Even though she is experienced, when Georgette creates a new flavor combination, an observer shouldn't perform a taste test. If she produces only low-calorie desserts, she limits her business prospects. To stop baking is out of the question.

4. H. Mom should give up and pack the lunch she knows will be eaten.

5. C. Frederick's parents should take away the credit card and not the computer. He is in college and needs to pay attention to his course work. If they take away the computer, Frederick will have a more difficult time doing the research and writing required for his college courses.

6. H. The syllable *leu* is found in all the example words that have to do with movement. Some are present tense; some are past tense. When the word is past tense, the suffix is *tio*. When the word is present tense, the ending is the syllable *leu*. The answer, which should be in present tense, must also end in the syllable *leu*.

7. B. All example words have the same suffix, *ep*, indicating a similarity. The answer word needs that same suffix. Also, all example words begin with the prefix, *preg*, so that needs to be part of the answer word.

8. J. These words have the same stem, *ionit*, possibly indicating the type of object that is mentioned. The answer requires this stem.

Test 6: Reading and Language Arts

1. **D.** This information is in the second paragraph.

2. **J.** The process is described in the third paragraph of the selection.

3. **C.** Because *it is expelled through the mouth,* **B** and **D** do not make sense. Choice **A** is clearly the opposite of what the process is intended to do.

4. **F.** While **G** and **J** are true statements, the passage also describes other important achievements by Dr. Heimlich.

5. **A.** The passage states that they are attached *only at the shoulder joint.*

6. **G.** Which choice can fly straight up and down, sideways, and backward like the hummingbird? Only the helicopter.

7. **A.** Because the bill is used for sipping, none of the other choices is possible.

8. **G.** The second and third sentences of paragraph two explain this answer.

9. **A.** This information is in the last paragraph of the selection.

10. **H.** Choice **G** is part of the lie that he plans to tell. Neither **F** nor **J** is supported by information in the passage.

11. **D.** To confront meets to challenge or to meet head on; it is a synonym for accost.

12. **G.** Although **F** and **J** might be true according to the passage, neither is the reason that he did not try to sleep.

13. **C.** **A** is not a good choice because, although Paul is afraid of rats and of waking up his father, it doesn't describe his attitude toward his home. **B** and **D** are contradicted by the description.

14. **H.** Although Paul does not want to be scolded by his father, that does not mean his father was unkind. However, nothing in the passage indicates his father is a kind man.

15. **A.** That the car wash benefits the environment is implied by its use of recycled water, but that is not the main subject of the passage, so **B** is not a good answer. The passage is objective; it does not stress the advantages of using an automatic car wash; therefore, **C** is not a good choice.

16. **H.** This information is in the third paragraph.

17. **C.** The passage states that there is an extra charge for waxing the car.

18. **G.** The content of the first paragraph explains this answer.

19. **B.** The question asks about the fictional character who the passage states was created by a nineteenth-century English novelist.

20. **J.** The passage answers the question about both the real and the fictional Dracula. It has little to do with **F,** and because there was a real Dracula, the word *legend* in **G** is inaccurate. The information in **H** might be true, but the passage is not about Bela Lugosi.

21. **A.** The phrase *strong rule* in the second paragraph is a clue to this answer.

22. **G.** The passage states that some historians believe his strong rule was needed to insure the independence of his country.

23. **D.** All this information is in the passage's last paragraph.

24. **H.** This is explained in the first paragraph.

25. **D.** None of the other choices makes sense in the first sentence of the second paragraph.

26. **F.** The examples in the passage lead to this answer. In the other choices, one of the words is accurate, but the other is not.

27. **C.** This information is in the second paragraph.

28. F. According to the poem's third and fourth lines, Lincoln carried the sword of power, meaning that the nation trusted him. This describes his role as president.

29. B. The third stanza says that this will be Lincoln's *proudest monument*.

30. J. The second stanza expresses grief, and all the other stanzas express admiration.

31. B. The words *anguish of a land* in the second stanza help to explain this answer.

32. F. By reading the rest of the passage, the meaning of this word becomes clear.

33. B. This is the only choice that states generally what the passage is about.

34. F. The second sentence of the passage contains this information.

35. C. The beginning of the second paragraph explains this answer.

36. J. In **F,** the plants and animals of the lake would be harmed. In **G,** although people are not hurt, damage to the street is not harmless.

37. C. Choice **A** is the mistake commonly made by Americans.

38. H. To commemorate is to remember an event of importance.

39. D. That the French ruler was able to tell an Austrian noble what to do implies that he controlled Austria. Aditionally, all the other choices are contradicted by information in the passage.

40. G. The second paragraph of the passage contains this information.

Test 7: Mathematics

1. C. $\frac{x+y}{y} = \frac{x}{y} + \frac{y}{y} = \frac{x}{y} + 1 = 7 + 1 = 8$

2. J. $(4.01 \times 10) + (4.01 \times 10^2) + (4.01 \times 10^4) = 40.1 + 401 + 40,100 = 40,541.1$

3. C. Note that $1\frac{1}{2} = \frac{3}{2}$ and $2\frac{3}{4} = \frac{11}{2}$. Therefore, the ratio is $\frac{\frac{3}{2}}{\frac{11}{2}} = \frac{3}{2} \times \frac{2}{11} = \frac{3}{11}$.

4. J. The volume of a cube with sides of length $\frac{1}{3}$ is $\left(\frac{1}{3}\right)^3 = \frac{1}{27}$. The volume of a cube with side 1 is $1^3 = 1$. Clearly, the number of cubes of volume $\frac{1}{27}$ that fit in a cube of volume 1 is 27.

5. B. This problem can be solved by setting up a proportion.

$\dfrac{\text{Boxes}}{\text{Dollars}} \begin{array}{l} \to \\ \to \end{array} \dfrac{r}{d} = \dfrac{7}{N}$ (Cross multiply.)

$rN = 7d$ (Divide both sides by r.)

$N = \dfrac{7d}{r}$

6. F. $\dfrac{64a^{12}b^6}{4a^4b^2} = 16a^{12-4}b^{6-2} = 16a^8b^4$

7. C. Let S equal the score that he needs to get on the fifth test. Then,

$\dfrac{88 + 89 + 93 + 81 + S}{5} = 90$

$\dfrac{351 + S}{5} = 90$ (Multiply both sides by 5.)

$351 + S = 450$ (Subtract 351 from both sides.)

$S = 99$

8. F. Follow the number line up and down as you add and subtract the numbers.

9. C. We are given the lengths of four of the five sides, so all we need to do is find the length of the missing side *HJ*. If we extend the figure to make a complete rectangle as shown in the following figure, it can be seen that *HJ* is the hypotenuse of a right triangle with legs of length 3 and 4.

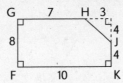

By the Pythagorean Theorem, the hypotenuse of such a triangle is 5. Therefore, the perimeter of the pentagon is $P = 10 + 8 + 7 + 4 + 5 = 34$.

10. J. $Q = P - (R - 1)T = 4 - (7 - 1)(-2) = 4 - 6(-2) = 4 - (-12) = 4 + 12 = 16$

11. D. Because the sum of two odd numbers is even, if *a* is odd, and $a + b$ is even, then *b* is odd as well. The difference of two odd numbers is even, so statement **A** is true. If you square or cube an odd number, the result is odd, so statements **B** and **C** are true. However, because $a + b$ is even, $(a + b)^2$ is also even, so **D** is false.

12. J. If the diameter of a circle is 9, the radius is $\frac{9}{2}$. Because the formula for the area of a circle is $A = \pi r^2$, we have $A = \pi \left(\frac{9}{2}\right)^2 = \pi \left(\frac{81}{4}\right)$, or $\frac{81}{4}\pi$.

13. A. The statement $a - b = 0$ is equivalent to $a = b$. Therefore, to evaluate $(2a - b)^2 - a^2$, we can substitute *a* for each appearance of *b*.

$(2a - b)^2 - a^2 = (2a - a)^2 - a^2 = (a)^2 - a^2 = a^2 - a^2 = 0.$

14. F. If a square has an area of 100, the dimensions of the square are 10×10. The side that increases by 10% becomes 11, while the side that decreases by 10% becomes 9. The area of the new rectangle, then, is $A = 9 \times 11 = 99$.

15. A. $\dfrac{\left(\frac{1}{7}\right)^3}{\left(\frac{1}{7}\right)^4} = \dfrac{\frac{1}{7^3}}{\frac{1}{7^4}} = \dfrac{1}{7^3} \times \dfrac{7^4}{1} = \dfrac{7^4}{7^3} = \dfrac{7}{1}$. Therefore, the ratio is 7 to 1.

16. G. $a = (b - 1)^{(b-1)^{(b-1)}} = (3 - 1)^{(3-1)^{(3-1)}} = 2^{2^2} = 4^2 = 16$

17. D. First, note that $\frac{4}{y} + \frac{3}{y} = \frac{7}{y}$. Thus, the equation becomes $\frac{7}{y} = \frac{1}{5}$. Cross multiply to get $7 \times 5 = y$, so $y = 35$.

18. H.

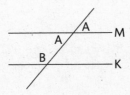

As the preceding diagram shows, the angle labeled *A* is congruent to the interior angle also labeled *A*. Note, then, that the angles *A* and *B* can be viewed as equivalent to interior angles on the same side of the transversal. Such angles are supplementary.

19. A. To find the average cost, take the total cost and divide by 8.

20. F. To find the common solution, add the two equations together.

$$\begin{array}{r} 2x - y = 7 \\ +\,3x + y = 3 \\ \hline 5x \quad\;\; = 10 \end{array}$$

Because $5x = 10$, it follows that $x = 2$.

21. **D.** As the following diagram shows, the rectangle has sides of length 5 and 8.

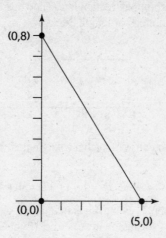

Therefore, the area is $A = 5 \times 8 = 40$.

22. **G.** The prime numbers that are less than 10 are 2, 3, 5, and 7. The numbers less than 10 that are the sum of two different prime numbers are 5 (which can be written as 2 + 3), 7 (which is 2 + 5), 9 (which is 2 + 7), and 8 (which is 3 + 5). Therefore, four such numbers exist.

23. **C.** We are told that $\frac{1}{8} a = 18$. If you multiply both sides of this equation by 8, you get $a = 18 \times 8 = 144$. Then, $\frac{1}{4} \times 144 = 36$.

24. **F.** The shaded figure is a triangle with a base of length 6 and a height of 4. The area is $A = \frac{1}{2} bh = \frac{1}{2}(6)(4) = 12$.

25. **B.** Begin by simplifying the compound fraction:

$$\frac{\frac{a}{b}}{\frac{c}{d}} = \frac{a}{b} \times \frac{d}{c} = \frac{ad}{bc}$$

Now, if d is tripled, the fraction becomes:

$$\frac{a(3d)}{bc} = \frac{3ad}{bc} = 3\frac{ad}{bc}$$

Therefore, the fraction becomes three times as big as it was.

26. **F.** Note that $20\% = \frac{1}{5}$. Therefore, Jimmy has saved $\frac{1}{5}$ of the money he hopes to save. The total amount he hopes to save, therefore, is $5 \times \$240 = \$1,200$.

27. **C.** $x^2 - 4^2 = (-4)^2 - 16 = 16 - 16 = 0$

28. **G.** The multiples of 6 that could possibly divide into 54 are 6, 12, 18, and 24. Of these, only 6 and 18 actually do divide evenly into 54. Thus, two numbers have the desired property.

29. **A.** $x = .2 \times .3 \times 250 = 0.06 \times 250 = 15$

30. **F.** The total number of people who voted is $276 + 535 + 489 = 1,300$. Therefore, out of the 2,000 residents, 700 did not vote. Now, simply note that $\frac{700}{2,000} = \frac{70}{200} = \frac{35}{100} = 35\%$.

31. **C.** The statement that is not true is **C** because the number 2 is in the product. The product of an even number and two odd numbers is always even.

32. **J.** $(z^2)^3 - z^3 = ((-3)^2)^3 - (-3)^3 = 9^3 - (-27) = 729 + 27 = 756$.

33. **D.** This is a trick question. Note that we are given that the length of one of the sides of the parallelogram is 5, but this side is *not* the height of the parallelogram. Because we do not know the height, we cannot find the length.

34. G. The area of circle A is πx^2, while the area of circle B is $\pi(2x)^2 = \pi(4x^2) = 4\pi x^2$. Therefore, the ratio of the areas is $\frac{4\pi x^2}{\pi x^2} = \frac{4}{1}$.

35. C. The least common denominator of the fractions is 16. Note that $\frac{1}{2} = \frac{8}{16}$, $\frac{3}{4} = \frac{12}{16}$, and $\frac{5}{8} = \frac{10}{16}$. Thus, we need to add $\frac{8}{16} + \frac{12}{16} + \frac{10}{16} + \frac{7}{16} = \frac{37}{16} = 2\frac{5}{16}$ hours.

36. H. The correct graph has an open dot at -3 to indicate that -3 is not included in the solution set, and a closed dot at 4 to indicate that 4 is included in the solution set.

37. A. $\frac{M-N}{C+D} = \frac{5-(-3)}{(-3)+(-1)} = \frac{5+3}{-4} = \frac{8}{-4} = -2$

38. F. $2 + 3(12 \div 4) - 4 = 2 + 3(3) - 4 = 2 + 9 - 4 = 11 - 4 = 7$.

39. D. Peter could answer each of four questions three ways. Therefore, the number of possible ways he could answer the questions is $3 \times 3 \times 3 \times 3 = 81$.

40. G. If K is Kimberly's age, then $2K$ is twice Kimberly's age, and 4 less than this is $2K - 4$.

Answer Sheet for Practice HSPT Exam 1

TEST 1 Verbal Skills

1 Ⓐ Ⓑ Ⓒ Ⓓ	13 Ⓐ Ⓑ Ⓒ Ⓓ	25 Ⓐ Ⓑ Ⓒ Ⓓ	37 Ⓐ Ⓑ Ⓒ	49 Ⓐ Ⓑ Ⓒ Ⓓ
2 Ⓐ Ⓑ Ⓒ Ⓓ	14 Ⓐ Ⓑ Ⓒ Ⓓ	26 Ⓐ Ⓑ Ⓒ Ⓓ	38 Ⓐ Ⓑ Ⓒ	50 Ⓐ Ⓑ Ⓒ
3 Ⓐ Ⓑ Ⓒ Ⓓ	15 Ⓐ Ⓑ Ⓒ Ⓓ	27 Ⓐ Ⓑ Ⓒ Ⓓ	39 Ⓐ Ⓑ Ⓒ Ⓓ	51 Ⓐ Ⓑ Ⓒ Ⓓ
4 Ⓐ Ⓑ Ⓒ Ⓓ	16 Ⓐ Ⓑ Ⓒ Ⓓ	28 Ⓐ Ⓑ Ⓒ Ⓓ	40 Ⓐ Ⓑ Ⓒ Ⓓ	52 Ⓐ Ⓑ Ⓒ Ⓓ
5 Ⓐ Ⓑ Ⓒ	17 Ⓐ Ⓑ Ⓒ Ⓓ	29 Ⓐ Ⓑ Ⓒ Ⓓ	41 Ⓐ Ⓑ Ⓒ Ⓓ	53 Ⓐ Ⓑ Ⓒ Ⓓ
6 Ⓐ Ⓑ Ⓒ Ⓓ	18 Ⓐ Ⓑ Ⓒ Ⓓ	30 Ⓐ Ⓑ Ⓒ	42 Ⓐ Ⓑ Ⓒ Ⓓ	54 Ⓐ Ⓑ Ⓒ Ⓓ
7 Ⓐ Ⓑ Ⓒ Ⓓ	19 Ⓐ Ⓑ Ⓒ	31 Ⓐ Ⓑ Ⓒ Ⓓ	43 Ⓐ Ⓑ Ⓒ Ⓓ	55 Ⓐ Ⓑ Ⓒ Ⓓ
8 Ⓐ Ⓑ Ⓒ Ⓓ	20 Ⓐ Ⓑ Ⓒ Ⓓ	32 Ⓐ Ⓑ Ⓒ Ⓓ	44 Ⓐ Ⓑ Ⓒ	56 Ⓐ Ⓑ Ⓒ Ⓓ
9 Ⓐ Ⓑ Ⓒ Ⓓ	21 Ⓐ Ⓑ Ⓒ Ⓓ	33 Ⓐ Ⓑ Ⓒ Ⓓ	45 Ⓐ Ⓑ Ⓒ Ⓓ	57 Ⓐ Ⓑ Ⓒ
10 Ⓐ Ⓑ Ⓒ Ⓓ	22 Ⓐ Ⓑ Ⓒ Ⓓ	34 Ⓐ Ⓑ Ⓒ Ⓓ	46 Ⓐ Ⓑ Ⓒ Ⓓ	58 Ⓐ Ⓑ Ⓒ Ⓓ
11 Ⓐ Ⓑ Ⓒ Ⓓ	23 Ⓐ Ⓑ Ⓒ Ⓓ	35 Ⓐ Ⓑ Ⓒ Ⓓ	47 Ⓐ Ⓑ Ⓒ Ⓓ	59 Ⓐ Ⓑ Ⓒ Ⓓ
12 Ⓐ Ⓑ Ⓒ	24 Ⓐ Ⓑ Ⓒ	36 Ⓐ Ⓑ Ⓒ Ⓓ	48 Ⓐ Ⓑ Ⓒ Ⓓ	60 Ⓐ Ⓑ Ⓒ Ⓓ

TEST 2 Quantitative Skills

61 Ⓐ Ⓑ Ⓒ Ⓓ	72 Ⓐ Ⓑ Ⓒ Ⓓ	83 Ⓐ Ⓑ Ⓒ Ⓓ	93 Ⓐ Ⓑ Ⓒ Ⓓ	103 Ⓐ Ⓑ Ⓒ Ⓓ
62 Ⓐ Ⓑ Ⓒ Ⓓ	73 Ⓐ Ⓑ Ⓒ Ⓓ	84 Ⓐ Ⓑ Ⓒ Ⓓ	94 Ⓐ Ⓑ Ⓒ Ⓓ	104 Ⓐ Ⓑ Ⓒ Ⓓ
63 Ⓐ Ⓑ Ⓒ Ⓓ	74 Ⓐ Ⓑ Ⓒ Ⓓ	85 Ⓐ Ⓑ Ⓒ Ⓓ	95 Ⓐ Ⓑ Ⓒ Ⓓ	105 Ⓐ Ⓑ Ⓒ Ⓓ
64 Ⓐ Ⓑ Ⓒ Ⓓ	75 Ⓐ Ⓑ Ⓒ Ⓓ	86 Ⓐ Ⓑ Ⓒ Ⓓ	96 Ⓐ Ⓑ Ⓒ Ⓓ	106 Ⓐ Ⓑ Ⓒ Ⓓ
65 Ⓐ Ⓑ Ⓒ Ⓓ	76 Ⓐ Ⓑ Ⓒ Ⓓ	87 Ⓐ Ⓑ Ⓒ Ⓓ	97 Ⓐ Ⓑ Ⓒ Ⓓ	107 Ⓐ Ⓑ Ⓒ Ⓓ
66 Ⓐ Ⓑ Ⓒ Ⓓ	77 Ⓐ Ⓑ Ⓒ Ⓓ	88 Ⓐ Ⓑ Ⓒ Ⓓ	98 Ⓐ Ⓑ Ⓒ Ⓓ	108 Ⓐ Ⓑ Ⓒ Ⓓ
67 Ⓐ Ⓑ Ⓒ Ⓓ	78 Ⓐ Ⓑ Ⓒ Ⓓ	89 Ⓐ Ⓑ Ⓒ Ⓓ	99 Ⓐ Ⓑ Ⓒ Ⓓ	109 Ⓐ Ⓑ Ⓒ Ⓓ
68 Ⓐ Ⓑ Ⓒ Ⓓ	79 Ⓐ Ⓑ Ⓒ Ⓓ	90 Ⓐ Ⓑ Ⓒ Ⓓ	100 Ⓐ Ⓑ Ⓒ Ⓓ	110 Ⓐ Ⓑ Ⓒ Ⓓ
69 Ⓐ Ⓑ Ⓒ Ⓓ	80 Ⓐ Ⓑ Ⓒ Ⓓ	91 Ⓐ Ⓑ Ⓒ Ⓓ	101 Ⓐ Ⓑ Ⓒ Ⓓ	111 Ⓐ Ⓑ Ⓒ Ⓓ
70 Ⓐ Ⓑ Ⓒ Ⓓ	81 Ⓐ Ⓑ Ⓒ Ⓓ	92 Ⓐ Ⓑ Ⓒ Ⓓ	102 Ⓐ Ⓑ Ⓒ Ⓓ	112 Ⓐ Ⓑ Ⓒ Ⓓ
71 Ⓐ Ⓑ Ⓒ Ⓓ	82 Ⓐ Ⓑ Ⓒ Ⓓ			

TEST 3 Reading

113 Ⓐ Ⓑ Ⓒ Ⓓ	126 Ⓐ Ⓑ Ⓒ Ⓓ	139 Ⓐ Ⓑ Ⓒ Ⓓ	151 Ⓐ Ⓑ Ⓒ Ⓓ	163 Ⓐ Ⓑ Ⓒ Ⓓ
114 Ⓐ Ⓑ Ⓒ Ⓓ	127 Ⓐ Ⓑ Ⓒ Ⓓ	140 Ⓐ Ⓑ Ⓒ Ⓓ	152 Ⓐ Ⓑ Ⓒ Ⓓ	164 Ⓐ Ⓑ Ⓒ Ⓓ
115 Ⓐ Ⓑ Ⓒ Ⓓ	128 Ⓐ Ⓑ Ⓒ Ⓓ	141 Ⓐ Ⓑ Ⓒ Ⓓ	153 Ⓐ Ⓑ Ⓒ Ⓓ	165 Ⓐ Ⓑ Ⓒ Ⓓ
116 Ⓐ Ⓑ Ⓒ Ⓓ	129 Ⓐ Ⓑ Ⓒ Ⓓ	142 Ⓐ Ⓑ Ⓒ Ⓓ	154 Ⓐ Ⓑ Ⓒ Ⓓ	166 Ⓐ Ⓑ Ⓒ Ⓓ
117 Ⓐ Ⓑ Ⓒ Ⓓ	130 Ⓐ Ⓑ Ⓒ Ⓓ	143 Ⓐ Ⓑ Ⓒ Ⓓ	155 Ⓐ Ⓑ Ⓒ Ⓓ	167 Ⓐ Ⓑ Ⓒ Ⓓ
118 Ⓐ Ⓑ Ⓒ Ⓓ	131 Ⓐ Ⓑ Ⓒ Ⓓ	144 Ⓐ Ⓑ Ⓒ Ⓓ	156 Ⓐ Ⓑ Ⓒ Ⓓ	168 Ⓐ Ⓑ Ⓒ Ⓓ
119 Ⓐ Ⓑ Ⓒ Ⓓ	132 Ⓐ Ⓑ Ⓒ Ⓓ	145 Ⓐ Ⓑ Ⓒ Ⓓ	157 Ⓐ Ⓑ Ⓒ Ⓓ	169 Ⓐ Ⓑ Ⓒ Ⓓ
120 Ⓐ Ⓑ Ⓒ Ⓓ	133 Ⓐ Ⓑ Ⓒ Ⓓ	146 Ⓐ Ⓑ Ⓒ Ⓓ	158 Ⓐ Ⓑ Ⓒ Ⓓ	170 Ⓐ Ⓑ Ⓒ Ⓓ
121 Ⓐ Ⓑ Ⓒ Ⓓ	134 Ⓐ Ⓑ Ⓒ Ⓓ	147 Ⓐ Ⓑ Ⓒ Ⓓ	159 Ⓐ Ⓑ Ⓒ Ⓓ	171 Ⓐ Ⓑ Ⓒ Ⓓ
122 Ⓐ Ⓑ Ⓒ Ⓓ	135 Ⓐ Ⓑ Ⓒ Ⓓ	148 Ⓐ Ⓑ Ⓒ Ⓓ	160 Ⓐ Ⓑ Ⓒ Ⓓ	172 Ⓐ Ⓑ Ⓒ Ⓓ
123 Ⓐ Ⓑ Ⓒ Ⓓ	136 Ⓐ Ⓑ Ⓒ Ⓓ	149 Ⓐ Ⓑ Ⓒ Ⓓ	161 Ⓐ Ⓑ Ⓒ Ⓓ	173 Ⓐ Ⓑ Ⓒ Ⓓ
124 Ⓐ Ⓑ Ⓒ Ⓓ	137 Ⓐ Ⓑ Ⓒ Ⓓ	150 Ⓐ Ⓑ Ⓒ Ⓓ	162 Ⓐ Ⓑ Ⓒ Ⓓ	174 Ⓐ Ⓑ Ⓒ Ⓓ
125 Ⓐ Ⓑ Ⓒ Ⓓ	138 Ⓐ Ⓑ Ⓒ Ⓓ			

CUT HERE

Answer Sheet for Practice HSPT Exam 1

TEST 4   Mathematics

175 Ⓐ Ⓑ Ⓒ Ⓓ	188 Ⓐ Ⓑ Ⓒ Ⓓ	201 Ⓐ Ⓑ Ⓒ Ⓓ	214 Ⓐ Ⓑ Ⓒ Ⓓ	227 Ⓐ Ⓑ Ⓒ Ⓓ
176 Ⓐ Ⓑ Ⓒ Ⓓ	189 Ⓐ Ⓑ Ⓒ Ⓓ	202 Ⓐ Ⓑ Ⓒ Ⓓ	215 Ⓐ Ⓑ Ⓒ Ⓓ	228 Ⓐ Ⓑ Ⓒ Ⓓ
177 Ⓐ Ⓑ Ⓒ Ⓓ	190 Ⓐ Ⓑ Ⓒ Ⓓ	203 Ⓐ Ⓑ Ⓒ Ⓓ	216 Ⓐ Ⓑ Ⓒ Ⓓ	229 Ⓐ Ⓑ Ⓒ Ⓓ
178 Ⓐ Ⓑ Ⓒ Ⓓ	191 Ⓐ Ⓑ Ⓒ Ⓓ	204 Ⓐ Ⓑ Ⓒ Ⓓ	217 Ⓐ Ⓑ Ⓒ Ⓓ	230 Ⓐ Ⓑ Ⓒ Ⓓ
179 Ⓐ Ⓑ Ⓒ Ⓓ	192 Ⓐ Ⓑ Ⓒ Ⓓ	205 Ⓐ Ⓑ Ⓒ Ⓓ	218 Ⓐ Ⓑ Ⓒ Ⓓ	231 Ⓐ Ⓑ Ⓒ Ⓓ
180 Ⓐ Ⓑ Ⓒ Ⓓ	193 Ⓐ Ⓑ Ⓒ Ⓓ	206 Ⓐ Ⓑ Ⓒ Ⓓ	219 Ⓐ Ⓑ Ⓒ Ⓓ	232 Ⓐ Ⓑ Ⓒ Ⓓ
181 Ⓐ Ⓑ Ⓒ Ⓓ	194 Ⓐ Ⓑ Ⓒ Ⓓ	207 Ⓐ Ⓑ Ⓒ Ⓓ	220 Ⓐ Ⓑ Ⓒ Ⓓ	233 Ⓐ Ⓑ Ⓒ Ⓓ
182 Ⓐ Ⓑ Ⓒ Ⓓ	195 Ⓐ Ⓑ Ⓒ Ⓓ	208 Ⓐ Ⓑ Ⓒ Ⓓ	221 Ⓐ Ⓑ Ⓒ Ⓓ	234 Ⓐ Ⓑ Ⓒ Ⓓ
183 Ⓐ Ⓑ Ⓒ Ⓓ	196 Ⓐ Ⓑ Ⓒ Ⓓ	209 Ⓐ Ⓑ Ⓒ Ⓓ	222 Ⓐ Ⓑ Ⓒ Ⓓ	235 Ⓐ Ⓑ Ⓒ Ⓓ
184 Ⓐ Ⓑ Ⓒ Ⓓ	197 Ⓐ Ⓑ Ⓒ Ⓓ	210 Ⓐ Ⓑ Ⓒ Ⓓ	223 Ⓐ Ⓑ Ⓒ Ⓓ	236 Ⓐ Ⓑ Ⓒ Ⓓ
185 Ⓐ Ⓑ Ⓒ Ⓓ	198 Ⓐ Ⓑ Ⓒ Ⓓ	211 Ⓐ Ⓑ Ⓒ Ⓓ	224 Ⓐ Ⓑ Ⓒ Ⓓ	237 Ⓐ Ⓑ Ⓒ Ⓓ
186 Ⓐ Ⓑ Ⓒ Ⓓ	199 Ⓐ Ⓑ Ⓒ Ⓓ	212 Ⓐ Ⓑ Ⓒ Ⓓ	225 Ⓐ Ⓑ Ⓒ Ⓓ	238 Ⓐ Ⓑ Ⓒ Ⓓ
187 Ⓐ Ⓑ Ⓒ Ⓓ	200 Ⓐ Ⓑ Ⓒ Ⓓ	213 Ⓐ Ⓑ Ⓒ Ⓓ	226 Ⓐ Ⓑ Ⓒ Ⓓ	

TEST 5   Language Skills

239 Ⓐ Ⓑ Ⓒ Ⓓ	251 Ⓐ Ⓑ Ⓒ Ⓓ	263 Ⓐ Ⓑ Ⓒ Ⓓ	275 Ⓐ Ⓑ Ⓒ Ⓓ	287 Ⓐ Ⓑ Ⓒ Ⓓ
240 Ⓐ Ⓑ Ⓒ Ⓓ	252 Ⓐ Ⓑ Ⓒ Ⓓ	264 Ⓐ Ⓑ Ⓒ Ⓓ	276 Ⓐ Ⓑ Ⓒ Ⓓ	288 Ⓐ Ⓑ Ⓒ Ⓓ
241 Ⓐ Ⓑ Ⓒ Ⓓ	253 Ⓐ Ⓑ Ⓒ Ⓓ	265 Ⓐ Ⓑ Ⓒ Ⓓ	277 Ⓐ Ⓑ Ⓒ Ⓓ	289 Ⓐ Ⓑ Ⓒ Ⓓ
242 Ⓐ Ⓑ Ⓒ Ⓓ	254 Ⓐ Ⓑ Ⓒ Ⓓ	266 Ⓐ Ⓑ Ⓒ Ⓓ	278 Ⓐ Ⓑ Ⓒ Ⓓ	290 Ⓐ Ⓑ Ⓒ Ⓓ
243 Ⓐ Ⓑ Ⓒ Ⓓ	255 Ⓐ Ⓑ Ⓒ Ⓓ	267 Ⓐ Ⓑ Ⓒ Ⓓ	279 Ⓐ Ⓑ Ⓒ Ⓓ	291 Ⓐ Ⓑ Ⓒ Ⓓ
244 Ⓐ Ⓑ Ⓒ Ⓓ	256 Ⓐ Ⓑ Ⓒ Ⓓ	268 Ⓐ Ⓑ Ⓒ Ⓓ	280 Ⓐ Ⓑ Ⓒ Ⓓ	292 Ⓐ Ⓑ Ⓒ Ⓓ
245 Ⓐ Ⓑ Ⓒ Ⓓ	257 Ⓐ Ⓑ Ⓒ Ⓓ	269 Ⓐ Ⓑ Ⓒ Ⓓ	281 Ⓐ Ⓑ Ⓒ Ⓓ	293 Ⓐ Ⓑ Ⓒ Ⓓ
246 Ⓐ Ⓑ Ⓒ Ⓓ	258 Ⓐ Ⓑ Ⓒ Ⓓ	270 Ⓐ Ⓑ Ⓒ Ⓓ	282 Ⓐ Ⓑ Ⓒ Ⓓ	294 Ⓐ Ⓑ Ⓒ Ⓓ
247 Ⓐ Ⓑ Ⓒ Ⓓ	259 Ⓐ Ⓑ Ⓒ Ⓓ	271 Ⓐ Ⓑ Ⓒ Ⓓ	283 Ⓐ Ⓑ Ⓒ Ⓓ	295 Ⓐ Ⓑ Ⓒ Ⓓ
248 Ⓐ Ⓑ Ⓒ Ⓓ	260 Ⓐ Ⓑ Ⓒ Ⓓ	272 Ⓐ Ⓑ Ⓒ Ⓓ	284 Ⓐ Ⓑ Ⓒ Ⓓ	296 Ⓐ Ⓑ Ⓒ Ⓓ
249 Ⓐ Ⓑ Ⓒ Ⓓ	261 Ⓐ Ⓑ Ⓒ Ⓓ	273 Ⓐ Ⓑ Ⓒ Ⓓ	285 Ⓐ Ⓑ Ⓒ Ⓓ	297 Ⓐ Ⓑ Ⓒ Ⓓ
250 Ⓐ Ⓑ Ⓒ Ⓓ	262 Ⓐ Ⓑ Ⓒ Ⓓ	274 Ⓐ Ⓑ Ⓒ Ⓓ	286 Ⓐ Ⓑ Ⓒ Ⓓ	298 Ⓐ Ⓑ Ⓒ Ⓓ

Practice HSPT Exam 1

Test 1: Verbal Skills

Time: 16 Minutes

Directions: Select the choice that best answers the following questions.

1. Talk is to shout as dislike is to:

   A. scream
   B. detest
   C. frighten
   D. admire

2. Conductor is to orchestra as shepherd is to:

   A. film
   B. canine
   C. control
   D. flock

3. Repeal most nearly means:

   A. abolish
   B. build
   C. support
   D. change

4. A poignant story is:

   A. absurd
   B. touching
   C. poisonous
   D. hilarious

5. Sue has a higher batting average than Ted. Rod has a higher batting average than Ellen, but it is not as high as Sue's. Ted has the highest batting average. If the first two statements are true, the third is:

   A. true
   B. false
   C. uncertain

6. Which word does *not* belong with the others?

   A. butter
   B. lard
   C. margarine
   D. suet

7. Which word does *not* belong with the others?

   A. incandescent
   B. florescent
   C. halogen
   D. laser

8. Passive is the *opposite* of:

   A. angry
   B. calm
   C. active
   D. conservative

9. Tool is to drill as poem is to:

   A. popular song
   B. sewing machine
   C. nursery rhyme
   D. mystery story

10. An archaic expression is:

    A. religious
    B. arched
    C. unattractive
    D. old-fashioned

11. Culmination most nearly means:

    A. combination
    B. beginning
    C. climax
    D. continuation

GO ON TO THE NEXT PAGE

12. All cows are grass eaters. Elsie eats grass. Elsie is a cow. If the first two statements are true, the third is:

A. true
B. false
C. uncertain

13. Which word does *not* belong with the others?

A. citrus
B. lemon
C. orange
D. lime

14. Which word does *not* belong with the others?

A. violin
B. trumpet
C. harp
D. cello

15. Recall is the *opposite* of:

A. remember
B. lose
C. forget
D. think

16. Civil is the *opposite* of:

A. illegal
B. rude
C. reveal
D. gracious

17. Tension is to stress as virus is to:

A. living
B. disease
C. bacteria
D. immunity

18. Undermines most nearly means:

A. asserts
B. tunnels
C. weakens
D. suggests

19. Blooms have more feathers than crats. Nefts have more feathers than pobs. Blooms have more feathers than pobs. If the first two statements are true, the third is:

A. true
B. false
C. uncertain

20. Which word does *not* belong with the others?

A. food
B. pizza
C. salad
D. jelly

21. Decay is the *opposite* of:

A. descend
B. grow
C. accept
D. find

22. Which word does *not* belong with the others?

A. aroma
B. stench
C. perfume
D. fragrance

23. Which word does *not* belong with the others?

A. durable
B. fragile
C. delicate
D. brittle

24. Broad Street is wider than Main Street. Main Street is narrower than First Street. Broad Street is wider than First Street. If the first two statements are true, the third is:

A. true
B. false
C. uncertain

25. A frivolous answer is:

A. relaxed
B. silly
C. serious
D. frilly

26. Exacerbate most nearly means:

A. worsen
B. scratch
C. improve
D. trap

27. Miser is to money as glutton is to:

A. food
B. envy
C. literature
D. nutrients

28. Proud is to humble as funny is to:

A. intellectual
B. energetic
C. serious
D. confident

29. Depicted most nearly means:

A. told
B. duplicated
C. showed
D. resemble

30. All rasks are striped blens. No flying blens are striped. No rasks fly. If the first two statements are true, the third is:

A. true
B. false
C. uncertain

31. Which word does *not* belong with the others?

A. crab
B. clam
C. shark
D. lobster

32. Which word does *not* belong with the others?

A. broccoli
B. spinach
C. brussel sprouts
D. tomato

33. Devoid is the *opposite* of:

A. lacking
B. emptying
C. having
D. taking

34. Bouquet is to vase as garbage is to:

A. urn
B. stomach
C. garbage can
D. carton

35. Something that is indeterminable is:

A. unknowable
B. partial
C. definite
D. transparent

36. Morphology most nearly means:

A. size
B. color
C. structure
D. material

37. A is south of B. B is south of C. C is north of A. If the first two statements are true, the third is:

A. true
B. false
C. uncertain

38. Nan runs faster than Pam. Mike runs faster than Nan but slower than Pat. Pam is the slowest runner. If the first two statements are true, the third is:

A. true
B. false
C. uncertain

39. Which word does *not* belong with the others?

A. steak
B. sugar
C. sandwich
D. stew

40. Which word does *not* belong with the others?

A. kindergarten
B. high school
C. college
D. education

GO ON TO THE NEXT PAGE

41. Prelude is the *opposite* of:

A. preclude
B. intermission
C. interlude
D. conclusion

42. Which word does *not* belong with the others?

A. tennis
B. wrestling
C. baseball
D. gymnastics

43. Which word does *not* belong with the others?

A. microscope
B. telescope
C. vision
D. magnifying glass

44. Carol is a student at State College. Residents of the state where the college is located do not pay tuition fees. Carol does not pay tuition fees. If the first two statements are true, the third is:

A. true
B. false
C. uncertain

45. A lucid explanation is:

A. light
B. confusing
C. clear
D. dull

46. Revere most nearly means:

A. esteem
B. pray
C. consider
D. age

47. Candid is to truthful as angry is to:

A. harmony
B. enraged
C. connected
D. unpleasant

48. Ooze is the *opposite* of:

A. pour
B. drink
C. river
D. zoo

49. Tradition is the *opposite* of:

A. custom
B. transition
C. novelty
D. treason

50. If grapes cost more than apples, fewer people buy grapes than apples. The price of grapes has risen above the price of apples. Sales of grapes have decreased. If the first two statements are true, the third is:

A. true
B. false
C. uncertain

51. Link is to undo as forget is to:

A. remember
B. think
C. careless
D. guess

52. Which word does *not* belong with the others?

A. suits
B. diamonds
C. clubs
D. hearts

53. Which word does *not* belong with the others?

A. key
B. can opener
C. combination
D. open

54. An audacious act is:

A. loud
B. cowardly
C. unimportant
D. bold

55. An austere room is:

    A. crowded
    B. tuneful
    C. frightening
    D. bare

56. Barometer is to pressure as ruler is to:

    A. cutting
    B. length
    C. thickness
    D. pliers

57. Nonrecycled paper is produced from wood pulp. My new computer was packed in a box made from wood pulp. The computer was in a paper box. If the first two statements are true, the third is:

    A. true
    B. false
    C. uncertain

58. Nadir most nearly means:

    A. pinnacle
    B. outstanding
    C. bottom
    D. average

59. Which word does *not* belong with the others?

    A. glove
    B. hat
    C. scarf
    D. swimsuit

60. Permit is the *opposite* of:

    A. license
    B. allow
    C. forbid
    D. persuade

IF YOU FINISH BEFORE TIME IS CALLED, CHECK YOUR WORK ON THIS SECTION ONLY. DO NOT WORK ON ANY OTHER SECTION IN THE TEST.

STOP

Test 2: Quantitative Skills

Time: 30 Minutes

Directions: Select the choice that best answers the following questions.

61. What number, when squared, is equal to the sum of 10 and 15?

    A. 3
    B. 4
    C. 5
    D. 6

62. What number should come next in the series 7, 11, 15, 19, ___?

    A. 21
    B. 22
    C. 23
    D. 24

63. Examine (a), (b), and (c) and find the best answer.

    (a) $2^2 + 3^2$
    (b) $(2 + 3)^2$
    (c) 5^2

    A. (a) is greater than (b) and (c).
    B. (a) is equal to (c) and less than (b).
    C. (b) and (c) are equal and greater than (a).
    D. (a), (b), and (c) are equal.

64. $\frac{1}{9}$ of what number is equal to $\frac{1}{10}$ of 70?

    A. 54
    B. 63
    C. 72
    D. 81

65. What number should come next in the series 1, 3, 9, 27, ___?

    A. 36
    B. 54
    C. 72
    D. 81

66. Examine the following figure, and select the best answer.

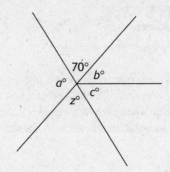

    A. $a = b + c = z$
    B. $z > a > b$
    C. $a = b + c > z$
    D. $b + c > z > a$

67. What number should fill in the blank in the series 8, 6, 9, 7, ___, 8?

    A. 9
    B. 10
    C. 11
    D. 12

68. The square of what number is equal to the cube of 4?

    A. 6
    B. 8
    C. 10
    D. 12

69. What number should come next in the series 16, 8, 4, 2, ___?

    A. 1
    B. 0
    C. −2
    D. −4

70. The number that is 15 more than 20 is the same as the product of 5 and what number?

   A.   7
   B.   9
   C.   11
   D.   13

71. Examine (a), (b), and (c) and find the best answer.

   (a) $(12 - 3)(2 + 1)$
   (b) $12 - 3(2 + 1)$
   (c) $12 - 3 \times 2 + 1$

   A.   (a) is greater than (b) and (c).
   B.   (a) is equal to (c) and less than (b).
   C.   (b) and (c) are equal and greater than (a).
   D.   (a), (b), and (c) are equal.

72. Lines l_1 and l_2 are parallel. Examine the figure and select the best answer.

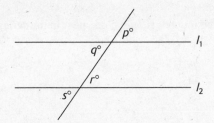

   A. $p = q = r = s$
   B. $p + q > r + s$
   C. $r + s > p + q$
   D. $r + q > p + s$

73. What number should come next in the series 2, 3, 5, 8, 12, ___?

   A.   14
   B.   16
   C.   17
   D.   19

74. If the difference of 25 and 17 is equal to 200% of a number, then the number is:

   A.   4
   B.   8
   C.   16
   D.   32

75. Examine (a), (b), and (c) and find the best answer.

   (a) $\sqrt{\dfrac{1}{4}}$
   (b) $\dfrac{1}{4}$
   (c) $\left(\dfrac{1}{4}\right)^2$

   A.   (a) is greater than (b) and (c).
   B.   (a) is equal to (c) and less than (b).
   C.   (b) and (c) are equal and greater than (a).
   D.   (a), (b), and (c) are equal.

76. One third of the sum of 10, 11, and 12 is equal to:

   A.   9
   B.   10
   C.   11
   D.   13

77. What number should fill in the blank in the series 5, −6, 7, −8, 9, ___, 11?

   A.   −11
   B.   −10
   C.   10
   D.   11

78. The following figure is a circle with center O. Examine the figure and choose the best answer.

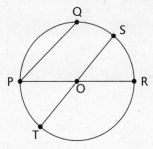

   A. $SO = RO = PQ$
   B. $ST = PR > PQ$
   C. $PQ = PO > PR$
   D. $PO + OR = SO + TO = 2PQ$

79. What number should come next in the series 12, 14, 18, 24, 32, ___?

   A.   36
   B.   38
   C.   40
   D.   42

GO ON TO THE NEXT PAGE

80. Ten percent of what number is equal to 50% of 16?

    A. 50

    B. 60

    C. 70

    D. 80

81. Examine (a), (b), and (c) and find the best answer.

    (a) 6.15×10^2

    (b) $61,500 \times 10^{-2}$

    (c) 61.5×10

    A. (a) is greater than (b) and (c).

    B. (a) is equal to (c) and less than (b).

    C. (b) and (c) are equal and greater than (a).

    D. (a), (b), and (c) are equal.

82. What number should come next in the series 1, 3, 2, 6, 3, 9, 4, ___?

    A. 8

    B. 10

    C. 11

    D. 12

83. If the product of 4 and a number is 24, then $\frac{1}{3}$ of the number is:

    A. 2

    B. 3

    C. 4

    D. 5

84. What number should come next in the series 9, 13, 18, 22, 27, ___?

    A. 31

    B. 32

    C. 33

    D. 35

85. Examine the following figure and select the best answer.

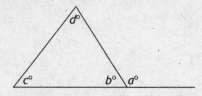

    A. $a = d > c$

    B. $a + b < c + d$

    C. $c > d > a$

    D. $a + b = b + c + d$

86. One eighth of the difference between 84 and 20 is equal to what number?

    A. 6

    B. 8

    C. 10

    D. 12

87. What number should come next in the series 12, 24, 20, 40, 36, ___?

    A. 48

    B. 54

    C. 68

    D. 72

88. Examine (a), (b), and (c) and find the best answer.

    (a) 52,491 rounded to the nearest hundred

    (b) 52,571 rounded to the nearest thousand

    (c) 53,021 rounded to the nearest hundred

    A. (a) is greater than (b) and (c).

    B. (a) is equal to (c) and less than (b).

    C. (b) and (c) are equal and greater than (a).

    D. (a), (b), and (c) are equal.

89. What number should come next in the series 78, 70, 63, 57, 52, ___?

    A. 50

    B. 48

    C. 47

    D. 46

90. Two thirds of what number is equal to $\frac{1}{8}$ of 64?

    A. 6
    B. 9
    C. 12
    D. 15

91. What number should come next in the series 72, 36, 12, 6, 2, ___?

    A. 1
    B. 0
    C. −1
    D. −2

92. *WXYZ* is a rectangle. Select the best answer.

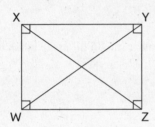

    A. $WY + YZ = XZ + WZ$
    B. $XZ = WY > XY$
    C. $XW = YZ > XZ$
    D. $WZ = XY = WY$

93. If the sum of 13 and 17 is equal to 25% of a number, then the number is equal to:

    A. 100
    B. 108
    C. 120
    D. 124

94. What number should fill in the blank in the series 36, 6, 25, 5, 16, ___, 9?

    A. 8
    B. 6
    C. 4
    D. 2

95. Examine (a), (b), and (c) and find the best answer.

    (a)   The least common multiple of 7 and 5
    (b)   The least common multiple of 8 and 4
    (c)   The least common multiple of 12 and 8

    A. (a) is greater than (b) and (c).
    B. (a) is equal to (c) and less than (b).
    C. (b) and (c) are equal and greater than (a).
    D. (a), (b), and (c) are equal.

96. What number, when tripled, is equal to twice the number 21?

    A. 7
    B. 12
    C. 14
    D. 15

97. What number should fill in the blank in the series 200, 180, 175, 155, 150, ___, 125?

    A. 145
    B. 140
    C. 135
    D. 130

98. The following figure shows a square and an isosceles triangle. In the triangle, $BE = ED$.

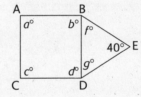

    A. $f = g < a$
    B. $c = d < f$
    C. $f + g > a + b$
    D. $a = b = f$

99. What number should come next in the series 35, 36, 34, 37, 33, ___?

    A. 38
    B. 36
    C. 35
    D. 33

GO ON TO THE NEXT PAGE

100. What number, when reduced by 10% of itself, is equal to 27?

    A. 30

    B. 32

    C. 34

    D. 36

101. What number is equal to 35% of the sum of 84 and 116?

    A. 35

    B. 70

    C. 105

    D. 140

102. Examine (a), (b), and (c) and find the best answer.

    (a) $\dfrac{0.03}{1,000}$

    (b) 0.03%

    (c) 0.3×0.001

    A. (a) is greater than (b) and (c).

    B. (a) is equal to (c) and less than (b).

    C. (b) and (c) are equal and greater than (a).

    D. (a), (b), and (c) are equal.

103. What number, when doubled and then increased by 3, is equal to 17?

    A. 6

    B. 7

    C. 8

    D. 9

104. What number should come next in the series 1, 2, 6, 24, 120, ___?

    A. 240

    B. 360

    C. 540

    D. 720

105. Three hundred percent of what number is equal to the square of 9?

    A. 18

    B. 21

    C. 24

    D. 27

106. In the following figure, *ABC* is an equilateral triangle. Select the best answer.

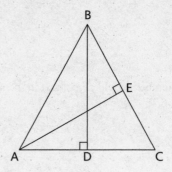

    A. $AE = BD = BC$

    B. $AC = BC > BD$

    C. $AB = BC < BD$

    D. $AE = BD < BC$

107. What number should fill in the blank in the series 12, 17, 27, 42, ___, 87?

    A. 47

    B. 52

    C. 57

    D. 62

108. What number, when squared and then decreased by 3, is equal to the product of 11 and 2?

    A. 5

    B. 6

    C. 7

    D. 8

109. Examine (a), (b), and (c) and find the best answer.

    (a) 7^5

    (b) 7^6

    (c) $(7^2)^3$

    A. (a) is greater than (b) and (c).

    B. (a) is equal to (c) and less than (b).

    C. (b) and (c) are equal and greater than (a).

    D. (a), (b), and (c) are equal.

110. In the following figure, all angles shown are right angles. Examine the figure and select the best answer.

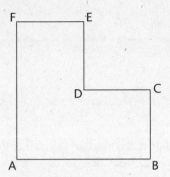

A. $EF = DE = BC$
B. $BC + DE = AF$
C. $EF + CD = AF$
D. $BC + CE > AF$

111. What number should fill in the blank in the series 20, 10, 18, 9, 16, 8, ___, 7

A. 15
B. 14
C. 13
D. 12

112. The following figure consists of two side-by-side squares. Examine the figure and sleect the best answer.

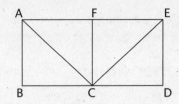

A. $AB + BC = AC + CE$
B. $AF < FC < AC$
C. $AC = CE > CD$
D. $CD = DE = AC$

IF YOU FINISH BEFORE TIME IS CALLED, CHECK YOUR WORK ON THIS SECTION ONLY. DO NOT WORK ON ANY OTHER SECTION IN THE TEST.

Test 3: Reading

Time: 25 Minutes

Directions: In this test, select the answer choice that best satisfies the question.

Comprehension

For questions 113–152, read each passage carefully. Then select the choice that best answers the questions that follow each passage.

Liberia is a nation in Africa that has special ties with the United States. In 1816, the American Colonization Society was founded to resettle freed American slaves in Africa. The <u>indigenous</u> rulers of the land granted a tract of land to the society. In 1820, Americans began arriving in the country. In 1824, an agent of the society named the land Liberia. The name is derived from the Latin word for free.

Many areas of the country are named for American states and cities. These include Maryland, New Georgia, and Providence Island. The capital, Monrovia, is named for American president James Monroe. English is the nation's official language. The Liberian constitution was modeled on that of the United States. Liberians pledge allegiance to their flag, which resembles the American flag, but it has only one star. Another tie with the United States is the country's electrical system. The Liberian and American systems are <u>compatible</u>. American appliances can be used by plugging them into a wall socket. No adapter or converter is needed.

Many natives wanted their children to be educated with the Americo-Liberians to learn their ways. Some Liberians dropped their African names and adopted American names. Americo-Liberians and the country's original peoples have intermarried. Thus, it is uncertain how many Liberians are descended only from the original American immigrants. Nevertheless, many Liberians view the United States as their mother country. Interestingly, some descendants of Americo-Liberians have performed a reverse migration. They now live in the United States.

113. Liberia was named by:

    A.   its native rulers
    B.   immigrants to the country
    C.   an American
    D.   James Madison

114. According to the passage, the goal of the American Colonization Society was:

    A.   to found a new nation
    B.   to transplant American culture to Africa
    C.   to help the people who already lived in the nation
    D.   to find a place for freed slaves to live

115. The word <u>indigenous</u>, as underlined and used in this passage, most nearly means:

    A.   angry
    B.   native
    C.   powerful
    D.   considerate

116. The flag of Liberia:

    A.   has red and white stripes
    B.   has stars representing the states in the country
    C.   looks strange to an American
    D.   uses native cultural designs

117. The word <u>compatible</u>, as underlined and used in this passage, most nearly means:

    A.   can be contrasted with
    B.   works the same way as
    C.   differs from
    D.   includes

118. The best title for this passage is:

    A.   A History of Liberia
    B.   An African Nation
    C.   America's Freed Slaves
    D.   Liberia and America

119. Which of the following is correct?

    A. All Americo-Liberians live in Liberia.

    B. Most Liberians live in Monrovia.

    C. Liberian laws follow the United States Constitution.

    D. Liberians pledge allegiance to their flag.

120. A reason for the American settlement in Liberia was to:

    A. found a new nation

    B. find a place to live in Africa for freed American slaves

    C. teach American ways to the native rulers of the land

    D. set up businesses and find trading partners

121. It is not clear how many Liberians are descendants of the original Americo-Liberians because:

    A. some Liberians changed their names

    B. the two peoples intermarried

    C. native Liberians adopted Americo-Liberian culture

    D. all of the above

122. Americans visiting Liberia:

    A. would feel they were in a very strange place

    B. need to buy converters for electrical appliances

    C. could easily use their own electric hair dryers

    D. might want to hire a translator

In an ordinary light bulb, when the filament is heated, electrons release energy and emit bits of light known as photons. But light can also be created without heat. When this occurs, the phenomenon is known as luminescence.

Some animals create light from within their bodies. This process is called bioluminescence. Fireflies are the most familiar bioluminescent creatures. Some sea creatures also make their own light. In fireflies, special cells in the insect's abdomen contain a chemical that makes light when combined with oxygen. An enzyme derived from the chemical speeds up the reaction with oxygen. The oxygen reaches the cells through a tube in the abdomen. The fireflies light up to attract a mate, but scientists do not know if the flashing of the light is controlled by nerve cells in the insect or by the supply of oxygen.

Luminescence is used in common objects like televisions, neon lights, and light sticks. These devices, of course, are not bioluminescent. In a light stick, the light is the product of a chemical reaction. Inside the light stick are two liquid chemical compounds separated by a small glass enclosure. The middle of the light stick contains another chemical that is an activator. When a person bends the light stick, the glass breaks open, and the two previously separated chemicals flow together. The activator causes the chemical reaction to begin. The reactions activate the electrons that then give off photons of light. The color of the light varies according to what dyes have been placed in the chemicals.

Because light sticks don't glow very brightly, they are not useful for lighting a room. But they are wonderful toys, especially for trick-or-treating at Halloween.

123. The word emit, as underlined and used in this passage, most nearly means:

    A. reduce

    B. release

    C. increase

    D. heat up

124. Fireflies light up to:

    A. control their oxygen supply

    B. react to nerve impulses

    C. communicate with each other

    D. attract a mate

125. Bioluminescence requires the presence of:

    A. oxygen

    B. water

    C. a filament

    D. heat

126. The word activate, as underlined and used in this passage, most nearly means:

    A. decrease the number of

    B. heat up

    C. set in motion

    D. shake

127. The author's purpose in writing this selection was most probably to:

    A. increase the sale of light sticks

    B. teach people how to make light sticks

    C. explain luminescence

    D. define the phenomenon of light

GO ON TO THE NEXT PAGE

128. The word <u>enclosure</u>, as underlined and used in this passage, most nearly means:

A. container
B. door
C. pump
D. vacuum

129. Neon lights glow because of:

A. luminescence
B. bioluminescence
C. heating of electrons
D. filaments within them

130. The glow of light sticks is produced by:

A. chemical reactions
B. biological reactions
C. combining heat and oxygen
D. the motion of liquids

131. Light sticks come in different colors as a result of:

A. glass
B. neon
C. photons
D. dyes

132. According to the information in this passage, light sticks might be useful:

A. in traffic lights
B. as flashlights
C. to light a kitchen
D. as toys

During the 1984 Summer Olympic Games, American Carl Lewis won four gold medals. He placed first in the 100 meter and 200 meter races, the 4 by 100 meter relay, and the long jump. No American had won four gold medals in track since Jesse Owen had accomplished the <u>feat</u> in 1936. But Carl Lewis never became a popular hero.

Stories about Lewis in the media suggested he was selfish and conceited. These <u>perceptions</u> of Lewis denied him the celebrity that would be expected as a result of his achievement.

The newspapers reported that Lewis decided not to live at the Olympic Village. Although Olympic officials argued with him, he eventually got his own way. His choice had not been a result of a desire to be alone; he wanted to avoid distractions. When he won the 100 meter race, he grabbed an American flag from someone in the stands and waved it during his victory lap. The media

accused him of showing off. But his reaction was one of joyous enthusiasm.

Contestants in the long jump can make three attempts. Lewis's distance on his first attempt assured him of first place. The crowd wanted him to use his two other attempts to try to break Bob Beamon's world record. But he did not jump again. A New York newspaper criticized him. He could have taken all his jumps in an attempt to break the record. He could have given his all and <u>thrown caution to the wind</u>, the article stated. The article implied that Lewis was either lazy or feared injury. But what would he have gained from the attempts? The long jump preceded the running events he had entered. Lewis needed to be prepared to win more medals. Breaking Bob Beamon's record would not help the American Olympic team.

133. Carl Lewis won:

A. three races
B. three events
C. two relays
D. four races

134. The word <u>feat</u>, as underlined and used in this passage, most nearly means:

A. serious problem
B. great victory
C. important decision
D. outstanding act

135. Lewis did not want to live at the Olympic Village because:

A. the officials told him not to
B. the village was far from the stadium where events were held
C. he wanted to stay focused on his events
D. he enjoyed breaking rules

136. The word <u>perceptions</u>, as underlined and used in this massage, most nearly means:

A. criticisms
B. discussions
C. impressions
D. comments

137. The author most likely:

A. thinks Lewis was an average athlete
B. wants Lewis to have tried to break the long jump record
C. believes Lewis was selfish
D. disagrees with the criticism of Lewis

138. According to the author, Lewis ran with the flag because of:

    A. showing off
    B. great emotion
    C. stealing it
    D. crowd applause

139. The world record holder in the long jump prior to the 1984 Olympics was:

    A. Carl Lewis
    B. Jesse Owens
    C. Bob Beamon
    D. none of the above

140. This passage would most likely have appeared in:

    A. an encyclopedia
    B. a magazine article
    C. the official records of the Olympics
    D. a history book

141. The phrase thrown caution to the wind, as underlined and used in this passage, most probably means:

    A. not worried about possible results
    B. ignored what people said
    C. run with the wind at his back
    D. given the event his best effort

142. The last sentence of the passage implies that the author thinks Lewis's decision was:

    A. unlikely
    B. unkind
    C. unselfish
    D. unimportant

If you touch a coral reef, it feels like stone. Most of the reef is stone—limestone. But the lifeless stone is the product of and the protection for great vitality in the ocean.

Corals are animals that have a cylindrical body and a saclike internal cavity. Their bodies contain great numbers of plants, tiny algae, which help the coral by absorbing its waste. They convert the waste to proteins for their own use, and, with the aid of sunlight, like most plants, produce carbohydrates. When they do this, like other plants, they release oxygen, which the coral needs to breathe.

The coral animal exudes limestone around itself to form a protective chamber. When the chamber has been built, the animal sends out tiny threads from which a new animal sprouts. The new animal then deposits limestone around itself, forming a shell open only at the top. This process buries the animal beneath it, which, having no access to food or oxygen, dies. As the animal on the bottom layer is buried, it dies, but its empty limestone shell remains. So the coral reef is a thin layer of living creatures on top of a mass of lifeless limestone.

Creatures proliferate around the reefs. The living coral provides food for fish. Some fish are able to grind up the limestone to reach the living animal. Other creatures suck the animal out.

Starfish squirt a fluid into the limestone that dissolves the animals, and the starfish sip the result. In addition to food, reefs provide excellent places to hide or to live. Clams and barnacles bore holes into the limestone to create a shelter. Eels wait in spaces between the branches of coral to dart out at their prey. Small fish hide in the coral's dense formation. Sea worms climb continuously around the network of branches.

143. The word vitality, as underlined and used in the passage, most nearly means:

    A. food
    B. depth
    C. verve
    D. life

144. The algae in corals:

    A. help themselves and the animals
    B. do not require sunlight
    C. breathe in oxygen
    D. do not use protein

145. As described in the passage, coral animals are closest in shape to:

    A. starfish
    B. algae
    C. clams
    D. worms

146. According to the passage, coral reproduce by:

    A. laying eggs
    B. a budding process
    C. sending out algae
    D. building a nest of threads

GO ON TO THE NEXT PAGE

147. The word <u>exudes</u>, as underlined and used in the passage, most nearly means:

A. oozes
B. hides
C. cuts
D. breathes

148. According to the passage, reefs help sea life by providing it with:

A. food
B. hiding places
C. places to breed
D. all of the above

149. Coral animals die because they:

A. grow old
B. have completed the reproductive cycle
C. are buried beneath living animals
D. no longer contain plants

150. The word <u>proliferate</u>, as underlined and used in the passage, most nearly means:

A. grow vigorously
B. swim quickly
C. dive quickly
D. eat frequently

151. A good title for this passage is:

A. "How Coral Grows"
B. "Life in the Coral Reef"
C. "Ocean Creatures"
D. "A Source of Limestone"

152. The author of the passage is most likely a:

A. marine biologist
B. deep sea diver
C. magazine writer
D. novelist

Vocabulary

For questions 153–174, select the word that means the same, or almost the same, as the underlined word.

153. <u>assent</u> to your request

A. false belief
B. commission
C. agreement
D. raid

154. to <u>suppress</u> the information

A. divide
B. refine
C. startle
D. subdue

155. She was <u>confounded</u> by the book.

A. perplexed
B. chatted
C. donated
D. adjusted

156. <u>Integrate</u> the pieces of the puzzle.

A. make into a whole
B. stir up
C. strengthen
D. make identical

157. the <u>serenity</u> of the surrounding

A. seriousness
B. calmness
C. self-satisfaction
D. simplicity

158. an <u>incorrigible</u> child

A. inappropriate
B. unmanageable
C. honest
D. disconnected

159. a <u>curt</u> response

A. secretive
B. vulgar
C. brief
D. greedy

160. <u>aloof</u> to all the people

A. flexible
B. watchful
C. soundless
D. reserved

161. a <u>blight</u> struck the country

    A. storm
    B. bomb
    C. plague
    D. asteroid

162. the mood began to <u>wane</u>

    A. joke
    B. reappear
    C. grieve
    D. decrease

163. <u>feigned</u> an illness

    A. pretended
    B. ignored
    C. achieved
    D. dreaded

164. <u>dubious</u> about her answer

    A. hateful
    B. suspicious
    C. frightened
    D. tired

165. <u>acute</u> hearing

    A. certain
    B. keen
    C. bitter
    D. genuine

166. <u>clientele</u> of the store

    A. legal body
    B. customers
    C. board of directors
    D. servants

167. <u>succumb</u> to the enemy

    A. follow
    B. help
    C. respond
    D. yield

168. walked with a <u>slouch</u>

    A. cane
    B. limp
    C. stoop
    D. skip

169. <u>infringe</u> on her privacy

    A. trespass
    B. expand
    C. disappoint
    D. weaken

170. <u>uncanny</u> ability to sleep anywhere

    A. ill-humored
    B. immature
    C. weird
    D. unrestrained

171. <u>submissive</u> to his teachers

    A. unintelligent
    B. underhanded
    C. meek
    D. enthusiastic

172. He was his <u>peer</u>.

    A. ancestor
    B. teacher
    C. judge
    D. equal

173. <u>Eulogize</u> his late uncle.

    A. kill
    B. apologize
    C. glorify
    D. soften

174. <u>Innovation</u> requires creativity.

    A. change
    B. prayer
    C. hint
    D. restraint

IF YOU FINISH BEFORE TIME IS CALLED, CHECK YOUR WORK ON THIS SECTION ONLY. DO NOT WORK ON ANY OTHER SECTION IN THE TEST.

Test 4: Mathematics

Time: 45 Minutes

Directions: Select the answer choice that best satisfies the question.

Mathematical Concepts

For questions 175–198, select the choice that best answers the following questions. You can use scratch paper to figure out your answers.

175. A bread recipe calls for $3\frac{1}{4}$ cups of flour. If you only have $2\frac{1}{8}$ cups, how much more flour is needed?

   A. $1\frac{1}{8}$

   B. $1\frac{1}{4}$

   C. $1\frac{3}{8}$

   D. $1\frac{3}{4}$

176. An employee earns $8.25 an hour. In 30 hours, what earnings are made?

   A. $240.00
   B. $247.50
   C. $250.00
   D. $255.75

177. There are 72 freshmen in the band. If freshmen make up $\frac{1}{3}$ of the entire band, the total number of students in the band is:

   A. 24
   B. 72
   C. 144
   D. 216

178. Brian uses a $20 bill to buy a magazine for $3.95. How much change should he receive?

   A. $16.05
   B. $16.95
   C. $17.05
   D. $17.95

179. One-eighth of a bookstore's magazines are sold on a Friday. If $\frac{1}{4}$ of the remaining magazines are sold the next day, what fractional part of the magazines remain at the end of the second day?

   A. $\frac{1}{32}$

   B. $\frac{1}{8}$

   C. $\frac{7}{32}$

   D. $\frac{21}{32}$

180. A machine can produce 8,000 gears in 3 hours. How many gears are produced in one day?

   A. 96,000
   B. 64,000
   C. 32,000
   D. 8,000

181. Jimmy buys 3 candy bars for 45 cents each and two packs of gum for 79 cents each. What is the total cost of this purchase?

   A. $1.24
   B. $2.93
   C. $6.20
   D. $6.24

182. Alex throws a football $7\frac{1}{3}$ yards. Keith throws it $2\frac{1}{2}$ times farther. How much farther did Keith's throw travel than Alex's?

   A. $2\frac{1}{2}$ yards

   B. $7\frac{1}{3}$ yards

   C. 11 yards

   D. $18\frac{1}{3}$ yards

183. This morning, Hazel drove 13 miles to the library and then returned home. In the afternoon, she drove 9 miles to the movies and returned home. How much farther did Hazel travel in the morning?

    A. 4 miles

    B. 6 miles

    C. 8 miles

    D. 9 miles

184. Find the value of $4^3 \times 3^2$.

    A. 343

    B. 576

    C. 16,807

    D. 248,832

185. Prime factor the number 48, and write the prime factorization using exponential notation.

    A. $2^4 \times 3$

    B. $2^3 \times 3^2$

    C. $2^5 \times 3$

    D. 6×8

186. What is the value of $(-1)^{100}(-2)^3$?

    A. -800

    B. -8

    C. 8

    D. 800

187. $4\frac{1}{4} \times 3\frac{2}{3} =$

    A. $7\frac{1}{6}$

    B. $12\frac{1}{6}$

    C. $15\frac{7}{12}$

    D. $15\frac{11}{12}$

188. A car is driven 750 miles in 25 hours. What is the rate of the car in miles per hour?

    A. 30

    B. 60

    C. 65

    D. 75

189. On opening night, 3,127 people attend a new play. The attendance for the next two nights is 2,944 and 3,009. What is the total number of people who saw the play on the first three nights?

    A. 8,070

    B. 8,080

    C. 9,080

    D. 9,800

190. Mark's car mileage in May was 2,374 miles. If 1,752 of those miles were driven for business purposes, how many miles were driven for other than business purposes?

    A. 522

    B. 622

    C. 1,622

    D. 4,126

191. If the average speed of an airplane is 525 miles per hour, how many miles can it travel in 6 hours?

    A. 3,050

    B. 3,120

    C. 3,150

    D. 8,750

192. An equilateral triangle is a triangle in which all three sides are the same length. What is the perimeter of an equilateral triangle whose sides are 5 inches?

    A. 5

    B. 10

    C. 15

    D. 20

193. Which of the following is equal to $12\frac{1}{2}\%$?

    A. $\frac{1}{6}$

    B. $\frac{1}{7}$

    C. $\frac{1}{8}$

    D. $\frac{1}{9}$

194. What is the value of $\left(\frac{1}{10}\right)^4 \times 10^2$?

    A. $\frac{1}{100}$

    B. 10

    C. 100

    D. 1,000,000

GO ON TO THE NEXT PAGE

195. What is the average of 0.5, 0.4, 0.2, 0.1, 0.0 and 0.0?

    A. 0.1

    B. 0.15

    C. 0.2

    D. 0.25

196. $5P - 3Q - (3P - 2Q) =$

    A. $2P - Q$

    B. $2P - 5Q$

    C. $8P - Q$

    D. $8P - 5Q$

197. If $x > y$, and z is positive, which of the following statements is *not* true?

    A. $x + z > y + z$

    B. $z - x > z - y$

    C. $xz > yz$

    D. $\frac{x}{z} > \frac{y}{z}$

198. What is the value of $\frac{14}{3 - y}$ if $y = -4$?

    A. -14

    B. -2

    C. 2

    D. 14

Problem Solving

For questions 199–238, select the choice that best answers the following questions. You can use scratch paper to figure out your answers.

199. How many omelets can be made from 2 dozen eggs if an omelet contains 3 eggs?

    A. 1

    B. 3

    C. 6

    D. 8

200. Two runners finished a race in 80 seconds, another runner finished the race in 72 seconds, and the final runner finished in 68 seconds. The average of these times is:

    A. 73 seconds

    B. 74 seconds

    C. 75 seconds

    D. 76 seconds

201. If 400 people can be seated in 8 subway cars, how many people can be seated in 5 subway cars?

    A. 200

    B. 250

    C. 300

    D. 350

202. Rachel receives $30 for her birthday and $15 for cleaning the garage. If she spends $16 on a CD, how much money does she have left?

    A. $29

    B. $27

    C. $14

    D. $1

203. A television is on sale for 20% off. If the sale price is $800, what was the original price?

    A. $160

    B. $640

    C. $960

    D. $1,000

204. Jasmine earns $9.50 an hour plus 3% commission on all sales made. If her total sales during a 30-hour work week were $500, how much did she earn?

    A. $15

    B. $250

    C. $285

    D. $300

205. The area of one circle is 4 times as large as a smaller circle with a radius of 3 inches. The radius of the larger circle is:

    A. 12 inches

    B. 9 inches

    C. 8 inches

    D. 6 inches

206. Standing by a pole, a boy $3\frac{1}{2}$ feet tall casts a 6 foot shadow. The pole casts a 24 foot shadow. How tall is the pole?

- **A.** 14 feet
- **B.** 18 feet
- **C.** 28 feet
- **D.** 41 feet

207. Peter earns $8.40 an hour plus an overtime rate equal to $1\frac{1}{2}$ times his regular pay for each hour worked beyond 40 hours. What are his total earnings for a 45-hour workweek?

- **A.** $336
- **B.** $370
- **C.** $399
- **D.** $567

208. A sweater originally priced at $40 is on sale for $30. What percent has the sweater been discounted?

- **A.** 25%
- **B.** 33%
- **C.** 70%
- **D.** 75%

209. A cardboard box has a length of 3 feet, a height of $2\frac{1}{2}$ feet and a depth of 2 feet. If the length and depth are doubled, by what percent does the volume of the box change?

- **A.** 200%
- **B.** 300%
- **C.** 400%
- **D.** 600%

210. Mr. Scalici earns a weekly salary of $300 plus 10% commission on all sales. If his total sales last week were $8,350, what were his total earnings?

- **A.** $835
- **B.** $865
- **C.** $1,135
- **D.** $1,835

211. Brett collects 300 stamps one week, 420 stamps the next week, and 180 stamps the last week. He can trade the stamps for collector coins. If 25 stamps earns him one coin, how many coins can Brett collect?

- **A.** 36
- **B.** 50
- **C.** 900
- **D.** 925

212. On a map, 1 centimeter represents 4 miles. A distance of 10 miles is represented by what length on the map?

- **A.** $1\frac{3}{4}$ cm
- **B.** 2 cm
- **C.** $2\frac{1}{2}$ cm
- **D.** 4 cm

213. Jared donates $\frac{4}{13}$ of his paycheck to his favorite charity. If he donates $26.80, what is the amount of his paycheck?

- **A.** $8.25
- **B.** $82.50
- **C.** $87.10
- **D.** $348.40

214. Rachel ran $\frac{1}{2}$ mile in 4 minutes. At this rate, how many miles can she run in 15 minutes?

- **A.** $1\frac{7}{8}$
- **B.** 4
- **C.** 30
- **D.** 60

215. Tiling costs $2.89 per square foot. What is the cost to tile a kitchen that has a dimension of 4 yards by 5 yards?

- **A.** $57.80
- **B.** $173.40
- **C.** $289.00
- **D.** $520.20

GO ON TO THE NEXT PAGE

216. Janet deposited $300 into a savings account earning $5\frac{1}{4}\%$ annually. What is her balance after one year?

A. $15.75
B. $315
C. $315.25
D. $315.75

217. One phone plan charges a $20 monthly fee and $0.08 per minute on every phone call made. Another phone plan charges a $12 monthly fee and $0.12 per minute on each call. After how many minutes is the charge the same for both plans?

A. 60 minutes
B. 90 minutes
C. 120 minutes
D. 200 minutes

218. The length of a rectangle is three times its width. If the perimeter of the rectangle is 48, what is its area?

A. 108
B. 96
C. 54
D. 48

219. Find the value of x in the following equation: $\frac{x}{4} = -9$.

A. -36
B. $-\frac{1}{9}$
C. $-\frac{1}{36}$
D. 13

220. If the sum of three consecutive integers is 57, find the smallest of the integers.

A. 17
B. 18
C. 19
D. 20

221. An airplane flies 50 miles due north, then turns and flies 120 miles due east. How far has the plane flown from its starting point?

A. 70 miles
B. 130 miles
C. 145 miles
D. 170 miles

222. Steve played in 14 basketball games. He scored a total of 53 field goals (2 points each) and 20 free throws (1 point each). What was his average score per game?

A. 5
B. 9
C. 11
D. 126

223. What is the cost of putting grass seed on a 480 square yard field, if a bag of grass seed covers 60 square yards and costs $7.45?

A. $44.70
B. $56.60
C. $57.20
D. $59.60

224. What is the perimeter, in inches, of a rectangular wall that measures 6 feet 4 inches by 8 feet 3 inches?

A. 87 1/2
B. 164
C. 175
D. 350

225. If $\frac{1}{2}$ of a number is 24, what is $\frac{2}{3}$ of the number?

A. 8
B. 16
C. 24
D. 32

226. What is the value of $2^7 - 7^2$?

A. 0
B. 15
C. 67
D. 79

227. Which of the following is equal to $\left(2 \times \frac{1}{10}\right) + \left(3 \times \frac{1}{100}\right) + \left(4 \times \frac{1}{1,000}\right)$?

A. 0.0234
B. 0.234
C. 2.34
D. 4,320

228. An investment of $90,000 is divided among 3 people in the ratio of $2:3:4$. What is the amount of the largest share?

    A. $30,000

    B. $35,000

    C. $37,500

    D. $40,000

229. If each sweater requires $3\frac{3}{4}$ yards of fabric, how many sweaters can be made from 600 yards of fabric?

    A. 150

    B. 160

    C. 170

    D. 180

230. If the length of one side of a $3'' \times 3''$ square is doubled, and the length of the adjacent side is tripled, the perimeter of the new rectangle is how many times bigger than the perimeter of the original square?

    A. 2

    B. $2\frac{1}{2}$

    C. 3

    D. $3\frac{1}{2}$

231. The solution set of the inequality $4x - 3 > 13$ is:

    A. $x < -4$

    B. $x > -4$

    C. $x < 4$

    D. $x > 4$

232. If $\frac{7}{4} = \frac{3}{x}$, then x is equal to:

    A. $\frac{4}{21}$

    B. $\frac{7}{12}$

    C. $\frac{12}{7}$

    D. $\frac{21}{4}$

233. Danny buys electric toothbrushes for $7.50 and sells them for $20. What is his total profit on 40 toothbrushes if there are no other expenses?

    A. $125

    B. $300

    C. $480

    D. $500

234. What is the radius of the largest circle that can be drawn inside a rectangle with the dimensions $10'' \times 6''$?

    A. 3"

    B. 5"

    C. 6"

    D. 10"

235. What is the value of $(2^4)^3 - (2^6)^2$?

    A. 0

    B. 4

    C. 8

    D. 16

236. If $(2x - 3) + (x + 4) + (3x - 7) = 0$, then $6x =$

    A. -6

    B. -1

    C. 1

    D. 6

237. If $x = \sqrt[3]{64}$, then $x^2 =$

    A. 2

    B. 4

    C. 8

    D. 16

238. If John is J years old, and Rusty is 2 years more than twice as old as John, which of the following expressions gives Rusty's age?

    A. $J(J + 2)$

    B. $2J - 2$

    C. $2J + 2$

    D. $\frac{J}{2} - 2$

IF YOU FINISH BEFORE TIME IS CALLED, CHECK YOUR WORK ON THIS SECTION ONLY. DO NOT WORK ON ANY OTHER SECTION IN THE TEST.

STOP

Test 5: Language Skills

Time: 25 Minutes

Directions: In each of the following questions, select that choice that best answers the question.

*In questions 239–250, look for errors in capitalization or punctuation. If you find no mistakes, mark **D** on your answer sheet.*

239.

A. I asked Maria, my cousin, to spend the weekend at my house.
B. "What time will you arrive?" I asked.
C. It's getting late; isn't it time to leave?
D. No mistakes.

240.

A. Let's share that last slice of cake.
B. There's a fly crawling on the icing!
C. Then, help yourself to the whole piece.
D. No mistakes.

241.

A. Kareem's backpack, jacket, and hat were missing from his locker.
B. Didn't he lock it when he left the room?
C. The locker's door was open.
D. No mistakes.

242.

A. "Carlos," asked the coach, "will you take over as the runner at first base?"
B. Craig who is tall plays center on the basketball team.
C. Alexandra's tennis match will be played next Friday.
D. No mistakes.

243.

A. Whose book is that?
B. I found the book under the table, and I took it to the lost and found office.
C. The campus security office wasn't busy.
D. No mistakes.

244.

A. Lee didn't enjoy math class, but he thought biology class was interesting.
B. Biology is one of the life sciences; chemistry is a physical science.
C. Mr. Kinsey teaches biology and Ms. Jong teaches physics.
D. No mistakes.

245.

A. On sunday, the track meet will start at 10:00 A.M.
B. Teams from every school in Queens County will participate.
C. This isn't an interstate competition.
D. No mistakes.

246.

A. The cat licked the last drops of milk from its dish.
B. "Come here, kitty," I said, hoping to pet her.
C. The stubborn cat's tail waved in the air.
D. No mistakes.

247.

A. Who said "If at first you don't succeed, try, try again"?
B. That saying could be from the book *The Little Engine That Could.*
C. It takes patience and desire to keep trying, I am not patient.
D. No mistakes.

248.

   A. "Help!" screamed the swimmer caught in a rip tide.

   B. The lifeguard asked if anyone had heard shouts?

   C. Maria had already pulled the swimmer to shore.

   D. No mistakes.

249.

   A. The children's toys lay scattered around the floor.

   B. The toy box's lid was wide open.

   C. The children spent the summer at their grandparents house.

   D. No mistakes.

250.

   A. Last month's trip to new mexico included a stop at Carlsbad Caverns.

   B. Have you ever seen underground caves before?

   C. Bats' nests hang from the roof of some caves.

   D. No mistakes.

*In questions 251–278, look for errors in usage. If you find no mistakes, mark **D** on your answer sheet.*

251.

   A. Sometimes a person can grow out of their allergies.

   B. School spirit and pride were very high.

   C. July has been more humid this year than it was last year.

   D. No mistakes.

252.

   A. The date of the surprise party will be a secret between you and me.

   B. That pizza is too hot to eat right now.

   C. I'm sure you're going to enjoy this story.

   D. No mistakes.

253.

   A. Whom did the director select to play the part of Hamlet?

   B. I could of been here earlier, but I didn't want to rush.

   C. There were many difficult problems on the math test.

   D. No mistakes.

254.

   A. The meeting between Ann and myself will be next week.

   B. What you have seen is a recreation of a real event.

   C. Each of the paintings is an original work.

   D. No mistakes.

255.

   A. There are the clues that will help to solve the puzzle.

   B. Helen is the fastest of the three runners on the team.

   C. Ron asked if he might go home early.

   D. No mistakes.

256.

   A. The play's third scene occurs in the kitchen.

   B. And the fourth scene's setting is the attic.

   C. Whom is responsible for collecting the tickets?

   D. No mistakes.

257.

   A. If one wants a larger vocabulary, you should study word roots.

   B. Learning the meaning of prefixes and suffixes increases vocabulary.

   C. Read as many different kinds of texts as you can.

   D. No mistakes.

258.

   A. No one enjoys working with a grouch.

   B. The dog smells bad; it needs a bath.

   C. After he washed the dog, he lay down for a nap.

   D. No mistakes.

GO ON TO THE NEXT PAGE

259.

    A. The patient felt himself shaking all over.
    B. He rung for a nurse.
    C. She calmed his fears.
    D. No mistakes.

260.

    A. The family wanted to find a home with a large back yard.
    B. High housing prices creates problems for families.
    C. The Garcias enjoyed their new house.
    D. No mistakes.

261.

    A. Few homes with basements are found in California.
    B. Earthquakes cause severe damage to structures.
    C. Tornadoes plague the mid-western states.
    D. No mistakes.

262.

    A. We three boys love baseball.
    B. Louise wanted to go to the World Series.
    C. Dan gave the tickets to Jim and I.
    D. No mistakes.

263.

    A. Looking at the wall, I seen a spider crawling up it.
    B. The life of most insects is brief.
    C. Bees and wasps belong to different families.
    D. No mistakes.

264.

    A. There's a hat on the chair.
    B. Who's hat is it?
    C. It's cold today.
    D. No mistakes.

265.

    A. There's nothing more fun than a picnic.
    B. My cousin and me hiked up Bear Mountain.
    C. State parks are supported by money from taxpayers.
    D. No mistakes.

266.

    A. If anybody wants a ride, they can go in my car.
    B. Mistakes are an effect of carelessness.
    C. Both of the children have their own rooms.
    D. No mistakes.

267.

    A. Sue and her brother went to the airport.
    B. We were enjoying the picnic, but then the rain starts.
    C. Consider the different possibilities.
    D. No mistakes.

268.

    A. Have you seen any films based on fairytales?
    B. Does practice make it easier to play tennis?
    C. Which of these two brands of toothpaste tastes best?
    D. No mistakes.

269.

    A. If you tune up the car, it will run smooth.
    B. Salad is the better of the two choices on the menu.
    C. It's too hot today.
    D. No mistakes.

270.

    A. When I saw the scene, I gasped.
    B. The server laid the plates in front of the diners.
    C. Make yourself useful by setting the table.
    D. No mistakes.

271.

    A. Water quenches thirst better than soda.
    B. Leave the rest of the books on my desk.
    C. The quarterback threw the ball out of bounds.
    D. No mistakes.

272.

    A. Selma eats a orange every morning.
    B. The poodle looked good after its bath.
    C. My aunt does not appreciate rap music.
    D. No mistakes.

273.

    A. Going to summer camp can be fun.

    B. She borrowed a bicycle from a friend with a basket.

    C. Jess will try to attend the meeting.

    D. No mistakes.

274.

    A. Laws have been past requiring cyclists to wear helmets.

    B. Do you own a motorcycle?

    C. Anita always buckles her seat belt.

    D. No mistakes.

275.

    A. Yankee Stadium is the larger of the two baseball parks in New York City.

    B. The Los Angeles Dodgers used to be Brooklyn's team.

    C. The Cardinals have always played in St. Louis.

    D. No mistakes

276.

    A. Adam asked more questions than myself.

    B. Trina was not affected by the change in plans.

    C. Each of the teachers is well qualified.

    D. No mistakes.

277.

    A. Mel agrees on Elaine's idea.

    B. Ms. Rodriguez is an authority on the subject.

    C. Dr. Boda specializes in surgery.

    D. No mistakes.

278.

    A. Crawling across the lawn, a caterpillar left a trail.

    B. The design of your house is different than mine.

    C. Each of the players has new shoes.

    D. No mistakes.

*In questions 279–288, look for mistakes in spelling only. If you find no mistakes, mark **D** on your answer sheet.*

279.

    A. I will finish this project by next Wensday.

    B. Saturday would be a good day to go to the park.

    C. Apparently, he does not work on weekends.

    D. No mistakes.

280.

    A. Sarah asked her teacher to recommend her for the tutoring job.

    B. Lee wanted to study medicine.

    C. Have you seen the skedule for next week's meeting?

    D. No mistakes.

281.

    A. People tend to exaggerate their own faults.

    B. They don't apprecate their strengths.

    C. Can learning psychology solve this problem?

    D. No mistakes.

282.

    A. It's possible that Lanisha won't come to the party.

    B. Draw a strait line from point A to point B.

    C. Clay is used to make pottery.

    D. No mistakes.

283.

    A. Rhythm in poetry and music is based on repetition.

    B. Unfortunately, Frank can't be here today.

    C. He is hoping to join us tomorrow.

    D. No mistakes.

284.

    A. Phil and Felicia had an arguement about whose turn it was to walk the dog.

    B. Rex sat there whining because he wanted to go out.

    C. The difference between the two shades of pink is not significant.

    D. No mistakes.

GO ON TO THE NEXT PAGE

285.

    A. I don't believe that doing well in school guarantees professional success.

    B. Good grammer is a requirement for clear communication.

    C. The grade of 90 means outstanding work.

    D. No mistakes.

286.

    A. I mailed your birthday present to you last Thursday.

    B. Have you recieved the package yet?

    C. Sometimes delivery services are slow.

    D. No mistakes.

287.

    A. Taylor has been studying for the chemistry test.

    B. Students usually take chemistry during their sophomore year.

    C. Athletes are not excused from taking the exam.

    D. No mistakes.

288.

    A. Dan did not like to listen to criticism of his work.

    B. There is a difference between helpful and harmful comments.

    C. You definately should make your advice positive.

    D. No mistakes.

For questions 289–298, look for errors in composition. Follow the directions for each question.

289. Choose the best word or words to join the thoughts together.

Many new shops have opened downtown; _____, most people still shop at the mall.

    A. therefore

    B. when

    C. however

    D. none of these

290. Choose the best word or words to join the thoughts together.

This calendar includes unusual information; _____ it lists the dates of full moons.

    A. for example,

    B. in contrast,

    C. sometimes

    D. none of the above

291. Which of these expresses the idea most clearly?

    A. Needing a tuneup, I took the car to a mechanic.

    B. I took the car to a mechanic needing a tuneup.

    C. I took the car to a mechanic because it needed a tuneup.

    D. A tuneup being needed by the car, I took it to a mechanic.

292. Choose the group of words that best completes this sentence.

Before I went to the beach,

_____.

    A. I will always use sunscreen

    B. sunscreen was something I would always use

    C. using sunscreen was what I always do

    D. I always used sunscreen

293. Which of these best fits under the topic "The Many Uses of Carbon"?

    A. The lead in lead pencils is graphite, a form of carbon.

    B. Diamonds are made up of crystals of carbon.

    C. Carbon is an element.

    D. None of these.

294. Which sentence does *not* belong in the paragraph?

(1) A strong wind was blowing, and our boat nearly turned over. (2) Heavy rain was falling. (3) Yesterday was sunny, so we had a picnic. (4) We should not have gone boating in this weather.

    A. sentence 1

    B. sentence 2

    C. sentence 3

    D. sentence 4

295. Which of these expresses the idea most clearly?

   A. My family discusses problems to avoid arguments.

   B. To avoid arguments in my family, we discuss problems.

   C. We discuss, to avoid arguments, problems in my family.

   D. Discussing problems to avoid arguments is what my family does.

296. Which of these expresses the idea most clearly?

   A. The students the author met often asked her questions about her childhood.

   B. Often, the students the author met asked her questions about her childhood.

   C. The author met students often who asked her questions about her childhood.

   D. Asking her questions about her childhood, the students often met the author.

297. Which topic is best for a one-paragraph theme?

   A. How to Prepare for College

   B. My Favorite Song

   C. My Childhood

   D. A History of Classical Music

298. Where should the sentence "This formation tends to trap harmful gases and particles" be placed in the following paragraph?

(1) Air pollution is difficult to control in Southern California. (2) The mountains surrounding the area on three sides create a basin. (3) In spite of efforts to reduce emissions from automobiles, the air remains dirty.

   A. after sentence 1.

   B. between sentences 1 and 2.

   C. between sentences 2 and 3.

   D. The sentence does not fit in this paragraph.

IF YOU FINISH BEFORE TIME IS CALLED, CHECK YOUR WORK ON THIS SECTION ONLY. DO NOT WORK ON ANY OTHER SECTION IN THE TEST.

Answer Key

Test 1: Verbal Skills

1. B	16. B	31. C	46. A
2. D	17. B	32. D	47. B
3. A	18. C	33. C	48. A
4. B	19. C	34. C	49. C
5. B	20. A	35. A	50. A
6. C	21. B	36. C	51. A
7. D	22. B	37. A	52. A
8. C	23. A	38. A	53. D
9. C	24. C	39. B	54. D
10. D	25. B	40. D	55. D
11. C	26. A	41. D	56. B
12. C	27. A	42. C	57. C
13. A	28. C	43. C	58. C
14. B	29. C	44. C	59. D
15. C	30. A	45. C	60. C

Test 2: Quantitative Skills

61. C	74. A	87. D	100. A
62. C	75. A	88. C	101. B
63. C	76. C	89. B	102. C
64. B	77. B	90. C	103. B
65. D	78. B	91. A	104. D
66. C	79. D	92. B	105. D
67. B	80. D	93. C	106. B
68. B	81. D	94. C	107. D
69. A	82. D	95. A	108. A
70. A	83. A	96. C	109. C
71. A	84. A	97. D	110. B
72. A	85. D	98. A	111. B
73. C	86. B	99. A	112. C

Test 3: Reading

113. A	**129.** A	**145.** D	**161.** C
114. D	**130.** A	**146.** B	**162.** D
115. B	**131.** D	**147.** A	**163.** A
116. A	**132.** D	**148.** D	**164.** B
117. B	**133.** A	**149.** C	**165.** B
118. D	**134.** D	**150.** A	**166.** B
119. D	**135.** C	**151.** B	**167.** D
120. B	**136.** C	**152.** C	**168.** C
121. D	**137.** D	**153.** C	**169.** A
122. C	**138.** B	**154.** D	**170.** C
123. B	**139.** C	**155.** A	**171.** C
124. D	**140.** B	**156.** A	**172.** D
125. A	**141.** A	**157.** B	**173.** C
126. C	**142.** C	**158.** B	**174.** A
127. C	**143.** D	**159.** C	
128. A	**144.** A	**160.** D	

Test 4: Mathematics

175. A	**191.** C	**207.** C	**223.** D
176. B	**192.** C	**208.** A	**224.** D
177. D	**193.** C	**209.** B	**225.** D
178. A	**194.** A	**210.** C	**226.** D
179. D	**195.** C	**211.** A	**227.** B
180. B	**196.** A	**212.** C	**228.** D
181. B	**197.** B	**213.** C	**229.** B
182. C	**198.** C	**214.** A	**230.** B
183. C	**199.** D	**215.** D	**231.** D
184. B	**200.** C	**216.** D	**232.** C
185. A	**201.** B	**217.** D	**233.** D
186. B	**202.** A	**218.** C	**234.** A
187. C	**203.** D	**219.** A	**235.** A
188. A	**204.** D	**220.** B	**236.** D
189. C	**205.** D	**221.** B	**237.** D
190. B	**206.** A	**222.** B	**238.** C

Test 5: Language Skills

239. D	**254.** A	**269.** A	**284.** A
240. C	**255.** D	**270.** D	**285.** B
241. D	**256.** C	**271.** D	**286.** B
242. B	**257.** A	**272.** A	**287.** D
243. D	**258.** D	**273.** B	**288.** C
244. C	**259.** B	**274.** A	**289.** C
245. A	**260.** B	**275.** D	**290.** A
246. D	**261.** D	**276.** A	**291.** C
247. C	**262.** C	**277.** A	**292.** D
248. B	**263.** A	**278.** B	**293.** A
249. C	**264.** B	**279.** A	**294.** C
250. A	**265.** B	**280.** C	**295.** B
251. A	**266.** A	**281.** B	**296.** B
252. D	**267.** B	**282.** B	**297.** B
253. B	**268.** C	**283.** D	**298.** C

Answers and Explanations

Test 1: Verbal Skills

1. **B.** The relationship is one of degree. Shouting is an intense form of talking, and detesting is an intense form of disliking.

2. **D.** Function explains the relationship. A conductor leads an orchestra; a shepherd leads a flock.

3. **A.** To repeal is to take back something previously established, like a law or a rule, making *abolish* the best choice.

4. **B.** Something *poignant* creates deep emotions. They can be positive or negative emotions. Therefore, choices **A** and **D** are incorrect. **C** doesn't make sense.

5. **B.** The third statement is contradicted by the first statement.

6. **C.** Margarine is a vegetable fat; the other choices are animal fat.

7. **D.** The other choices are used in lamps. Lasers are not presently used to light homes.

8. **C.** *Passive* means not reacting; the opposite is *active.*

9. **C.** A drill is part of the category tools, and a nursery rhyme is part of the category poems.

10. **D.** *Archaic* means out of date, something used in the past but not the present.

11. **C.** The culmination is what a series of events or statements lead up to, a *climax.*

12. **C.** Other animals also eat grass, so Elsie might or might not be a cow.

13. **A.** Citrus is the general category; the other items are specifics in that category.

14. **B.** All the other choices are musical instruments that have strings.

15. **C.** *Recall* means remember; *forget* is the opposite.

16. **B.** One meaning of *civil* is polite; do not be confused by another meaning of civil, referring to citizens and their relationship with a state. *Rude* is the correct choice.

17. **B.** The basis of the analogy is cause. Tension is a cause of stress, and a virus is a cause of disease.

18. **C.** When you undermine something, you take away that which is supporting it, so you *weaken* it.

19. **C.** The first two statements give no information about the relative numbers of feathers on blooms and pobs.

20. **A.** *Food* is a general term; the other choices are kinds of food.

21. **B.** To *decay* is to break down or rot; *grow* is the opposite.

22. **B.** The other choices means something that smells pleasant; a *stench* is an unpleasant odor.

23. **A.** *Durable* objects are sturdy; the other choices describe objects that break easily.

24. **C.** No information is given about whether First Street is wider or narrower than Broad Street.

25. **B.** *Frivolous* means not serious or unimportant. *Silly* is a good synonym for the word.

26. **A.** This is a tricky word. It means to make more intense is a negative way, which is why *improve,* **C,** is not the correct choice.

27. **A.** A miser cares excessively about money, and a glutton cares excessively about food.

28. **C.** The relationship is one of opposites.

29. **C.** To *depict* something is to draw a picture of it or portray it.

30. A. Because all rasks are in the category striped blens, and none of the flying blens are striped, the rasks, which are striped, can't be blens.

31. C. The other choices are marine animals that have shells.

32. D. All choices except *tomato* have green exteriors.

33. C. To be *devoid* is to lack; *having* is the opposite.

34. C. A proper location for a bouquet is a vase; garbage should be put into a garbage can.

35. A. The prefix *-in* is your clue that the correct choice is a word meaning something is *not*.

36. C. The prefix *morph-* refers to form or shape.

37. A. Because B is south of C, C is north of both B and A.

38. A. If the first two statements are true, all the runners are faster than Pam.

39. B. Choices **A, C,** and **D** are meals or parts of meals, while sugar is a condiment.

40. D. The other choices are places where education is the main activity.

41. D. A *prelude* is at the beginning of a work of music or literature; therefore, *conclusion* is the best choice.

42. C. The other choices are individual sports; baseball is a team sport.

43. C. *Vision* is the word telling what the other choices are used to sharpen.

44. C. The information in the first two statements doesn't tell whether Carol is or is not a resident of the state where the college is located.

45. C. Choice **A** is confusing. Does *light* mean the opposite of heavy? Or does it mean the same as bright? Even if the latter is the case, **C** is a better answer.

46. A. Although **B,** pray, is a way of revering something, prayer is not the only means of reverence. Therefore, **A** is the best choice.

47. B. The relationship is one of synonyms. *Enraged* means the same as *angry*.

48. A. To *ooze* is to seep out slowly; if something flows out quickly, it *pours*.

49. C. A *tradition* is something done now that was also done in the past, and *novelty* is the opposite.

50. A. According to the first statement, fewer people buy more expensive grapes. Thus, when the price of grapes rises, the sales decline.

51. A. The relationship is one of opposites.

52. A. Suits is the general term for the specific names of categories of cards given in the other choices.

53. D. The other choices are used to open something. (A combination opens a lock.)

54. D. To act audaciously is to act in a daring manner.

55. D. When something is *austere*, it lacks decorations or adornments.

56. B. The relationship is one of function. A barometer measures pressure; a ruler measures length.

57. C. The computer might or might not have come in a paper box. The box could have been made of some other material, such as cardboard or wood.

58. C. *Nadir* refers to the utmost depths.

59. D. The other choices are clothing that keeps you warm, usually worn in winter. Swimsuits are most often worn during the summer.

60. C. Although *permit* can be a noun, in this item it is used as a verb, and *forbid* is the opposite.

Test 2: Quantitative Skills

61. C. The sum of 10 and 15 is 25, which is equal to **5** squared because $5^2 = 25$.

62. C. The pattern is 7 (+ 4), 11 (+ 4), 15 (+ 4), 19 (+ 4), which is equal to **23.**

63. C. Note that (a) $2^2 + 3^2 = 4 + 9 = 13$, (b) $(2 + 3)^2 = 5^2 = 25$, and (c) $5^2 = 25$. Thus, (b) and (c) are equal and greater than (a).

64. B. One tenth of $70 = \frac{1}{10} \times 70 = 7$. Thus, we need to determine the number $\frac{1}{9}$ of which is 7. Call this number x.

$$\frac{1}{9}x = 7$$

Multiply both sides by 9.

$$x = 7 \times 9 = 63.$$

65. D. The pattern is 1 ($\times$ 3), 3 ($\times$ 3), 9 ($\times$ 3), 27 ($\times$ 3), which is equal to **81.**

66. C. To begin, $z = 70$ because the angle labeled z is vertical to the angle labeled 70°. Next, $a = 180° - 70° = 110°$ because the angle labeled a is supplementary to the angle labeled 70°. Also note that $a = b + c$ by the property of vertical angles. Thus, it is true that $a = b + c > z$.

67. B. The pattern is 8 (− 2), 6 (+ 3), 9 (− 2), 7 (+ 3), **10** (− 2), which is equal to 8.

68. B. The cube of 4 is $4^3 = 64$. This is also equal to 8^2.

69. A. The pattern is 16 (÷ 2), 8 (÷ 2), 4 (÷ 2), 2 (÷ 2), which is equal to **1.**

70. A. The number that is 15 more than 20 is 35. This is the same as 5×7.

71. A. Note that (a) $(12 − 3)(2 + 1) = (9)(3) = 27$, (b) $12 − 3(2 + 1) = 12 − 3(3) = 12 − 9 = 3$, and (c) $12 − 3 \times 2 + 1 = 12 − 6 + 1 = 7$. Therefore (a) is greater than (b) and (c).

72. A. All four labeled angles are equal because they are either alternate interior or vertical angles of each other. Thus, $p = q = r = s$.

73. C. The pattern is 2 (+ 1), 3 (+ 2), 5 (+ 3), 8 (+ 4), 12 (+ 5), which is equal to **17.**

74. A. The difference of 25 and 17 is $25 − 17 = 8$. Note that 200% of **4** is also equal to 8.

75. A. Note that (a) is $\sqrt{\frac{1}{4}} = \frac{1}{2}$, (b) is $\frac{1}{4}$, and (c) is $\left(\frac{1}{4}\right)^2 = \frac{1}{16}$. Therefore (a) is greater than (b) and (c).

76. C. The sum of 10, 11, and 12 is $10 + 11 + 12 = 33$. One third of 33 is **11.**

77. B. In this pattern, the numbers ascend in numerical order, and alternate positive and negative. Thus, we have 5, −6, 7, −8, 9, **−10,** 11.

78. B. Because O is the center of the circle, ST and PR are both diameters, and therefore equal. In addition, PQ is a chord of the circle, and is therefore shorter than the diameters. Thus, $ST = PR > PQ$.

79. D. The pattern is 12 (+ 2), 14 (+ 4), 18 (+ 6), 24 (+ 8), 32 (+ 10), which is equal to **42.**

80. D. Fifty percent of 16 is equal to 8. Note that 10% of **80** is also equal to 8.

81. D. Note that (a) $6.15 \times 10^2 = 615$, (b) $61,500 \times 10^{-2} = 615$, and (c) $61.5 \times 10 = 615$. Therefore, (a), (b), and (c) are equal.

82. D. In this pattern, the number 1 is followed by $1 \times 3 = 3$, then the number 2 is followed by $2 \times 3 = 6$. Continuing, the number 3 is followed by $3 \times 3 = 9$. The next number is 4, so the missing number must be $4 \times 3 = $ **12.**

83. A. The product of 4 and 6 is 24, and 1/3 of 6 is **2.**

84. A. The pattern is 9 (+ 4), 13 (+ 5), 18 (+ 4), 22 (+ 5), 27 (+ 4), which is equal to **31.**

85. D. The sum of the angles of a triangle is equal to 180°, so $b + c + d = 180$. Also, $b + a = 180$ because the two angles associated with these measures are supplementary. Thus, $a + b = b + c + d$.

86. B. The difference between 84 and 20 is 64. One-eighth of 64 is **8.**

87. D. The pattern is 12 ($\times$ 2), 24 ($-$ 4), 20 ($\times$ 2), 40 ($-$ 4), 36 ($\times$ 2), which is equal to **72.**

88. C. Note that (a) 52,491 rounded to the nearest hundred is 52,500, (b) 52,571 rounded to the nearest thousand is 53,000, and (c) 53,021 rounded to the nearest hundred is 53,000. Thus, (b) and (c) are equal and greater than (a).

89. B. The pattern is 78 ($-$ **8**), 70 ($-$ **7**), 63 ($-$ **6**), 57 ($-$ **5**), 52 ($-$ **4**), which is equal to **48.**

90. C. One eighth of 64 is 8. Note that $\frac{2}{3}$ of 12 is also 8.

91. A. The pattern is 72 ($\div$ 2), 36 ($\div$ 3), 12 ($\div$ 2), 6 ($\div$ 3), 2 ($\div$ 2), which is equal to **1.**

92. B. To begin, XZ and WY are both diagonals of the same rectangle, and therefore are equal. Because the diagonal of a rectangle is longer than either the length or the width, it follows that $XZ = WY > XY$.

93. C. The sum of 13 and 17 is 30. Note that 25% of **120** is also 30.

94. C. This pattern begins with a perfect square, 36, and then lists its square root. The next number is the next smaller perfect square, 25, followed by its square root. Then next number is 16, which should then be followed by its square root, **4.**

95. A. Note that (a) the least common multiple of 7 and 5 is 35; (b) the least common multiple of 8 and 4 is 8; and (c) the least common multiple of 12 and 8 is 24. Therefore, (a) is greater than (b) and (c).

96. C. Twice 21 is equal to 42. If you divide 42 by 3, you obtain the number that, when tripled, is equal to 42. Note that $\frac{42}{3} = 14$.

97. D. The pattern is 200 ($-$ 20), 180 ($-$ 5), 175 ($-$ 20), 155 ($-$ 5), 150 ($-$ 20), **130** ($-$5), which is equal to 125.

98. A. Because $BE = ED$, the angles opposite these two sides must also be equal, that is, $f = g$. Because there are 180° in a triangle and the third angle is 40°, it must be true that $f = g = 70$. Further, because all the angles in a square are right angles, it follows that $a = 90$. Thus, $f = g < a$.

99. A. The pattern is 35 ($+$ 1), 36 ($-$ 2), 34 ($+$ 3), 37 ($-$ 4), 33 ($+$ 5), which is equal to **38.**

100. A. Ten percent of **30** is equal to 3, and when 30 is reduced by 3, the result is 27.

101. B. The sum of 84 and 116 is 200, and 35% of 200 = $.35 \times 200 =$ **70.**

102. C. Note that (a) $\frac{0.03}{1,000} = 0.00003$, (b) 0.03% $= 0.0003$, and (c) $0.3 \times 0.001 = 0.0003$. Therefore, (b) and (c) are equal and greater than (a).

103. B. When **7** is doubled, the result is 14. Increasing this by 3 gives 17.

104. D. The pattern is 1 ($\times$ 2), 2 ($\times$ 3), 6 ($\times$ 4), 24 ($\times$ 5), 120 ($\times$ 6), which is equal to **720.**

105. D. The square of 9 is $9^2 = 81$. Note that 300% of **27** $= 3 \times 27 = 81$.

106. B. The lengths of the sides of an equilateral triangle are all equal, and the altitude is always shorter than the sides. Thus, $AC = BC > BD$.

107. D. In this pattern, the numbers increase by multiples of 5. Thus, 12 ($+$ 5), 17 ($+$ 10), 27 ($+$ 15), 42 ($+$ 20), **62** ($+$ 25), 87.

108. A. The product of 11 and 2 is $11 \times 2 = 22$. Note that $5^2 = 25$, and that when this is decreased by 3, the result is 22.

109. C. It is not necessary to evaluate the quantities. Note that (a) is 7^5, (b) is 7^6, and (c) is $(7^2)^3 = 7^6$. Thus, (b) and (c) are equal and greater than (a).

110. B. The length of AF represents the vertical distance from the bottom of the figure to the top. The same distance is represented by the sums of the lengths of BC and DE. Thus, $BC + DE = AF$.

111. B. If you notice that the first, third, and fifth entries decrease by 2, that is, 20 ($-$ 2), 18 ($-$ 2), 16, the pattern is easier to follow. The first number is 20, and this is followed by half of 20. The third number is 2 less than the first number,

20 − 2 = 18, and this is followed by half of 18. The fifth number is 2 less than the third number, 18 − 2 = 16, and this is followed by half of 16. The missing number, then, should be 2 less than the fifth number, 16 − 2 = **14,** and this is followed by half of 14, which is 7.

112. C. The two squares share a common side, *CF*, and therefore the two squares must be of the same size. It follows that the lengths of their diagonals must also be the same, and so *AC* = *CE*. Finally, because the diagonals of a square are longer than the sides, *AC* = *CE* > *CD*.

Test 3: Reading

113. A. The paragraph states it was named by an agent of the American Colonization Society.

114. D. Although choices **A, B,** and **C** sound logical, none of them is given as the society's purpose in the passage.

115. B. *Indigenous* people are those who are native to an area.

116. A. Because the passage says the flag resembles the American flag, you can infer that it has stripes. **B** is incorrect because the passage states that the flag has only one star.

117. B. Something that is *compatible* with something else can integrate or work with it.

118. D. The other choices refer to content that is part of the passage, but the focus of the passage is on the relationship between the two countries.

119. D. **A** is contradicted by the last sentence of the passage. **C** is incorrect because the fact that the Liberian constitution was modeled on America's does not mean the laws are the same. Nothing in the passage gives information about **B.**

120. B. This is stated in the first paragraph of the passage.

121. D. This content is in the passage's third paragraph.

122. C. This is the correct choice because the passage states that American appliances can be used.

123. B. To *emit* means to release or give off.

124. D. Choices **A** and **B** are incorrect because the passage states that scientists don't know which of these causes fireflies to flash.

125. A. The explanation of bioluminescence does not refer to any of the other choices.

126. C. According to the passage, something happens after the electrons are *activated*. Therefore, *activate* means to set in motion or to begin a process.

127. C. While the passage explains how light sticks work, it does not give enough information for you to make one after reading it, so **B** is incorrect. **D** is a more general subject than the passage deals with, and because the passage is not written like an advertisement, **A** is wrong.

128. A. The passage states that the glass breaks open; therefore, before it breaks, it *encloses* its contents.

129. A. The lights are given as one of the general examples of luminescence. Because they are not living, **B** cannot be correct. **C** and **D** are related to the kind of light found in ordinary lightbulbs.

130. A. Although **D** might be a choice because the chemicals in the light sticks are liquids, **A** is a more exact response based on the passage.

131. D. This is stated at the end of the third paragraph.

132. D. Because light sticks don't glow very brightly, and because they must be bent to begin the process of creating light. They are somewhat useless for anything other than toys or for trick-or-treating at Halloween.

133. A. The long jump event is not a race.

134. D. A *feat* is an action that is notable or special. Although **B** sounds logical, a feat can be something negative as well as something positive.

135. C. The passage states that he wanted to *avoid distractions*; in other words, he wanted to focus on what he had to do.

136. C. Perceptions are impressions, which might or might not be true.

137. D. The last two sentences of the second paragraph and the last three sentences of the third paragraph make this the correct choice.

138. B. *Joyous enthusiasm* indicates that Lewis was filled with emotion.

139. C. This information appears in the third paragraph.

140. B. Encyclopedias, choice **A**, usually do not present an author's opinion about a subject. While history books, choice **D**, do present analyses, they attempt to be objective. Choice **C** might contain the information that Lewis won the four medals, but the rest of the passage would not be part of official records.

141. A. The word *wind* in this expression is not meant literally.

142. C. Because the author indicates that Lewis could have been thinking about the American team, this is the correct choice.

143. D. The word *but* in the sentence indicates a contrast. *Life* is the opposite of *lifeless*.

144. A. According to the third paragraph, the plants both use the protein they create and provide oxygen for the animals.

145. D. The animals are described as *cylindrical*. That word does not describe choices **A**, **B**, or **C**.

146. B. The animal sends out threads from which a new animal *sprouts*. Thus, the new animal is like a bud of the old one.

147. A. Because the limestone is described as coming from *itself*, this is the best answer.

148. D. This information is in the last paragraph of the passage.

149. C. The passage states that the old animal is buried beneath the new one.

150. A. The rest of the paragraph gives specific examples of this vigorous growth.

151. B. Choices **A** and **D** describe only part of the content of the passage. Choice **C** is too general.

152. C. Choice **D** can be eliminated because novelists usually don't write nonfiction. The passage does not use technical and specialized terms, so **A** is not likely. **B** is a possibility, but divers do not necessarily study coral. That the tone of the passage is somewhat informal (the reader is addressed as you) also suggests that **C** is the best choice.

153. C.	**159.** C.	**165.** B.	**171.** C.
154. D.	**160.** D.	**166.** B.	**172.** D.
155. A.	**161.** C.	**167.** D.	**173.** C.
156. A.	**162.** D.	**168.** C.	**174.** A.
157. B.	**163.** A.	**169.** A.	
158. B.	**164.** B.	**170.** C.	

Test 4: Mathematics

175. A. $3\frac{1}{4} - 2\frac{1}{8} = \frac{13}{4} - \frac{17}{8} = \frac{26}{8} - \frac{17}{8} = \frac{9}{8} = 1\frac{1}{8}$ more cups of flour.

176. B. The earnings for 30 hours are $8.25 \times 30 = $247.50.

177. D. Let n represent the number of students in the band. Then $\frac{1}{3} n = 72$, so $n = 72 \times 3 = 216$.

178. A. $20 - $3.95 = $16.05.

179. D. At the end of the first day, there are $1 - \frac{1}{8} = \frac{7}{8}$ of the magazines remaining. $\frac{7}{8} \times \frac{1}{4} = \frac{7}{32}$ sold the next day. So, at the end of the second day, $\frac{7}{8} - \frac{7}{32} = \frac{28}{32} - \frac{7}{32} = \frac{21}{32}$ of the magazines remain.

180. B. If a machine produces 8,000 gears in 3 hours, it produces $\frac{8000}{3}$ gears in one hour. There are 24 hours in a day, so $\frac{8000}{3} \times 24$ or 64,000 gears are produced in one day.

181. B. The total cost of the purchase is $(3 \times \$0.45) + (2 \times \$0.79) = \$1.35 + \$1.58 = \$2.93$.

182. C. Keith's throw went $7\frac{1}{3} \times 2\frac{1}{2} = \frac{22}{3} \times \frac{5}{2} = \frac{110}{6} = 18\frac{1}{3}$ yards. The difference between the two throws is $18\frac{1}{3} - 7\frac{1}{3} = 11$ yards.

183. C. The total distance traveled in the morning was $13 \times 2 = 26$ miles. The total distance traveled in the afternoon was $9 \times 2 = 18$ miles. The difference between the two distances is $26 - 18 = 8$ miles.

184. B. $4^3 \times 3^2 = (4 \times 4 \times 4) \times (3 \times 3) = 64 \times 9 = 576$

185. A. $48 = 6 \times 8 = 2 \times 2 \times 2 \times 2 \times 3 = 2^4 \times 3$

186. B. $(-1)^{100}(-2)^3 = (+1)(-8) = -8$

187. C. $4\frac{1}{4} \times 3\frac{2}{3} = \frac{17}{4} \times \frac{11}{3} = \frac{187}{12} = 15\frac{7}{12}$

188. A. The rate of the car is $\frac{750 \text{ miles}}{25 \text{ hours}}$. Dividing 25 into 750 gives 30, so the car is traveling 30 miles per hour.

189. C. To find the total number of people who saw the play, add 3,127 and 2,944 and 3,009 to get 9,080.

190. B. To solve this problem, we need to subtract 1,752 from 2,374. This tells us how many miles the car was driven for purposes other than business. Because $2,374 - 1,752 = 622$, the car went 622 miles for purposes other than business.

191. C. Previously, we saw that the formula for distance is $d = r \times t$, that is, distance = rate × time. In this case, distance = $525 \times 6 = 3,150$ miles.

192. C. Three sides of length 5 gives a perimeter of $3 \times 5 = 15$ inches.

193. C. $12\frac{1}{2}\% = \frac{12.5}{100} = \frac{125}{1,000} = \frac{125 \div 125}{1,000 \div 125} = \frac{1}{8}$

194. A. $\left(\frac{1}{10}\right)^4 \times 10^2 = \frac{10^2}{10^4} = \frac{1}{10^{4-2}} = \frac{1}{10^2} = \frac{1}{100}$

195. C. $\frac{0.5 + 0.4 + 0.2 + 0.1 + 0.0 + 0.0}{6} = \frac{1.2}{6} = 0.2$

196. A. $5P - 3Q - (3P - 2Q) = 5P - 3P - 3Q + 2Q = 2P - Q$

197. B. Because z is positive, z can be added to both sides of the inequality without changing the direction of the inequality, as in **A**. Both sides can also be multiplied by z and divided by z, as in **C** and **D**. However, in **B**, a larger number is being subtracted from z on the left than on the right, so the number on the left ends up being smaller than the number on the right. Thus, **B** is not true.

198. C. $\frac{14}{3-y} = \frac{14}{3-(-4)} = \frac{14}{3+4} = \frac{14}{7} = 2$

199. D. Two dozen eggs is equal to 24 eggs. If 3 eggs are in an omelet, then $24 \div 3$, or 8 omelets can be made.

200. C. Because two runners finished in 80 seconds, the average of 80, 80, 72, and 68 must be found. This average is $\frac{80 + 80 + 72 + 68}{3} = \frac{300}{4} = 75$ seconds.

201. B. If 400 people fit in 8 subway cars, then $400 \div 8$, or 50, people fit in one subway car. Therefore, 50×5, or 250, people fit in 5 subway cars.

202. A. Add the amount of money received and subtract the amount spent: $\$30 + \$15 - \$16 = \$29$.

203. D. If an item is discounted 20%, the sale price is 80% of the original price. Let p represent the original price. Then $\$800 = 80\% \times p$ and $p = \frac{800}{80\%} = \frac{800}{.80} = \$1,000$.

204. D. For a 30-hour week with $500 in sales, total earnings are $(30 \times \$9.50) + (3\% \times \$500) = \$285 + \$15 = \$300$.

205. D. The area of the circle with a radius of 3 is $\pi r^2 = \pi 3^2 = 9\pi$. The area of the larger circle is $4 \times 9\pi = 36\pi$. Therefore, $r^2 = 36$, so $r = \sqrt{36} = 6$. The radius of the larger circle is 6.

206. A. Using the ratio $\frac{\text{height}}{\text{shadow}}$, the proportion $\frac{3\frac{1}{2}}{6} = \frac{x}{24}$ models this situation, where x represents the height of the pole. Cross multiply: $3\frac{1}{2} \times 24 = 6x$, so $x = \frac{84}{6} = 14$ feet.

207. C. The overtime rate is $\$8.40 \times 1.5 = \$12.60$. Five hours of overtime were completed, so the total earnings are $(\$8.40 \times 40) + (\$12.60 \times 5) = \$336 + \$63 = \$399$.

208. A. The amount of discount is $\$40 - \$30 = \$10$. The percent of discount is the amount of discount divided by the original price. $\frac{10}{40} = \frac{1}{4} = 25\%$

209. B. The volume of the original box is $3 \times 2\frac{1}{2} \times 2 = 15$. The volume of the box with the length and depth doubled is $6 \times 2\frac{1}{2} \times 4 = 60$. The amount of change in volume is $60 - 15 = 45$. The percent change is the amount of change in volume divided by the original volume. $\frac{45}{15} = 3 = 300\%$.

210. C. The amount of commission is $10\% \times \$8,350 = \$835$. Total earnings are $\$300 + \$835$ commission $= \$1,135$.

211. A. The total number of stamps collected is $300 + 420 + 180 = 900$. The number of coins that can be collected is $\frac{900}{25} = 36$.

212. C. The proportion $\frac{1 \text{ cm}}{4 \text{ miles}} = \frac{x \text{ cm}}{10 \text{ miles}}$ models this situation. Cross multiply: $1 \times 10 = 4x$, so $10 = 4x$, and $x = 2\frac{1}{2}$.

213. C. Let p represent the amount of the paycheck. $\frac{4}{13}p = \$26.80$, so $p = \$26.80 \times \frac{13}{4} = \$87.10$.

214. A. The proportion $\frac{\frac{1}{2} \text{ mile}}{4 \text{ minutes}} = \frac{x \text{ miles}}{15 \text{ minutes}}$ models this situation. Cross multiply: $\frac{1}{2} \times 15 = 4x$, so $\frac{15}{2} = 4x$ and $x = \frac{15}{2} \cdot \frac{1}{4} = \frac{15}{8} = 1\frac{7}{8}$ miles.

215. D. Three feet are in a yard, so a kitchen 4 yards by 5 yards is equivalent to (4×3) feet by (5×3) feet, or 12 feet by 15 feet. The area of the kitchen is $12 \times 15 = 180$ square feet. The cost to tile is $\$2.89 \times 180 = \$520.20$.

216. D. Interest earned in one year is $\$300 \times 5\frac{1}{4}\% = \$15.75$. The total amount of the account after one year is $\$300 + \$15.75 = \$315.75$.

217. D. Let m represent the length of the phone calls in minutes. The monthly charge for the first plan is $20 + 0.08m$. The monthly charge for the second plan is $12 + 0.12m$. When the monthly charges are the same, $20 + 0.08m = 12 + 0.12m$. Solve for m to find the number of minutes after which both plans have the same rate.

$$20 + 0.08m - 0.08m = 12 + 0.12m - 0.08m$$
$$20 = 12 + 0.04m$$
$$20 - 12 = 12 + 0.04m - 12$$
$$8 = 0.04m \text{ so } m = \frac{8}{0.04} = \frac{800}{4} = 200 \text{ minutes}$$

218. C. The perimeter of a rectangle is $l + w + l + w = 48$. Because $l = 3w$, the perimeter is $3w + w + 3w + w = 48$, so $8w = 48$, and $w = 6$. Therefore, the length is 3×6, or 18, and the area of the rectangle is $l \times w = 18 \times 3 = 54$.

219. A. $\frac{x}{4} = -9$. Multiplying both sides by 4 gives $x = -36$.

220. B. Let N = the smallest integer. Then, $N + 1$ is the middle integer, and $N + 2$ is the largest.

$N + (N+1) + (N+2) = 57$ or $3N + 3 = 57$, so $3N = 54$, or $N = 18$.

221. B. The flight path of the plane forms the two legs of a right triangle. The total distance that the plane has flown from its starting point is the length of the hypotenuse of the triangle. In other words, we need to use the Pythagorean theorem to find the hypotenuse of a right triangle with legs of 50 and 120.

$$50^2 + 120^2 = h^2$$
$$2500 + 14,400 = h^2$$
$$16,900 = h^2$$
$$130 = h$$

Therefore, the plane flew 130 miles from its starting point.

222. B. This problem has several steps. To begin, we need to determine the number of points he scored. The 53 field goals give him $53 \times 2 = 106$ points. Adding the 20 free throws gives him 126 points. The average per game is $126 \div 14 = 9$ points.

223. D. Because $480 \div 60 = 8$, we need 8 bags to cover the yard. Because each bag costs $7.45, the total cost is $7.45 \times 8 = \$59.60$.

224. D. To begin, find the length of each side in inches: 6 feet, 4 inches is equal to 72 inches + 4 inches = 76 inches; 8 feet, 3 inches is the same as 96 inches + 3 inches = 99 inches. The perimeter is $76 \times 2 + 99 \times 2 = 152 + 198 = 350$ inches.

225. D. Begin by noting that $\frac{1}{2}$ of 48 is 24. Next, compute $\frac{2}{3} \times 48 = 32$.

226. D. Here, $7^2 = 49$, and $2^7 = 128$. Thus, $128 - 49 = 79$.

227. B. $\left(2 \times \frac{1}{10}\right) + \left(3 \times \frac{1}{100}\right) + \left(4 \times \frac{1}{1,000}\right) = 0.2 + 0.03 + 0.004 = 0.234$

228. D. Consider the investment of $90,000 partitioned into $2 + 3 + 4 = 9$ equal amounts of $10,000. The smallest share, then, consists of 2 of the 9 $10,000 amounts; the middle share is 3 of the $10,000 amounts, and the largest share is 4 of the $10,000 amounts, or $40,000.

229. B. Express $3\frac{3}{4}$ as 3.75, and divide into 600.

$$\frac{600}{3.75} = 160$$

230. B. The perimeter of the original square is $4 \times 3" = 12"$. The new rectangle has a width of $2 \times 3" = 6"$ and a length of $3 \times 3" = 9"$. Its perimeter, thus, is $6" + 6" + 9" + 9" = 30"$. The new perimeter, then, is $30 \div 12 = 2\frac{1}{2}$ times as big as the original.

231. D.

$4x - 3 > 13$

Add 3 to both sides.

$4x > 16$

Divide both sides by 4.

$x > 4$

232. C.

$\frac{7}{4} = \frac{3}{x}$

Cross multiply.

$7x = 12$

Divide both sides by 7.

$x = \frac{12}{7}$

233. D. The profit on each toothbrush is $20 − $7.50 = $12.50. The profit on 40 toothbrushes is $12.50 × 40 = $500.

234. A. The largest circle that fits has a diameter of 6"; any circle with a larger diameter extends outside the rectangle. The radius of a circle with a diameter of 6" is, of course, 3".

235. A. To begin, $(2^4)^3 = 2^{4 \times 3} = 2^{12}$. Similarly, $(2^6)^2 = 2^{12}$. Therefore, these two quantities are identical, and, when subtracted, the result is 0.

236. D.

$$(2x − 3) + (x + 4) + (3x − 7) = 0$$

Combine like terms on the left.

$$6x − 6 = 0$$

Add 6 to both sides.

$$6x = 6$$

237. D. Because $4 \times 4 \times 4 = 64$, it follows that $\sqrt[3]{64} = 4$. If $x = 4$, $x^2 = 4^2 = 16$.

238. C. John is J years old, so twice John's age is $2J$ years. Rusty is two years older than this, and is, therefore, $2J + 2$ years old.

Test 5: Language Skills

239. D. All answer choices are correct.

240. C. No comma is required after the introductory word.

241. D. In a series of items, a comma should appear after each item, including before the word *and* that introduces the last item: *Kareem's backpack, jacket, and hat.*

242. B. Place commas around a descriptive phrase that does not restrict the noun it follows, or that is not necessary to the main idea of the sentence. Leaving out the commas makes this sentence mean that there is more than one Craig! Craig who is tall, Craig who has blue eyes, Craig who is average height. Which Craig is meant? Corrected, the sentence refers to only one Craig, who plays center and is tall. *Craig, who is tall, plays center on the basketball team.*

243. D. All answer choices are correct.

244. C. When two independent clauses are separated by a coordinating conjunction, a comma is required before the conjunction. *Mr. Kinsey teaches biology, and Mrs. Jong teaches physics.*

245. A. The names of days of the week are capitalized.

246. D. All answer choices are correct.

247. C. Two independent clauses should be separated by a semicolon, not a comma.

248. B. An indirect question is not followed by a question mark.

249. C. A plural word is made possessive by adding an apostrophe after the *s*; the correct form is *grandparents'*.

250. A. Capitalize the names of states: *New Mexico.*

251. A. A pronoun must agree in number with what it refers to. *Their* is incorrect because it refers to *person*.

252. D. All answer choices are correct.

253. B. Do not confuse *of* with *have*.

254. A. The objective form of the pronoun is *me*. The reflexive form (*myself*) is not used when the personal pronoun can be used without changing the meaning of the sentence.

255. D. All answer choices are correct.

256. C. Use *who*, not *whom*, as the subject of a sentence. If the question form is confusing, think of the sentence as a statement. He or she, not him or her, is responsible for the collection of tickets.

257. A. Do not shift from third person to second person pronouns.

258. D. All answer choices are correct.

259. B. The past tense of *ring* is *rang*.

260. B. The verb must agree with the subject in number. *Prices* is plural. The verb should be *create*.

261. D. All answer choices are correct.

262. C. Use *me* when the pronoun is the object of a preposition.

263. A. The past tense of *see* is *saw*.

264. B. *Who's* means *who is*. *Whose* is the interrogative pronoun.

265. B. You should use the pronoun *I* instead of *me* when it is the subject of the sentence.

266. A. Do not shift from singular to plural. If you want to avoid using *he* to refer to both males and females, make the pronoun's antecedent plural. *If people want a ride, they can go in my car.*

267. B. Do not shift illogically from past to present tense.

268. C. When only two items are compared, use the comparative form, *better*, rather than the superlative form, *best*.

269. A. Use an adverb, not an adjective, to modify a verb: *It will run smoothly.*

270. D. All answer choices are correct.

271. D. All answer choices are correct.

272. A. Use *an*, not *a*, before words beginning with a vowel.

273. B. According to this sentence, the friend has a basket. The writer meant that the bicycle had a basket. Place modifiers as close as possible to what they modify.

274. A. *Past* can be a noun or an adjective. The verb is *pass*, and its past tense is *passed*.

275. D. All answer choices are correct.

276. A. Do not use a reflexive pronoun when a personal pronoun can replace it.

277. A. The correct idiom is *agree with*.

278. B. *Different from* is correct usage in almost all circumstances.

279. A. Wednesday

280. C. schedule

281. B. appreciate

282. B. straight

283. D. All answer choices are correct.

284. A. argument

285. B. grammar

286. B. received

287. D. All answer choices are correct.

288. C. definitely

289. C. The relation between the two halves of the sentence is a contrast.

290. A. The second half of the sentence gives an example of unusual information.

291. C. In **A,** the person needs a tuneup. In **B,** the mechanic needs a tuneup. **D** is wordy and unnecessarily uses a passive construction.

292. D. Because the first half of the sentence is in past tense, the second half should also be in past tense.

293. A. The other sentences are about carbon, but not about how it is used.

294. C. The paragraph tells about something happening on a stormy day.

295. B. This answer shows the cause/effect relationship of the ideas most clearly.

296. B. In **A,** it isn't clear whether the students meet the author often, or if they ask questions often. Does **C** mean that the author sometimes met students who did not ask questions?

297. B. In one paragraph, it is possible to name your favorite song and list the reasons that you like it.

298. C. The words *this formation* tell you that the sentence must refer to something named in the preceding sentence.

Answer Sheet for Practice HSPT Exam 2

TEST 1 Verbal Skills

1 Ⓐ Ⓑ Ⓒ Ⓓ	13 Ⓐ Ⓑ Ⓒ Ⓓ	25 Ⓐ Ⓑ Ⓒ Ⓓ	37 Ⓐ Ⓑ Ⓒ Ⓓ	49 Ⓐ Ⓑ Ⓒ Ⓓ
2 Ⓐ Ⓑ Ⓒ Ⓓ	14 Ⓐ Ⓑ Ⓒ Ⓓ	26 Ⓐ Ⓑ Ⓒ Ⓓ	38 Ⓐ Ⓑ Ⓒ	50 Ⓐ Ⓑ Ⓒ Ⓓ
3 Ⓐ Ⓑ Ⓒ Ⓓ	15 Ⓐ Ⓑ Ⓒ Ⓓ	27 Ⓐ Ⓑ Ⓒ Ⓓ	39 Ⓐ Ⓑ Ⓒ Ⓓ	51 Ⓐ Ⓑ Ⓒ Ⓓ
4 Ⓐ Ⓑ Ⓒ	16 Ⓐ Ⓑ Ⓒ Ⓓ	28 Ⓐ Ⓑ Ⓒ Ⓓ	40 Ⓐ Ⓑ Ⓒ	52 Ⓐ Ⓑ Ⓒ Ⓓ
5 Ⓐ Ⓑ Ⓒ Ⓓ	17 Ⓐ Ⓑ Ⓒ	29 Ⓐ Ⓑ Ⓒ	41 Ⓐ Ⓑ Ⓒ Ⓓ	53 Ⓐ Ⓑ Ⓒ Ⓓ
6 Ⓐ Ⓑ Ⓒ Ⓓ	18 Ⓐ Ⓑ Ⓒ Ⓓ	30 Ⓐ Ⓑ Ⓒ Ⓓ	42 Ⓐ Ⓑ Ⓒ Ⓓ	54 Ⓐ Ⓑ Ⓒ Ⓓ
7 Ⓐ Ⓑ Ⓒ Ⓓ	19 Ⓐ Ⓑ Ⓒ Ⓓ	31 Ⓐ Ⓑ Ⓒ Ⓓ	43 Ⓐ Ⓑ Ⓒ Ⓓ	55 Ⓐ Ⓑ Ⓒ Ⓓ
8 Ⓐ Ⓑ Ⓒ Ⓓ	20 Ⓐ Ⓑ Ⓒ Ⓓ	32 Ⓐ Ⓑ Ⓒ Ⓓ	44 Ⓐ Ⓑ Ⓒ Ⓓ	56 Ⓐ Ⓑ Ⓒ Ⓓ
9 Ⓐ Ⓑ Ⓒ Ⓓ	21 Ⓐ Ⓑ Ⓒ Ⓓ	33 Ⓐ Ⓑ Ⓒ Ⓓ	45 Ⓐ Ⓑ Ⓒ	57 Ⓐ Ⓑ Ⓒ Ⓓ
10 Ⓐ Ⓑ Ⓒ Ⓓ	22 Ⓐ Ⓑ Ⓒ	34 Ⓐ Ⓑ Ⓒ Ⓓ	46 Ⓐ Ⓑ Ⓒ Ⓓ	58 Ⓐ Ⓑ Ⓒ
11 Ⓐ Ⓑ Ⓒ Ⓓ	23 Ⓐ Ⓑ Ⓒ	35 Ⓐ Ⓑ Ⓒ Ⓓ	47 Ⓐ Ⓑ Ⓒ Ⓓ	59 Ⓐ Ⓑ Ⓒ Ⓓ
12 Ⓐ Ⓑ Ⓒ	24 Ⓐ Ⓑ Ⓒ Ⓓ	36 Ⓐ Ⓑ Ⓒ Ⓓ	48 Ⓐ Ⓑ Ⓒ Ⓓ	60 Ⓐ Ⓑ Ⓒ Ⓓ

TEST 2 Quantitative Skills

61 Ⓐ Ⓑ Ⓒ Ⓓ	72 Ⓐ Ⓑ Ⓒ Ⓓ	83 Ⓐ Ⓑ Ⓒ Ⓓ	93 Ⓐ Ⓑ Ⓒ Ⓓ	103 Ⓐ Ⓑ Ⓒ Ⓓ
62 Ⓐ Ⓑ Ⓒ Ⓓ	73 Ⓐ Ⓑ Ⓒ Ⓓ	84 Ⓐ Ⓑ Ⓒ Ⓓ	94 Ⓐ Ⓑ Ⓒ Ⓓ	104 Ⓐ Ⓑ Ⓒ Ⓓ
63 Ⓐ Ⓑ Ⓒ Ⓓ	74 Ⓐ Ⓑ Ⓒ Ⓓ	85 Ⓐ Ⓑ Ⓒ Ⓓ	95 Ⓐ Ⓑ Ⓒ Ⓓ	105 Ⓐ Ⓑ Ⓒ Ⓓ
64 Ⓐ Ⓑ Ⓒ Ⓓ	75 Ⓐ Ⓑ Ⓒ Ⓓ	86 Ⓐ Ⓑ Ⓒ Ⓓ	96 Ⓐ Ⓑ Ⓒ Ⓓ	106 Ⓐ Ⓑ Ⓒ Ⓓ
65 Ⓐ Ⓑ Ⓒ Ⓓ	76 Ⓐ Ⓑ Ⓒ Ⓓ	87 Ⓐ Ⓑ Ⓒ Ⓓ	97 Ⓐ Ⓑ Ⓒ Ⓓ	107 Ⓐ Ⓑ Ⓒ Ⓓ
66 Ⓐ Ⓑ Ⓒ Ⓓ	77 Ⓐ Ⓑ Ⓒ Ⓓ	88 Ⓐ Ⓑ Ⓒ Ⓓ	98 Ⓐ Ⓑ Ⓒ Ⓓ	108 Ⓐ Ⓑ Ⓒ Ⓓ
67 Ⓐ Ⓑ Ⓒ Ⓓ	78 Ⓐ Ⓑ Ⓒ Ⓓ	89 Ⓐ Ⓑ Ⓒ Ⓓ	99 Ⓐ Ⓑ Ⓒ Ⓓ	109 Ⓐ Ⓑ Ⓒ Ⓓ
68 Ⓐ Ⓑ Ⓒ Ⓓ	79 Ⓐ Ⓑ Ⓒ Ⓓ	90 Ⓐ Ⓑ Ⓒ Ⓓ	100 Ⓐ Ⓑ Ⓒ Ⓓ	110 Ⓐ Ⓑ Ⓒ Ⓓ
69 Ⓐ Ⓑ Ⓒ Ⓓ	80 Ⓐ Ⓑ Ⓒ Ⓓ	91 Ⓐ Ⓑ Ⓒ Ⓓ	101 Ⓐ Ⓑ Ⓒ Ⓓ	111 Ⓐ Ⓑ Ⓒ Ⓓ
70 Ⓐ Ⓑ Ⓒ Ⓓ	81 Ⓐ Ⓑ Ⓒ Ⓓ	92 Ⓐ Ⓑ Ⓒ Ⓓ	102 Ⓐ Ⓑ Ⓒ Ⓓ	112 Ⓐ Ⓑ Ⓒ Ⓓ
71 Ⓐ Ⓑ Ⓒ Ⓓ	82 Ⓐ Ⓑ Ⓒ Ⓓ			

TEST 3 Reading

113 Ⓐ Ⓑ Ⓒ Ⓓ	126 Ⓐ Ⓑ Ⓒ Ⓓ	139 Ⓐ Ⓑ Ⓒ Ⓓ	151 Ⓐ Ⓑ Ⓒ Ⓓ	163 Ⓐ Ⓑ Ⓒ Ⓓ
114 Ⓐ Ⓑ Ⓒ Ⓓ	127 Ⓐ Ⓑ Ⓒ Ⓓ	140 Ⓐ Ⓑ Ⓒ Ⓓ	152 Ⓐ Ⓑ Ⓒ Ⓓ	164 Ⓐ Ⓑ Ⓒ Ⓓ
115 Ⓐ Ⓑ Ⓒ Ⓓ	128 Ⓐ Ⓑ Ⓒ Ⓓ	141 Ⓐ Ⓑ Ⓒ Ⓓ	153 Ⓐ Ⓑ Ⓒ Ⓓ	165 Ⓐ Ⓑ Ⓒ Ⓓ
116 Ⓐ Ⓑ Ⓒ Ⓓ	129 Ⓐ Ⓑ Ⓒ Ⓓ	142 Ⓐ Ⓑ Ⓒ Ⓓ	154 Ⓐ Ⓑ Ⓒ Ⓓ	166 Ⓐ Ⓑ Ⓒ Ⓓ
117 Ⓐ Ⓑ Ⓒ Ⓓ	130 Ⓐ Ⓑ Ⓒ Ⓓ	143 Ⓐ Ⓑ Ⓒ Ⓓ	155 Ⓐ Ⓑ Ⓒ Ⓓ	167 Ⓐ Ⓑ Ⓒ Ⓓ
118 Ⓐ Ⓑ Ⓒ Ⓓ	131 Ⓐ Ⓑ Ⓒ Ⓓ	144 Ⓐ Ⓑ Ⓒ Ⓓ	156 Ⓐ Ⓑ Ⓒ Ⓓ	168 Ⓐ Ⓑ Ⓒ Ⓓ
119 Ⓐ Ⓑ Ⓒ Ⓓ	132 Ⓐ Ⓑ Ⓒ Ⓓ	145 Ⓐ Ⓑ Ⓒ Ⓓ	157 Ⓐ Ⓑ Ⓒ Ⓓ	169 Ⓐ Ⓑ Ⓒ Ⓓ
120 Ⓐ Ⓑ Ⓒ Ⓓ	133 Ⓐ Ⓑ Ⓒ Ⓓ	146 Ⓐ Ⓑ Ⓒ Ⓓ	158 Ⓐ Ⓑ Ⓒ Ⓓ	170 Ⓐ Ⓑ Ⓒ Ⓓ
121 Ⓐ Ⓑ Ⓒ Ⓓ	134 Ⓐ Ⓑ Ⓒ Ⓓ	147 Ⓐ Ⓑ Ⓒ Ⓓ	159 Ⓐ Ⓑ Ⓒ Ⓓ	171 Ⓐ Ⓑ Ⓒ Ⓓ
122 Ⓐ Ⓑ Ⓒ Ⓓ	135 Ⓐ Ⓑ Ⓒ Ⓓ	148 Ⓐ Ⓑ Ⓒ Ⓓ	160 Ⓐ Ⓑ Ⓒ Ⓓ	172 Ⓐ Ⓑ Ⓒ Ⓓ
123 Ⓐ Ⓑ Ⓒ Ⓓ	136 Ⓐ Ⓑ Ⓒ Ⓓ	149 Ⓐ Ⓑ Ⓒ Ⓓ	161 Ⓐ Ⓑ Ⓒ Ⓓ	173 Ⓐ Ⓑ Ⓒ Ⓓ
124 Ⓐ Ⓑ Ⓒ Ⓓ	137 Ⓐ Ⓑ Ⓒ Ⓓ	150 Ⓐ Ⓑ Ⓒ Ⓓ	162 Ⓐ Ⓑ Ⓒ Ⓓ	174 Ⓐ Ⓑ Ⓒ Ⓓ
125 Ⓐ Ⓑ Ⓒ Ⓓ	138 Ⓐ Ⓑ Ⓒ Ⓓ			

CUT HERE

Answer Sheet for Practice HSPT Exam 2

TEST 4 Mathematics

175 Ⓐ Ⓑ Ⓒ Ⓓ	188 Ⓐ Ⓑ Ⓒ Ⓓ	201 Ⓐ Ⓑ Ⓒ Ⓓ	214 Ⓐ Ⓑ Ⓒ Ⓓ	227 Ⓐ Ⓑ Ⓒ Ⓓ
176 Ⓐ Ⓑ Ⓒ Ⓓ	189 Ⓐ Ⓑ Ⓒ Ⓓ	202 Ⓐ Ⓑ Ⓒ Ⓓ	215 Ⓐ Ⓑ Ⓒ Ⓓ	228 Ⓐ Ⓑ Ⓒ Ⓓ
177 Ⓐ Ⓑ Ⓒ Ⓓ	190 Ⓐ Ⓑ Ⓒ Ⓓ	203 Ⓐ Ⓑ Ⓒ Ⓓ	216 Ⓐ Ⓑ Ⓒ Ⓓ	229 Ⓐ Ⓑ Ⓒ Ⓓ
178 Ⓐ Ⓑ Ⓒ Ⓓ	191 Ⓐ Ⓑ Ⓒ Ⓓ	204 Ⓐ Ⓑ Ⓒ Ⓓ	217 Ⓐ Ⓑ Ⓒ Ⓓ	230 Ⓐ Ⓑ Ⓒ Ⓓ
179 Ⓐ Ⓑ Ⓒ Ⓓ	192 Ⓐ Ⓑ Ⓒ Ⓓ	205 Ⓐ Ⓑ Ⓒ Ⓓ	218 Ⓐ Ⓑ Ⓒ Ⓓ	231 Ⓐ Ⓑ Ⓒ Ⓓ
180 Ⓐ Ⓑ Ⓒ Ⓓ	193 Ⓐ Ⓑ Ⓒ Ⓓ	206 Ⓐ Ⓑ Ⓒ Ⓓ	219 Ⓐ Ⓑ Ⓒ Ⓓ	232 Ⓐ Ⓑ Ⓒ Ⓓ
181 Ⓐ Ⓑ Ⓒ Ⓓ	194 Ⓐ Ⓑ Ⓒ Ⓓ	207 Ⓐ Ⓑ Ⓒ Ⓓ	220 Ⓐ Ⓑ Ⓒ Ⓓ	233 Ⓐ Ⓑ Ⓒ Ⓓ
182 Ⓐ Ⓑ Ⓒ Ⓓ	195 Ⓐ Ⓑ Ⓒ Ⓓ	208 Ⓐ Ⓑ Ⓒ Ⓓ	221 Ⓐ Ⓑ Ⓒ Ⓓ	234 Ⓐ Ⓑ Ⓒ Ⓓ
183 Ⓐ Ⓑ Ⓒ Ⓓ	196 Ⓐ Ⓑ Ⓒ Ⓓ	209 Ⓐ Ⓑ Ⓒ Ⓓ	222 Ⓐ Ⓑ Ⓒ Ⓓ	235 Ⓐ Ⓑ Ⓒ Ⓓ
184 Ⓐ Ⓑ Ⓒ Ⓓ	197 Ⓐ Ⓑ Ⓒ Ⓓ	210 Ⓐ Ⓑ Ⓒ Ⓓ	223 Ⓐ Ⓑ Ⓒ Ⓓ	236 Ⓐ Ⓑ Ⓒ Ⓓ
185 Ⓐ Ⓑ Ⓒ Ⓓ	198 Ⓐ Ⓑ Ⓒ Ⓓ	211 Ⓐ Ⓑ Ⓒ Ⓓ	224 Ⓐ Ⓑ Ⓒ Ⓓ	237 Ⓐ Ⓑ Ⓒ Ⓓ
186 Ⓐ Ⓑ Ⓒ Ⓓ	199 Ⓐ Ⓑ Ⓒ Ⓓ	212 Ⓐ Ⓑ Ⓒ Ⓓ	225 Ⓐ Ⓑ Ⓒ Ⓓ	238 Ⓐ Ⓑ Ⓒ Ⓓ
187 Ⓐ Ⓑ Ⓒ Ⓓ	200 Ⓐ Ⓑ Ⓒ Ⓓ	213 Ⓐ Ⓑ Ⓒ Ⓓ	226 Ⓐ Ⓑ Ⓒ Ⓓ	

TEST 5 Language Skills

239 Ⓐ Ⓑ Ⓒ Ⓓ	251 Ⓐ Ⓑ Ⓒ Ⓓ	263 Ⓐ Ⓑ Ⓒ Ⓓ	275 Ⓐ Ⓑ Ⓒ Ⓓ	287 Ⓐ Ⓑ Ⓒ Ⓓ
240 Ⓐ Ⓑ Ⓒ Ⓓ	252 Ⓐ Ⓑ Ⓒ Ⓓ	264 Ⓐ Ⓑ Ⓒ Ⓓ	276 Ⓐ Ⓑ Ⓒ Ⓓ	288 Ⓐ Ⓑ Ⓒ Ⓓ
241 Ⓐ Ⓑ Ⓒ Ⓓ	253 Ⓐ Ⓑ Ⓒ Ⓓ	265 Ⓐ Ⓑ Ⓒ Ⓓ	277 Ⓐ Ⓑ Ⓒ Ⓓ	289 Ⓐ Ⓑ Ⓒ Ⓓ
242 Ⓐ Ⓑ Ⓒ Ⓓ	254 Ⓐ Ⓑ Ⓒ Ⓓ	266 Ⓐ Ⓑ Ⓒ Ⓓ	278 Ⓐ Ⓑ Ⓒ Ⓓ	290 Ⓐ Ⓑ Ⓒ Ⓓ
243 Ⓐ Ⓑ Ⓒ Ⓓ	255 Ⓐ Ⓑ Ⓒ Ⓓ	267 Ⓐ Ⓑ Ⓒ Ⓓ	279 Ⓐ Ⓑ Ⓒ Ⓓ	291 Ⓐ Ⓑ Ⓒ Ⓓ
244 Ⓐ Ⓑ Ⓒ Ⓓ	256 Ⓐ Ⓑ Ⓒ Ⓓ	268 Ⓐ Ⓑ Ⓒ Ⓓ	280 Ⓐ Ⓑ Ⓒ Ⓓ	292 Ⓐ Ⓑ Ⓒ Ⓓ
245 Ⓐ Ⓑ Ⓒ Ⓓ	257 Ⓐ Ⓑ Ⓒ Ⓓ	269 Ⓐ Ⓑ Ⓒ Ⓓ	281 Ⓐ Ⓑ Ⓒ Ⓓ	293 Ⓐ Ⓑ Ⓒ Ⓓ
246 Ⓐ Ⓑ Ⓒ Ⓓ	258 Ⓐ Ⓑ Ⓒ Ⓓ	270 Ⓐ Ⓑ Ⓒ Ⓓ	282 Ⓐ Ⓑ Ⓒ Ⓓ	294 Ⓐ Ⓑ Ⓒ Ⓓ
247 Ⓐ Ⓑ Ⓒ Ⓓ	259 Ⓐ Ⓑ Ⓒ Ⓓ	271 Ⓐ Ⓑ Ⓒ Ⓓ	283 Ⓐ Ⓑ Ⓒ Ⓓ	295 Ⓐ Ⓑ Ⓒ Ⓓ
248 Ⓐ Ⓑ Ⓒ Ⓓ	260 Ⓐ Ⓑ Ⓒ Ⓓ	272 Ⓐ Ⓑ Ⓒ Ⓓ	284 Ⓐ Ⓑ Ⓒ Ⓓ	296 Ⓐ Ⓑ Ⓒ Ⓓ
249 Ⓐ Ⓑ Ⓒ Ⓓ	261 Ⓐ Ⓑ Ⓒ Ⓓ	273 Ⓐ Ⓑ Ⓒ Ⓓ	285 Ⓐ Ⓑ Ⓒ Ⓓ	297 Ⓐ Ⓑ Ⓒ Ⓓ
250 Ⓐ Ⓑ Ⓒ Ⓓ	262 Ⓐ Ⓑ Ⓒ Ⓓ	274 Ⓐ Ⓑ Ⓒ Ⓓ	286 Ⓐ Ⓑ Ⓒ Ⓓ	298 Ⓐ Ⓑ Ⓒ Ⓓ

Practice HSPT Exam 2

Test 1: Verbal Skills

Time: 16 Minutes

Directions: Select the choice that best answers the following questions.

1. Dentist is to teeth as plumber is to:

    A. bones
    B. shovel
    C. drill
    D. pipes

2. Contradict most nearly means:

    A. discuss
    B. predict
    C. listen to
    D. disagree with

3. An ambiguous answer is:

    A. unclear
    B. positive
    C. unkind
    D. deliberate

4. Spice cookies cost less than chocolate cookies.
   Frosted cookies cost more than spice cookies.
   Chocolate cookies cost more than frosted cookies.

   If the first two statements are true, the third is:

    A. true
    B. false
    C. uncertain

5. Which word does *not* belong with the others?

    A. whale
    B. monkey
    C. snake
    D. cow

6. Which word does *not* belong with the others?

    A. lilac
    B. rose
    C. violet
    D. lavender

7. Somber is the *opposite* of:

    A. straight
    B. bright
    C. cloudy
    D. miserable

8. Professor is to lecture as actor is to:

    A. script
    B. performance
    C. tests
    D. stage

9. Duet is to solo as quart is to:

    A. single
    B. trio
    C. pint
    D. gallon

10. Emit most nearly means:

    A. hide
    B. hope for
    C. let out
    D. disturb

11. Evoke most nearly means:

    A. hold back
    B. call forth
    C. change
    D. tease

GO ON TO THE NEXT PAGE

12. In New City, all the park benches are painted green. Maria sees a green park bench.

She is visiting New City. If the first two statements are true, the third is:

- **A.** true
- **B.** false
- **C.** uncertain

13. Which word does *not* belong with the others?

- **A.** fingernails
- **B.** skin
- **C.** teeth
- **D.** bones

14. Which word does *not* belong with the others?

- **A.** durable
- **B.** fragile
- **C.** sturdy
- **D.** tough

15. Freeze is to cold as boil is to:

- **A.** steam
- **B.** ice
- **C.** smoke
- **D.** heat

16. Mar most nearly means:

- **A.** sell
- **B.** spoil
- **C.** move
- **D.** upset

17. Ian's voice is deeper than Ken's. Max's voice is higher than Ken's. Ian has a deeper voice than Max. If the first two statements are true, the third is:

- **A.** true
- **B.** false
- **C.** uncertain

18. Which word does *not* belong with the others?

- **A.** horse
- **B.** donkey
- **C.** camel
- **D.** hippopotamus

19. Indispensable is the *opposite* of:

- **A.** unnecessary
- **B.** ridiculous
- **C.** trashy
- **D.** cheap

20. Which word does *not* belong with the others?

- **A.** fiction
- **B.** novel
- **C.** myth
- **D.** legend

21. Which word does *not* belong with the others?

- **A.** ice
- **B.** snow
- **C.** rain
- **D.** frost

22. Yawps live in underground caves. Wiffy is a yawp. Wiffy lives underground. If the first two statements are true, the third is:

- **A.** true
- **B.** false
- **C.** uncertain

23. Nina has taken more math classes than Patrick. Patrick has taken fewer math classs than Carl. Nina has taken more math classes than Carl. If the first two statements are true, the third is:

- **A.** true
- **B.** false
- **C.** uncertain

24. A punctual student is:

- **A.** late
- **B.** prompt
- **C.** missing
- **D.** quick

25. A vital item is:

- **A.** healthy
- **B.** useless
- **C.** necessary
- **D.** wasted

26. Deny is to contradict as obtain is to:

    A. acquire
    B. lose
    C. disagree
    D. stubborn

27. Food is to nutrition as soap is to:

    A. dirt
    B. suds
    C. cleanliness
    D. health

28. Scurry most nearly means:

    A. clean
    B. dash
    C. stroll
    D. fall

29. Helen is taller than Polly. Ann is shorter than Polly. Helen is taller than Ann. If the first two statements are true, the third is:

    A. true
    B. false
    C. uncertain

30. Divulge most nearly means:

    A. care for
    B. leave
    C. reveal
    D. injure

31. Which word does *not* belong with the others?

    A. cap
    B. sneaker
    C. turban
    D. beret

32. Which word does *not* belong with the others?

    A. bee
    B. bat
    C. fly
    D. gnat

33. Which word does *not* belong with the others?

    A. wrench
    B. tool
    C. hammer
    D. saw

34. Which word does *not* belong with the others?

    A. cake
    B. pie
    C. dessert
    D. fruit

35. Infant is to adult as kid is to:

    A. goat
    B. baby
    C. joke
    D. calf

36. Clash most nearly means:

    A. conflict
    B. soot
    C. dance
    D. delight

37. Heed most nearly means:

    A. avoid
    B. agree with
    C. hear
    D. pay attention to

38. All gorgons have scales. No griffins are gorgons. No griffins have scales. If the first two statements are true, the third is:

    A. true
    B. false
    C. uncertain

39. Which word does *not* belong with the others?

    A. calendar
    B. month
    C. day
    D. hour

GO ON TO THE NEXT PAGE

Practice HSPT Exam 2

40. Green grapes are sweeter than red grapes but not as sweet as purple grapes. Purple grapes are less sweet than pink grapes. Pink grapes are sweeter than red grapes. If the first two statements are true, the third is:

A. true
B. false
C. uncertain

41. Startle most nearly means:

A. surprise
B. climb
C. draw
D. sparkle

42. An irritating remark is:

A. annoying
B. itchy
C. funny
D. gloomy

43. Tight is to loose as gritty is to:

A. coarse
B. relaxed
C. pavement
D. smooth

44. Seep most nearly means:

A. fall
B. rain
C. ooze
D. climb

45. State Street is narrower than Smith Street. Main Street is wider than Smith Street. State Street is narrower than Main Street . If the first two statements are true, the third is:

A. true
B. false
C. uncertain

46. Which word does *not* belong with the others?

A. ripe
B. mature
C. ready
D. rotten

47. Which word does *not* belong with the others?

A. nouns
B. verbs
C. words
D. adjectives

48. Familiar is the *opposite* of:

A. lonesome
B. well known
C. relative
D. strange

49. Cease is the *opposite* of:

A. stop
B. forget
C. change
D. continue

50. Vacant is the *opposite* of:

A. full
B. empty
C. relaxed
D. nervous

51. Which word does *not* belong with the others?

A. seaweed
B. beach
C. sand
D. shells

52. Which word does *not* belong with the others?

A. cup
B. canteen
C. thermos
D. water

53. Rotor is to helicopter as tuner is to:

A. radio
B. piano
C. airplane
D. dial

54. Slow is to snail as thin is to:

A. skinny
B. kitten
C. heavy
D. twig

55. Incite most nearly means:

    A. calm down
    B. stir up
    C. continue
    D. intend

56. Concur is the *opposite* of:

    A. shout
    B. argue
    C. agree
    D. discuss

57. Sparse is the *opposite* of:

    A. plentiful
    B. skinny
    C. ashy
    D. dry

58. Zax has a red nose. Burbs have red noses. Zax is a burb. If the first two statements are true, the third is:

    A. true
    B. false
    C. uncertain

59. Hostile is the *opposite* of:

    A. sorry
    B. generous
    C. homely
    D. friendly

60. Stingy is the *opposite* of:

    A. calming
    B. generous
    C. frugal
    D. wealthy

Practice HSPT Exam 2

IF YOU FINISH BEFORE TIME IS CALLED, CHECK YOUR WORK ON THIS SECTION ONLY. DO NOT WORK ON ANY OTHER SECTION IN THE TEST.

Test 2: Quantitative Skills

Time: 30 Minutes

Directions: Select the choice that best answers the following questions.

61. What number should come next in the series 6, 11, 16, 21, 26, ___?

    A. 29
    B. 31
    C. 33
    D. 35

62. What number, when divided by 4, is equal to the product of 2 and 5?

    A. 36
    B. 40
    C. 44
    D. 48

63. Examine (a), (b), and (c) and find the best answer.

    (a) -5^2
    (b) $(-5)^2$
    (c) 5^2

    A. (a) is greater than (b) and (c).
    B. (a) is equal to (c) and less than (b).
    C. (b) and (c) are equal and greater than (a).
    D. (a), (b), and (c) are equal.

64. Twenty percent of what number is equal to 5% of 200?

    A. 40
    B. 48
    C. 50
    D. 60

65. The following triangle is isosceles, with $XY = YZ$. Examine the figure and determine which of the following is true.

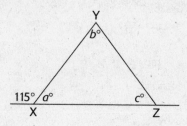

    A. $a > c > b$
    B. $a = c > b$
    C. $a = c < b$
    D. $a = c = b$

66. What number should come next in the series 8, 16, 32, 64, ___?

    A. 72
    B. 96
    C. 128
    D. 132

67. Examine (a), (b), and (c) and find the best answer.

    (a) $5 + 3(2 + 4)$
    (b) $(5 + 3)2 + 4$
    (c) $5 + (3 \times 2) + 4$

    A. (a) is greater than (b) and (c).
    B. (a) is equal to (c) and less than (b).
    C. (b) and (c) are equal and greater than (a).
    D. (a), (b), and (c) are equal.

68. Three fourths of what number is equal to $\frac{9}{11}$ of 33?

    A. 24
    B. 28
    C. 32
    D. 36

69. In the following figure, line *l* and line *m* are parallel. Examine the figure, and determine which of the following relationships must be true.

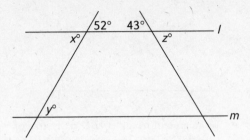

- **A.** $x = y > z$
- **B.** $x = z > y$
- **C.** $x = z > y$
- **D.** $x = y = z$

70. Examine (a), (b), and (c) and find the best answer.

- (a) $(-1)^3$
- (b) $(-1)^2$
- (c) $(-1)^4$

- **A.** (a) is greater than (b) and (c).
- **B.** (a) is equal to (c) and less than (b).
- **C.** (b) and (c) are equal and greater than (a).
- **D.** (a), (b), and (c) are equal.

71. What number should fill in the blank in the series 4, 3, 10, 9, ___, 15?

- **A.** 11
- **B.** 14
- **C.** 16
- **D.** 18

72. The number that is 12 less than 26 is the same as the product of 7 and what number?

- **A.** 1
- **B.** 2
- **C.** 4
- **D.** 6

73. The following figure shows a circle with center *O*. Which of the following relationships is true?

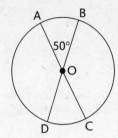

- **A.** The length of arc *AB* < the length of arc *DC* = the length of arc *BC*.
- **B.** The length of arc *AB* = the length of arc *DC* < the length of arc *BC*.
- **C.** The length of arc *BC* > the length of arc *AD* > the length of arc *AB*.
- **D.** The length of arc *AB* = the length of arc *BC* < the length of arc *AB*.

74. What number should come next in the series 24, 4, 12, 2, 6, ___?

- **A.** 8
- **B.** 4
- **C.** 2
- **D.** 1

75. Three fifths of the sum of 25, 30, and 45 is equal to:

- **A.** 60
- **B.** 65
- **C.** 70
- **D.** 75

76. Examine (a), (b), and (c) and find the best answer.

- (a) 2.06×10^{-2}
- (b) 0.000206×10^{2}
- (c) 0.0206

- **A.** (a) is greater than (b) and (c).
- **B.** (a) is equal to (c) and less than (b).
- **C.** (b) and (c) are equal and greater than (a).
- **D.** (a), (b), and (c) are equal.

GO ON TO THE NEXT PAGE

77. What number, when doubled, is equal to the number 24 when tripled?

    A. 28

    B. 34

    C. 36

    D. 38

78. Examine the following figure and determine which of the following relationships must be true.

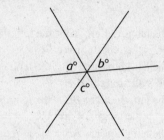

    A. $a + b + c > 180$

    B. $a + b + c < 180$

    C. $a + b + c = 180$

    D. $a = b = c$

79. What number, when cubed and then increased by 6, is equal to the product of 7 and 10?

    A. 4

    B. 6

    C. 8

    D. 10

80. Examine (a), (b), and (c) and find the best answer.

    (a) 4.268 rounded to the nearest tenth

    (b) 4.328 rounded to the nearest tenth

    (c) 4.352 rounded to the nearest tenth

    A. (a) is greater than (b) and (c).

    B. (a) is equal to (b) and less than (c).

    C. (b) and (c) are equal and greater than (a).

    D. (a), (b), and (c) are equal.

81. Sixty percent of what number is equal to 15% of 300?

    A. 27

    B. 75

    C. 80

    D. 125

82. In the following figure, *ABCD* is a rectangle. Based on the figure, which of the following must be true?

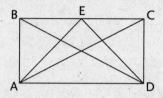

    A. The area of triangle *ABD* = the area of triangle *ADC* < the area of triangle *AED*.

    B. The area of triangle *ABD* = the area of triangle *ADC* > the area of triangle *AED*.

    C. The area of triangle *ABD* > the area of triangle *ADC* > the area of triangle *AED*.

    D. The area of triangle *ABD* = the area of triangle *ADC* = the area of triangle *AED*.

83. What number, when tripled and then decreased by 12, is equal to 48?

    A. 18

    B. 20

    C. 22

    D. 24

84. What number should come next in the series 1, 4, 2, 8, 3, 12, 4, ___?

    A. 10

    B. 12

    C. 16

    D. 18

85. One fifth of what number is equal to $\frac{1}{6}$ of 24?

    A. 10

    B. 15

    C. 20

    D. 25

86. Examine (a), (b), and (c) and find the best answer.

    (a) The largest prime factor of 28

    (b) The largest prime factor of 64

    (c) The largest prime factor of 72

    A. (a) is greater than (b) and (c).

    B. (a) is equal to (c) and less than (b).

    C. (b) and (c) are equal and greater than (a).

    D. (a), (b), and (c) are equal.

87. What number should come next in the series 81, 27, 9, 3, ___?

    A. 6
    B. 1
    C. 0
    D. −3

88. The square of what number is equal to the number 2 raised to the fourth power?

    A. 4
    B. 6
    C. 8
    D. 12

89. The following figure contains two right triangles. Examine the following statements and determine which one is true.

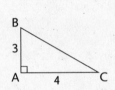
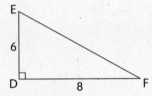

    A. Twice the perimeter of triangle *ABC* = the perimeter of triangle *DEF*.
    B. The perimeter of triangle *ABC* + 7 = the perimeter of triangle *DEF*.
    C. Three times the perimeter of triangle *ABC* = the perimeter of triangle *DEF*.
    D. The perimeter of triangle *ABC* + 5 = the perimeter of triangle *DEF*.

90. What number should come next in the series 20, 15, 11, 8, 6, ___?

    A. 5
    B. 4
    C. 3
    D. 2

91. If the product of 3 and a number is 36, then 50% of the number is:

    A. 4
    B. 5
    C. 6
    D. 8

92. What number should come next in the series 0, 3, 9, 18, 30, 45, ___?

    A. 54
    B. 57
    C. 60
    D. 63

93. Examine (a), (b), and (c) and find the best answer.

    (a) 350%

    (b) 0.035×100

    (c) $\dfrac{14}{4}$

    A. (a) is greater than (b) and (c).
    B. (a) is equal to (c) and less than (b).
    C. (b) and (c) are equal and greater than (a).
    D. (a), (b), and (c) are equal.

94. One sixth of the difference between 102 and 12 is equal to:

    A. 12
    B. 13
    C. 14
    D. 15

95. Examine the triangle in the following figure and determine the best answer.

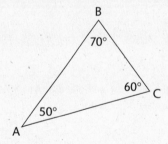

    A. $AB > AC > BC$
    B. $AC > AB > BC$
    C. $BC > AB > AC$
    D. $AC > BC > AB$

96. What number should come next in the series 5, 15, 10, 30, 25, 75, ___?

    A. 65
    B. 70
    C. 150
    D. 225

GO ON TO THE NEXT PAGE

97. If the difference of 37 and 15 is equal to 20% of a number, then the number is:

A. 90
B. 110
C. 120
D. 140

98. What number should come next in the series 2, 6, 4, 12, 10, ___?

A. 14
B. 20
C. 26
D. 30

99. Examine (a), (b), and (c) and find the best answer.

(a) The value of $2x + 3y$ if $x = 6$ and $y = 0$

(b) The value of $2x + 3y$ if $x = 0$ and $y = 4$

(c) The value of $2x + 3y$ if $x = 12$ and $y = -6$

A. (a) is greater than (b) and (c).
B. (a) is equal to (b) and greater than (c).
C. (b) and (c) are equal and greater than (a).
D. (a), (b), and (c) are equal.

100. What number should fill in the blank in the series 99, 89, 80, ___, 65?

A. 76
B. 74
C. 72
D. 70

101. If the product of 9 and 6 is equal to 300% of a number, then the number is:

A. 12
B. 15
C. 18
D. 21

102. The following figure is a semicircle with center O. Select the best answer from the following choices.

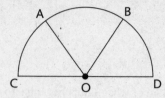

A. $CD > AO > BO$
B. $CD = AO + BO$
C. $CO = DO > AO$
D. $CO > BO > AO$

103. What number should fill in the blank in the series 0, 1, 4, 9, 16, ___, 36?

A. 18
B. 20
C. 24
D. 25

104. What number, when reduced by 20% of itself, is equal to 48?

A. 50
B. 56
C. 60
D. 68

105. What number should come next in the series 49, 7, 64, 8, 81, ___?

A. 9
B. 18
C. 27
D. 54

106. What number is equal to 25% of the product of 8 and 16?

A. 24
B. 32
C. 36
D. 42

107. What number should come next in the series 4, −4, 8, −24, 96, ___?

A. −480
B. −240
C. 240
D. 480

108. What number should fill in the blank in the series 9, 13, 16, 20, 23, ___, 30?

A. 25
B. 26
C. 27
D. 28

109. Four hundred percent of what number is equal to the square of 10?

A. 15
B. 20
C. 25
D. 50

110. What number should fill in the blank in the series 11, 14, 20, 29, ___, 56?

A. 39
B. 40
C. 41
D. 42

111. What number should fill in the blank in the series 33, 11, 30, 10, 27, 9, ___, 8?

A. 26
B. 24
C. 22
D. 21

112. What number should come next in the series 5, 6, 11, 17, 28, 45, ___?

A. 56
B. 62
C. 67
D. 73

IF YOU FINISH BEFORE TIME IS CALLED, CHECK YOUR WORK ON THIS SECTION ONLY. DO NOT WORK ON ANY OTHER SECTION IN THE TEST.

STOP

Practice HSPT Exam 2

Test 3: Reading

Time: 25 Minutes

Directions: In this test, select the answer choice that best satisfies the question.

Comprehension

For questions 113–152, read each passage carefully. Then select the choice that best answers the questions that follow each passage.

More than 10,000 species of bees exist. The most commonly known species is the honeybee, the only bee that produces honey and wax. Humans use the wax in making candles, lipsticks, and other products, and they use the honey as a food. While gathering the nectar and pollen with which they make honey, bees are <u>simultaneously</u> helping to fertilize the flowers on which they land. Many fruits and vegetables would not survive if bees did not carry the pollen from blossom to blossom.

A beehive is a nest with storage space for the honey. Each type of bee performs a unique function. Some worker bees carry nectar to the hive in a special stomach called a honey stomach. Other workers make beeswax and shape it into a honeycomb, which is a waterproof mass of six-sided <u>compartments</u>, or cells. The cells contain honey. The queen lays eggs in completed cells. As the workers build more cells, the queen lays more eggs.

All workers are female, but the workers are smaller than the queen. The male honeybees are called drones; they do no work and cannot sting. They are developed from unfertilized eggs. Their only job is to mate with the queen. The queen then can lay worker eggs. During the season when less honey is available and the drone is of no further use, the workers block the drones from eating the honey. The drones starve to death, leaving more honey for the workers.

113. The best title for this passage is:

    A. The Many Species of Bees
    B. The Useless Drone
    C. The Lives of Honeybees
    D. Making Honey

114. As underlined and used in this passage, the word <u>simultaneously</u> most nearly means:

    A. with great skill
    B. preparing to
    C. at the same time
    D. while flying

115. According to the passage, a hive is:

    A. a type of honey
    B. a nest
    C. a type of bee
    D. a storage space

116. According to the passage, the drone:

    A. collects less honey than workers
    B. mates with the queen and has no other purpose
    C. comes from eggs fertilized by other drones
    D. can be male or female

117. As underlined and used in this passage, the word <u>compartments</u> most nearly means:

    A. rooms
    B. portions
    C. enclosures
    D. hexagons

118. Honey is carried to the hive in a honey stomach by the:

    A. queens
    B. drones
    C. males
    D. workers

119. All the following statements are true of a honeycomb except:

    A. It contains six-sided sections.
    B. It is made of honey.
    C. It is made of wax.
    D. It keeps honey dry.

120. Bees are useful in nature because they:

    A. pollinate fruit and vegetable plants
    B. make marvelous creations from wax
    C. kill the dangerous drones
    D. create storage spaces

121. The passage suggests that beeswax is:

    A. absorbent
    B. flexible
    C. clean
    D. sweet

122. Drones are prevented from eating honey:

    A. when plenty of honey is available
    B. because the worker bees are female
    C. so that more food is available for workers
    D. as soon as they have mated with the queen

When I was a boy, there was but one permanent ambition among my comrades in our village on the west bank of the Mississippi River. That was to be a steamboatman. We had transient ambitions of other sorts, but they were only transient. When a circus came and went, it left us all burning to become clowns; the first minstrel show that ever came to our area left us all suffering to try that kind of life; now and then we had a hope that, if we lived and were good, God would permit us to be pirates. These ambitions faded out, each in its turn, but the ambition to be a steamboatman always remained.

Once a day, a steamboat arrived upward from St. Louis, and another downward from Keokuk. Before these events, the day was glorious with expectancy, after them, the day was a dead and empty thing. Not only the boys, but the whole village, felt this. After all these years I can picture that old time to myself now, just as it was then: the white town drowsing in the sunshine of a summer's morning, the streets empty, or pretty nearly so, one or two clerks sitting in front of the Water Street stores with their chairs tilted back against the walls, chins on breasts, hats slouched over their faces, asleep. A sow and a litter of pigs loafing along the sidewalk, two or three piles of freight scattered about the levee, nobody to listen to the peaceful lapping of the wavelets against the head of the pier; the great Mississippi, the majestic the magnificent Mississippi, rolling its mile-wide tide along shining in the sun; the dense forest away on the other side, the point above the town, and the point below bounding the river-glimpse and turning it into a sort of sea, a very still and brilliant and lonely one.

Presently a film of dark smoke appears above one of those remote points and a worker famous for his quick eye and prodigious voice lifts up the cry "Steamboat a-coming!" The clerks wake up, a furious clatter of carts follows, every house and store pours out a human contribution, and all in a twinkling the dead town is alive and moving.

From "Life on the Mississippi" by Mark Twain

123. The word transient as underlined and used in this passage most nearly means:

    A. traveling
    B. honest
    C. serious
    D. temporary

124. The expression *if we lived and were good, God would permit us to be pirates* is ironic because:

    A. the boys were too young to go to sea
    B. pirates are not good people
    C. there were no pirates on the Mississippi River
    D. the boys fear they might die before they grow up

125. Steamboats arrived in the town:

    A. once each day
    B. twice each day
    C. every night
    D. every week

126. Based on the description of the river in the passage, what impressed the author most about the Mississippi was its:

    A. brightness
    B. stillness
    C. size
    D. tides

127. The word expectancy as underlined and used in this passage most nearly means:

    A. dreams
    B. anticipation
    C. ambition
    D. nervousness

GO ON TO THE NEXT PAGE

128. The best pair of words to describe the town before the steamboat arrives and when it arrives is:

    A. sick/healthy

    B. waiting/hoping

    C. dark/bright

    D. asleep/awake

129. The smoke that appears comes from:

    A. a fire on one of the points

    B. the smokestack of a steamboat

    C. railroad trains passing the town

    D. the cooking stoves in houses in the town

130. The word <u>prodigious</u> as underlined and used in this passage most nearly means:

    A. impressive

    B. arguing

    C. deep

    D. miniature

131. It is most likely the boys want to be steamboatmen because:

    A. they like the idea of working on the river

    B. the boats and their crew were important and exciting to people

    C. it would be impossible for them to grow up to be clowns or pirates

    D. that would give them a chance to leave their homes

132. The main subject of this passage is:

    A. the author's feelings about the Mississippi River

    B. the lives of steamboatmen

    C. a memory of the past

    D. boys' ambitions

Lightning has been a mystery since early times. People of ancient civilizations believed angry gods threw lightning bolts from the sky. Nobody understood that lightning resulted from electricity until Ben Franklin flew a kite with a key dangling from the string, and it was struck by lightning.

Now forecasters know what causes lightning. Within a storm cloud, friction from water- and ice-laden clouds creates a negative charge at the bottom of the cloud. When that charge grows too great for the air to hold it back, it is united with a positive charge from the Earth. This creates a channel of electricity that flows between the two points. The charge remains invisible as it moves toward the ground until it meets the charge rising from the ground. When they meet, an extremely hot current superheats the air around the channel, resulting in an explosion of sound known as thunder. Lightning is much harder to forecast than a storm. Forecasters can tell when a storm is likely to produce lightning, but they have no way of knowing when or where the lightning will strike. It can strike up to 25 miles from the center of a storm. This occurs when lightning originates under a cloud but travels horizontally for a time before turning toward earth. Thunder is only heard up to 10 miles from where lightning strikes, so it is possible to be struck by lightning without even realizing a storm is in the area.

Generally, people are injured by lightning when they are in the open, near or in water, or near tall structures like trees. Golfers, swimmers, beach-goers, and outdoor workers are in the greatest danger. More males than females are victims. It is thought that this is because males are more likely to be in the places where lightning strikes. When lightning is about to strike, one feels an odd, tingling sensation, and one's hair stands on end. Of course, there is little chance to do anything about it because the full blow occurs within a second and is over in a couple of seconds. The victim might be thrown, lose consciousness, be burned, die, or suffer injury. Some injured people recover completely, but others do not.

133. The first recorded evidence that lightning came from electricity was discovered by:

    A. people of ancient civilizations

    B. Ben Franklin

    C. researchers from the 1400s

    D. modern researchers

134. As underlined and used in this passage, the word <u>dangling</u> most nearly means:

    A. connected

    B. hanging

    C. tied

    D. sewed into

135. The relationship between the charge in the cloud and the charge from earth is that:

    A. they meet each other in the sky

    B. they are the same polarity

    C. the charge from earth travels to the cloud

    D. the charge from the cloud reaches the ground before they meet

136. The primary cause of the charge in the storm cloud is:

 A. ice buildup
 B. friction
 C. unknown
 D. water

137. As underlined and used in this passage, the word <u>channel</u> most nearly means:

 A. station
 B. lake
 C. path
 D. clap

138. The passage suggests that as the lightning comes toward earth, but before it strikes,

 A. it can be seen in the sky
 B. it can turn back
 C. its approach can be felt by someone about to be struck
 D. thunder is heard several miles away

139. Thunder is created when:

 A. the charge from the earth meets the charge from the cloud
 B. lightning strikes the ground
 C. friction occurs in the cloud
 D. lightning leaves the cloud

140. The author indicates that lightning can strike far from the center of a storm when:

 A. it travels horizontally first
 B. the storm cloud is large
 C. lightning has already come from the same cloud
 D. it comes from a positive charge in the cloud

141. It is possible that more males than females are struck by lightning because:

 A. females don't play golf
 B. males attract electricity more easily than females
 C. females are usually shorter than males
 D. males are more likely to be outdoors

142. This passage was probably printed in a:

 A. science book
 B. newspaper
 C. safety guide
 D. golf magazine

The story of the slave ship *L'Amistad*, which was re-told in a 1997 movie, began in early 1839. In Havana, a Spanish colony at that time, 53 people who had been captured and imprisoned in West Africa and then transported to Cuba were sold to two Spanish men, Pedro Montez and Jose Ruiz. These men wanted to transport the Africans to another Cuban city to resell them. The enslaved Africans were put in chains and locked in the lowest part of the ship for the voyage. Montez and Ruiz <u>accompanied</u> them; they would thus arrive with their slaves for the sale.

A man called Cinque by his <u>captors</u> used a nail to free himself and his fellow Africans four days after the voyage began. The freed men killed the ship's cook and captain. Wanting to return to Africa, and not knowing how to sail the ship themselves, they ordered Montez and Ruiz to sail the ship. The two Spanish men sailed slowly toward the sun each morning, heading east toward Africa. But at night, when the Africans would not know in which direction the ship was sailing, the Spaniards headed northwest and sailed more quickly.

Two months after leaving Cuba, the ship landed on Long Island where the U. S. Navy seized it. A series of legal actions followed. The Africans were charged with murder. Several parties claimed they owned the ship and asked the courts to hear their claims. Montez and Ruiz claimed they owned the Africans who should be turned over to the Spanish government. If this happened, they would be returned to Cuba for trial on the charge of murder. Eventually, the case reached the U.S. Supreme Court. The Court noted that if the people on *L'Amistad* had been born in Cuba, where slavery was legal, they could be returned there. But because they were Africans, they had been unlawfully forced to Cuba. Thus, Ruiz and Montez could not claim to own them.

After the decision, they were released from confinement. Abolitionists raised money to return them to West Africa, and they left in 1842. The decision was not a direct challenge to the institution of slavery in the United States. However, it suggested that blacks were entitled to the same rights as whites when they were involved in a legal action.

143. The prisoners on *L'Amistad* came from:

 A. Cuba
 B. Spain
 C. the United States
 D. Africa

GO ON TO THE NEXT PAGE

144. The word <u>accompanied</u>, as underlined and used in the passage, most nearly means:

    A. went with

    B. entertained

    C. controlled

    D. listened to

145. According to the selection, the Africans asked Montez and Ruiz to sail the ship because:

    A. they were unable to do so

    B. Montez and Ruiz owned the ship

    C. the ship needed to head toward the east

    D. sailing at night was difficult

146. Montez's and Ruiz's sailing of the ship is best described as a:

    A. contest

    B. trick

    C. vacation

    D. trek

147. The word <u>captors</u> as underlined and used in the passage, most nearly means:

    A. leaders

    B. sailors

    C. prisoners

    D. jailers

148. After the ship landed on Long Island, legal actions began because:

    A. the ship landed in American territory

    B. a crime had been committed

    C. the ship's ownership was in dispute

    D. both **A** and **B**

149. The Africans were ordered to be freed by:

    A. the U. S. Navy

    B. the U. S. Supreme Court

    C. the Spanish government

    D. the governor of Cuba

150. The Africans on *L'Amistad* could have been returned to Cuba if they had been born there because:

    A. this was what Montez and Ruiz requested

    B. the U. S. government agreed to do so

    C. ownership of the ship was in dispute

    D. slavery was legal in Cuba

151. The author's purpose in writing this selection was most probably to:

    A. describe the ship and the events

    B. contrast the United States and Cuba

    C. explain why the story has historical importance

    D. make people aware of the film version of the story

152. The Supreme Court's decision did not affect slavery laws in the United States because:

    A. the slaves had been born in Africa

    B. abolitionists thought it did not go far enough

    C. slavery was already illegal in some states

    D. no Americans were involved in the sale or purchase of the slaves

Vocabulary

For questions 153–174, select the word that means the same, or almost the same, as the underlined word.

153. <u>appraise</u> the value

- **A.** excite
- **B.** estimate
- **C.** agree
- **D.** flatter

154. an <u>ordeal</u> by war

- **A.** revenge
- **B.** compromise
- **C.** severe trial
- **D.** strong demand

155. A <u>trite</u> message bored them.

- **A.** lengthy
- **B.** wordy
- **C.** stale
- **D.** sly

156. <u>Entreat</u> your mother to let us go.

- **A.** give up
- **B.** comfort
- **C.** finish
- **D.** beg

157. <u>vigilant</u> over his baby sister

- **A.** watchful
- **B.** imaginary
- **C.** spiteful
- **D.** poisonous

158. <u>glower</u> with anger

- **A.** broil
- **B.** praise
- **C.** collect
- **D.** scowl

159. a <u>pacific</u> sigh

- **A.** deep
- **B.** huge
- **C.** peaceful
- **D.** swift

160. <u>cantankerous</u> and annoying man

- **A.** diseased
- **B.** ill tempered
- **C.** outspoken
- **D.** ridiculous

161. <u>Augment</u> my allowance.

- **A.** increase
- **B.** withdraw
- **C.** prophesy
- **D.** dignify

162. an <u>austere</u> demeanor

- **A.** severe
- **B.** powerful
- **C.** isolated
- **D.** false

163. <u>Solicit</u> new orders.

- **A.** request
- **B.** worry
- **C.** command
- **D.** deny

164. <u>perturbed</u> by the noise

- **A.** pierced
- **B.** filtered
- **C.** calculated
- **D.** agitated

165. walked with a <u>jaunty</u> step

- **A.** bored
- **B.** lively
- **C.** quarrelsome
- **D.** chatty

166. I never heard such <u>drivel</u>.

- **A.** shrill laughter
- **B.** foolish talk
- **C.** untidy dress
- **D.** quaint humor

GO ON TO THE NEXT PAGE

167. <u>frugal</u> with his money

    A. sickly
    B. saving
    C. slow
    D. foolish

168. an <u>iota</u> of good sense

    A. first step
    B. sacred picture
    C. ornamental scroll
    D. very small quantity

169. Don't <u>poach</u> here.

    A. squander
    B. trespass
    C. outwit
    D. bully

170. <u>Defect</u> to the United States.

    A. delay
    B. slander
    C. respect
    D. desert

171. Don't <u>masticate</u> so loudly.

    A. chew
    B. slaughter
    C. walk
    D. cough

172. an <u>analogy</u> between walk and stroll

    A. imitation
    B. research
    C. calendar
    D. similarity

173. a <u>lucrative</u> project

    A. profitable
    B. wasteful
    C. sterling
    D. strange

174. a <u>bizarre</u> movie

    A. charitable
    B. joyous
    C. flattering
    D. insane

IF YOU FINISH BEFORE TIME IS CALLED, CHECK YOUR WORK ON THIS SECTION ONLY. DO NOT WORK ON ANY OTHER SECTION IN THE TEST.

Test 4: Mathematics

Time: 45 Minutes

Directions: Select the answer choice that best satisfies the question.

Mathematical Concepts

For questions 175–198, select the choice that best answers the following questions. You can use scratch paper to figure out your answers.

175. Fides walked 45 yards north, 36 yards west and 41 yards south. Peter walked 16 yards north, 49 yards west and 33 yards south. How much farther did Fides walk than Peter?

  A. 20 yards
  B. 22 yards
  C. 24 yards
  D. 28 yards

176. The sum of 2 feet $2\frac{1}{2}$ inches, 4 feet $3\frac{3}{8}$ inches, and 3 feet $9\frac{3}{4}$ inches is:

  A. 9 feet $\frac{7}{8}$ inches
  B. 9 feet $9\frac{5}{8}$ inches
  C. 10 feet $\frac{5}{8}$ inches
  D. 10 feet $3\frac{5}{8}$ inches

177. How much change do you get back from a $20.00 bill if you purchase 8 CD covers that cost $1.59 each?

  A. $7.28
  B. $10.41
  C. $12.00
  D. $18.41

178. A 10-foot rope is to be cut into equal segments measuring 8 inches each. The total number of segments is:

  A. 1
  B. 8
  C. 15
  D. 40

179. Rachel can read 1 page in 2 minutes. If a book has 80 pages, how long does it take her to read?

  A. 160 minutes
  B. 120 minutes
  C. 80 minutes
  D. 40 minutes

180. Dennis ran a race in 2.2 minutes. Kayla ran the same race in 124 seconds. What is the difference between these two times?

  A. 2 seconds
  B. 8 seconds
  C. 14 seconds
  D. 22 seconds

181. You have 40 nickels and 12 dimes. What is the total amount of money that you have?

  A. $0.52
  B. $3.20
  C. $4.60
  D. $5.20

182. A nut mixture consists of $1\frac{1}{8}$ pounds of almonds, $2\frac{3}{4}$ pounds of cashews, and $3\frac{1}{3}$ pounds of peanuts. The total weight of the mixture is:

  A. $6\frac{1}{3}$
  B. $6\frac{23}{24}$
  C. $7\frac{5}{24}$
  D. $7\frac{7}{12}$

GO ON TO THE NEXT PAGE

183. Mary has an appointment in 50 minutes. It is now 3:50 p.m. When is Mary's appointment?

    A. 3:00 p.m.
    B. 4:00 p.m.
    C. 4:40 p.m.
    D. 4:45 p.m.

184. Marty has 16 pencils and 4 times as many erasers. How many more erasers than pencils does Marty have?

    A. 4
    B. 32
    C. 48
    D. 64

185. Last week, Craig ran a race in $13\frac{2}{3}$ minutes. This week, he ran the same race in $12\frac{5}{12}$ minutes. By how many seconds did his time improve?

    A. 15
    B. 75
    C. 120
    D. 150

186. A check register shows a $512.33 beginning balance, a deposit of $120.30, withdrawals of $35 and $60, another deposit of $21.84 and a withdrawal of $36.89. What is the ending balance?

    A. $238.30
    B. $522.58
    C. $596.36
    D. $786.36

187. Danielle is decorating a package with ribbons. If she cuts a 5-foot piece of ribbon into 4-inch pieces, how many smaller ribbons are there?

    A. 12
    B. 15
    C. 18
    D. 24

188. You have 7 quarters. How many more quarters are needed to fill a $10.00 quarter wrapper?

    A. 3
    B. 13
    C. 28
    D. 33

189. Find the value of $(2 \times 3)^2$

    A. 10
    B. 12
    C. 25
    D. 36

190. Evaluate $18 - 3(5 - 2)$

    A. 0
    B. 1
    C. 9
    D. 45

191. What is the value of $\frac{(+12)(-4)}{(-2)(-8)}$?

    A. -3
    B. $-1\ 1/2$
    C. $1\ 1/2$
    D. 3

192. $\frac{4}{5} \div \frac{7}{10}$

    A. $\frac{14}{25}$
    B. $\frac{7}{8}$
    C. $1\frac{1}{7}$
    D. $1\frac{1}{5}$

193. A 15-lb roast contains 45 servings of meat. What is the rate in servings per pound?

    A. 2
    B. 3
    C. 4
    D. $6\frac{3}{4}$

194. George bowls three games. His scores are 222, 208, and 197. What is his average score for the three games?

    A. 206
    B. 207
    C. 208
    D. 209

195. In the election for Union County Comptroller, Mr. Heine got 33,172 votes, and Mr. Palisano got 25,752 votes. By how many votes did Mr. Heine win the election?

- A. 7,420
- B. 8,420
- C. 18,420
- D. 58,924

196. Jimmy earns an annual salary of $26,124. What is his average monthly salary?

- A. $2,107
- B. $2,177
- C. $2,179
- D. $5,024

197. How many yards of fencing are needed to enclose a rectangular yard that is 42-feet long and 84-feet wide?

- A. 42 yards
- B. 84 yards
- C. 112 yards
- D. 252 yards

198. Which of the following fractions is larger than $\frac{3}{5}$?

- A. $\frac{7}{25}$
- B. $\frac{59}{100}$
- C. $\frac{3}{10}$
- D. $\frac{39}{50}$

Problem Solving

For questions 199–238, select the choice that best answers the following questions. You can use scratch paper to figure out your answers.

199. A cylinder whose height is 8 inches has a volume of 128π cm^3. If the radius is doubled and its height is cut in half, the volume of the resulting cylinder is:

- A. 64π cm^3
- B. 128π cm^3
- C. 256π cm^3
- D. 512π cm^3

200. Doug earns 15% commission on all sales over $5,000. Last month, his sales totaled $12,500. What were Doug's earnings?

- A. $750
- B. $1,125
- C. $1,875
- D. $2,625

201. Fencing costs $4.75 per foot. Posts cost $12.50 each. How much does it cost to fence a garden if 10 posts and 34 feet of fencing are needed?

- A. $472.50
- B. $336.50
- C. $315.50
- D. $286.50

202. The scale on a map shows 50 miles for every $\frac{1}{4}$ inch. If two cities are 6 inches apart on the map, what is the actual distance they are apart?

- A. 12.5 miles
- B. 75 miles
- C. 200 miles
- D. 1,200 miles

203. One gallon of paint covers 400 square feet. How many gallons are needed to cover 2,225 square feet?

- A. 5 gallons
- B. 6 gallons
- C. 7 gallons
- D. 8 gallons

204. Three boxes are needed to hold 18 reams of paper. How many boxes are needed for 90 reams?

- A. 5
- B. 6
- C. 9
- D. 15

GO ON TO THE NEXT PAGE

205. In the following figure, *ABCD* is a square. The area of the figure is:

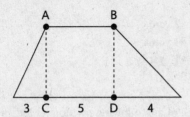

A. 42.5
B. 47
C. 52.5
D. 60

206. Cards normally sell for $3.00 each. How much is saved if 5 cards are purchased on sale at a price of 2 for $5.00?

A. $2.50
B. $5.00
C. $12.50
D. $15.00

207. A restaurant bill without tax and tip comes to $38.40. If a 15% tip is included after a 6% tax is added to the amount, how much is the tip?

A. $6.11
B. $5.76
C. $5.15
D. $2.30

208. The following figure contains 5 equal squares. If the area is 405, what is the perimeter?

A. 81
B. 90
C. 108
D. 144

209. Jennifer eats $\frac{1}{4}$ of a peach pie and divides the remainder of the pie among her four friends. What fraction of the pie does each of her friends receive?

A. $\frac{1}{3}$
B. $\frac{7}{12}$
C. $\frac{3}{16}$
D. $\frac{1}{8}$

210. Max weighs 209 pounds. If he loses 2 pounds per week, how much does he weigh in 7 weeks?

A. 191 lbs
B. 195 lbs
C. 202 lbs
D. 207 lbs

211. An appliance originally costing $1,000 goes on sale one week for 25% off. The following week, it is discounted an additional 10%. What is the new sale price of the appliance?

A. $650
B. $675
C. $750
D. $900

212. A taxi ride costs $3.00 for the first mile and $1.00 each additional half mile. What is the cost of a 10 mile ride?

A. $10
B. $12
C. $13
D. $21

213. If 3 cans of soup cost $5.00, how much do 10 cans cost?

A. $15.00
B. $16.45
C. $16.67
D. $17.33

214. Kyle ran 3 miles in $17\frac{1}{2}$ minutes on Saturday, $4\frac{1}{2}$ miles in 22 minutes on Sunday, and 2 miles in 9 minutes on Monday. What was Kyle's average rate of speed while running?

    A. 1.6 minutes per mile
    B. 5.1 minutes per mile
    C. 16.2 minutes per mile
    D. 17.8 minutes per mile

215. A savings account earns $2\frac{1}{4}$ % interest each year. How much interest is earned on a $1,000 deposit after a 5-year period?

    A. $22.50
    B. $100.00
    C. $112.50
    D. $150.00

216. Jill put some water in the freezer. When she removed it, the water's temperature was 0° C. Leaving it out raises the temperature 4° F each hour. At this rate, when is the water's temperature 52° F?

    A. after 4 hours
    B. after 5 hours
    C. after 13 hours
    D. after 52 hours

217. Stanley can type 35 words per minute. If it takes him a half hour to type a document, about how many words are in the document?

    A. 900
    B. 1,050
    C. 1,500
    D. 2,100

218. Sandy bought $4\frac{1}{2}$ lbs of apples and 6 kiwi fruits. Brandon bought $3\frac{1}{4}$ lbs of apples and 9 kiwi fruits. If apples cost $1.39 per lb and kiwis are 2 for $1.00, how much more money did Sandy spend than Brandon?

    A. $0.24
    B. $0.94
    C. $1.54
    D. $2.32

219. Brian agrees to pay back a $50,000 loan over a 10-year period. If the interest rate is 8%, what is his monthly payment?

    A. $450
    B. $540
    C. $3,333
    D. $5,400

220. Grace earned $520 last week. Her pay is based on a 6% commission of all sales. What were Grace's total sales last week?

    A. $31.20
    B. $86.67
    C. $3,120.00
    D. $8,666.67

221. Trey can tie 45 knots in 8 minutes. At this rate, how long does it take him to tie 60 knots?

    A. 10 minutes
    B. $10\frac{2}{3}$ minutes
    C. 12 minutes
    D. $12\frac{1}{2}$ minutes

222. Security answered 5 calls between 5:00 and 6:00, 3 calls between 6:00 and 7:00, no calls between 7:00 and 8:00 and 8 calls between 8:00 and 9:00. What was the average number of calls per hour answered during this time?

    A. 4
    B. $5\frac{1}{3}$
    C. 6
    D. 16

223. A recliner originally priced at $900 is discounted 30%. Because it didn't sell, it was reduced another 20%. What is the total percent of discount?

    A. 56%
    B. 50%
    C. 48%
    D. 44%

GO ON TO THE NEXT PAGE

224. A circular swimming pool that is 5 feet high has a volume of 125π cubic feet. What is the distance across the widest part of the pool?

   A. 5 feet
   B. 10 feet
   C. 20 feet
   D. 25 feet

225. Mrs. Ladner plans to put flowers in her yard except in each corner, as shown in the following figure. What area of her yard is designated for the flowers?

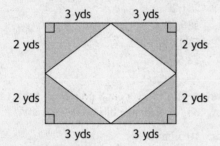

   A. 24 square yards
   B. 18 square yards
   C. 12 square yards
   D. 6 square yards

226. Charles takes out a loan of $600 that charges an annual interest rate of 15%. If he repays the loan in monthly installments over a one-year period, how much are his monthly payments?

   A. $690.00
   B. $90.00
   C. $57.50
   D. $7.50

227. Admission to a museum costs $15.50 per adult and $8.75 per child. What is the cost for a family of 2 adults and 4 children to see the museum?

   A. $52.50
   B. $66.00
   C. $79.50
   D. $93.00

228. Find the value of a in the equation $2(a - 3) = 14 - 3a$

   A. −8
   B. $\frac{17}{5}$
   C. 4
   D. 8

229. If a number is added to twice the same number, and the result is equal to 8 less than 5 times the number, what is the number?

   A. 4
   B. 6
   C. 8
   D. 12

230. Assume that a circle fits exactly inside a square. If the circumference of the circle is 10π, what is the area of the square?

   A. 5
   B. 10
   C. 20
   D. 100

231. Fred wishes to enclose a square garden whose side measures 20 feet with wire. If he decides to have the wire go around the garden five times, how much will the wire cost him if wire costs 40 cents for a spool of 50 feet?

   A. $1.60
   B. $3.20
   C. $6.40
   D. $10.00

232. Janet wants to carpet a 12-foot by 15-foot rectangular room. If carpet costs $11.50 per square yard, how much does it cost her to carpet the room?

   A. $230
   B. $690
   C. $1,380
   D. $2,070

233. What is the area, in square inches, of a square piece of carpet that measures 6 feet 2 inches on a side?

   A. 296
   B. 384
   C. 2,738
   D. 5,476

234. Brian jogged for $\frac{1}{3}$ of a mile, rested, and then jogged for $\frac{1}{2}$ of a mile. What fractional part of a mile must he still jog to have jogged an entire mile?

    A. $\frac{1}{12}$

    B. $\frac{1}{6}$

    C. $\frac{2}{5}$

    D. $\frac{5}{6}$

235. The square root of 25 is what percent of 25?

    A. 20%

    B. 25%

    C. 30%

    D. $33\frac{1}{3}\%$

236. If one side of a square increases by 30% and the adjacent side decreases by 10%, by what percent does its area increase?

    A. 14%

    B. 15%

    C. 17%

    D. 20%

237. If p boxes of pens cost c cents, how much do 8 boxes cost at the same rate?

    A. $8cp$

    B. $\frac{8c}{p}$

    C. $\frac{c}{8p}$

    D. $\frac{8p}{c}$

238. Michael gets a paycheck every other week. On each of his paychecks, $42 is deducted for income taxes. How much is deducted from his checks for income taxes over the course of the entire year?

    A. $504

    B. $546

    C. $1,092

    D. $2,184

IF YOU FINISH BEFORE TIME IS CALLED, CHECK YOUR WORK ON THIS SECTION ONLY. DO NOT WORK ON ANY OTHER SECTION IN THE TEST.

Test 5: Language Skills

Time: 25 Minutes

Directions: In each of the following questions, select that choice that best answers the question.

*In questions 239–250, look for errors in capitalization or punctuation. If you find no mistakes, mark **D** on your answer sheet.*

239.

    A. The McDonald's chain was founded by brothers Richard and Maurice McDonald.
    B. For whom is Wendy's named?
    C. Carl's Junior is named after the Son of Carl Karcher.
    D. No mistakes.

240.

    A. "Is the fish fresh today?" the customer asked.
    B. Shrimp, crab, and lobster are sold frozen.
    C. If the clam's shell doesn't open, the clam is spoiled.
    D. No mistakes.

241.

    A. Anna, who lived in Mexico for a year, learned to speak Spanish.
    B. It's easy to learn a new language when you are young.
    C. The roads are icy today; be careful!
    D. No mistakes.

242.

    A. Ben wanted to go swimming, but the water was too cold.
    B. "The beach is three miles from my house," he said.
    C. I like horror films, even though they scare me.
    D. No mistakes.

243.

    A. The coach assigned the players to their positions, and then gave a pep talk.
    B. "How far from the base should I stand?" the first baseman asked.
    C. Rita, who bats left handed, plays centerfield.
    D. No mistakes.

244.

    A. Every tuesday Bobby bathes his dog.
    B. The dog's name is Lucky.
    C. Who gave the dog such an ordinary name?
    D. No mistakes.

245.

    A. Please lock the door when you leave the house.
    B. After you close the windows, close the curtains.
    C. Can you help me clean the house on Saturday, or do you have homework to do?
    D. No mistakes.

246.

    A. "I'm too busy to talk to you now!" yelled the manager.
    B. "When are you going on vacation" Susan asked?
    C. The students knew the stories about Cuchalain, a legendary Irish warrior.
    D. No mistakes.

247.

    A. "Ladies and gentlemen," said the announcer, "here is the starting lineup for today's game."
    B. What time would you like to take your lunch break today?
    C. Look before you leap is a proverb meaning don't jump into action without thinking.
    D. No mistakes.

248.

   A. Monopoly—a game that has been popular for decades, has undergone no changes.

   B. The advertisement claimed that the low prices were for "a limited time only."

   C. Have you found any bargains by looking at advertisements?

   D. No mistakes.

249.

   A. Each of the house's roofs was a different color.

   B. When did you decide you wanted to move to Nashville?

   C. "Help me decide which shirt is better looking," my sister said.

   D. No mistakes.

250.

   A. I can't understand why Pete is always late for class.

   B. Ella takes a bus to school; Nancy prefers to walk.

   C. "Hilary," the teacher said, please repeat your answer."

   D. No mistakes.

*In questions 251–278, look for errors in usage. If you find no mistakes, mark **D** on your answer sheet.*

251.

   A. It's too hot today to play tennis.

   B. Although Mel knows all the words to most songs, he sings badly.

   C. There is a few pieces of candy left in the box.

   D. No mistakes.

252.

   A. Which of the two buildings is taller?

   B. My cousin and me went to the movies last night.

   C. Three of the exotic birds escaped from their cages.

   D. No mistakes.

253.

   A. The grumpy man spoke sourly.

   B. The student taking three science classes have lots of homework.

   C. The effect of overwork is mental fatigue.

   D. No mistakes.

254.

   A. Are there any volunteers for this project?

   B. What can I do to help you?

   C. Whose going to dry the dishes tonight?

   D. No mistakes.

255.

   A. All my friends have bikes that are newer than mine.

   B. Scrabble is always a close game between my friend and me.

   C. Tim felt badly about the mistake he'd made.

   D. No mistakes.

256.

   A. Both Julio and me were chosen for the track team.

   B. The coach insisted that we run in the relay race.

   C. Long-distance racing is too challenging for beginning runners.

   D. No mistakes.

257.

   A. Don't let minor problems affect you.

   B. Is there a public library in your neighborhood?

   C. When watching a movie on television, advertisements are annoying.

   D. No mistakes.

GO ON TO THE NEXT PAGE

258.

    A. Although fast food are cheap and convenient, they often are high in fat.

    B. Having dropped the hamburger on the floor, Rita let her dog eat it.

    C. Each of us will try to win the race.

    D. No mistakes.

259.

    A. Nobody has difficulty assembling something when the instructions are clear.

    B. We helped a upper-class student who was new to our school find a locker.

    C. Neither John nor Mary is happy about the result of the experiment.

    D. No mistakes.

260.

    A. The missing child was last seen leaving school at 3:00 p.m.

    B. An effect of the flu is a high fever.

    C. There are the papers I thought I had lost.

    D. No mistakes.

261.

    A. Shortly after we arrived at the park, it begins to rain.

    B. Some dictionaries list synonyms as well as definitions.

    C. One of the artists has had his work shown at the Metropolitan Museum.

    D. No mistakes.

262.

    A. Jane and I go to the library every Thursday.

    B. Because of the storm, the game was postponed.

    C. If anyone notices suspicious activity, they should report it to the police.

    D. No mistakes

263.

    A. After braiding Kate's hair, Sue decorated them with ribbons.

    B. The dog's breath smelled bad.

    C. Each of the Girl Scouts wears a uniform.

    D. No mistakes.

264.

    A. Kindness and consideration strengthen friendships.

    B. Tom Sawyer's Aunt Polly lived simply.

    C. Thank the hostess for inviting me to the party.

    D. No mistakes.

265.

    A. Many seashells washed up on the beach.

    B. Extreme sports has become quite popular.

    C. Supposedly, the ninth wave in a sequence is the largest.

    D. No mistakes.

266.

    A. The company was suppose to deliver the merchandise last Thursday.

    B. Contradicting the officer's order, the soldier sat down.

    C. Employees can leave work early for medical appointments.

    D. No mistakes.

267.

    A. First prize goes to the person who earns the most points.

    B. Hanging on the line, the clothes flapped in the breeze.

    C. When she turns 21 next January, Katherine wanted to buy a car.

    D. No mistakes.

268.

    A. Of the three brands of orange juice, Calflor tastes better.

    B. Crossword puzzles can be challenging.

    C. The ancient mariner told his story to whoever would listen to it.

    D. No mistakes.

269.

    A. Eric's first three days at Boy Scout Camp was exciting.

    B. When baking an apple pie, set the oven temperature to 400 degrees.

    C. The tutor to whom I was assigned was very helpful.

    D. No mistakes.

270.

A. Except when pickled, I don't like cucumbers.
B. The fresh tomatoes tasted wonderful.
C. Seeing a roadside stand, I stopped to buy some cider.
D. No mistakes.

271.

A. Saving your pennies can add up to dollars.
B. If it were not raining, we could go fishing.
C. The agreement between yourself and the company can be signed next week.
D. No mistakes.

272.

A. Next Sunday, Roseanne sang her solo at the recital.
B. The charm was worn on a chain around the wizard's neck.
C. Francis Scott Key wrote the words to "The Star Spangled Banner."
D. No mistakes.

273.

A. Which of the two cats is fuzzier?
B. You don't know him like I do.
C. Teresa explained the problem very well.
D. No mistakes.

274.

A. Let's keep this a secret between you and me.
B. Books about spies are very exciting.
C. My brother and me have a close relationship.
D. No mistakes.

275.

A. I built the table by myself.
B. The monster's hair looks like a bird built a nest in it.
C. Consider your choice carefully.
D. No mistakes.

276.

A. A large amount of people attended the county fair.
B. Too few areas have adopted antipollution laws.
C. The citizens wrote to their representatives about the problem.
D. No mistakes.

277.

A. Paul is younger than his brother Tim, so he does less chores.
B. It's difficult to guess how many jelly beans there are in that jar.
C. Swimming quickly, the lifeguard reached the struggling child.
D. No mistakes.

278.

A. Learning to use a word-processing program is not difficult.
B. Keeping aquarium fish healthy requires that the tank be cleaned.
C. Making sure the door was locked, I will leave the house.
D. No mistakes.

*In questions 279–288, look for mistakes in spelling only. If you find no mistakes, mark **D** on your answer sheet.*

279.

A. Professor Gray teaches history.
B. Kate wants to develope her public speaking skills.
C. The novel was written in 1995.
D. No mistakes.

280.

A. Lee is an amature golfer.
B. Every afternoon he practices at the driving range.
C. He tries to improve his performance.
D. No mistakes.

GO ON TO THE NEXT PAGE

281.

   A. The state experienced a severe drought.
   B. Zoology is the study of animals.
   C. Electricity can be generated by nucular power plants.
   D. No mistakes.

282.

   A. The circus tent was set up in the field.
   B. Clowns crowded into tiny cars.
   C. I probly will go to the show on Friday.
   D. No mistakes.

283.

   A. Most libraries use computer catalogs.
   B. Ted kept his shirts and socks in separate drawers.
   C. Are you familiar with the new system?
   D. No mistakes.

284.

   A. The colonists celebrated their independance.
   B. It's likely that rain will fall on Monday.
   C. The mayor's speech was applauded by the crowd.
   D. No mistakes.

285.

   A. Do you plan to attend colledge?
   B. A laboratory science is a required course for graduation.
   C. The officer relieved the guard from her post.
   D. No mistakes.

286.

   A. In February, Alice moved to Florida.
   B. Did you go skiing last winter?
   C. This dress and that one are very similar.
   D. No mistakes.

287.

   A. Nancy enjoyed her mathmatics class.
   B. Take advantage of this wonderful opportunity.
   C. Multiply the length by the width.
   D. No mistakes.

288.

   A. Nina planned her project carefully.
   B. Do not start untill you hear the instructions.
   C. Using a dictionary can make you a better speller.
   D. No mistakes.

For questions 289–298, look for errors in composition. Follow the directions for each question.

289. Choose the best word or words to join the thoughts together.

I always read the directions carefully _____ I use a new appliance.

   A. after
   B. because
   C. when
   D. whenever

290. Which of these expresses the idea most clearly?

   A. The robbery suspect riding a bike on the pier claimed she owned it.
   B. The robbery suspect on the pier riding a bike she claimed she owned.
   C. The robbery suspect claimed she owned the bike she was riding on the pier.
   D. On the pier, the robbery suspect claimed she owned the bike which she was riding.

291. Which of these expresses the idea most clearly?

   A. In my room, the rain was coming down heavily outside on the balcony.
   B. Outside on the balcony, the rain was coming down in my room.
   C. In my room, I heard the rain coming down heavily outside on the balcony.
   D. I heard the rain in my room coming down heavily outside on the balcony.

292. Which sentence does *not* belong in the paragraph?

(1) Building roads in the wilderness encourages the spread of nonnative plants. (2) The blooms of roadside plants provide welcome color. (3) Cars and trucks carry their seeds on their tires and on the dirt underneath the car. (4) The clearings made for road building give the nonnative plants room to grow.

A. sentence 1
B. sentence 2
C. sentence 3
D. sentence 4

293. Choose the best word or words to join the thoughts together.

Being neighborly is kind, _____ if you overdo it, you might be considered nosy.

A. once
B. but
C. and
D. when

294. Which topic is best for a one-paragraph theme?

A. What Teenagers Enjoy in Their Spare Time
B. The Sport of Surfing
C. A Description of My City
D. A Skateboard Trick

295. Which of these best fits under the topic "Is There Life on Mars?"

A. Jupiter is further from Earth than Mars.
B. Mars has two moons.
C. Many science fiction novels are set on Mars.
D. None of these.

296. Which of these expresses the idea most clearly?

A. Both Mr. Greg and Mr. Moor suffered a leg fracture as a result of the accident.
B. Mr. Greg and Mr. Moor each suffered a fracture in his leg as a result of the accident.
C. Mr. Greg and Mr. Moor each suffered a fracture in their leg as a result of the accident.
D. As a result of the accident, the leg of Mr. Greg and the leg of Mr. Moor suffered a fracture.

297. Where should the sentence "Modern golf clubs are light, so they are easy to swing" be placed in the following paragraph?

(1) Today's golfers often hit the ball farther than golfers did in the past. (2) Many golfers spend time physically conditioning themselves. (3) Therefore, they are strong.

A. Before sentence 1.
B. After sentence 1.
C. Between sentences 2 and 3.
D. The sentence does not fit in the paragraph.

298. Choose the group of words that best completes this sentence.

When I came back from my vacation,

_____

A. I will feel rested and ready to begin working.
B. I am rested and ready to begin working.
C. I can feel that I have rested and would be ready to begin working.
D. I felt rested and ready to begin working.

IF YOU FINISH BEFORE TIME IS CALLED, CHECK YOUR WORK ON THIS SECTION ONLY. DO NOT WORK ON ANY OTHER SECTION IN THE TEST.

Answer Key

Test 1: Verbal Skills

1. D	16. B	31. B	46. D
2. D	17. A	32. B	47. C
3. A	18. D	33. B	48. D
4. C	19. A	34. C	49. D
5. C	20. A	35. A	50. A
6. B	21. C	36. A	51. B
7. B	22. A	37. D	52. D
8. B	23. C	38. C	53. A
9. C	24. B	39. A	54. D
10. C	25. C	40. A	55. B
11. B	26. A	41. A	56. B
12. C	27. C	42. A	57. A
13. B	28. B	43. D	58. C
14. B	29. A	44. C	59. D
15. D	30. C	45. A	60. B

Test 2: Quantitative Skills

61. B	74. D	87. B	100. C
62. B	75. A	88. A	101. C
63. C	76. D	89. A	102. B
64. C	77. C	90. A	103. D
65. B	78. C	91. C	104. C
66. C	79. A	92. D	105. A
67. A	80. B	93. D	106. B
68. D	81. B	94. D	107. A
69. A	82. D	95. B	108. C
70. C	83. B	96. B	109. C
71. C	84. C	97. B	110. C
72. B	85. C	98. D	111. B
73. B	86. A	99. B	112. D

Test 3: Reading

113. C	**129.** B	**145.** A	**161.** A
114. C	**130.** A	**146.** B	**162.** A
115. B	**131.** B	**147.** D	**163.** A
116. B	**132.** A	**148.** D	**164.** D
117. C	**133.** B	**149.** B	**165.** B
118. D	**134.** B	**150.** D	**166.** B
119. B	**135.** A	**151.** C	**167.** B
120. A	**136.** B	**152.** D	**168.** D
121. B	**137.** C	**153.** B	**169.** B
122. C	**138.** C	**154.** C	**170.** D
123. D	**139.** A	**155.** C	**171.** A
124. B	**140.** A	**156.** D	**172.** D
125. B	**141.** D	**157.** A	**173.** A
126. C	**142.** A	**158.** D	**174.** D
127. B	**143.** D	**159.** C	
128. D	**144.** A	**160.** B	

Test 4: Mathematics

175. C	**191.** A	**207.** A	**223.** D
176. D	**192.** C	**208.** C	**224.** B
177. A	**193.** B	**209.** C	**225.** C
178. C	**194.** D	**210.** B	**226.** C
179. A	**195.** A	**211.** B	**227.** B
180. B	**196.** B	**212.** D	**228.** C
181. B	**197.** B	**213.** C	**229.** A
182. C	**198.** D	**214.** B	**230.** D
183. C	**199.** C	**215.** C	**231.** B
184. C	**200.** B	**216.** B	**232.** A
185. B	**201.** D	**217.** B	**233.** D
186. B	**202.** D	**218.** A	**234.** B
187. B	**203.** B	**219.** A	**235.** A
188. D	**204.** D	**220.** D	**236.** C
189. D	**205.** A	**221.** B	**237.** B
190. C	**206.** A	**222.** A	**238.** C

Test 5: Language Skills

239. C	**254.** C	**269.** A	**284.** A
240. D	**255.** C	**270.** A	**285.** A
241. D	**256.** A	**271.** C	**286.** D
242. C	**257.** C	**272.** A	**287.** A
243. A	**258.** A	**273.** B	**288.** B
244. A	**259.** B	**274.** C	**289.** C
245. D	**260.** D	**275.** D	**290.** C
246. B	**261.** A	**276.** A	**291.** C
247. C	**262.** C	**277.** A	**292.** B
248. A	**263.** A	**278.** C	**293.** B
249. A	**264.** D	**279.** B	**294.** D
250. C	**265.** B	**280.** A	**295.** D
251. C	**266.** A	**281.** C	**296.** A
252. B	**267.** C	**282.** C	**297.** B
253. B	**268.** A	**283.** D	**298.** D

Answers and Explanations

Test 1: Verbal Skills

1. **D.** A dentist works on teeth, and a plumber works on pipes.

2. **D.** To contradict someone is to say that what the person said is wrong—to *disagree*.

3. **A.** Something that is *ambiguous* can be understood in more than one way.

4. **C.** Spice cookies cost less than the other two kinds, but the first two statements don't give the relative prices of chocolate and frosted cookies.

5. **C.** The other choices are mammals; a snake is a reptile.

6. **B.** Rose is a shade of red, as well as the name of a flower. The other choices are shades of purple, and they are also the names of flowers.

7. **B.** *Somber* means dark and gloomy; *bright* is the best choice.

8. **B.** A professor gives a lecture, and an actor gives a performance. An actor might read a script, but the actor's job is to give a performance.

9. **C.** The relationship is that of more to less, or greater to smaller.

10. **C.** *Emit* means to *give off* or *let out*.

11. **B.** *Evoke* means to *call forth*.

12. **C.** Other cities might also have green park benches.

13. **B.** Skin is soft; the other choices are parts of the body that are hard.

14. **B.** *Fragile* objects break easily; the other choices are words describing objects that are strong.

15. **D.** The relationship is that of an effect to its cause. Choices **A** and **C** are cause to effect.

16. **B.** When something has been marred, for example a window that has a crack in it, it is *spoiled*.

17. **A.** Ian has the deepest voice.

18. **D.** People don't ride on a hippopotamus.

19. **A.** Something *indispensable* is required or necessary.

20. **A.** The other choices are examples of the general category *fiction*.

21. **C.** All the words are related to weather; only *rain* does not necessarily include cold temperature.

22. **A.** Wiffy is part of the class of beings (*yawps*) that live in underground caves.

23. **C.** Both Nina and Carl have taken more math classes than Patrick, but which of the two has taken more classes than the other is not stated.

24. **B.** To be *punctual* means to be on time. *Prompt* is a good synonym.

25. **C.** Something *vital* is something that cannot be done without.

26. **A.** The words are synonyms.

27. **C.** The relationship is one of purpose. Food is eaten for nutrition; soap is used to maintain cleanliness.

28. **B.** *Scurry* means to move quickly—to *dash*.

29. **A.** Helen is the tallest of the three.

30. **C.** The word usually suggests telling something that had been secret or hidden.

31. **B.** The other choices are objects that are worn on the head.

32. **B.** All the choices can fly, but bats are not insects.

33. **B.** The other choices are examples of the general category *tools*.

34. **C.** *Dessert* is the general category the other items are members of.

35. **A.** You might not know that a kid is a baby goat. But the relationship of the first two words is from younger to older. None of the other choices fits.

36. **A.** *Clash* means a *conflict* or a *fight*.

37. **D.** To *heed* advice or an instruction means not only to listen to it, but to follow it.

38. **C.** The first two statements don't say whether griffins have scales. Griffins might or might not have scales.

39. **A.** A calendar shows what day of the month it is; the other choices are all measurements of time.

40. **A.** Pink grapes are the sweetest, followed by purple, green, and red grapes.

41. **A.** *Startle* means *surprise*.

42. **A.** Don't be confused by **B**. While an itch is irritating, itchy is not what the word means.

43. **D.** The relationship is one of opposites.

44. **C.** Something that seeps slowly trickles out of where it was.

45. **A.** If Main Street is wider than Smith Street (statement 2) and Smith Street is wider than State Street (statement 1), then Main Street is wider than State Street.

46. **D.** You wouldn't eat a *rotten* fruit, but all the other words describe a fruit that would be good to eat.

47. **C.** *Words* is the general category. The other choices describe different types of words.

48. **D.** Choice **B** means the same as *familiar*.

49. **D.** Although **C** might seem like a good choice, to *cease* is to stop what is already in motion, so *continue* is a better answer.

50. **A.** If your mind is *vacant,* you might be *relaxed* (choice **C**), but *vacant* means *empty*, so *full* is the best choice.

51. **B.** The other choices are found on a beach.

52. **D.** *Water* can be carried in or drunk from the other choices.

53. **A.** The relationship is that of a part to the whole.

54. **D.** The relationship is between an object and its characteristic. A snail is slow, and a twig is a thin branch of a tree.

55. **B.** *Incite* means to *stir up* or to *urge*.

56. **B.** To *concur* is to agree; to *argue* implies disagreement.

57. **A.** *Sparse* means thin or meager; *plentiful* is its opposite.

58. **C.** Both the individual (Zax) and the group (Burbs) have red noses, but other groups might have red noses, and Zax might be a member of one of those groups if Zax is not a Burb.

59. **D.** To be *hostile* means to dislike or treat someone as an enemy. *Friendly* is the opposite.

60. **B.** Choice **C** is a synonym for *stingy*. Do not be confused by choice **D**. Not all wealthy people are stingy.

Test 2: Quantitative Skills

61. B. The pattern is 6 (+ 5), 11 (+ 5), 16 (+ 5), 21 (+ 5), 26 (+ 5), which is equal to **31**.

62. B. The product of 2 and 5 is 10. Note that when **40** is divided by 4, the result is also 10.

63. C. Note that (a) $-5^2 = -25$, (b) $(-5)^2 = 25$, and (c) $5^2 = 25$. Therefore, (b) and (c) are equal and greater than (a).

64. C. Five percent of 200 is equal to 10. Note that 20% of **50** is also equal to 10.

65. B. First note that $a = 65$ because it is supplementary to a 115° angle. Also, $c = 65$ because the base angles in an isosceles triangle are equal. Finally, because there are 180° in a triangle, $b = 180 - 65 - 65 = 50$. Thus, $a = c > b$.

66. C. The pattern is 8 ($\times$ 2), 16 ($\times$ 2), 32 ($\times$ 2), 64 ($\times$ 2), which is equal to **128**.

67. A. Note that (a) $5 + 3(2 + 4) = 5 + 3(6) = 5 + 18 = 23$, (b) $(5 + 3)2 + 4 = (8)2 + 4 = 16 + 4 = 20$, and (c) $5 + (3 \times 2) + 4 = 5 + 6 + 4 = 15$. Therefore, (a) is greater than (b) and (c).

68. D. $\frac{9}{11}$ of 33 is equal to $\frac{9}{11} \times 33 = 27$. Note that $\frac{3}{4}$ of **36** is also equal to 27.

69. A. To begin, $x = 52$ because it forms a vertical angle with the angle labeled 52. Also, $z = 43$ for the same reason. Finally, $y = 52$ because it is an alternate interior angle to the angle labeled x. Thus, $x = y > z$.

70. C. Note that (a) $(-1)^3 = -1$, (b) $(-1)^2 = 1$, and (c) $(-1)^4 = 1$. Therefore, (b) and (c) are equal and greater than (a).

71. C. The pattern is 4 (− 1), 3 (+ 7), 10 (− 1), 9 (+ 7), 16 (− 1), which is equal to 15.

72. B. Twelve less than 26 is equal to $26 - 12 = 14$. This is the same as the product of 7 and **2**.

73. B. We are told that the measure of $\angle AOB = 50$. Because $\angle DOC$ is vertical to this angle, it also measures 50. Thus, the arcs opposite these two angles are of equal length. Now, the measures of $\angle BOC$ and $\angle AOD$ are both equal to 130° because they are supplementary to 50° angles. Therefore, the arcs opposite these two angles are also equal in length, but are longer than the other two arcs because they are opposite larger angles. All in all, then, we can conclude that the length of arc AB = the length of arc DC < the length of arc BC.

74. D. The pattern is 24 ($\div$ 6), 4 ($\times$ 3), 12 ($\div$ 6), 2 ($\times$ 3), 6 ($\div$ 6), which is equal to **1**.

75. A. The sum of 25, 30, and 45 is equal to 100. $\frac{3}{5}$ of 100 is equal to $\frac{3}{5} \times 100 = $ **60**.

76. D. In this problem, (a) $2.06 \times 10^{-2} = 0.0206$, (b) $0.000206 \times 10^2 = 0.0206$, and (c) $= 0.0206$. Therefore, (a), (b), and (c) are equal.

77. C. When 24 is tripled, the result is 72. The same result is obtained by doubling **36**.

78. C. The angle between a and b is equal to c by the property of vertical angles. Note that the angles labeled $a°$, $b°$, and $c°$ form a straight line, so $a + b + c = 180$.

79. A. The product of 7 and 10 is 70. Note that when **4** is cubed, the result is $4^3 = 64$ and that, when 64 is increased by 6, the result is 70.

80. B. Note that (a) 4.268 rounded to the nearest tenth is 4.3, (b) 4.328 rounded to the nearest tenth is 4.3, and (c) 4.352 rounded to the nearest tenth is 4.4. Therefore, (a) is equal to (b) and less than (c).

81. B. 15% of 300 is equal to 45. Note that 60% of 75 is also equal to 45.

82. D. All three triangles have the same area because they all have the same base, and their heights are also the same.

83. B. When **20** is tripled, the result is 60, and when this is decreased by 12, the result is 48.

84. C. The pattern begins with the first positive integer, 1, followed by $1 \times 4 = 4$. Then, the second positive integer, 2, is followed by $2 \times 4 = 8$. The third positive integer, 3, is followed by $3 \times 4 = 12$, so, the fourth positive integer, 4, should be followed by $4 \times 4 = $ **16**.

85. C. $\frac{1}{6}$ of 24 is equal to $\frac{1}{6} \times 24 = 4$. Note that $\frac{1}{5}$ of 20 is equal to $\frac{1}{5} \times 20 = 4$.

86. A. Note that (a) the largest prime factor of 28 is 7; (b) the largest prime factor of 64 is 2; and (c) the largest prime factor of 72 is 3. Therefore, (a) is greater than (b) and (c).

87. B. The pattern is 81 ($\div$ 3), 27 ($\div$ 3), 9 ($\div$ 3), 3 ($\div$ 3), which is equal to **1**.

88. A. Two to the fourth power = 16. Note that 4^2 is also 16.

89. A. By the Pythagorean Theorem, $BC = 5$, and $EF = 10$. Thus, the perimeter of triangle ABC is $3 + 4 + 5 = 12$, and the perimeter of triangle DEF is $6 + 8 + 10 = 24$. Thus, twice the perimeter of ABC = the perimeter of DEF.

90. A. The pattern is 20 ($-$ 5), 15 ($-$ 4), 11 ($-$ 3), 8 ($-$ 2), 6 ($-$ 1), which is equal to **5**.

91. C. Note that the product of 3 and 12 is 36. Also, 50% of 12 is **6**.

92. D. The pattern is 0 ($+$ 3), 3 ($+$ 6), 9 ($+$ 9), 18 ($+$ 12), 30 ($+$ 15), 45 ($+$ 18), which is equal to **63**.

93. D. In this problem, (a) 350% = 3.5, (b) $0.035 \times 100 = 3.5$, and (c) $\frac{14}{4} = 3.5$. Therefore, (a), (b), and (c) are equal.

94. D. The difference between 102 and 12 is 90. Further, $\frac{1}{6}$ of $90 = \frac{1}{6} \times 90 = $ **15**.

95. B. In a triangle, the longest side is opposite the largest angle, and the shortest side is opposite the smallest angle. Therefore, $AC > AB > BC$.

96. B. The pattern is 5 ($\times$ 3), 15 ($-$ 5), 10 ($\times$ 3), 30 ($-$ 5), 25 ($\times$ 3), 75 ($-$ 5), which is equal to **70**.

97. B. The difference between 37 and 15 is 22. Note that 20% of **110** is also equal to 22.

98. D. The pattern is 2 ($\times$ 3), 6 ($-$ 2), 4 ($\times$ 3), 12 ($-$ 2), 10 ($\times$ 3), which is equal to **30**.

99. B. Here, (a) the value of $2x + 3y$ if $x = 6$ and $y = 0$ is 12; (b) the value of $2x + 3y$ if $x = 0$ and $y = 4$ is 12; and (c) the value of $2x + 3y$ if $x = 12$ and $y = -6$ is $24 - 18 = 6$. Therefore, (a) is equal to (b) and greater than (c).

100. C. The pattern is 99 ($-$ 10), 89 ($-$ 9), 80 ($-$ 8), 72 ($-$ 7), which is equal to 65.

101. C. The product of 9 and 6 is 54. Note that $54 \div 3 = 18$, so 300% of **18** is equal to 54.

102. B. Note that OC, OD, OA, and OB are all radiuses of the semicircle, and therefore are all equal. Also, CD is a diameter and therefore is equal to two radiuses. It follows that $CD = AO + BO$.

103. D. The list of numbers here is the squares of the whole numbers, in ascending order. The missing square is $5^2 = $ **25**.

104. C. Twenty percent of **60** is 12, so when 60 is reduced by 20% of itself, the result is $60 - 12 = 48$.

105. A. The first two numbers are perfect squares, followed by their square roots. We then have the next largest perfect square, followed by its square root. The fifth number is the next largest perfect square, 81, and should be followed by its square root, **9**.

106. B. The product of 8 and 16 is $8 \times 16 = 128$. Then, 25% of $128 = .25 \times 128 = $ **32**.

107. A. The pattern is 4 ($\times -1$), -4 ($\times -2$), 8 ($\times -3$), -24 ($\times -4$), 96 ($\times -5$), which is equal to -480.

108. C. The pattern is 9 ($+$ 4), 13 ($+$ 3), 16 ($+$ 4), 20 ($+$ 3), 23 ($+$ 4), **27** ($+$ 3), which is equal to 30.

109. C. The square of 10 is $10^2 = 100$. Because $100 \div 4 = 25$, 400% of **25** is equal to 100.

110. C. The pattern is 11 ($+$ 3), 14 ($+$ 6), 20 ($+$ 9), 29 ($+$ 12), **41** ($+$ 15), which is equal to 56.

111. B. This pattern becomes easier to recognize if you notice that the third number is 3 less than the first, and that the fifth number is 3 less than the third. The pattern is 33, followed by $33 \div 3 = 11$. Then, the number 3 less than the first number, $33 - 3 = 30$, is followed by $30 \div 3 = 10$. In the same way, $30 - 3 = 27$ is followed by $27 \div 3 = 9$. The missing number, then, should be 3 less than 27, or $27 - 3 = $ **24**, which would be followed by $24 \div 3 = 8$.

112. D. The first two numbers are added to get the third, $5 + 6 = 11$. Then, the second and third numbers are added to get the fourth, $6 + 11 = 17$. Next, $11 + 17 = 28$, and $17 + 28 = 45$. The missing number would be $28 + 45 = $ **73**.

Test 3: Reading

113. C. Choice **A** is too general; **B** and **D** are too specific.

114. C. The word *while* is a clue to the meaning of *simultaneously*.

115. B. **D** is incorrect because the passage states that the storage space is a part of the nest.

116. B. This is stated in the third paragraph of the passage.

117. C. Choices **A** and **B** seem logical, but because the compartments are cells, sealed off from each other, **C** is a better choice. **D** simply restates that the cells have six sides.

118. D. This information is in the second paragraph.

119. B. According to the passage, honey is contained in the comb, but the comb is not made of honey.

120. A. The last two sentences of the first paragraph explain this choice.

121. B. Because the bees shape the wax, it must be flexible.

122. C. The last sentence of the paragraph explains this choice.

123. D. The ambitions *faded out*, so they were *temporary*.

124. B. **A** is a true statement, but the quoted expression indicates that they know they are only children. The irony of **B** is that the boys think they have to be good to be pirates, people who are known for bad deeds.

125. B. Read carefully. The boats arrived from two different directions each day.

126. C. The author calls the river *majestic* and *magnificent*, words that suggest great size. He refers to *mile-wide* tides and says it looks like a *sea*.

127. B. Because everyone awaited the arrival of the boats, this is the best choice.

128. D. In **B,** there is little difference between the two descriptive words. **A** and **C** do contrast a positive and negative word, but because the town is described as *drowsing* and then becomes active when the boat is arriving, **D** is the best choice.

129. B. Nothing in the passage indicates that any of the other choices are correct.

130. A. If the man's voice could wake up the whole town, clearly it was *impressive*.

131. B. Choice **A** is a restatement of the idea that they wanted to be steamboatmen using different words. **C** might be a true statement, but the focus of the passage is on what the steamboats mean to the town.

132. A. Although **C** is a possibility, the author reminisces about the Mississippi and the steamboatmen.

133. B. This information is in the first paragraph of the passage.

134. B. To *dangle* means to hang from something.

135. A. The charge moves toward the ground and is met by a charge rising from the ground.

136. B. This is stated in the second paragraph.

137. C. Because the electricity *flows*, the word must mean something that creates a place it can move through— a *path*.

138. C. The passage states that one can feel an *odd sensation* when lightning is about to strike.

139. A. This is explained in the second paragraph of the passage.

140. A. According to the passage, lightning can strike as far as 25 miles from the center of a storm when it travels horizontally before turning toward earth.

141. D. Choices **A** and **B** are false. Choice **C** might be true, but nothing in the passage indicates that this is connected to why more males than females are struck by lightning.

142. A. The information is too detailed for a newspaper, choice **B**. It doesn't tell how to avoid being struck by lightning, so **C** is not a good answer. Although golf is mentioned in the passage, the information is about lightning and how it is created, so **D** is a poor choice.

143. D. The information is in the second sentence of the selection.

144. A. While **C** is a possibility, the logic of the sentence emphasizes that they were with the slaves.

145. A. The other choices might be true according to the selection, but none of them is given as a reason for asking the Spaniards to sail the ship.

146. B. The selection indicates that the men changed direction when the Africans did not know what was happening; they were trying to *trick* them.

147. D. Montez and Ruiz were imprisoning Cinque, so this is the best choice.

148. D. Both of these reasons for legal action are stated in the third paragraph.

149. B. Although no sentence in the passage states this, paragraph three shows that the Supreme Court determined the fate of the Africans.

150. D. This is explained in paragraph three.

151. C. The end of a selection is often where the main idea or emphasis occurs. In this selection, the story leads to the conclusion, which is an explanation of its historical significance.

152. D. Choices **B** and **C** might be true statements, but they do not explain why the laws were not affected by the decision.

153. B.	**159.** C.	**165.** B.	**171.** A.
154. C.	**160.** B.	**166.** B.	**172.** D.
155. C.	**161.** A.	**167.** B.	**173.** A.
156. D.	**162.** A.	**168.** D.	**174.** D.
157. A.	**163.** A.	**169.** B.	
158. D.	**164.** D.	**170.** D.	

Test 4: Mathematics

175. C. Fides walked $45 + 36 + 41 = 122$ yards. Peter walked $16 + 49 + 33 = 98$ yards. The difference between these two distances is $122 - 98 = 24$ yards.

176. D. First add the number of feet together, and then add the number of inches.

$2 \text{ ft} + 4 \text{ ft} + 3 \text{ ft} = 9 \text{ ft}$

$2\frac{1}{2} \text{ inches} + 3\frac{3}{8} \text{ inches} + 9\frac{3}{4} \text{ inches} = \frac{5}{2} + \frac{27}{8} + \frac{39}{4} = \frac{20}{8} + \frac{27}{8} + \frac{78}{8} = \frac{125}{8} = 15\frac{5}{8} \text{ inches}$

$15\frac{5}{8} \text{ inches} = 1 \text{ foot } 3\frac{5}{8} \text{ inches}$, so all together, $9 \text{ feet} + 1 \text{ foot } 3\frac{5}{8} \text{ inches} = 10 \text{ feet } 3\frac{5}{8} \text{ inches}$.

177. A. The cost of the 8 CD covers is $8 \times \$1.59 = \$12.72$. The change received is $\$20.00 - \$12.72 = \$7.28$.

178. C. The total number of inches in a 10-foot rope is $10 \times 12 = 120$ inches. The number of 8 inch segments that can be cut is $\frac{120}{8} = 15$.

179. A. If 1 page can be read in 2 minutes, then 80 pages can be read in 80×2 or 160 minutes.

180. B. Convert 2.2 minutes to seconds. $2.2 \times 60 = 132$ seconds. The difference in the two times is $132 - 124 = 8$ seconds.

181. B. The total amount of money is $(40 \times \$0.05) + (12 \times \$0.10) = \$2.00 + \$1.20 = \$3.20$.

182. C. $1\frac{1}{8} + 2\frac{3}{4} + 3\frac{1}{3} = \frac{9}{8} + \frac{11}{4} + \frac{10}{3} = \frac{27}{24} + \frac{66}{24} + \frac{80}{24} = \frac{173}{24} = 7\frac{5}{24}$ pounds.

183. C. If it is 3:50, there are 10 minutes until 4:00 and an additional 40 minutes afterward, so the time is 4:40.

184. C. There are 4×16, or 64 erasers. So there are $64 - 16$, or 48 more erasers.

185. B. Convert minutes to seconds. $13\frac{2}{3}$ minutes $= 13\frac{2}{3} \times 60 = 820$ seconds. $12\frac{5}{12}$ minutes $= 12\frac{5}{12} \times 60 = 745$ seconds. The overall improvement is $820 - 745 = 75$ seconds.

186. B. Deposits are added to the balance; withdrawals are subtracted. $\$512.33 + \$120.30 = \$632.63 - \$35 = \$597.63 - \$60 = \$537.63 + \$21.84 = \$559.47 - \$36.89 = \$522.58$.

187. B. There are $12 \times 5 = 60$ inches in a 5-foot piece of ribbon. If this is divided into 4-inch pieces, there are $\frac{60}{4} = 15$.

188. D. Four quarters are in \$1.00. So 40 quarters are needed to fill a \$10.00 quarter wrapper. If there are 7 quarters, then $40 - 7 = 33$ quarters are still needed.

189. D. $(2 \times 3)^2 = (6)^2 = 36$.

190. C. $18 - 3(5 - 2) = 18 - 3(3) = 18 - 9 = 9$.

191. A. $\frac{(+12)(-4)}{(-2)(-8)} = \frac{-48}{+16} = -3$.

192. C. $\frac{4}{5} \div \frac{7}{10} = \frac{4}{5} \times \frac{10}{7} = \frac{40}{35} = 1\frac{5}{35} = 1\frac{1}{7}$.

193. B. The rate is $\frac{45 \text{ servings}}{15 \text{ pounds}}$. Dividing 15 into 45 gives 3, so 3 servings are in each pound.

194. D. To find the average of three numbers, begin by adding the numbers, and then divide by 3. Because $222 + 208 + 197 = 627$, and $627 \div 3 = 209$, his average score is 209.

195. A. We need to determine how many more votes Mr. Heine got than Mr. Palisano. Because $33,172 - 25,752 = 7,420$, Mr. Heine got 7,420 more votes.

196. B. Because 12 months are in each year, Jimmy's average monthly salary is $\$26,124 \div 12 = \$2,177$.

197. B. Because we are asked for the number of yards of fencing required to enclose the garden, begin by expressing the length and width in yards. Since there are 3 feet in a yard, divide the length and width by 3 to determine that 42 feet is equal to 14 yards, and 84 feet is equal to 28 yards. Then, the perimeter is $P = 2 \times 14 + 2 \times 28 = 28 + 56 = 84$ yards.

198. D. One way to answer this question is to convert each fraction to an equivalent fraction with a denominator of 100. To begin, $\frac{3}{5} \times \frac{20}{20} = \frac{60}{100}$. Also, note that $\frac{7}{25} \times \frac{4}{4} = \frac{28}{100}$, $\frac{59}{100} \times \frac{1}{1} = \frac{59}{100}$, $\frac{3}{10} \times \frac{10}{10} = \frac{30}{100}$, and $\frac{39}{50} \times \frac{2}{2} = \frac{78}{100}$. Thus, only $\frac{39}{50}$ is larger than $\frac{3}{5}$.

199. C. The volume of a cylinder is $\pi r^2 h$. In the original cylinder, $\pi r^2 8 = 128\pi$, so $r^2 = \frac{128\pi}{8\pi} = 16$, and the radius, r, equals $\sqrt{16} = 4$. In the new cylinder, the radius is doubled to 8, and the height is cut in half to 4. The resulting volume is $\pi 8^2 4 = 256\pi$ cm³.

200. B. The amount of commissions over \$5,000 is $\$12,500 - \$5,000 = \$7,500$. Earnings are $\$7,500 \times 15\% = \$1,125$.

201. D. The total cost for the posts and fencing is $(10 \times \$12.50) + (34 \times \$4.75) = \$125.00 + \$161.50 = \$286.50$.

202. D. The proportion $\frac{50 \text{ mi}}{\frac{1}{4} \text{ in}} = \frac{x \text{ mi}}{6 \text{ in}}$ can be used to find the actual distance. Cross multiply. $50 \times 6 = \frac{1}{4} x$, so $300 = \frac{1}{4} x$ and $x = 300 \times 4 = 1,200$ miles.

203. B. If one gallon covers 400 square feet, then $\frac{2,225}{400} = 5.5625$, or 6 whole gallons are need to cover 2,225 square feet.

204. D. The proportion $\frac{3 \text{ boxes}}{18 \text{ reams}} = \frac{x \text{ boxes}}{90 \text{ reams}}$ can be used to find the number of boxes. Cross multiply: $3 \times 90 = 18x$, so $270 = 18x$, and $x = \frac{270}{18} = 15$ boxes.

205. A. Add the areas of the two triangles and the square to find the total area. The area of the square is $5^2 = 25$. Both triangles have a height of 5. The area of one triangle is $\frac{1}{2} bh = \frac{1}{2} \times 3 \times 5 = \frac{15}{2} = 7.5$. The area of the other triangle is $\frac{1}{2} bh = \frac{1}{2} \times 4 \times 5 = \frac{20}{2} = 10$. The total area is $25 + 7.5 + 10 = 42.5$.

206. A. Five cards at $3.00 each cost $5 \times \$3.00 = \$15.00$. If cards are 2 for $5.00, the cost per cards is $\frac{\$5.00}{2} = \$2.50$, so 5 cards cost $\$2.50 \times 5 = \$12.50$. The amount saved is $\$15.00 - \$12.50 = \$2.50$.

207. A. The tax on the bill is $\$38.40 \times 6\% = \$2.30$. The amount, including tax, is $\$38.40 + \$2.30 = \$40.70$. The tip is $\$40.70 \times 15\% = \$6.11$.

208. C. The area of one square is $\frac{405}{5} = 81$. So the length of each side is $\sqrt{81} = 9$. The total number of sides in the figure is 12, so the perimeter is $9 \times 12 = 108$.

209. C. After eating $\frac{1}{4}$ of a pie, what remains is $1 - \frac{1}{4} = \frac{3}{4}$. If 4 friends share the remainder, then each received $\frac{3}{4} \div 4 = \frac{3}{4} \times \frac{1}{4} = \frac{3}{16}$.

210. B. If 2 pounds are lost each week, then after 7 weeks, $7 \times 2 = 14$ pounds are lost. The weight after 7 weeks is $209 - 14 = 195$ pounds.

211. B. The discounted amount after the first week is $\$1,000 \times 25\% = \$250$, so the sale price is $\$1,000 - \$250 = \$750$. The discounted amount after the second week is $\$750 \times 10\% = \$75$, so the sale price is $\$750 - \$75 = \$675$.

212. D. In a 10-mile trip, after the first mile, 9 miles remain. If each additional half mile is $1, then an additional mile is $2. The cost of the trip is $3 for the first mile + ($2 \times 9$) for the additional miles. $\$3 + \$18 = \$21$.

213. C. The proportion $\frac{\$5.00}{3 \text{ cans}} = \frac{\$x}{10 \text{ cans}}$ can be used to find the cost of 10 cans. Cross multiply: $5 \times 10 = 3x$, so $50 = 3x$, and $\frac{50}{3} = 16.67$.

214. B. The average is the total time divided by the total miles run. The total time is $17.5 + 22 + 9 = 48.5$ minutes. The total number of miles run is $3 + 4.5 + 2 = 9.5$. The average is $\frac{48.5}{9.5} = 5.1$ minutes per mile.

215. C. Interest = principle × rate × time. Interest $= \$1,000 \times 2\frac{1}{4}\% \times 5 = \$1,000 \times 0.0225 \times 5 = \$112.50$.

216. B. Zero degrees Celsius is equivalent to a Fahrenheit temperature of $0° \left(\frac{9}{5} \right) + 32 = 32°$ F. To reach $52°$ F, the temperature must rise $20°$ F. If it rises $4°$ F every hour, then $\frac{20}{4}$ or 5 hours later, it is at $52°$ F.

217. B. Thirty minutes are in a half hour: $30 \times 35 = 1,050$ words.

218. A. The cost of Sandy's purchase is $\left(4\frac{1}{2} \times \$1.39 \right) + (6 \times \$0.50) = \$9.26$. The cost of Brandon's purchase is $\left(3\frac{1}{4} \times \$1.39 \right) + (9 \times \$0.50) = \$9.02$. Sandy spent $\$9.26 - \$9.02 = \$0.24$ more.

219. A. The interest on a $50,000 loan is $\$50,000 \times 8\% = \$4,000$. The amount that must be paid back is $\$50,000 + \$4,000 = \$54,000$. There are 120 months in 10 years. If this is to be paid over a 10-year period, each monthly payment is $\frac{\$54,000}{120} = \$450$.

220. D. Earnings = sales × commission rate. So $520 = sales × 6\%$. Therefore, sales $= \frac{\$520}{6\%} = \frac{\$520}{0.06} = \$8,666.67$.

221. B. The proportion $\frac{45 \text{ knots}}{8 \text{ minutes}} = \frac{60 \text{ knots}}{x \text{ minutes}}$ can be used to find the number of minutes to tie 60 knots. Cross multiply: $45x = 8 \times 60$, so $45x = 480$, and $x = \frac{480}{45} = 10\frac{2}{3}$ minutes.

222. A. The average is found by adding the total number of calls answered and dividing by the number of hours. The total number of calls is $5 + 3 + 0 + 8 = 16$. The number of hours between 5:00 and 9:00 is 4. So the average is $\frac{16}{4} = 4$.

223. D. The total percent discounted is the total dollar amount discounted divided by the original price. The first discounted amount is $\$900 \times 30\% = \$270$. The second discounted amount is 20% of the reduced price. So $\$900 - \$270 = \$630 \times 20\% = \$126$. The total dollar amount discounted is $\$270 + \$126 = \$396$. The percent discounted is $\frac{396}{900} = 0.44 = 44\%$.

224. B. The distance across the widest part of the pool is equivalent to the pool's diameter. The diameter is twice the radius. The volume of a circular pool is $\pi r^2 h$. So, $125\pi = \pi r^2 5$. $r^2 = \frac{125\pi}{5\pi} = 25$, and $r = \sqrt{25} = 5$. Therefore, the diameter of the pool is $5 \times 2 = 10$ feet.

225. C. Find the total area of the figure and subtract each shaded region. The dimensions of the figure are 6 yards by 4 yards, so the area of the total figure is $6 \times 4 = 24$ square yards. Each shaded region is a triangle with a base of 2 yards and a height of 3 yards. The area of each triangle is $\frac{1}{2} bh = \frac{1}{2} \times 2 \times 3 = 3$. Because there are 4 triangles, the area of the shaded region is $4 \times 3 = 12$ square yards. The area remaining for the flowers is $24 - 12 = 12$ square yards.

226. C. The interest on the loan is $\$600 \times 15\% = \$90$. The total amount to be repaid is $\$600 + \$90 = \$690$. If this is paid in monthly installments, the amount paid each month is $\frac{690}{12} = \$57.50$.

227. B. The cost for 2 adults is $2 \times \$15.50 = \$31.00$. The cost for 4 children is $4 \times \$8.75 = \$35.00$. The total cost for the family is $\$31.00 + \$35.00 = \$66.00$.

228. C. $2(a - 3) = 14 - 3a$. Distribute to get $2a - 6 = 14 - 3a$. Add +6 and +3a to get $5a = 20$. Thus, $a = 4$.

229. A. Let N equal the number. Then $N + 2N = 5N - 8$, or $3N = 5N - 8$. Subtract $5N$ to get $-2N = -8$. Divide by -2 to get $N = 4$.

230. D. The circumference of the circle is $2\pi r = 10\pi$, so the radius of the circle is 5. Then, the diameter of the circle is 10. Because the side of the square is equal to the diameter of the circle, the area of the square is $10^2 = 100$.

231. B. The perimeter of the garden is $20 \times 4 = 80$ feet, so $5 \times 80 = 400$ feet is needed to go around it five times. Now, dividing 400 feet by 50 feet, we get 8, which means we need to buy 8 spools. Finally, 8 spools at 40 cents per spool costs $3.20.

232. A. Be careful with this one. Note that the measurement of the room is given in feet, but the cost of the carpet is given in square yards. The easiest way to deal with this is to express the measurement of the room in yards; 12 feet by 15 feet is the same as 4 yards by 5 yards, so the room measures 20 square yards. At $11.50 per square yard, the cost to carpet the room is $20 \times \$11.50 = \$230$.

233. D. Because they ask for the area in square inches, let's express the length of the side in inches. A length of 6 feet 2 inches is $6 \times 12 + 2 = 72 + 2 = 74$ inches. The area, then, is 74×74 inches $= 5,476$ square inches.

234. B. So far, Brian has jogged $\frac{1}{2} + \frac{1}{3} = \frac{3}{6} + \frac{2}{6} = \frac{5}{6}$ of a mile. Therefore, he has $1 - \frac{5}{6} = \frac{1}{6}$ of a mile left to run.

235. A. Because $\sqrt{25} = 5$, we need to determine what percent 5 is of 25. Note that 5 is $\frac{1}{5}$ of 25, and because $\frac{1}{5} = 20\%$, 5 is 20% of 25.

236. C. Let's say that the side of the square is originally 10. Then, the original area is 100. If one side increases by 30%, it becomes 13, and if the other side decreases by 10%, it becomes 9. The rectangle formed is $13 \times 9 = 117$. Overall, then, the area has gone from 100 to 117, an increase of 17%.

237. B. If E represents the cost of 8 boxes, we can set up the proportion:

$$\frac{p \text{ boxes}}{c \text{ cents}} = \frac{8 \text{ boxes}}{E \text{ cents}}.$$

Then, cross multiply.

$$pE = 8c$$

Divide both sides by p.

$$E = \frac{8c}{p}$$

238. C. If he gets paid every other week, then he receives $\frac{52}{2} = 26$ paychecks per year. If \$42 is deducted from each check, the total amount deducted is $26 \times \$42 = \$1,092$.

Test 5: Language Skills

239. C. The word *son* should not be capitalized. It is not part of the person's name, nor is it a title like senator or professor.

240. D. All answer choices are correct.

241. D. All answer choices are correct.

242. C. No comma is needed between a main clause and a clause that modifies it.

243. A. No comma is needed when the main subject in a sentence is followed by two verbs, unless the second verb also has a subject.

244. A. The names of days of the week are capitalized.

245. D. All answer choices are correct.

246. B. Question marks are placed inside quotation marks when the quoted material is a question.

247. C. Because "look before you leap" is referred to as a proverb, it is a quotation and should be enclosed in quotation marks.

248. A. Enclose parenthetical material either between two dashes, between two commas, or in parentheses. Do not use one dash and one comma.

249. A. When a possessive plural ends in the letter *s*, the apostrophe follows the letter *s*.

250. C. A quotation mark is needed before the word *please*.

251. C. When a sentence begins with *there* followed by a form of the verb *to be*, the subject follows the verb. In this sentence, the subject is *pieces,* so the verb should be plural.

252. B. Use *I* for the subject of a sentence.

253. B. Don't be confused by words coming between the subject and verb. The subject is *student*, so the verb should be singular.

254. C. *Whose* is an interrogative pronoun. *Who's* is the contraction for *who is*.

255. C. *Badly* is an adverb describing a verb. A predicate adjective, *bad*, should be used to describe Tim.

256. A. Use *I* as the subject of a sentence.

257. C. Which word in the sentence tells who or what was watching the movie? *Advertisements* can't watch a movie.

258. A. The subject of the verb *food* is singular.

259. B. Use *an* before words beginning with a vowel.

260. D. All answer choices are correct.

261. A. The verb tense in the sentence unnecessarily shifts from past to present.

262. C. The antecedent of the pronoun is *anyone*, which is singular, so the pronoun should be *he*. However, some people object to using the masculine pronoun when either sex is meant. The best correction is to make the antecedent plural. *If people notice suspicious activity.*

263. A. Nothing in the sentence indicates what was *decorated*.

264. D. All answer choices are correct.

265. B. *Sports* is the subject, so a plural verb is required.

266. A. *Supposed* is the past participle of suppose.

267. C. The sentence illogically shifts from future to past tense.

268. A. Use the superlative, *best*, when comparing more than two things.

269. A. The subject, *days*, requires a plural verb.

270. A. According to the sentence, the person speaking is sometimes pickled!

271. C. Do not use a reflexive pronoun instead of the normal objective form.

272. A. The sentence shifts from future tense (next Sunday) to past tense (sang). The correct phrase should be *will sing*.

273. B. *Like* is a preposition that can only be followed by a noun phrase. A subordinating conjunction, *as*, is required to introduce a clause.

274. C. Use *I* in subject phrases.

275. D. All answer choices are correct.

276. A. *Amount* is used to describe something that cannot be counted. Use *number* to describe things that can be counted.

277. A. *Less* describes an amount that can be measured. *Fewer* describes things that can be counted.

278. C. The sentence illogically shifts from past to future tense.

279. B. develop.

280. A. amateur.

281. C. nuclear.

282. C. probably.

283. D. All answer choices are correct.

284. A. independence.

285. A. college.

286. D. All answer choices are correct.

287. A. mathematics.

288. B. until.

289. C. A doesn't make sense; why read the directions *after* you do something? The sentence does not present a cause/effect relationship, so B is not a good choice. Choice D is not as good as C because the word *always* means every time, making *whenever* repetitious.

290. C. In A, the suspect claims to own the pier. B is a sentence fragment. D changes the meaning by making the pier the place where the robbery suspect made the claim rather than the place where she was riding the bike.

291. C. In **A, B,** and **D,** it is raining inside the writer's room and outside on the balcony at the same time.

292. B. The paragraph is about how building roads affects plant life, not about the advantages of roadside plants.

293. B. Choices **A** and **D** don't make sense in the context of the sentence. **C** is a possibility; however the word *but* is used to show a contrast between *kind* and *nosy*.

294. D. Choices **A, B,** and **C** are very general subjects that would be hard to write about in one paragraph. It would be possible to describe a skateboard trick in one paragraph, making **D** the only choice.

295. D. Although all the other choices mention Mars, none of them contains information about whether there is or is not life on Mars.

296. A. In **B,** *in his leg* is confusing because two people are referred to. **C** seems to solve this problem by changing the phrase to *in their leg*, but that sounds like they both have the same leg. **D** is unnecessarily wordy and uses a passive voice.

297. B. The paragraph gives reasons to explain sentence 1. The sentence doesn't fit between sentences 2 and 3 because sentence 3 is directly related to sentence 2.

298. D. The first part of the sentence is in the past tense, so the rest of the sentence should also be in the past tense.

Answer Sheet for Practice HSPT Exam 3

TEST 1 Verbal Skills

1 Ⓐ Ⓑ Ⓒ Ⓓ	13 Ⓐ Ⓑ Ⓒ Ⓓ	25 Ⓐ Ⓑ Ⓒ Ⓓ	37 Ⓐ Ⓑ Ⓒ Ⓓ	49 Ⓐ Ⓑ Ⓒ Ⓓ
2 Ⓐ Ⓑ Ⓒ Ⓓ	14 Ⓐ Ⓑ Ⓒ Ⓓ	26 Ⓐ Ⓑ Ⓒ Ⓓ	38 Ⓐ Ⓑ Ⓒ	50 Ⓐ Ⓑ Ⓒ Ⓓ
3 Ⓐ Ⓑ Ⓒ Ⓓ	15 Ⓐ Ⓑ Ⓒ Ⓓ	27 Ⓐ Ⓑ Ⓒ Ⓓ	39 Ⓐ Ⓑ Ⓒ	51 Ⓐ Ⓑ Ⓒ Ⓓ
4 Ⓐ Ⓑ Ⓒ Ⓓ	16 Ⓐ Ⓑ Ⓒ Ⓓ	28 Ⓐ Ⓑ Ⓒ Ⓓ	40 Ⓐ Ⓑ Ⓒ Ⓓ	52 Ⓐ Ⓑ Ⓒ
5 Ⓐ Ⓑ Ⓒ Ⓓ	17 Ⓐ Ⓑ Ⓒ Ⓓ	29 Ⓐ Ⓑ Ⓒ Ⓓ	41 Ⓐ Ⓑ Ⓒ Ⓓ	53 Ⓐ Ⓑ Ⓒ Ⓓ
6 Ⓐ Ⓑ Ⓒ	18 Ⓐ Ⓑ Ⓒ Ⓓ	30 Ⓐ Ⓑ Ⓒ Ⓓ	42 Ⓐ Ⓑ Ⓒ Ⓓ	54 Ⓐ Ⓑ Ⓒ Ⓓ
7 Ⓐ Ⓑ Ⓒ Ⓓ	19 Ⓐ Ⓑ Ⓒ	31 Ⓐ Ⓑ Ⓒ Ⓓ	43 Ⓐ Ⓑ Ⓒ	55 Ⓐ Ⓑ Ⓒ Ⓓ
8 Ⓐ Ⓑ Ⓒ Ⓓ	20 Ⓐ Ⓑ Ⓒ Ⓓ	32 Ⓐ Ⓑ Ⓒ	44 Ⓐ Ⓑ Ⓒ	56 Ⓐ Ⓑ Ⓒ Ⓓ
9 Ⓐ Ⓑ Ⓒ	21 Ⓐ Ⓑ Ⓒ	33 Ⓐ Ⓑ Ⓒ Ⓓ	45 Ⓐ Ⓑ Ⓒ Ⓓ	57 Ⓐ Ⓑ Ⓒ Ⓓ
10 Ⓐ Ⓑ Ⓒ Ⓓ	22 Ⓐ Ⓑ Ⓒ Ⓓ	34 Ⓐ Ⓑ Ⓒ Ⓓ	46 Ⓐ Ⓑ Ⓒ Ⓓ	58 Ⓐ Ⓑ Ⓒ Ⓓ
11 Ⓐ Ⓑ Ⓒ Ⓓ	23 Ⓐ Ⓑ Ⓒ Ⓓ	35 Ⓐ Ⓑ Ⓒ Ⓓ	47 Ⓐ Ⓑ Ⓒ Ⓓ	59 Ⓐ Ⓑ Ⓒ Ⓓ
12 Ⓐ Ⓑ Ⓒ Ⓓ	24 Ⓐ Ⓑ Ⓒ Ⓓ	36 Ⓐ Ⓑ Ⓒ Ⓓ	48 Ⓐ Ⓑ Ⓒ Ⓓ	60 Ⓐ Ⓑ Ⓒ Ⓓ

TEST 2 Quantitative Skills

61 Ⓐ Ⓑ Ⓒ Ⓓ	72 Ⓐ Ⓑ Ⓒ Ⓓ	83 Ⓐ Ⓑ Ⓒ Ⓓ	93 Ⓐ Ⓑ Ⓒ Ⓓ	103 Ⓐ Ⓑ Ⓒ Ⓓ
62 Ⓐ Ⓑ Ⓒ Ⓓ	73 Ⓐ Ⓑ Ⓒ Ⓓ	84 Ⓐ Ⓑ Ⓒ Ⓓ	94 Ⓐ Ⓑ Ⓒ Ⓓ	104 Ⓐ Ⓑ Ⓒ Ⓓ
63 Ⓐ Ⓑ Ⓒ Ⓓ	74 Ⓐ Ⓑ Ⓒ Ⓓ	85 Ⓐ Ⓑ Ⓒ Ⓓ	95 Ⓐ Ⓑ Ⓒ Ⓓ	105 Ⓐ Ⓑ Ⓒ Ⓓ
64 Ⓐ Ⓑ Ⓒ Ⓓ	75 Ⓐ Ⓑ Ⓒ Ⓓ	86 Ⓐ Ⓑ Ⓒ Ⓓ	96 Ⓐ Ⓑ Ⓒ Ⓓ	106 Ⓐ Ⓑ Ⓒ Ⓓ
65 Ⓐ Ⓑ Ⓒ Ⓓ	76 Ⓐ Ⓑ Ⓒ Ⓓ	87 Ⓐ Ⓑ Ⓒ Ⓓ	97 Ⓐ Ⓑ Ⓒ Ⓓ	107 Ⓐ Ⓑ Ⓒ Ⓓ
66 Ⓐ Ⓑ Ⓒ Ⓓ	77 Ⓐ Ⓑ Ⓒ Ⓓ	88 Ⓐ Ⓑ Ⓒ Ⓓ	98 Ⓐ Ⓑ Ⓒ Ⓓ	108 Ⓐ Ⓑ Ⓒ Ⓓ
67 Ⓐ Ⓑ Ⓒ Ⓓ	78 Ⓐ Ⓑ Ⓒ Ⓓ	89 Ⓐ Ⓑ Ⓒ Ⓓ	99 Ⓐ Ⓑ Ⓒ Ⓓ	109 Ⓐ Ⓑ Ⓒ Ⓓ
68 Ⓐ Ⓑ Ⓒ Ⓓ	79 Ⓐ Ⓑ Ⓒ Ⓓ	90 Ⓐ Ⓑ Ⓒ Ⓓ	100 Ⓐ Ⓑ Ⓒ Ⓓ	110 Ⓐ Ⓑ Ⓒ Ⓓ
69 Ⓐ Ⓑ Ⓒ Ⓓ	80 Ⓐ Ⓑ Ⓒ Ⓓ	91 Ⓐ Ⓑ Ⓒ Ⓓ	101 Ⓐ Ⓑ Ⓒ Ⓓ	111 Ⓐ Ⓑ Ⓒ Ⓓ
70 Ⓐ Ⓑ Ⓒ Ⓓ	81 Ⓐ Ⓑ Ⓒ Ⓓ	92 Ⓐ Ⓑ Ⓒ Ⓓ	102 Ⓐ Ⓑ Ⓒ Ⓓ	112 Ⓐ Ⓑ Ⓒ Ⓓ
71 Ⓐ Ⓑ Ⓒ Ⓓ	82 Ⓐ Ⓑ Ⓒ Ⓓ			

TEST 3 Reading

113 Ⓐ Ⓑ Ⓒ Ⓓ	126 Ⓐ Ⓑ Ⓒ Ⓓ	139 Ⓐ Ⓑ Ⓒ Ⓓ	151 Ⓐ Ⓑ Ⓒ Ⓓ	163 Ⓐ Ⓑ Ⓒ Ⓓ
114 Ⓐ Ⓑ Ⓒ Ⓓ	127 Ⓐ Ⓑ Ⓒ Ⓓ	140 Ⓐ Ⓑ Ⓒ Ⓓ	152 Ⓐ Ⓑ Ⓒ Ⓓ	164 Ⓐ Ⓑ Ⓒ Ⓓ
115 Ⓐ Ⓑ Ⓒ Ⓓ	128 Ⓐ Ⓑ Ⓒ Ⓓ	141 Ⓐ Ⓑ Ⓒ Ⓓ	153 Ⓐ Ⓑ Ⓒ Ⓓ	165 Ⓐ Ⓑ Ⓒ Ⓓ
116 Ⓐ Ⓑ Ⓒ Ⓓ	129 Ⓐ Ⓑ Ⓒ Ⓓ	142 Ⓐ Ⓑ Ⓒ Ⓓ	154 Ⓐ Ⓑ Ⓒ Ⓓ	166 Ⓐ Ⓑ Ⓒ Ⓓ
117 Ⓐ Ⓑ Ⓒ Ⓓ	130 Ⓐ Ⓑ Ⓒ Ⓓ	143 Ⓐ Ⓑ Ⓒ Ⓓ	155 Ⓐ Ⓑ Ⓒ Ⓓ	167 Ⓐ Ⓑ Ⓒ Ⓓ
118 Ⓐ Ⓑ Ⓒ Ⓓ	131 Ⓐ Ⓑ Ⓒ Ⓓ	144 Ⓐ Ⓑ Ⓒ Ⓓ	156 Ⓐ Ⓑ Ⓒ Ⓓ	168 Ⓐ Ⓑ Ⓒ Ⓓ
119 Ⓐ Ⓑ Ⓒ Ⓓ	132 Ⓐ Ⓑ Ⓒ Ⓓ	145 Ⓐ Ⓑ Ⓒ Ⓓ	157 Ⓐ Ⓑ Ⓒ Ⓓ	169 Ⓐ Ⓑ Ⓒ Ⓓ
120 Ⓐ Ⓑ Ⓒ Ⓓ	133 Ⓐ Ⓑ Ⓒ Ⓓ	146 Ⓐ Ⓑ Ⓒ Ⓓ	158 Ⓐ Ⓑ Ⓒ Ⓓ	170 Ⓐ Ⓑ Ⓒ Ⓓ
121 Ⓐ Ⓑ Ⓒ Ⓓ	134 Ⓐ Ⓑ Ⓒ Ⓓ	147 Ⓐ Ⓑ Ⓒ Ⓓ	159 Ⓐ Ⓑ Ⓒ Ⓓ	171 Ⓐ Ⓑ Ⓒ Ⓓ
122 Ⓐ Ⓑ Ⓒ Ⓓ	135 Ⓐ Ⓑ Ⓒ Ⓓ	148 Ⓐ Ⓑ Ⓒ Ⓓ	160 Ⓐ Ⓑ Ⓒ Ⓓ	172 Ⓐ Ⓑ Ⓒ Ⓓ
123 Ⓐ Ⓑ Ⓒ Ⓓ	136 Ⓐ Ⓑ Ⓒ Ⓓ	149 Ⓐ Ⓑ Ⓒ Ⓓ	161 Ⓐ Ⓑ Ⓒ Ⓓ	173 Ⓐ Ⓑ Ⓒ Ⓓ
124 Ⓐ Ⓑ Ⓒ Ⓓ	137 Ⓐ Ⓑ Ⓒ Ⓓ	150 Ⓐ Ⓑ Ⓒ Ⓓ	162 Ⓐ Ⓑ Ⓒ Ⓓ	174 Ⓐ Ⓑ Ⓒ Ⓓ
125 Ⓐ Ⓑ Ⓒ Ⓓ	138 Ⓐ Ⓑ Ⓒ Ⓓ			

CUT HERE

Answer Sheet for Practice HSPT Exam 3

TEST 4 Mathematics

175 Ⓐ Ⓑ Ⓒ Ⓓ	188 Ⓐ Ⓑ Ⓒ Ⓓ	201 Ⓐ Ⓑ Ⓒ Ⓓ	214 Ⓐ Ⓑ Ⓒ Ⓓ	227 Ⓐ Ⓑ Ⓒ Ⓓ
176 Ⓐ Ⓑ Ⓒ Ⓓ	189 Ⓐ Ⓑ Ⓒ Ⓓ	202 Ⓐ Ⓑ Ⓒ Ⓓ	215 Ⓐ Ⓑ Ⓒ Ⓓ	228 Ⓐ Ⓑ Ⓒ Ⓓ
177 Ⓐ Ⓑ Ⓒ Ⓓ	190 Ⓐ Ⓑ Ⓒ Ⓓ	203 Ⓐ Ⓑ Ⓒ Ⓓ	216 Ⓐ Ⓑ Ⓒ Ⓓ	229 Ⓐ Ⓑ Ⓒ Ⓓ
178 Ⓐ Ⓑ Ⓒ Ⓓ	191 Ⓐ Ⓑ Ⓒ Ⓓ	204 Ⓐ Ⓑ Ⓒ Ⓓ	217 Ⓐ Ⓑ Ⓒ Ⓓ	230 Ⓐ Ⓑ Ⓒ Ⓓ
179 Ⓐ Ⓑ Ⓒ Ⓓ	192 Ⓐ Ⓑ Ⓒ Ⓓ	205 Ⓐ Ⓑ Ⓒ Ⓓ	218 Ⓐ Ⓑ Ⓒ Ⓓ	231 Ⓐ Ⓑ Ⓒ Ⓓ
180 Ⓐ Ⓑ Ⓒ Ⓓ	193 Ⓐ Ⓑ Ⓒ Ⓓ	206 Ⓐ Ⓑ Ⓒ Ⓓ	219 Ⓐ Ⓑ Ⓒ Ⓓ	232 Ⓐ Ⓑ Ⓒ Ⓓ
181 Ⓐ Ⓑ Ⓒ Ⓓ	194 Ⓐ Ⓑ Ⓒ Ⓓ	207 Ⓐ Ⓑ Ⓒ Ⓓ	220 Ⓐ Ⓑ Ⓒ Ⓓ	233 Ⓐ Ⓑ Ⓒ Ⓓ
182 Ⓐ Ⓑ Ⓒ Ⓓ	195 Ⓐ Ⓑ Ⓒ Ⓓ	208 Ⓐ Ⓑ Ⓒ Ⓓ	221 Ⓐ Ⓑ Ⓒ Ⓓ	234 Ⓐ Ⓑ Ⓒ Ⓓ
183 Ⓐ Ⓑ Ⓒ Ⓓ	196 Ⓐ Ⓑ Ⓒ Ⓓ	209 Ⓐ Ⓑ Ⓒ Ⓓ	222 Ⓐ Ⓑ Ⓒ Ⓓ	235 Ⓐ Ⓑ Ⓒ Ⓓ
184 Ⓐ Ⓑ Ⓒ Ⓓ	197 Ⓐ Ⓑ Ⓒ Ⓓ	210 Ⓐ Ⓑ Ⓒ Ⓓ	223 Ⓐ Ⓑ Ⓒ Ⓓ	236 Ⓐ Ⓑ Ⓒ Ⓓ
185 Ⓐ Ⓑ Ⓒ Ⓓ	198 Ⓐ Ⓑ Ⓒ Ⓓ	211 Ⓐ Ⓑ Ⓒ Ⓓ	224 Ⓐ Ⓑ Ⓒ Ⓓ	237 Ⓐ Ⓑ Ⓒ Ⓓ
186 Ⓐ Ⓑ Ⓒ Ⓓ	199 Ⓐ Ⓑ Ⓒ Ⓓ	212 Ⓐ Ⓑ Ⓒ Ⓓ	225 Ⓐ Ⓑ Ⓒ Ⓓ	238 Ⓐ Ⓑ Ⓒ Ⓓ
187 Ⓐ Ⓑ Ⓒ Ⓓ	200 Ⓐ Ⓑ Ⓒ Ⓓ	213 Ⓐ Ⓑ Ⓒ Ⓓ	226 Ⓐ Ⓑ Ⓒ Ⓓ	

TEST 5 Language Skills

239 Ⓐ Ⓑ Ⓒ Ⓓ	251 Ⓐ Ⓑ Ⓒ Ⓓ	263 Ⓐ Ⓑ Ⓒ Ⓓ	275 Ⓐ Ⓑ Ⓒ Ⓓ	287 Ⓐ Ⓑ Ⓒ Ⓓ
240 Ⓐ Ⓑ Ⓒ Ⓓ	252 Ⓐ Ⓑ Ⓒ Ⓓ	264 Ⓐ Ⓑ Ⓒ Ⓓ	276 Ⓐ Ⓑ Ⓒ Ⓓ	288 Ⓐ Ⓑ Ⓒ Ⓓ
241 Ⓐ Ⓑ Ⓒ Ⓓ	253 Ⓐ Ⓑ Ⓒ Ⓓ	265 Ⓐ Ⓑ Ⓒ Ⓓ	277 Ⓐ Ⓑ Ⓒ Ⓓ	289 Ⓐ Ⓑ Ⓒ Ⓓ
242 Ⓐ Ⓑ Ⓒ Ⓓ	254 Ⓐ Ⓑ Ⓒ Ⓓ	266 Ⓐ Ⓑ Ⓒ Ⓓ	278 Ⓐ Ⓑ Ⓒ Ⓓ	290 Ⓐ Ⓑ Ⓒ Ⓓ
243 Ⓐ Ⓑ Ⓒ Ⓓ	255 Ⓐ Ⓑ Ⓒ Ⓓ	267 Ⓐ Ⓑ Ⓒ Ⓓ	279 Ⓐ Ⓑ Ⓒ Ⓓ	291 Ⓐ Ⓑ Ⓒ Ⓓ
244 Ⓐ Ⓑ Ⓒ Ⓓ	256 Ⓐ Ⓑ Ⓒ Ⓓ	268 Ⓐ Ⓑ Ⓒ Ⓓ	280 Ⓐ Ⓑ Ⓒ Ⓓ	292 Ⓐ Ⓑ Ⓒ Ⓓ
245 Ⓐ Ⓑ Ⓒ Ⓓ	257 Ⓐ Ⓑ Ⓒ Ⓓ	269 Ⓐ Ⓑ Ⓒ Ⓓ	281 Ⓐ Ⓑ Ⓒ Ⓓ	293 Ⓐ Ⓑ Ⓒ Ⓓ
246 Ⓐ Ⓑ Ⓒ Ⓓ	258 Ⓐ Ⓑ Ⓒ Ⓓ	270 Ⓐ Ⓑ Ⓒ Ⓓ	282 Ⓐ Ⓑ Ⓒ Ⓓ	294 Ⓐ Ⓑ Ⓒ Ⓓ
247 Ⓐ Ⓑ Ⓒ Ⓓ	259 Ⓐ Ⓑ Ⓒ Ⓓ	271 Ⓐ Ⓑ Ⓒ Ⓓ	283 Ⓐ Ⓑ Ⓒ Ⓓ	295 Ⓐ Ⓑ Ⓒ Ⓓ
248 Ⓐ Ⓑ Ⓒ Ⓓ	260 Ⓐ Ⓑ Ⓒ Ⓓ	272 Ⓐ Ⓑ Ⓒ Ⓓ	284 Ⓐ Ⓑ Ⓒ Ⓓ	296 Ⓐ Ⓑ Ⓒ Ⓓ
249 Ⓐ Ⓑ Ⓒ Ⓓ	261 Ⓐ Ⓑ Ⓒ Ⓓ	273 Ⓐ Ⓑ Ⓒ Ⓓ	285 Ⓐ Ⓑ Ⓒ Ⓓ	297 Ⓐ Ⓑ Ⓒ Ⓓ
250 Ⓐ Ⓑ Ⓒ Ⓓ	262 Ⓐ Ⓑ Ⓒ Ⓓ	274 Ⓐ Ⓑ Ⓒ Ⓓ	286 Ⓐ Ⓑ Ⓒ Ⓓ	298 Ⓐ Ⓑ Ⓒ Ⓓ

Test 1: Verbal Skills

Time: 16 Minutes

Directions: Select the choice that best answers the following questions.

1. Bold is to tame as polite is to:

   A. gentle
   B. brave
   C. rude
   D. dirty

2. Zest most nearly means:

   A. enjoyment
   B. sadness
   C. anger
   D. concentration

3. Sway most nearly means:

   A. fall down
   B. move back and forth
   C. laugh loudly
   D. jump around

4. Which word does *not* belong with the others?

   A. squirrel
   B. chicken
   C. lizard
   D. cat

5. Contradict is the *opposite* of:

   A. dislike
   B. agree
   C. pronounce
   D. meet

6. Los Angeles gets less rain annually than Chicago. Seattle gets more rain than Los Angeles. Chicago gets more rain than Seattle. If the first two statements are true, the third is:

   A. true
   B. false
   C. uncertain

7. Green is to plant as hard is to:

   A. diamond
   B. water
   C. flower
   D. inventor

8. Static is the *opposite* of:

   A. dynamic
   B. quiet
   C. funny
   D. laborious

9. No chickens have teeth. Penny has no teeth. Penny is a hen. If the first two statements are true, the third is:

   A. true
   B. false
   C. uncertain

10. A deft worker is:

    A. skillful
    B. courageous
    C. insane
    D. clumsy

11. Which word does *not* belong with the others?

    A. chalk
    B. charcoal
    C. pencil
    D. ashes

12. Which word does *not* belong with the others?

    A. breeze
    B. draft
    C. tornado
    D. flood

GO ON TO THE NEXT PAGE

13. Clumsy is to trip as late is to:

   A. walk
   B. early
   C. forgive
   D. hurry

14. Ancient is the *opposite* of:

   A. faint
   B. useful
   C. antique
   D. modern

15. Which word does *not* belong with the others?

   A. deft
   B. clumsy
   C. skillful
   D. adroit

16. Which word does *not* belong with the others?

   A. oxygen
   B. element
   C. copper
   D. chlorine

17. Bland most nearly means:

   A. blind
   B. tasteless
   C. raw
   D. comforting

18. A grotesque mask is:

   A. gigantic
   B. magical
   C. ugly
   D. hidden

19. Clear Lake is shallower than Blue Lake. Frost Lake is deeper than Blue Lake. Clear Lake is deeper than Blue Lake. If the first two statements are true, the third is:

   A. true
   B. false
   C. uncertain

20. Mock most nearly means:

   A. make fun of
   B. cheer loudly
   C. listen to
   D. hit directly

21. Cross Creek flows faster than May Creek. Witch Creek flows faster than Cross Creek but slower than Hunt Creek. May Creek flows the most slowly. If the first two statements are true, the third is:

   A. true
   B. false
   C. uncertain

22. Dispose is the *opposite* of:

   A. throw
   B. acquire
   C. consolidate
   D. oppose

23. Fall is to winter as bud is to:

   A. leaf
   B. spring
   C. root
   D. curl

24. Ruin is to spoil as jump is to:

   A. surprise
   B. leap
   C. run
   D. stand

25. Temporary is the *opposite* of:

   A. permanent
   B. late
   C. fragile
   D. written

26. Familiar is the *opposite* of:

   A. akin
   B. lost
   C. strange
   D. maternal

27. Which word does *not* belong with the others?

    A. walk
    B. laugh
    C. speak
    D. race

28. Which word does *not* belong with the others?

    A. green
    B. red
    C. blue
    D. yellow

29. Which word does *not* belong with the others?

    A. weep
    B. sob
    C. bawl
    D. shout

30. Bay is to ocean as pebble is to:

    A. dust
    B. rock
    C. lake
    D. salt

31. Destroy is the *opposite* of:

    A. decimate
    B. restore
    C. history
    D. change

32. All zebs are flying boks. No swimming boks fly. No zebs swim. If the first two statements are true, the third is:

    A. true
    B. false
    C. uncertain

33. A uniform rule is:

    A. unfair
    B. shapely
    C. consistent
    D. hateful

34. Impose most nearly means:

    A. protect
    B. require
    C. stop
    D. surround

35. Which word does *not* belong with the others?

    A. height
    B. inch
    C. depth
    D. weight

36. Abandon most nearly means:

    A. please
    B. beg
    C. forbid
    D. desert

37. Specify most nearly means:

    A. name
    B. command
    C. forget
    D. select

38. A is north of B. B is north of C. C is north of A. If the first two statements are true, the third is:

    A. true
    B. false
    C. uncertain

39. Carco makes reliable vehicles. Stan's new truck is very reliable. Stan bought a Carco truck. If the first two statements are true, the third is:

    A. true
    B. false
    C. uncertain

40. Mathematics is to algebra as biology is to:

    A. alive
    B. animals
    C. botany
    D. science

GO ON TO THE NEXT PAGE

41. Lead is to heavy as water is to:

   A. wet
   B. light
   C. ice
   D. solid

42. Important is the *opposite* of:

   A. useful
   B. settled
   C. imaginary
   D. trivial

43. Box M is heavier than box N but lighter than box P. Box P is lighter than box R. Box R is heavier than box N. If the first two statements are true, the third is:

   A. true
   B. false
   C. uncertain

44. Laura owns more books than Fred. Fred owns more books than Terry. Laura owns fewer books than Terry. If the first two statements are true, the third is:

   A. true
   B. false
   C. uncertain

45. A minute amount is:

   A. tiny
   B. huge
   C. timely
   D. needed

46. Consider most nearly means:

   A. learn from
   B. question
   C. think about
   D. care for

47. Which word does *not* belong with the others?

   A. screwdriver
   B. wrench
   C. hammer
   D. ratchet

48. Which word does *not* belong with the others?

   A. meat
   B. beef
   C. lamb
   D. chicken

49. Which word does *not* belong with the others?

   A. dirty
   B. soiled
   C. clean
   D. foul

50. Manual is to explain as stapler is to:

   A. staples
   B. fasten
   C. define
   D. paper

51. Completely is the *opposite* of:

   A. totally
   B. sadly
   C. partially
   D. thoughtlessly

52. Some mushrooms are poisonous. The cook served fried mushrooms at dinner. Some of the diners will become ill. If the first two statements are true, the third is:

   A. true
   B. false
   C. uncertain

53. A critical idea is:

   A. negative
   B. useless
   C. helpful
   D. important

54. Pity most nearly means:

   A. sympathy
   B. friendship
   C. sadness
   D. harmony

55. Which word does *not* belong with the others?

    A. giraffes
    B. mammals
    C. reptiles
    D. birds

56. Which word does *not* belong with the others?

    A. skip
    B. run
    C. walk
    D. hop

57. Which word does *not* belong with the others?

    A. and
    B. but
    C. yet
    D. however

58. An incredible story is:

    A. fascinating
    B. mysterious
    C. frightening
    D. unbelievable

59. Which word does *not* belong with the others?

    A. candid
    B. frank
    C. truthful
    D. false

60. Depth is to trench as height is to:

    A. empty
    B. size
    C. hole
    D. hill

IF YOU FINISH BEFORE TIME IS CALLED, CHECK YOUR WORK ON THIS
SECTION ONLY. DO NOT WORK ON ANY OTHER SECTION IN THE TEST.

Test 2: Quantitative Skills

Time: 30 Minutes

Directions: Select the choice that best answers the following questions.

61. What number should come next in the series 9, 16, 23, 30, ___?

    A. 33
    B. 35
    C. 37
    D. 41

62. What number, when multiplied by 3, is equal to the difference of 31 and 10?

    A. 5
    B. 6
    C. 7
    D. 8

63. Examine (a), (b), and (c), and find the best answer.

    (a) $(2 \times 3)^2$

    (b) $2^2 \times 3^2$

    (c) 6^2

    A. (a) is greater than (b) and (c).
    B. (a) is equal to (c) and less than (b).
    C. (b) and (c) are equal and greater than (a).
    D. (a), (b), and (c) are equal.

64. What number should come next in the series 5, 20, 80, 320, ___?

    A. 640
    B. 960
    C. 1,280
    D. 1,600

65. Twenty-five percent of what number is equal to 15% of 200?

    A. 60
    B. 90
    C. 120
    D. 150

66. In the following figure, *AB* is parallel to *CD*. Which of the following statements must be true?

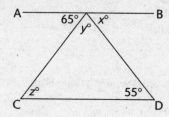

    A. $x > y > z$
    B. $z > x > y$
    C. $z > y > x$
    D. $y > z > x$

67. What number should fill in the blank in the series 6, 9, 4, 7, ___, 5?

    A. 1
    B. 2
    C. 3
    D. 4

68. Two fifths of what number is equal to $\frac{4}{5}$ of 30?

    A. 20
    B. 25
    C. 40
    D. 60

69. What number should fill in the blank in the series 64, 32, 16, 8, ___, 2?

    A. 6
    B. 5
    C. 4
    D. 3

70. If the product of 5 and 16 is a number, then $\frac{1}{4}$ of the number is:

    A. 20
    B. 22
    C. 24
    D. 26

71. Examine (a), (b), and (c), and find the best answer.

(a) $5 - (3 + 5)$

(b) $5 - 3 + 5$

(c) $(5 - 3) + 5$

 A.   (a) is greater than (b) and (c).
 B.   (a) is equal to (c) and less than (b).
 C.   (b) and (c) are equal and greater than (a).
 D.   (a), (b), and (c) are equal.

72. Examine the following figure and determine which of the following statements must be true.

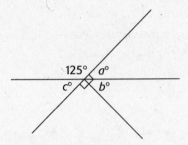

 A. $a = c < b$
 B. $a = c > b$
 C. $a > c > b$
 D. $a = b = c$

73. The number that is equal to the sum of 12 and 15 is the same as the product of 9 and what number?

 A.   1
 B.   2
 C.   3
 D.   4

74. What number should fill in the blank in the series 7, −10, 13, −16, ___, −22?

 A.   −19
 B.   −18
 C.   18
 D.   19

75. Examine (a), (b), and (c), and find the best answer.

(a) $(-3)^3$

(b) -3^3

(c) -27

 A.   (a) is greater than (b) and (c).
 B.   (a) is equal to (c) and less than (b).
 C.   (b) and (c) are equal and greater than (a).
 D.   (a), (b), and (c) are equal.

76. What number should fill in the blank in the series 12, 13, 10, 11, 8, ___, 6?

 A.   5
 B.   7
 C.   9
 D.   10

77. If the sum of 12 and 40 is equal to 400% of a number, then that number is:

 A.   11
 B.   12
 C.   13
 D.   14

78. Examine the triangle in the following figure, and determine which of the following statements must be true.

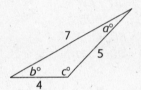

 A. $b > a > c$
 B. $b > c > a$
 C. $c > a > b$
 D. $c > b > a$

79. What number should come next in the series 10, 13, 17, 22, 28, ___?

 A.   34
 B.   35
 C.   36
 D.   37

80. Examine (a), (b), and (c), and find the best answer.

(a) $10^{-2} \times 10^3$

(b) $10^{-3} \times 10^5$

(c) $10^{-4} \times 10^6$

 A.   (a) is greater than (b) and (c).
 B.   (a) is equal to (c) and less than (b).
 C.   (b) and (c) are equal and greater than (a).
 D.   (a), (b), and (c) are equal.

GO ON TO THE NEXT PAGE

81. What number should fill in the blank in the series 1, 2, 6, 12, ___, 72?

   A. 24
   B. 30
   C. 36
   D. 48

82. In the following figure, *ABCD* is a square. Select the best answer from the following choices.

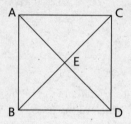

   A. $BC > BD > ED$
   B. $BC > AD > ED$
   C. $BE = BD = CD$
   D. $AD = BD = CD$

83. $\frac{5}{12}$ of the product of 4, 5, and 6 is equal to:

   A. 50
   B. 52
   C. 54
   D. 58

84. What number, when quadrupled, is equal to 16 tripled?

   A. 8
   B. 9
   C. 10
   D. 12

85. Examine (a), (b), and (c), and find the best answer.

   (a) 529.52 rounded to the nearest whole number

   (b) 532.79 rounded to the nearest ten

   (c) 529.5 rounded to the nearest whole number

   A. (a) is greater than (b) and (c).
   B. (a) is equal to (c) and less than (b).
   C. (b) and (c) are equal and greater than (a).
   D. (a), (b), and (c) are equal.

86. What number should come next in the series 2, 8, 3, 12, 7, ___?

   A. 14
   B. 21
   C. 28
   D. 35

87. $\frac{1}{7}$ of what number is equal to $\frac{1}{9}$ of 45?

   A. 21
   B. 28
   C. 35
   D. 42

88. What number should come next in the series 20, 8, 16, 4, 8, –4, ___?

   A. –8
   B. –6
   C. 2
   D. 8

89. In the following figure, *O* is the center of the circle. Select the best answer.

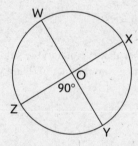

   A. The length of arc *ZY* = the length of arc *WX* > the length of arc *XY*.
   B. The length of arc *ZY* < the length of arc *WX* = the length of arc *XY*.
   C. The length of arc *WZ* = the length of arc *XY* < the length of arc *ZY*.
   D. The length of arc *ZY* = the length of arc *XY* = the length of arc *WX*.

90. The square of what number is equal to 2 raised to the 6th power?

   A. 4
   B. 6
   C. 8
   D. 12

91. What number should come next in the series −7, −2, 2, 5, 7, ___?

    A. 8
    B. 9
    C. 10
    D. 12

92. Examine (a), (b), and (c), and find the best answer.

    (a) The greatest common divisor of 20 and 15
    (b) The greatest common divisor of 5 and 10
    (c) The greatest common divisor of 45 and 70

    A. (a) is greater than (b) and (c).
    B. (a) is equal to (c) and less than (b).
    C. (b) and (c) are equal and greater than (a).
    D. (a), (b), and (c) are equal.

93. $\frac{2}{3}$ of the difference between 84 and 12 is equal to:

    A. 40
    B. 42
    C. 44
    D. 48

94. What number should come next in the series 4, 16, 13, 52, 49, ___?

    A. 190
    B. 193
    C. 196
    D. 199

95. In the following figure, *ABGH, BCDG,* and *DEFG* are congruent squares. Select the most appropriate answer.

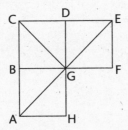

    A. $CD = GH > AG$
    B. AE = twice the length of CG
    C. $AE > AH > CG$
    D. $CG = EG < AB$

96. What number, when reduced by 30% of itself, is equal to 63?

    A. 80
    B. 85
    C. 88
    D. 90

97. Examine (a), (b), and (c), and find the best answer.
    (a) $\frac{21}{4}$
    (b) 0.0525×10^2
    (c) 525%

    A. (a) is greater than (b) and (c).
    B. (a) is equal to (c) and less than (b).
    C. (b) and (c) are equal and greater than (a).
    D. (a), (b), and (c) are equal.

98. What number should come next in the series 1, 1, 2, 8, 3, 27, 4, ___?

    A. 24
    B. 48
    C. 64
    D. 72

99. What number is equal to 15% of the difference between 98 and 18?

    A. 12
    B. 13
    C. 14
    D. 15

100. What number should fill in the blank in the series 9, 15, 20, 26, ___, 37?

    A. 29
    B. 31
    C. 33
    D. 35

101. Three hundred percent of what number is equal to the square of 6?

    A. 8
    B. 10
    C. 12
    D. 14

GO ON TO THE NEXT PAGE

102. What number should fill in the blank in the series 17, 16, 18, 15, 19, ___, 20?

    A. 18
    B. 17
    C. 16
    D. 14

103. Examine the triangles in the following figure, and then select the most appropriate answer.

  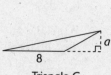

    Triangle A   Triangle B   Triangle C

    A. The area of triangle A = the area of triangle B = the area of triangle C.
    B. The area of triangle B > the area of triangle A > the area of triangle C.
    C. The area of triangle A = the area of triangle B > the area of triangle C.
    D. The area of triangle A > the area of triangle B > the area of triangle C.

104. What number should come next in the series 7, 11, 19, 31, 47, ___?

    A. 67
    B. 78
    C. 80
    D. 82

105. What number, when quadrupled and then decreased by 8, is equal to the product of 6 and 10?

    A. 13
    B. 15
    C. 17
    D. 19

106. Examine (a), (b), and (c), and find the best answer.

    (a) The value of $5a - 2b$ if $a = -2$ and $b = -3$
    (b) The value of $5a - 2b$ if $a = -3$ and $b = -2$
    (c) The value of $5a - 2b$ if $a = -4$ and $b = -6$

    A. (a) is greater than (b) and (c).
    B. (a) is equal to (c) and less than (b).
    C. (b) and (c) are equal and greater than (a).
    D. (a), (b), and (c) are equal.

107. The following figure is a circle with center O. Select the most appropriate answer.

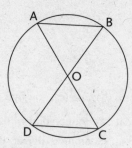

    A. $AC > AB = CD$
    B. $AC > AB > CD$
    C. $BD > CD > AB$
    D. $BD = AC = CD$

108. What number should come next in the series 3, 3, 6, 9, 15, 24, ___?

    A. 33
    B. 36
    C. 39
    D. 46

109. What number, when squared and then increased by 19, is equal to the product of 20 and 5?

    A. 6
    B. 7
    C. 8
    D. 9

110. Examine the following figure, and select the most appropriate answer.

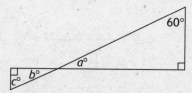

    A. $b = a > c$
    B. $c > b > a$
    C. $c > b = a$
    D. $c > a > b$

111. What number should fill in the blank in the series 48, 12, 44, 11, 40, 10, ___, 9?

    A. 36
    B. 37
    C. 38
    D. 39

112. Examine the following figure, and select the best answer.

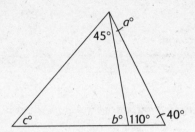

- **A.** $c > b > a$
- **B.** $a > b > c$
- **C.** $b > c > a$
- **D.** $b > a > c$

IF YOU FINISH BEFORE TIME IS CALLED, CHECK YOUR WORK ON THIS SECTION ONLY. DO NOT WORK ON ANY OTHER SECTION IN THE TEST.

Practice HSPT Exam 3

319

Test 3: Reading

Time: 25 Minutes

Directions: In this test, select the answer choice that best satisfies the question.

Comprehension

For questions 113–152, read each passage carefully. Then select the choice that best answers the questions that follow each passage.

Sometimes people worry about the germs that they come into contact with. But many microbes, tiny life forms, inhabit a human's body at any given time. Some of the natural species that regularly come into contact with our bodies include mites, lice, yeast, and fungus. We are, in fact, an ecosystem much like a rain forest is for the natural plants and animals that call it home.

Lice, or nits, are particularly disgusting to most people. To learn that a child has been found in school with head lice can cause shock and shame. People think that having lice is a symptom of being unclean, although one can be infected by contact with somebody else who has them. Although lice are not common generally, children can easily get them because of their close contact with other children at school or play.

Mites are always present on the human body, and cleanliness does not eliminate the chance of having them. They are also microscopic, so they are invisible to the naked eye. A number of different species of mites exist, two of which live on the human face, particularly the skin of the forehead. Others are very content in human hair, living among the follicles of the eyelashes, eyebrows, and scalp hair.

Not all such inhabitants are harmful. In fact, even the annoying mite lives on dead skin cells, actually doing us a favor by removing them. The dreaded dust mite, for example, blamed for causing allergies, removes dead skin from bed coverings. And harmless bacteria often keep potentially harmful bacteria from surviving.

Besides the tiny inhabitants, we are also regularly harassed by insects that feed on our bodies, like mosquitoes, ticks, and fleas. They sometimes deposit harmful illnesses at the same time they probe the skin for the blood on which they live. Mosquitoes can spread malaria and yellow fever as well as encephalitis. Fleas have transmitted bubonic plague, and ticks have caused lime disease.

Just like a river, an ocean, a rain forest, or any other natural wonder in which numerous species survive, feeding on other inhabitants, our bodies are natural providers of nutrition and life for various small and microscopic species.

113. The word <u>inhabit</u>, as underlined and used in this passage, most nearly means:

A. escape
B. live in
C. feed on
D. abuse

114. The author's purpose in writing this selection was most probably to:

A. explain the dangerous ailments that can result from insects and microbes
B. describe how the human body is host to harmful and harmless inhabitants and visitors
C. warn people about the dangers of being attacked by small life forms
D. describe how to rid oneself of bacteria and insects

115. According to the selection, lice and mites are different in that:

A. mites are totally unavoidable, while lice might be avoidable
B. lice are not harmful, but mites are
C. mites live only on the skin, and lice live only in the hair
D. mites are treatable, and lice are not

116. The word <u>shame</u>, as underlined and used in this passage, most nearly means:

A. embarrassment
B. anger
C. disbelief
D. contentment

117. Lice are also known as:

- **A.** nits
- **B.** microbes
- **C.** yeast
- **D.** ticks

118. What does the author mean by *Not all such inhabitants are harmful*?

- **A.** Microbes are the same as yeast.
- **B.** Some microbes benefit people.
- **C.** Some mites eat other harmful mites.
- **D.** The diseases mites carry do not pass to humans.

119. Insects deposit germs in humans while the insects are:

- **A.** flying
- **B.** feeding
- **C.** sleeping
- **D.** bleeding

120. Some bacteria are helpful because they:

- **A.** destroy other bacteria that could be harmful
- **B.** remove dead skin cells
- **C.** are not a result of being dirty
- **D.** are invisible

121. The word <u>harassed</u>, as underlined and used in this passage, most nearly means:

- **A.** tickled
- **B.** infected
- **C.** hurried
- **D.** bothered

122. The writer of this selection:

- **A.** has provided a factual report
- **B.** is disgusted by the creatures that live on the human body
- **C.** thinks the human body is like a marvelous environment
- **D.** makes fun of people who are afraid of germs

A word is a symbol. The marks on a page or the sounds made when the word is pronounced represent a thing or a thought. *Arbre* is the symbol in French that represents the same thing as the English symbol *tree*. *Laugh* is the English symbol that represents the same action as the French word *rire*. The words are different, but what is represented is the same. Words that represent things we can <u>perceive</u> through our senses, like *tree* or *laugh*, are called concrete words. Words that represent ideas or feelings, like *democracy* or *love*, are called abstract words.

Words can be general or specific. Although this idea applies to all parts of speech, it is most easily understood by using nouns as an example. The most general words and phrases represent a category or group of many items. The most specific words and phrases represent something that is <u>unique</u>. *Tool* is a general category that includes smaller categories like tools used for building things, tools used for cooking, and tools used for writing. Tools used for building things include the more specific words *hammer, screwdriver,* and *wrench*. There are two more specific kinds of screwdrivers: slot-head and Phillips. To get to the most specific wording, making the item <u>unique</u>, we use a phrase like "the Phillips screwdriver made by Toolco that I bought at the hardware store."

But words do more than simply point to items. What the word represents is its meaning. But words also suggest feelings and associations. These are called the words' connotations. *Aroma* and *smell* mean the same thing, but *aroma* always suggests something with a pleasant scent, while *smell* could refer to a rose or a full garbage pail. Connotations are not always positive or negative. *Clothes* and *outfit* both represent what we wear, but they have slightly different associations. Connotations might differ from person to person. For example, for most people, the word *flowers* is associated with ideas about beauty, color, and pleasant scents. But for a person who has allergies, the word might bring to mind associations of sneezing, runny eyes, and discomfort.

123. The word <u>perceive</u>, as underlined and used in this passage, most nearly means:

- **A.** divide
- **B.** harden
- **C.** recognize
- **D.** learn

124. The same word might have different associations for different people because:

- **A.** words can have more than one meaning
- **B.** people have had different experiences with what the word represents
- **C.** dictionaries do not explain the connotations of words
- **D.** they are symbols

GO ON TO THE NEXT PAGE

125. This selection would most likely have appeared in:

    A. a newspaper article

    B. instructions about how to solve puzzles

    C. an advertisement

    D. a textbook for an English class

126. According to the information in this selection, which of the following is the most specific?

    A. citrus fruits

    B. food

    C. navel orange

    D. lemon

127. The word unique, as underlined and used in this passage, most nearly means:

    A. unusual for something of that type

    B. the only one of its kind

    C. members of a group

    D. very special

128. The idea that words and phrases can be general or specific applies to:

    A. nouns

    B. verbs

    C. adjectives

    D. all of the above

129. Words that represent ideas or feelings are called:

    A. abstract

    B. concrete

    C. democracy

    D. nouns

130. The word connotations, as underlined and used in this passage, most nearly means:

    A. suggestions

    B. contrasts

    C. meanings

    D. writings

131. The symbols *arbre* and *tree*:

    A. are part of the same language

    B. have different connotations to the same person

    C. represent a feeling or idea

    D. represent the same thing

132. The author of this selection probably:

    A. works with tools for building things

    B. enjoys doing crossword puzzles

    C. is allergic to flowers and perfume

    D. visits museums frequently

Charles Elmer Hires was the father of root beer. His first job was working in a pharmacy. But he was determined to open his own business. He studied pharmacy in night school and eventually borrowed money to open his own drugstore. The company records note that one of the store's features was an elaborate soda fountain made of marble. This might have been an <u>omen</u> of Hires' future.

Shortly after he married, he took his wife on a vacation. They stayed in a boarding house where the landlady served them a special tea she had brewed made of a blend of roots, herbs, and spices, including sassafras bark. Hires thought it was delicious. He had been thinking about starting a business that would be more interesting than the daily routine of the pharmacy. The tea suggested that he could create a tasty soft drink that could be sold to the public. He experimented with a variety of formulas until he tasted what he thought would sell.

Although the recipe for Hires Root Beer is a secret, it is known that one of the key flavoring ingredients is not sassafras bark but the root of the sarsaparilla, a plant related to the lily and the onion. The beverage succeeded not only because of its taste, but also because of Hires' clever marketing and advertising. He had wanted to call it "root tea," but a friend told him that the word "tea" suggested something for sick people or women, and he suggested "root beer." Although there is no alcohol in the drink, and none of its ingredients affect the body, the name would suggest strength and vitality.

Hires began to market the ingredients for the drink to drugstore soda fountains in 1876. In 1893, he introduced bottled root beer. The drink was marketed as being <u>beneficial</u> as well as tasty. One of the early advertisements for the drink included the slogan "Hires to your health." Another claimed it would <u>induce</u> "health for the baby, pleasure for the parents, and new life for the old folks." But taste and convenience were not ignored. Hires was "a pure delicious beverage for the home in bottles and at fountains." As other companies began to market a product that they claimed was the same, Hires' ads read "Because of the real root juices, Hires has a finer flavor than imitation root beers."

Hires grew rich. But root beer was not his only source of his wealth. He was an early developer of the condensed milk business and organized a chain of factories to process it in the eastern United States and Canada. He sold that business in 1917, but he continued to supervise the root beer company until his death in 1937.

133. Root beer contains:

   A.   sassafras
   B.   tea
   C.   alcohol
   D.   sarsaparilla

134. The word <u>omen</u>, as underlined and used in this passage, most nearly means:

   A.   sign
   B.   criticism
   C.   reward
   D.   conclusion

135. Based on this selection, the best word to describe Charles Hires is:

   A.   artistic
   B.   ambitious
   C.   sympathetic
   D.   violent

136. Hires began experimenting with a new drink because:

   A.   his wife had enjoyed the taste of the tea the landlady served
   B.   he had been thinking about starting a new business
   C.   the pharmacy business was not making enough money
   D.   the recipe for root beer is a secret

137. According to the selection, the word *tea* was associated with:

   A.   health
   B.   English people
   C.   vacations
   D.   weakness

138. The word <u>beneficial</u>, as underlined and used in this passage, most nearly means:

   A.   blessed
   B.   nutritious
   C.   helpful
   D.   medicinal

139. A good title for this passage might be:

   A.   The Life of Charles Elmer Hires
   B.   A Drink for Your Health
   C.   The History of Root Beer
   D.   Mr. Hires' New Beverage

140. The word <u>induce</u>, as underlined and used in this passage, most nearly means:

   A.   consider
   B.   take away
   C.   lead to
   D.   desire

141. The advertisements for root beer mentioned its:

   A.   healthfulness and flavor
   B.   price and convenience
   C.   taste and novelty
   D.   none of the above

142. Hires was a pioneer in the:

   A.   pharmacy business
   B.   promotion of tea
   C.   development of one product
   D.   development of two products

For a time, the Hubble telescope was the subject of jokes and the object of wrath because some people believed the U.S. government had spent too much money on space projects that served no purpose. The Hubble was sent into orbit with a satellite by the Space Shuttle Discovery in 1990. There were great hopes and expectations for its possible uses. But after it was in position, it simply did not work because the primary mirror was not shaped correctly. However, in 1993, the crew of the Shuttle Endeavor arrived like roadside mechanics, opened the hatch that was installed for the purpose, and replaced the defective mirror with a good one.

Suddenly, all that had originally been expected came true. The Hubble telescope was indeed the "window on the universe," as it had originally been <u>dubbed</u>. When you look deep into space, you are actually looking back through time, because even though light travels at 186,000 miles a second, it requires time to get from one place to another. In fact, it is said that in some cases, the Hubble telescope is looking back eleven billion years to see galaxies already forming. The distant galaxies are speeding away from Earth, some traveling at the speed of light.

GO ON TO THE NEXT PAGE

Hubble has viewed exploding stars such as the Eta Carinae. This star clearly displayed clouds of gas and dust billowing outward from its poles at 1.5 million miles an hour. Before Hubble, it was visible from traditional telescopes on earth, but its details could not be seen clearly. But now, the evidence of the explosion is obvious. Hubble has also provided a close look at black holes, which can be described as cosmic drains. Gas and dust swirl around the drain and are slowly sucked in by the extremely strong gravity.

The Hubble telescope was named after Edwin Hubble, a 1920s astronomer. He developed a formula that expresses the relationship of distances between clusters of galaxies and the speeds at which they travel. Astronomers use stars known as Cepheid variables to measure distances in space. These stars dim and brighten from time to time, and they are photographed over time and charted. All the discoveries made by Hubble have allowed astronomers to learn more about the formation of early galaxies.

143. The Hubble telescope was not always popular at first because:

A. people were afraid of what might be found
B. many people believed space exploration was a waste of money
C. it had a mirror that was not shaped correctly
D. it was more expensive than most space shuttles

144. The word <u>wrath</u>, as underlined and used in the passge, most nearly means:

A. interest
B. contentment
C. anger
D. pleasure

145. The passage suggests that at the time the Hubble telescope was initially sent into space:

A. there was little attention paid to it
B. all attention was focused on the space shuttle, not the Hubble telescope
C. there was considerable excitement about what it would be able to do
D. it was already known that the mirror was defective

146. The author compares the astronauts of the Endeavor to:

A. astronomers
B. scientists
C. mechanics
D. politicians

147. According to the passage, Edward Hubble:

A. developed the Hubble telescope
B. was the first person to use the Hubble telescope
C. developed a mathematical formula to measure speed and distances between galaxies
D. was a politician who sponsored funding in Congress

148. The word <u>dubbed</u>, as underlined and used in this passage, most nearly means:

A. flown
B. named
C. hoped
D. bought

149. When viewing a distant galaxy through the Hubble telescope:

A. you are actually looking back in time
B. the new mirror distorts the image
C. the view from Hubble is not accurate, but it is interesting
D. you cannot determine distance or time with any kind of accuracy

150. A Cepheid variable is:

A. a star
B. a Hubble calculation
C. the dimming and brightening of a star
D. a mirror

151. The Eta Carinae was previously viewed from other telescopes, but:

A. its details could not be seen well
B. its speed and distance were not known
C. its location was not known
D. it had not been named

152. The author suggests that a black hole is similar to:

    A. water draining in a bathtub
    B. a galaxy
    C. a group of stars
    D. a cloud

Vocabulary

For questions 153–174, select the word that means the same, or almost the same, as the underlined word.

153. Don't <u>dawdle</u> with your friends.

    A. hang loosely
    B. waste time
    C. paint
    D. splash

154. They were an <u>impartial</u> group.

    A. unlawful
    B. incomplete
    C. unprejudiced
    D. unfaithful

155. the <u>militant</u> organization

    A. political
    B. mighty
    C. aggressive
    D. peaceable

156. an <u>eminent</u> scientist

    A. noted
    B. moral
    C. future
    D. low

157. I can <u>perceive</u> the solution.

    A. resolve
    B. observe
    C. organize
    D. stick in

158. It's his <u>idiosyncrasy</u>.

    A. stupidity
    B. virtue
    C. personal peculiarity
    D. foreign dialect

159. They erected an <u>edifice</u>.

    A. tool
    B. large building
    C. garden
    D. mushroom

160. in a <u>seedy</u> neighborhood

    A. dishonest
    B. helpless
    C. shabby
    D. nervous

161. You can't <u>supplant</u> it with new information.

    A. spend
    B. unite
    C. recall
    D. replace

162. asked to <u>desist</u> from singing

    A. loiter
    B. stand
    C. hurry
    D. stop

163. They won't <u>collaborate</u> on the project.

    A. act jointly
    B. converse
    C. arrange in order
    D. provide proof

164. the <u>futility</u> of running uphill

    A. uselessness
    B. timelessness
    C. stinginess
    D. happiness

GO ON TO THE NEXT PAGE

165. His bones were <u>intact</u>.

    A. blunt
    B. strong
    C. hidden
    D. uninjured

166. The group's <u>fervor</u> was exciting.

    A. originality
    B. justice
    C. zeal
    D. productivity

167. with <u>unerring</u> aim

    A. modest
    B. illogical
    C. ghostly
    D. unfailing

168. <u>Refute</u> the politician's statement.

    A. polish
    B. disprove
    C. throw away
    D. break up

169. Their <u>consensus</u> helped us win.

    A. steadfastness of purpose
    B. general agreement
    C. lack of harmony
    D. informal vote

170. The dog was <u>compliant</u>.

    A. tangled
    B. grumbling
    C. submissive
    D. treacherous

171. no <u>access</u> to that road

    A. agreement
    B. rapidity
    C. welcome
    D. approach

172. a <u>prudent</u> investment

    A. wise
    B. overcritical
    C. famous
    D. dull

173. Don't <u>incur</u> your brother's anger.

    A. take to heart
    B. anticipate
    C. bring down on oneself
    D. impress by repetition

174. He lectured from the <u>rostrum</u>.

    A. easy chair
    B. platform
    C. dance hall
    D. grandstand

IF YOU FINISH BEFORE TIME IS CALLED, CHECK YOUR WORK ON THIS SECTION ONLY. DO NOT WORK ON ANY OTHER SECTION IN THE TEST.

Test 4: Mathematics

Time: 45 Minutes

Directions: Select the answer choice that best satisfies the question.

Mathematical Concepts

For questions 175–198, select the choice that best answers the following questions. You can use scratch paper to figure out your answers.

175. John spent 30 minutes vacuuming, 12 minutes dusting, 37 minutes washing dishes, and 45 minutes resting. How many minutes did John spend cleaning?

   A.   34
   B.   79
   C.   100
   D.   124

176. Rockford is 439 miles from Springville and 638 miles from Davenport. How much closer is Rockford to Springville than Rockford to Davenport?

   A.   199 miles
   B.   201 miles
   C.   439 miles
   D.   1,077 miles

177. The basketball game starts at 8:00. If it is now 5:30, how much time is left before the game starts?

   A.   1 hour, 30 minutes
   B.   2 hours, 30 minutes
   C.   3 hours, 30 minutes
   D.   4 hours, 30 minutes

178. Janice buys a quart of milk and two dozen eggs. If milk costs $1.39 and eggs are $1.28 a dozen, how much change does Janice get back if she pays with a $10.00 bill?

   A. $3.95
   B. $5.94
   C. $6.05
   D. $7.33

179. Kim's favorite movie is 144 minutes long. Justin's favorite movie is 127 minutes long. How much longer is Kim's favorite movie?

   A.   17 minutes
   B.   23 minutes
   C.   36 minutes
   D.   44 minutes

180. Roger collects bottle caps. Each cap can be traded for 5 cents. If Roger receives $40.50, how many bottle caps did he trade?

   A.   810
   B.   405
   C.   200
   D.   8

181. A piece of wood measuring 16.5 inches long is cut into 2.75-inch pieces. How many smaller pieces of wood are there?

   A.   3
   B.   5
   C.   6
   D.   8

182. Lauren has 17 quarters, 33 dimes, and 8 pennies. The total amount of money is:

   A. $7.63
   B. $7.95
   C. $5.80
   D. $15.55

183. The value of 18 quarters, 6 dimes, and 24 nickels is:

    A. $5.34
    B. $6.30
    C. $18.84
    D. $24.24

184. What is the greatest common factor of 42 and 28?

    A. 6
    B. 7
    C. 14
    D. 21

185. $(+8) - (+2) - (-7) =$

    A. -1
    B. 3
    C. 13
    D. 17

186. $\frac{8}{9} - \frac{1}{3} =$

    A. $\frac{5}{9}$

    B. $\frac{2}{3}$

    C. $\frac{7}{9}$

    D. $\frac{7}{6}$

187. Light travels 744,000 miles in 4 seconds. What is its speed in miles per second?

    A. 186,000
    B. 187,000
    C. 188,000
    D. 189,000

188. A baseball stadium has 1,350 box seats, 3,527 reserve seats, 2,007 general admission seats, and 4,275 bleacher seats. What is the total number of seats in the stadium?

    A. 10,059
    B. 10,159
    C. 11,149
    D. 11,159

189. Bob buys 25 pads of paper, each of which contains 70 pieces of paper. What is the total number of pieces of paper that Bob has purchased?

    A. 1,750
    B. 1,770
    C. 2,800
    D. 3,571

190. Mr. Norwalk bought 24 gallons of gasoline, which enables him to drive 648 miles. On average, how many miles does he get per gallon of gasoline?

    A. 24
    B. 25
    C. 26
    D. 27

191. The distance from Mark's house to Peter's house is 12 yards, 1 foot, and 17 inches. How far apart are the houses, in inches?

    A. 173
    B. 360
    C. 449
    D. 461

192. Which of the following is closest to 31.49?

    A. 32
    B. 31.4
    C. 31.5
    D. 31.45

193. The difference between 2^6 and 6^2 is:

    A. 0
    B. 4
    C. 24
    D. 28

194. What is the value of $\sqrt{\frac{36}{64}}$?

    A. $\frac{3}{4}$

    B. $\frac{9}{16}$

    C. $\frac{1}{4}$

    D. $\frac{3}{16}$

195. $(2.3 \times 10) + (2.3 \times 10^2) + (2.3 \times 10^3) =$

    A. 25.53
    B. 255.3
    C. 2,553
    D. 25,530

196. Which of the following numbers is the smallest?

    A. 0.199
    B. 0.1987
    C. 0.23
    D. 1.007

197. Which of the following expresses the number 630 as a product of prime numbers?

    A. $2 \times 2 \times 3 \times 5 \times 7$
    B. $2 \times 3 \times 3 \times 5 \times 7$
    C. $2 \times 5 \times 7 \times 9$
    D. $2 \times 3 \times 5 \times 5 \times 7$

198. If the number $57,28p$ is divisible by 5, then the digit that the p stands for must be:

    A. 0
    B. 3
    C. 5
    D. 0 or 5

Problem Solving

For questions 199–238, select the choice that best answers the following questions. You can use scratch paper to figure out your answers.

199. Jack lives $6\frac{1}{2}$ miles from the library. If he walks $\frac{1}{3}$ of the way and takes a break, what is the remaining distance to the library?

    A. $5\frac{5}{6}$ miles
    B. 4 miles
    C. $4\frac{1}{3}$ miles
    D. $2\frac{1}{6}$ miles

200. Amelia casts a shadow 5 feet long. Her father, who is 6 feet tall, casts a shadow 8 feet long. How tall is Amelia?

    A. 6 feet 8 inches
    B. 4 feet 10 inches
    C. 4 feet 6 inches
    D. 3 feet 9 inches

201. A recipe calls for 3 cups of wheat and white flour combined. If $\frac{3}{8}$ of this is wheat flour, how many cups of white flour are needed?

    A. $1\frac{1}{8}$
    B. $1\frac{7}{8}$
    C. $2\frac{3}{8}$
    D. $2\frac{5}{8}$

202. Jared rents 3 videos for $8.00. What is the cost of 2 video rentals?

    A. $1.33
    B. $5.00
    C. $5.33
    D. $6.00

203. A winter coat is on sale for $150. If the original price was $200, what percent has the coat been discounted?

    A. 50%
    B. 40%
    C. 33%
    D. 25%

204. A square garden is to be built inside a circular area. Each corner of the square touches the circle. If the radius of the circle is 2, how much greater is the area of the circle than the square?

    A. $4 - 4\pi$
    B. $4 - 8\pi$
    C. $4\pi - 4$
    D. $4\pi - 8$

GO ON TO THE NEXT PAGE

205. A blueprint has a scale of 3 feet per $\frac{1}{2}$ inch. If a bathroom is $1\frac{1}{2}$ inches × 2 inches, what are its actual dimensions?

    A. $4\frac{1}{2}$ feet × 6 feet

    B. 6 feet × $7\frac{1}{2}$ feet

    C. $7\frac{1}{2}$ feet × 9 feet

    D. 9 feet × 12 feet

206. A barrel holds 60 gallons of water. If a crack in the barrel causes $\frac{1}{2}$ of a gallon to leak out each day, how many gallons of water remain after 2 weeks?

    A. 30
    B. 53
    C. $56\frac{1}{2}$
    D. 59

207. How many blocks 6" × 4" × 4" can fit in a box 8' × 6' × 4'?

    A. 2
    B. 48
    C. 576
    D. 3,456

208. Eight hundred employees work at a company. If 60% drive to work and 30% take the train, how many employees arrive to work by car?

    A. 240
    B. 480
    C. 540
    D. 600

209. Jillian reads 3 hardcover mysteries and 4 soft-cover mysteries. She reads 3 times as many nonfiction books as she does mysteries. How many nonfiction books does Jillian read?

    A. 9
    B. 12
    C. 18
    D. 21

210. The volume of a cube is 343 cm³. The surface area of the cube is:

    A. 7 cm²
    B. 49 cm²
    C. 294 cm²
    D. 2,401 cm²

211. Debby eats $\frac{3}{8}$ of a pizza and divides the rest among her two friends. What percent of the pizza do her friends each receive?

    A. 62.50%
    B. 37.50%
    C. 31.25%
    D. 18.75%

212. A batch of cookies requires 2 cups of milk and 4 eggs. If you have 9 cups of milk and 9 eggs, how many batches of cookies can you make?

    A. 9
    B. 6
    C. 4
    D. 2

213. While dining out, Chad spent $25.00. If the bill totaled $21.00 before the tip was added, approximately what percent tip did Chad leave?

    A. 16%
    B. 19%
    C. 21%
    D. 25%

214. A right triangle has an area of 24 feet. If one leg is 3 times as long as the other, what is the length of the longest side?

    A. 12.6 feet
    B. 12 feet
    C. 8.4 feet
    D. 6.3 feet

215. Interest earned on an account totals $100. If the interest rate is $7\frac{1}{4}$ %, what is the principle amount?

   A. $725
   B. $1,333
   C. $1,379
   D. $1,428

216. Eric can read 2 pages in 3 minutes. At this rate, how long does it take him to read a 360-page book?

   A. 30 minutes
   B. 2 hours
   C. 6 hours
   D. 9 hours

217. Tanya's bowling scores this week are 112, 156, 179, and 165. Last week, her average score was 140. How many points did her average improve?

   A. 18
   B. 13
   C. 11
   D. 8

218. Felix buys 3 books for $8.95 each. How much does he owe if he uses a $12.73 credit toward his purchase?

   A. $39.58
   B. $26.85
   C. $21.68
   D. $14.12

219. Find the value of $-3a + 4b$ if $a = 2$ and $b = -3$.

   A. -30
   B. -18
   C. -6
   D. 18

220. A piece of wood that is 27 inches long is cut into two pieces, such that one piece is twice as long as the other. Find the length of the shorter piece.

   A. 6 in
   B. 9 in
   C. 12 in
   D. 18 in

221. In the following diagram, $x =$

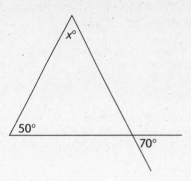

   A. 50°
   B. 60°
   C. 65°
   D. 70°

222. How many feet of baseboard are needed to go around a rectangular room if the room has a length of 12 feet and a width of $7\frac{1}{2}$ feet, and 4 feet must be deducted for a doorway?

   A. 15 1/2
   B. 31
   C. 35
   D. 39

223. How much does it cost per month to rent a rectangular office that measures 20 feet by 30 feet if the cost per square foot per month is $8?

   A. $800
   B. $4,800
   C. $5,600
   D. $7,500

224. Paul studied for $\frac{1}{4}$ of an hour on Monday, $\frac{3}{8}$ of an hour on Tuesday, $\frac{7}{12}$ of an hour on Wednesday, and $\frac{9}{16}$ of an hour on Thursday. How much time did he spend studying on these days, in total?

   A. $1\frac{5}{11}$ hours
   B. $1\frac{3}{4}$ hours
   C. $1\frac{9}{16}$ hours
   D. $1\frac{37}{48}$ hours

GO ON TO THE NEXT PAGE

225. The price of a portable CD player is marked up from $180 to $240. What is the percent of increase in the price of the CD player?

A. 25%
B. 30%
C. $33\frac{1}{3}$%
D. 75%

226. If $x = -1$, what is the value of $x^3 - x^2 + x - 1$?

A. -4
B. -2
C. 2
D. 4

227. Brian earned three times as much during the month of August as in each of the other 11 months. What fraction of his total year's earnings did he earn in August?

A. $\frac{1}{4}$
B. $\frac{3}{14}$
C. $\frac{3}{11}$
D. $\frac{3}{4}$

228. At a college football game, $\frac{1}{4}$ of the fans at the game were girls, and $\frac{1}{3}$ of the fans at the game were boys. What fraction of the fans at the game were children?

A. $\frac{2}{7}$
B. $\frac{5}{12}$
C. $\frac{3}{8}$
D. $\frac{7}{12}$

229. If Jimmy can do a job in x minutes, what fraction of the job can he do in 15 minutes?

A. $\frac{15}{x}$
B. $\frac{x}{15}$
C. $\frac{15x}{1}$
D. $\frac{1}{4x}$

230. How many cubes that measure $\frac{1}{2}$ inch on a side can fit in a cubic box that measures 2 inches on a side?

A. 4
B. 16
C. 48
D. 64

231. $\frac{1}{5}$ is what part of $\frac{3}{4}$?

A. $\frac{3}{20}$
B. $\frac{4}{15}$
C. $\frac{15}{4}$
D. $\frac{20}{3}$

232. Which of the following pairs of numbers is the common solution to the system of equations $2x + 3y = 6$ and $x + y = 3$?

A. $(0, 2)$
B. $(3, 0)$
C. $(1, 2)$
D. $(2, 1)$

233. If a square foot of carpeting costs $5, how much does it cost to carpet a room that measures 3 yards by 4 yards?

A. $60
B. $180
C. $540
D. $600

234. What is the value of $\dfrac{\frac{4}{5} - \frac{1}{3}}{\frac{1}{2}}$?

A. $\dfrac{7}{15}$

B. $\dfrac{14}{15}$

C. $\dfrac{15}{14}$

D. $\dfrac{15}{7}$

235. A candy store sells gumballs for 10 cents. Bobby has one penny, one nickel, one dime, one quarter, and one half dollar in his pocket. If he reaches into his pocket and takes out a coin at random, what is the probability that he is able to buy a gumball with it?

A. $\dfrac{1}{5}$

B. $\dfrac{1}{3}$

C. $\dfrac{2}{5}$

D. $\dfrac{3}{5}$

236. How many minutes does it take Susan to type a 600-word essay if she can type 5 words in 20 seconds?

A. 4
B. 20
C. 30
D. 40

237. Brett deposited $1,500 in a bank account at the start of the year. If, at the end of the year, $1,605 is in the account, what interest did Brett earn, assuming that no deposits or withdrawals were made during the year?

A. $5\dfrac{1}{2}\%$

B. 6%

C. 7%

D. $7\dfrac{1}{4}\%$

238. A diamond ring, which initially cost $6,000, is marked down 30% and then an additional 20%. What is the final price of the ring?

A. $3,640
B. $3,360
C. $3,000
D. $2,840

IF YOU FINISH BEFORE TIME IS CALLED, CHECK YOUR WORK ON THIS SECTION ONLY. DO NOT WORK ON ANY OTHER SECTION IN THE TEST.

STOP

Test 5: Language Skills

Time: 25 Minutes

Directions: In each of the following questions, select that choice that best answers the question.

*In questions 239–250, look for errors in capitalization or punctuation. If you find no mistakes, mark **D** on your answer sheet.*

239.

   A. *Frankenstein* was written by Mary Shelley.
   B. People wrongly call the creature Frankenstein, that is the name of his creator.
   C. Percy Bysshe Shelley, Mary's husband, was a famous poet.
   D. No mistakes.

240.

   A. *Mr. Popper's Penguins* was my favorite book when I was a child.
   B. Large pet stores sell everything for your dogs and cat's needs.
   C. Where, in this library, is the Reference section?
   D. No mistakes.

241.

   A. The fans are eager to hear the score of today's football game.
   B. "And the final score is Giants 21, Colts 14," said the broadcaster.
   C. "Folks, she added, "that was a really exciting game."
   D. No mistakes.

242.

   A. Who's going to prepare tonight's dinner?
   B. The chef is ill; the owner of the café will need to find a substitute.
   C. "I'll do the cooking myself," the owner said.
   D. No mistakes.

243.

   A. "Have you seen both of the *Harry Potter* films?" Ruth asked.
   B. "No, but Ive read all the books," Kevin answered.
   C. Ruth said that her favorite character was Dumbledore.
   D. No mistakes.

244.

   A. He talked to uncle Fred.
   B. Professor Montero teaches Italian.
   C. I sent an e-mail to my cousin who lives in Arizona.
   D. No mistakes.

245.

   A. At Carnegie Hall in New York, many famous musicians have played.
   B. Classical, jazz, and popular instrumentalists and singers have appeared.
   C. Have you ever visited New York City?
   D. No mistakes.

246.

   A. The radio station is sponsoring a contest.
   B. If you guess the names of 10 songs in 20 seconds you win a prize.
   C. I don't believe anyone can do that.
   D. No mistakes.

247.

   A. "When did you last see your aunt?" asked my mother.
   B. "I know I should visit her more often," I said.
   C. Aunt Tina always enjoys my visits; she says I make her laugh.
   D. No mistakes.

248.

A. Dorothy, Toto, and the Scarecrow were on the road to Oz.
B. "We're off to see the wizard," they sang.
C. But would the wizard be able to help them.
D. No mistakes.

249.

A. The X Games include motocross, bike, and skateboard events.
B. The contestants style, creativity and the difficulty of the stunt are judged.
C. "Are these events as dangerous as they look?" asked my grandmother.
D. No mistakes.

250.

A. Elaine's chores made her very tired.
B. "Wherefore art thou Romeo?" Juliet asked.
C. The soup was very hot but, it tasted delicious.
D. No mistakes.

*In questions 251–278, look for errors in usage. If you find no mistakes, mark **D** on your answer sheet.*

251.

A. When you go to the beach, be sure to take sunscreen.
B. The glare from snow can cause severe sunburn.
C. In our town, the police gets involved in supporting youth sports.
D. No mistakes.

252.

A. The American editions of the *Harry Potter* books are different than the British editions.
B. British expressions unfamiliar to Americans were changed.
C. The characters and the story remain the same.
D. No mistakes.

253.

A. Closing the door quietly, I tiptoed away from the room.
B. My shopping list includes milk, butter, and bread.
C. There goes that annoying dog; he's barking again.
D. No mistakes.

254.

A. When I have lost something, I try to remember where I last saw it.
B. After finishing my homework, that pizza tasted great.
C. If Jean asks Sue and me who will help her, I will volunteer.
D. No mistakes.

255.

A. Drive slow when there's snow on the roads.
B. In the fog, turn on your low-beam headlights.
C. Be sure your windshield wipers work properly.
D. No mistakes.

256.

A. The language of many native peoples is disappearing.
B. Fewer children are taught the trades their ancestors practiced.
C. My grandfather learned me about our family's traditions.
D. No mistakes.

257.

    A. I enjoy reading books about penguins.

    B. Paco's Pet Supplies sells everything your dog and cat needs.

    C. When Tina went to Canada, she visited Niagara Falls.

    D. No mistakes.

258.

    A. Helen scolded herself for her carelessness.

    B. Of all my books, this one is my favorite.

    C. Did Tony told you that he'd be here by 8:00 p.m.?

    D. No mistakes.

259.

    A. School spirit and pride was very high.

    B. Our baseball team would appear in the state championship game.

    C. All the uniforms were cleaned and pressed.

    D. No mistakes.

260.

    A. Each of the tools have a different use.

    B. It's important to choose the right tool for the job.

    C. Electric drills can be easier to use than manual drills.

    D. No mistakes.

261.

    A. This restaurant's atmosphere is supposed to be romantic.

    B. I can't hardly read the menu because the light is so dim.

    C. When the candles were lit, they did not provide much illumination.

    D. No mistakes.

262.

    A. The hurricane raced swiftly across the state.

    B. Large areas were affected by the storm's force.

    C. High tides and rain created flooded conditions on the highways.

    D. No mistakes.

263.

    A. Of Philadelphia, Scranton, and Erie, the first is the largest city.

    B. At the age of 7, my family moved from Dallas to Houston.

    C. Three different cities have been the capital of the United States.

    D. No mistakes.

264.

    A. The letter was addressed to my sister and myself.

    B. The mail delivery arrived later on Thursday than on Wednesday.

    C. Packages and magazines are too large to fit through the mail slot.

    D. No mistakes.

265.

    A. Each of the winners receives their medal at the event's conclusion.

    B. The twins wore their matching outfits to the birthday party.

    C. None of the mice used in the experiment became ill.

    D. No mistakes.

266.

    A. Steve and I were playing catch in the backyard.

    B. He threw the ball too high for me to catch it.

    C. Looking under the car, the missing baseball was found.

    D. No mistakes.

267.

    A. What effect does the star of the film have on its popularity?

    B. I haven't had no chance to see that movie yet.

    C. Many moviegoers eat popcorn while watching a film.

    D. No mistakes.

268.

A. Neither Lucy nor Desi wants to join the club.
B. Sheet music and tap shoes are required for the audition.
C. Either Bob or Ted forgot to take his jacket from the coatroom.
D. No mistakes.

269.

A. There's three songs that I want to hear Maria sing.
B. She knows that they are my favorites.
C. Their tunes and words were written by Cole Porter.
D. No mistakes.

270.

A. The broken umbrella looked like a spider.
B. Missing the deadline, I was unable to enter the contest.
C. Walking around the block, the rain began.
D. No mistakes.

271.

A. Next week Tina will begin her exercise classes.
B. I might have fallen down, but I grabbed the rail to steady myself.
C. Sam did good on the test.
D. No mistakes.

272.

A. If I were on the committee, I would vote for the new rules.
B. Intending to return immediately, I leave the door open when I went out.
C. Will you or I be the first person to leave the room?
D. No mistakes.

273.

A. The basket was filled with sweet-smelling bars of soap.
B. Each scent was different.
C. Lilac was the odor I found most pleasant.
D. No mistakes.

274.

A. Mike has three brothers, two of which have red hair.
B. Whose car is parked in the driveway?
C. The dog knocked over its bowl of water.
D. No mistakes.

275.

A. Part-time work does not pay as well as full-time work.
B. Trying to earn money for a vacation, I took a second job.
C. The bank will make loans to people of any size.
D. No mistakes.

276.

A. All the jurors question the witness's truthfulness.
B. The lawyer stated that the victim suffered serious injuries.
C. The judge explained the law to the jury.
D. No mistakes.

277.

A. While preparing dinner, the telephone rang.
B. The chef dislikes interruptions while she is cooking.
C. Placing the pot of stew to one side, she answered the telephone.
D. No mistakes.

278.

A. My brother and I take turns doing household chores.
B. Who's turn is it to take out the garbage?
C. Our parents said we should finish our homework before doing chores.
D. No mistakes.

GO ON TO THE NEXT PAGE

*In questions 279–288, look for mistakes in spelling only. If you find no mistakes, mark **D** on your answer sheet.*

279.

    A.   Mandy usually eats breakfast at 9:00 a.m.

    B.   Ms. Lee tries to make sure her children have a balanced diet.

    C.   The cabinet's heigth is 36 inches.

    D.   No mistakes.

280.

    A.   The play *Death of a Salesman* is a modern tradegy.

    B.   The critic preferred plays written in Shakespeare's time.

    C.   The hero of the play is named Willy Loman.

    D.   No mistakes.

281.

    A.   In the mayor's absence, the deputy chaired the city council meeting.

    B.   Cats move gracefully and rarely seem awkward.

    C.   Edna tried to persuade Tom to vote for the new program.

    D.   No mistakes.

282.

    A.   Human activity is not the only cause of pollution of the envinronment.

    B.   Eruptions of volcanoes are a possible cause of bad air.

    C.   Forbidding the use of gasoline engines would not be practical.

    D.   No mistakes.

283.

    A.   The comedian thought she was humorous, but I didn't laugh at her jokes.

    B.   The earthquake led to disastrous floods because the dam crumbled.

    C.   Jay wanted to pursue a career in medicine.

    D.   No mistakes.

284.

    A.   I will sacrifice my free time to practice playing the violin.

    B.   Having a driver's license is a privilege, not a right.

    C.   The house acrost the street from ours is for sale.

    D.   No mistakes.

285.

    A.   The chair appointed Ms. Montez to the Finance Comittee.

    B.   Pleasant weather created the right atmosphere for the picnic.

    C.   The American Red Cross offers courses in water safety.

    D.   No mistakes.

286.

    A.   We suggest that you study the manual before taking the test.

    B.   New construction can often interfere with traffic.

    C.   A new biznes center opened next to the mall.

    D.   No mistakes.

287.

    A.   The railroad tracks ran paralel to the highway.

    B.   Saul was grateful for the gift his aunt gave him on his birthday.

    C.   One benefit of regular exercise is increased muscular strength.

    D.   No mistakes.

288.

    A.   On the eighth day of the festival, closing ceremonies were held.

    B.   Excellent fireworks displays concluded the activities.

    C.   The occasion was a complete success.

    D.   No mistakes.

For questions 289–298, look for errors in composition. Follow the directions for each question.

289. Building sand castles seems useless _____ the tide always knocks them down.

    A. although
    B. because
    C. while
    D. when

290. Which of these expresses the idea most clearly?

    A. Treat your kids to delicious frozen grapes by putting them in the freezer.
    B. Grapes put in the freezer make themselves into a delicious treat for your kids.
    C. Frozen grapes are delicious; treat your kids by putting them in the freezer.
    D. Putting grapes in the freezer makes them a delicious treat for your kids.

291. Which sentence does *not* belong in the paragraph?

(1) Service dogs help people with their lives and work. (2) They assist blind people going about their daily routines; they cheer up people in hospitals; they work with the police. (3) An organization named Paws to Recognize gives awards to these well-trained dogs. (4) My dog is also very well trained and can do many tricks.

    A. sentence 1
    B. sentence 2
    C. sentence 3
    D. sentence 4

292. Choose the pair of sentences that best develops this topic sentence.

The March on Washington for Jobs and Freedom in 1963 was a major event in the civil rights movement.

    A. It was the occasion for Dr. Martin Luther King Jr.'s famous "I Have a Dream Speech." The march and the speech influenced the passage of the Civil Rights Act of 1964.
    B. More than 200,000 people gathered in front of the Lincoln Memorial. They had come on foot, by car, by bus, and by train.
    C. In 1965, the Voting Rights Act was passed. It forbids practices that had made it difficult for minorities to vote.
    D. Martin Luther King, Jr. wrote "Letter from Birmingham Jail" after being imprisoned for leading a march without getting a permit. This letter became famous.

293. Which of these expresses the idea most clearly?

    A. When the jockey fell from the horse, eventually he suffered a broken leg.
    B. Falling from the horse, the leg of the jockey broke.
    C. When the jockey fell from the horse, he suffered a broken leg.
    D. The jockey was falling from the horse, and he suffered a broken leg.

294. Choose the group of words that best completes this sentence.

Having begun at 9:00 a.m., by noon, Saul had:

    A. almost cleaned the whole house.
    B. cleaned almost the whole house.
    C. cleaned the whole house almost.
    D. almost the whole house cleaned.

GO ON TO THE NEXT PAGE

295. Which of these best fits under the topic "Endangered Sea Turtles"?

    A. Four species of sea turtles spend time in United States waters off the coast of California.

    B. The turtles' diet includes sea grass and algae.

    C. Female turtles come ashore and dig nests on sandy beaches in which to lay their eggs.

    D. Eating turtle meat on special occasions is a tradition in some places.

296. Choose the best word or words to join the thoughts together.

He wanted to write a composition _____ his visit to Yellowstone Park.

    A. dealing with

    B. on

    C. about

    D. coming from

297. Where should the sentence "In the summer, Americans travel more than they do at other times of year" be placed in the following paragraph?

(1) When many people want to buy a product, the price usually goes up. (2) They might take planes or trains, and many families drive to their vacation spots. (3) So it is not surprising that gasoline prices usually rise in July and August.

    A. Before sentence 1.

    B. Between sentences 1 and 2.

    C. Between sentences 2 and 3.

    D. The sentence does not fit in the paragraph.

298. Which of the following sentences offers the *least* support of the topic "Pizza–A Nutritious Snack"?

    A. The tomato sauce on pizza contains Vitamin C and provides fiber.

    B. Pepperoni is the most frequently ordered pizza topping.

    C. Calcium, needed for healthy bones, is supplied by the cheese.

    D. The bread-like crust provides carbohydrates.

IF YOU FINISH BEFORE TIME IS CALLED, CHECK YOUR WORK ON THIS SECTION ONLY. DO NOT WORK ON ANY OTHER SECTION IN THE TEST.

Answer Key

Test 1: Verbal Skills

1. C	16. B	31. B	46. C
2. A	17. B	32. A	47. C
3. B	18. C	33. C	48. A
4. B	19. B	34. B	49. C
5. B	20. A	35. B	50. B
6. C	21. A	36. D	51. C
7. A	22. B	37. A	52. C
8. A	23. A	38. B	53. D
9. C	24. B	39. C	54. A
10. A	25. A	40. C	55. A
11. D	26. C	41. A	56. D
12. D	27. C	42. D	57. A
13. D	28. A	43. A	58. D
14. D	29. D	44. B	59. D
15. B	30. B	45. A	60. D

Test 2: Quantitative Skills

61. C	74. D	87. C	100. B
62. C	75. D	88. A	101. C
63. D	76. C	89. D	102. D
64. C	77. C	90. C	103. B
65. C	78. D	91. A	104. A
66. C	79. B	92. D	105. C
67. B	80. C	93. D	106. A
68. D	81. C	94. C	107. A
69. C	82. A	95. B	108. C
70. A	83. A	96. D	109. D
71. C	84. D	97. D	110. C
72. B	85. D	98. C	111. A
73. C	86. C	99. A	112. C

Test 3: Reading

113. B	129. A	145. C	161. D
114. B	130. C	146. C	162. D
115. A	131. D	147. C	163. A
116. A	132. B	148. B	164. A
117. A	133. D	149. A	165. D
118. B	134. A	150. A	166. C
119. B	135. B	151. A	167. D
120. A	136. B	152. A	168. B
121. D	137. D	153. B	169. B
122. C	138. C	154. C	170. C
123. C	139. D	155. C	171. D
124. B	140. C	156. A	172. A
125. D	141. A	157. B	173. C
126. C	142. D	158. C	174. B
127. B	143. B	159. B	
128. D	144. C	160. C	

Test 4: Mathematics

175. B	191. D	207. D	223. B
176. A	192. C	208. B	224. D
177. B	193. D	209. D	225. C
178. C	194. A	210. C	226. A
179. A	195. C	211. C	227. B
180. A	196. B	212. D	228. D
181. C	197. B	213. B	229. A
182. A	198. D	214. A	230. D
183. B	199. C	215. C	231. B
184. C	200. D	216. D	232. B
185. C	201. B	217. B	233. C
186. A	202. C	218. D	234. B
187. A	203. D	219. B	235. D
188. D	204. D	220. B	236. D
189. A	205. D	221. B	237. C
190. D	206. B	222. C	238. B

Test 5: Language Skills

239. B	**254.** B	**269.** A	**284.** C
240. B	**255.** A	**270.** C	**285.** A
241. C	**256.** C	**271.** C	**286.** C
242. D	**257.** B	**272.** B	**287.** A
243. B	**258.** C	**273.** D	**288.** D
244. A	**259.** A	**274.** A	**289.** B
245. D	**260.** A	**275.** C	**290.** D
246. B	**261.** B	**276.** D	**291.** D
247. D	**262.** D	**277.** A	**292.** A
248. C	**263.** B	**278.** B	**293.** C
249. B	**264.** A	**279.** C	**294.** B
250. C	**265.** A	**280.** A	**295.** D
251. C	**266.** C	**281.** D	**296.** C
252. A	**267.** B	**282.** A	**297.** B
253. D	**268.** D	**283.** D	**298.** B

Answers and Explanations

Test 1: Verbal Skills

1. **C.** The relationship is one of opposites.

2. **A.** To have *zest* for something is to be enthusiastic about it, to *enjoy* it.

3. **B.** *Sway* suggests a gentle movement, so the other choices are not appropriate.

4. **B.** Chickens have two legs; the other animals listed have four legs.

5. **B.** To *contradict* is to say the opposite of what has been said; the opposite is *agree*.

6. **C.** Los Angeles gets less rain than the other two cities, but the first two statements don't indicate whether Seattle or Chicago gets more rain.

7. **A.** To be green is a characteristic of plants, and to be hard is a characteristic of a diamond.

8. **A.** *Static* means motionless or inert; *dynamic*, meaning *lively* or *energetic,* is the best choice.

9. **C.** Penny might or might not be a chicken. Other creatures also lack teeth.

10. **A.** To be *deft* at a task is to be able to do it well.

11. **D.** The other items can be used to draw or to write.

12. **D.** A flood is a quantity of water. The other words describe winds.

13. **D.** The relationship is that of cause to effect. To be clumsy can cause one to trip, and to be late can cause one to hurry.

14. **D.** Choice **C,** *antique*, is a synonym. *Modern* is the opposite.

15. **B.** The other words describe the ability to do something well.

16. **B.** *Element* is general; the other words are examples of elements.

17. **B.** Something *bland* has no strong flavor; it is mild.

18. **C.** The other choices might be used to describe something that is also *grotesque,* but they are not synonyms for the word.

19. **B.** The third statement is contradicted by the first statement.

20. **A.** To *mock* means to *tease* or *make fun of.*

21. **A.** If the first two statements are true, all the creeks flow more quickly than May Creek.

22. **B.** To *dispose* is to throw away or get rid of something; to *acquire* is to get or obtain something.

23. **A.** The relationship is between items in a sequence. Fall comes before winter, and a bud appears before a leaf opens.

24. **B.** The words are synonyms.

25. **A.** Something temporary only lasts for a period of time; something *permanent* lasts forever.

26. **C.** Don't be confused by **A.** *Familiar* does not mean of the family.

27. **C.** This is a difficult question. Each of the other words can be used as a noun or a verb. *Speak* is only a verb. The noun form is *speech.*

28. **A.** Red, blue, and yellow are the primary colors. All other colors, like green, are a mixture of the primary colors.

29. **D.** All the words except *shout* mean cry.

30. B. A bay is a small body of salt water, and an ocean is a large body of salt water. A pebble is small, and a rock is large.

31. B. Choice **A** is a synonym. To *restore*, to bring back to the original condition, is the opposite of to *destroy*.

32. A. Because all zebs are flying boks, and none of the swimming boks fly, the zebs can't swim.

33. C. The prefix *uni-* means one. So a *uniform* rule is the same for everyone.

34. B. To *impose* means to order or demand.

35. B. *Inch* is a specific measurement; the other words describe a quality to be measured.

36. D. *Abandon* means to leave or go away from.

37. A. When something is *specified*, it is named exactly.

38. B. The order from north to south is A, B, C.

39. C. Stan's truck might or might not be a Carco. The first statement doesn't mean that only Carco vehicles are reliable.

40. C. Whole to part is the relationship. Algebra is a branch of mathematics; botany is a branch of biology.

41. A. Characteristics are the key to this analogy. Lead is heavy; water is wet.

42. D. *Trivial,* meaning small or unimportant, is the best choice.

43. A. Box R is the heaviest, followed by box P, box M, and box N.

44. B. Laura owns more books than Fred and Terry.

45. A. In this question, the word is an adjective, not a noun.

46. C. Do not be confused by **D**, which is a synonym for considerate.

47. C. All the other choices are tools used to tighten or loosen something.

48. A. *Meat* is the general term; the other choices are kinds of meat.

49. C. *Clean* means the opposite of the other three choices.

50. B. The function of a manual is to explain something, and the function of a stapler is to fasten things.

51. C. A is a synonym for *completely.*

52. C. Nothing indicates whether the mushrooms prepared by the cook were poisonous. They might or might not have been.

53. D. Something critical is essential. Critical does not always mean a negative comment.

54. A. Although if one feels pity, they feel sad (**C**), the word implies feelings for someone, so **A** is the best choice.

55. A. Choices **B, C,** and **D** are classes of animals. A giraffe is an example of a mammal.

56. D. You hop on one leg; the other actions use both legs.

57. A. All the other words indicate a contrast or difference between to words or ideas.

58. D. Although *incredible* is incorrectly used in speech to replace the other answer choices, those words are not synonyms.

59. D. *False* means the opposite of the other choices.

60. D. Depth is a characteristic of a trench, and height is a characteristic of a hill.

Test 2: Quantitative Skills

61. C. The pattern is 9 (+ 7), 16 (+ 7), 23 (+ 7), 30 (+ 7), which is equal to **37.**

62. C. The difference of 31 and 10 is 21. When **7** is tripled, the result is 21.

63. D. In this problem, (a) $(2 \times 3)^2 = 6^2 = 36$, (b) $2^2 \times 3^2 = 4 \times 9 = 36$, and (c) $6^2 = 36$. Therefore, (a), (b), and (c) are equal.

64. C. The pattern is 5 (× 4), 20 (× 4), 80 (× 4), 320 (× 4), which is equal to **1,280.**

65. C. Fifteen percent of 200 is 30. Note that 25% of **120** is also equal to 30.

66. C. To begin, we have $x = 55$ because it is an alternate interior angle with angle D. In the same way, $z = 65$. Finally, because 180° are in each triangle, $y = 180 - 55 - 65 = 60$. Therefore, $z > y > x$.

67. B. The pattern is 6 (+ 3), 9 (− 5), 4 (+ 3), 7 (− 5), 2 (+ 3), which is equal to 5.

68. D. $\frac{4}{5}$ of 30 is equal to $\frac{4}{5} \times 30 = 24$. Note that $\frac{2}{5}$ of **60** is also equal to 24.

69. C. The pattern is 64 (÷ 2), 32 (÷ 2), 16 (÷ 2), 8 (÷ 2), **4** (÷ 2), which is equal to 2.

70. A. The product of 5 and 16 is 80. Note that $\frac{1}{4}$ of 80 is 20.

71. C. Here, (a) $5 - (3 + 5) = 5 - 8 = -3$, (b) $5 - 3 + 5 = 2 + 5 = 7$, and (c) $(5 - 3) + 5 = 2 + 5 = 7$. Therefore, (b) and (c) are equal and greater than (a).

72. B. Here, $a = 55$ because it is supplementary to the 125° angle. Next, note that $b = 35$ because it is complementary to a 55° angle. Finally, $c = 55$ because the angle labeled c is vertical to the angle labeled a.

73. C. The sum of 12 and 15 is 27. This is the same as the product of 9 and **3.**

74. D. In this pattern, ignoring the signs, each number is 3 bigger than the previous number. The numbers alternate from positive to negative to positive and so on. Thus, the missing number is 19.

75. D. In this problem, (a) $(-3)^3 = -27$, (b) $-3^3 = -27$, and (c) = −27. Therefore, (a), (b), and (c) are equal.

76. C. The pattern is 12 (+ 1), 13 (− 3), 10 (+ 1), 11 (− 3), 8 (+ 1), 9 (− 3), which is equal to 6.

77. C. The sum of 12 and 40 is 52. Because 52 ÷ 4 = 13, 400% of **13** is 52.

78. D. In a triangle, the largest angle is always opposite the longest side, and the shortest angle is opposite the shortest side.

79. B. The pattern is 10 (+ 3), 13 (+ 4), 17 (+ 5), 22 (+ 6), 28 (+ 7), which is equal to **35.**

80. C. Note that (a) $10^{-2} \times 10^3 = 10$, (b) $10^{-3} \times 10^5 = 10^2$, and (c) $10^{-4} \times 10^6 = 10^2$. Therefore, (b) and (c) are equal and greater than (a).

81. C. The pattern is 1 (× 2), 2 (× 3), 6 (× 2), 12 (× 3), **36** (× 2), which is equal to 72.

82. A. All sides of the square have the same length. The diagonals are equal to each other and longer than the sides of the square. However, the sides of the square are longer than half the length of the diagonal. Thus, $BC > BD > ED$.

83. A. The product of 4, 5, and 6 is $4 \times 5 \times 6 = 120$. Then, $\frac{5}{12}$ of $120 = \frac{5}{12} \times 120 = $ **50.**

84. D. When 16 is tripled, the result is 48. The same result is obtain when **12** is quadrupled.

85. D. Note that (a) 529.52 rounded to the nearest whole number is 530, (b) 532.79 rounded to the nearest ten is 530, and (c) 529.5 rounded to the nearest whole number is 530. Therefore, (a), (b), and (c) are equal.

86. C. The pattern is 2 (× 4), 8 (− 5), 3 (× 4), 12 (− 5), 7 (× 4), which is equal to **28.**

87. C. $\frac{1}{9}$ of $45 = \frac{1}{9} \times 45 = 5$. Note that $\frac{1}{7}$ of **35** is also 5.

88. A. The pattern is 20 (− 12), 8 (× 2), 16 (− 12), 4 (× 2), 8 (− 12), −4 (× 2), which is equal to **−8.**

89. D. The length of arc ZY = the length of arc XY = the length of arc WX.

90. C. The value of 2^6 is 64. This is the same as the value of 8^2.

91. A. The pattern is -7 $(+5)$, -2 $(+4)$, 2 $(+3)$, 5 $(+2)$, 7 $(+1)$, which is equal to 8.

92. D. In this problem, (a) the greatest common divisor of 20 and 15 is 5, (b) the greatest common divisor of 5 and 10 is 5, and (c) the greatest common divisor of 45 and 70 is 5. Therefore, (a), (b), and (c) are equal.

93. D. The difference between 84 and 12 is 72. Then, $\frac{2}{3}$ of 72 is $\frac{2}{3} \times 72 = \mathbf{48.}$

94. C. The pattern is 4 $(\times 4)$, 16 (-3), 13 $(\times 4)$, 52 (-3), 49 $(\times 4)$, which is equal to **196.**

95. B. Because the three squares are of the same size, all the diagonals are equal. Note that the length of AE is equal to the length of two diagonals. Thus, $AE = 2CG$.

96. D. Note that 30% of 90 is 27, so that when 90 is reduced by 30% of itself, the result is $\mathbf{90} - 27 = 63$.

97. D. In this problem, (a) $\frac{21}{4} = 5.25$, (b) $0.0525 \times 10^2 = 5.25$, and (c) $525\% = 5.25$. Therefore, (a), (b), and (c) are equal.

98. C. In this pattern, each successive positive integer is followed by its cube. Thus, 1 is followed by $1^3 = 1$. Then, 2 is followed by $2^3 = 8$, and 3 is followed by $3^3 = 27$. The number 4 must then be followed by $4^3 = \mathbf{64.}$

99. A. The difference between 98 and 18 is $98 - 18 = 80$. Then, 15% of 80 is $.15 \times 80 = \mathbf{12.}$

100. B. The pattern is 9 $(+6)$, 15 $(+5)$, 20 $(+6)$, 26 $(+5)$, **31** $(+6)$, which is equal to 37.

101. C. The square of 6 is equal to $6^2 = 36$. Because $36 \div 3 = \mathbf{12,}$ 300% of 12 is 36.

102. D. The pattern is 17 (-1), 16 $(+2)$, 18 (-3), 15 $(+4)$, 19 (-5), **14** $(+6)$, which is equal to 20.

103. B. The bases of all three triangles are the same. Therefore, the triangle with the greatest height has the greatest area, and the triangle with the shortest height has the smallest area.

104. A. The pattern is 7 $(+4)$, 11 $(+8)$, 19 $(+12)$, 31 $(+16)$, 47 $(+20)$, which is equal to **67.**

105. C. The product of 6 and 10 is 60. Note that when **17** is quadrupled, the result is 68, and that when 68 is reduced by 8, the result is 60.

106. A. Here, (a) the value of $5a - 2b$ if $a = -2$ and $b = -3$ is $5(-2) - 2(-3) = -10 + 6 = -4$. Further, (b) the value of $5a - 2b$ if $a = -3$ and $b = -2$ is $5(-3) - 2(-2) = -15 + 4 = -11$. Finally, (c) the value of $5a - 2b$ if $a = -4$ and $b = -6$ is $5(-4) - 2(-6) = -20 + 12 = -8$. Thus, (a) is greater than (b) and (c).

107. A. The length of AB is the same as the length of CD because they are opposite equal angles. However, both AB and CD are shorter than AC because AC is a diameter.

108. C. The sum of the first two numbers is the third number, $3 + 3 = 6$. Then, the sum of the second and third numbers is the fourth number, $3 + 6 = 9$. In the same way, $9 + 15 = 24$. To finish, $15 + 24 = \mathbf{39.}$

109. D. The product of 20 and 5 is 100. Note that, when **9** is squared, the result is 81, and that, when 81 is increased by 19, the result is 100.

110. C. To begin, $a = 45$ because 180° are in a triangle. Further, $b = 30$ because it is vertical to a. Finally, $c = 60$ because 180° are in a triangle. Thus, $c > b = a$.

111. A. The pattern is easier to recognize if you note that the third number is 4 less than the first, and that the fifth number is 4 less than the third. Now, the first number is 48, and the second number is $48 \div 4 = 12$. The third number is 4 less than the first number, $48 - 4 = 44$, and the fourth number is $44 \div 4 = 11$. The fifth number is 4 less than the third, $44 - 4 = 40$, and the sixth number is $40 \div 4 = 10$. Thus, the missing number should be 4 less than 40, or $40 - 4 = \mathbf{36.}$ Finally, $36 \div 4 = 9$.

112. C. Here, $a = 45$ because 180° are in a triangle. Next, $b = 70$ because it is supplementary to a 110° angle. Finally, $c = 65$ because, once again, there are 180° in a triangle. Thus, $b > c > a$.

Test 3: Reading

113. B. In this early portion of the passage, no information is provided about what microbes do, so **C** and **D** are not good choices.

114. B. Although some portions of the selection relate to **A, C,** and **D,** none of these are a good description of the entire passage.

115. A. The second paragraph indicates that lice can be avoided by keeping away from those infected with them.

116. A. The sentence that follows *shame* shows what the word means.

117. A. The information is in the first sentence of the second paragraph.

118. B. If they are not harmful, they can be beneficial.

119. B. The words *probe the skin for blood on which they live* means they are feeding.

120. A. This information is at the end of the fourth paragraph.

121. D. **B** is not correct because the insects *regularly harass* people, but they only *sometimes* transmit illnesses.

122. C. That this is the author's attitude is revealed by the last sentence of the first paragraph and the last paragraph of the selection.

123. C. The examples help to explain the meaning of the word.

124. B. The example of the different associations of *flowers* provides this answer.

125. D. The passage provides information about a subject one might study in school, so it would not be likely to appear in a newspaper or an advertisement, choices **A** and **C.** Although it might be of interest to someone who solves puzzles, it doesn't tell how to solve them, so **B** is not correct.

126. C. The choices, from general to specific, are food, citrus fruits, lemon, navel orange (a specific type of orange).

127. B. The content of the paragraph and the example define the word. Although *unique* is frequently used in speech to mean something unusual or out of the ordinary, that is incorrect usage.

128. D. The second sentence of the second paragraph explains this answer.

129. A. This information is in the first paragraph.

130. C. The third paragraph of the selection contains this information.

131. D. The words are an example of the idea that different languages use different symbols to represent the same thing.

132. B. **A** might seem like a good choice because building tools are used as an example. But because the selection is about words and how they work, it is safe to assume that the author enjoys playing with words. Doing crossword puzzles is a word game.

133. D. Choice **A,** sassafras, was in the tea served to Hires, not in root beer.

134. A. The word means a prediction or a sign of the future.

135. B. The details add up to this conclusion. Hires went to night school, borrowed money to start his own business, and developed two new products.

136. B. This information is in the second paragraph of the selection.

137. D. The association with sick people suggests weakness.

138. C. While choices **B** and **D** look like good possibilities, they are specific, and the claims made in the advertisements are general.

139. D. This choice combines the two main subjects of the passage, the man and his product.

140. C. *Induce* means to produce something or to lead to it.

141. A. Choices **B** and **C** state one property mentioned in the ads, but they add another property the ads do not mention.

142. D. He not only invented root beer, he also developed condensed milk.

143. B. This is stated in the first sentence of the passage.

144. C. If you don't know the meaning of *wrath,* you can still choose this answer because all the other words are positive, and the sentence requires a word that suggests a negative feeling.

145. C. The words *hopes and expectations* in the passage indicate this is the correct choice.

146. C. The passage states that they *arrived like roadside mechanics*.

147. C. Although the telescope is named for him, the passage does not say that he developed it, as stated in choice **A.**

148. B. Because the phrase *window on the universe* is in quotation marks, it is the name given to the telescope.

149. A. This information is in the second paragraph of the passage.

150. A. This information is in the last paragraph of the passage.

151. A. This is explained in the second paragraph of the passage.

152. A. The author writes that the gas and dust *swirl around the drain and are slowly sucked in.*

153. B.	**159. B.**	**165. D.**	**171. D.**
154. C.	**160. C.**	**166. C.**	**172. A.**
155. C.	**161. D.**	**167. D.**	**173. C.**
156. A.	**162. D.**	**168. B.**	**174. B.**
157. B.	**163. A.**	**169. B.**	
158. C.	**164. A.**	**170. C.**	

Test 4: Mathematics

175. B. The time cleaning was 30 minutes + 12 minutes + 37 minutes = 79 minutes.

176. A. The difference in miles is $638 - 439 = 199$.

177. B. At 5:30, there are 30 minutes until 6:00 and 2 additional hours until 8:00, for a total of 2 hours and 30 minutes.

178. C. The cost of milk and 2 dozen eggs is $\$1.39 + (2 \times \$1.28) = \$3.95$. The change is $\$10.00 - \$3.95 = \$6.05$.

179. A. The difference in time is $144 - 127 = 17$ minutes.

180. A. Let c represent the number of caps traded in. Then $0.05c = 40.50$ and $c = \frac{40.50}{0.05}$.

181. C. The number of smaller pieces is $\frac{16.5}{2.75} = 6$.

182. A. The total amount is $(17 \times \$0.25) + (33 \times \$0.10) + (8 \times \$0.01) = \$4.25 + \$3.30 + \$0.08 = \$7.63$.

183. B. The total is $(18 \times \$0.25) + (6 \times \$0.10) + (24 \times \$0.05) = \$4.50 + \$0.60 + \$1.20 = \$6.30$.

184. C. The factors of 42 are 1, 2, 3, 6, 7, 14, 21, and 42. The factors of 28 are 1, 2, 4, 7, 14, and 28. The greatest common factor, therefore, is 14.

185. C. $(+8) - (+2) - (-7) = (+8) + (-2) + (+7) = +13$.

186. A. $\frac{8}{9} - \frac{1}{3} = \frac{8}{9} - \frac{3}{9} = \frac{5}{9}$.

187. A. The speed (rate) is $\frac{744,000 \text{ miles}}{4 \text{ seconds}}$. Dividing 4 into 744,000 gives 186,000 miles per second.

188. D. The total number of seats is $1,350 + 3,527 + 2,007 + 4,275 = 11,159$.

189. A. To solve this problem, we need to multiply the number of pads times the number of pieces of paper in a pad. Because $25 \times 70 = 1,750$, this is the total number of sheets of paper he bought.

190. D. He got $\frac{648 \text{ miles}}{24 \text{ gallons}}$. Dividing 648 by 24 gives 27 miles per gallon.

191. D. Because 36 inches are in a yard, 12 yards is the same as $12 \times 36 = 432$ inches. In the same way, 1 foot contains 12 inches, and the total distance is 432 inches + 12 inches + 17 inches = 461 inches.

192. C. The number 31.5 is the closest, differing by only 0.01.

193. D. $2^6 - 6^2 = 64 - 36 = 28$.

194. A. $\sqrt{\frac{36}{64}} = \frac{\sqrt{36}}{\sqrt{64}} = \frac{6}{8} = \frac{3}{4}$.

195. C. $(2.3 \times 10) + (2.3 \times 10^2) + (2.3 \times 10^3) = 23 + 230 + 2,300 = 2,553$.

196. B. It is easy to tell which of the numbers is the smallest by adding 0's to the end of each number and ignoring the decimal points. Thus, compare:

0.1990

0.1987

0.2300

1.0070

It is easy to see that 0.1987 is the smallest.

197. B. Note that $630 = 63 \times 10 = 7 \times 9 \times 2 \times 5 = 2 \times 3 \times 3 \times 5 \times 7$.

198. D. A number that ends in 5 or 0 is divisible by 5.

199. C. $\frac{1}{3}$ of $6\frac{1}{2}$ miles is $\frac{1}{3} \times 6\frac{1}{2} = \frac{1}{3} \times \frac{13}{2} = \frac{13}{6}$ miles walked. The remaining distance is $6\frac{1}{2} - \frac{13}{6} = \frac{13}{2} - \frac{13}{6} = \frac{39}{6} - \frac{13}{6} = \frac{26}{6} = 4\frac{1}{3}$ miles.

200. D. Using the ratio $\frac{\text{height}}{\text{shadow}}$, the proportion $\frac{x \text{ feet}}{5 \text{ feet}} = \frac{6 \text{ feet}}{8 \text{ feet}}$ can be used to find the unknown height. Cross multiply: $8x = 5 \times 6$, so $8x = 30$, and $x = \frac{30}{8} = 3\frac{3}{4}$ feet. Convert $\frac{3}{4}$ feet to inches: $\frac{3}{4} \times 12 = 9$ inches. Therefore, the height is 3 feet 9 inches.

201. B. If $\frac{3}{8}$ is wheat flour, then $1 - \frac{3}{8}$ or $\frac{5}{8}$ is white flour. So $3 \times \frac{5}{8} = \frac{15}{8} = 1\frac{7}{8}$ cups of white flour are needed.

202. C. Using the ratio $\frac{\text{price}}{\text{video}}$, the proportion $\frac{8}{3} = \frac{x}{2}$ can be used to find the cost to rent two videos. Cross multiply: $8 \times 2 = 3x$, so $16 = 3x$, and $x = \frac{16}{3} = \$5.33$.

203. D. The percent discounted is the amount discounted divided by the original price. The amount discounted is $\$200 - \$150 = \$50$. The percent discounted is $\frac{50}{200} = 0.25 = 25\%$.

204. D. Find the difference between the area of circle and the area of the square. The area of the circle is $\pi r^2 = \pi 2^2 = 4\pi$. The area of the square is s^2, where s represents the length of the square. The radius is half the length of the square's diagonal, so the diagonal is 4. By the Pythagorean Theorem $s^2 + s^2 = 4^2$. $2s^2 = 16$. $2s^2 = 16$, so $s^2 = 8$. The difference in area is $4\pi - 8$.

205. D. If the blueprint shows $\frac{1}{2}$ inch for every 3 feet, then 1 inch represents 6 feet. The actual dimensions of a room $1\frac{1}{2}$ inches $\times$ 2 inches are $(1\frac{1}{2} \times 6)$ by (2×6) or 9 feet by 12 feet.

206. B. In 2 weeks, or 14 days, $\frac{1}{2} \times 14 = 7$ gallons leak out, leaving $60 - 7 = 53$ gallons.

207. D. Convert the dimensions of the box from feet to inches. $8' \times 6' \times 4'$ is equivalent to $(8 \times 12 \text{ in}) \times (6 \times 12 \text{ in}) \times (4 \times 12 \text{ in}) = 96 \text{ in} \times 72 \text{ in} \times 48 \text{ in}$. The volume $= 96 \times 72 \times 48 = 331,776$. The volume of each block is $6 \times 4 \times 4 = 96$. The number of blocks that fit in the box is $\frac{331,776}{96} = 3,456$.

208. B. Sixty percent arrive to work by car, so $800 \times 60\% = 480$.

209. D. Jillian read a total of $3 + 4$, or 7, mysteries. Therefore, she read 3×7, or 21, nonfiction books.

210. C. The volume of a cube is s^3, where s represents the length of an edge. Surface area is $6s^2$. If the volume $= 343 \text{ cm}^3$, then $\sqrt[3]{343} = \sqrt[3]{7 \times 7 \times 7} = 7$. So the surface area is $6 \times 7^2 = 49 = 294 \text{cm}^2$.

211. C. If $\frac{3}{8}$ of the pizza is eaten, then $1 - \frac{3}{8} = \frac{5}{8}$ remains. If that is divided by 2, then each receives $\frac{5}{8} \div 2 = \frac{5}{8} \times \frac{1}{2} = \frac{5}{16} = 0.3125 = 31.25\%$.

212. D. With 9 cups of milk, $\frac{9}{2} = 4\frac{1}{2}$, or 4 full batches, can be made. However, with 9 eggs, only $\frac{9}{4} = 2\frac{1}{4}$, or 2 full batches, can be made. At most, only 2 batches can be made with the given ingredients.

213. B. The percent tip is the amount of tip over the total before tip. The amount of the tip is $\$25.00 - \$21.00 = \$4.00$. The percent of the tip is $\frac{4}{21} = 0.19 = 19\%$.

214. A. The area of a triangle is $\frac{1}{2}bh$. Let b represent the length of one leg. Then $h = 3b$, so the area is $\frac{1}{2}bh = \frac{1}{2} \times b \times 3b = \frac{3}{2}b^2 = 24$, so $\frac{2}{3} \times \frac{3}{2}b^2 = \frac{2}{3} \times 24$, and $b^2 = 16$. $b = \sqrt{16} = 4$, and $h = 3 \times 4 = 12$. The longest side of a right triangle is the hypotenuse. Using the Pythagorean Theorem, $\text{leg}^2 + \text{leg}^2 = \text{hypotenuse}^2$, so $4^2 + 12^2 = c^2$, and $16 + 144 = c^2$. Therefore, $160 = c^2$, and $c = \sqrt{160} = 12.6$.

215. C. Interest = principle × rate. Let p represent the principle. Then $\$100 = p \times 7\frac{1}{4}\%$, so $p = \frac{\$100}{7\frac{1}{4}\%} = \frac{\$100}{0.0725} = \$1,379$.

216. D. Using the ratio $\frac{\text{pages}}{\text{minutes}}$, the proportion $\frac{2}{3} = \frac{360}{x}$ can be used to find the time. Cross multiply: $2x = 3 \times 360$, so $2x = 1080$, and $x = \frac{1080}{2} = 540$ minutes. Convert minutes to hours. Sixty minutes are in one hour, so $\frac{540}{60} = 9$ hours.

217. B. The average is found by adding up all the scores and dividing by the total number of scores. The average this week is $\frac{112 + 156 + 179 + 165}{4} = \frac{612}{4} = 153$. The amount of improvement is $153 - 140 = 13$.

218. D. The total cost of the purchase is $\$8.95 \times 3 = \$26.85$. With a $12.73 credit, the amount owed is $\$26.85 - \$12.73 = \$14.12$.

219. B. $-3a + 4b = -3(2) + 4(-\!\!-\!\!=s3) = -6 - 12 = -18$.

220. B. Let S = the length of the shorter piece. Then, the longer piece is of length $2S$, and $S + 2S = 27$, or $3S = 27$, so $S = 9$.

221. B. The unlabeled angle of the triangle has the same measure as the angle labeled 70°. Thus, the triangle has angles of 70° and 50°. The missing angle must be 60° so that the three angles add up to 180°.

222. C. The perimeter of the room is $2 \times 12 + 2 \times 7.5 = 24 + 15 = 39$ feet. Subtracting 4 feet for the doorway leaves 35 feet of baseboard needed.

223. B. The area of the office is 20 feet × 30 feet = 600 square feet. At $8 a square foot, the total cost is $600 \times \$8 = \$4,800$ a month.

224. D. Paul studied for $\frac{1}{4} + \frac{3}{8} + \frac{7}{12} + \frac{9}{16} = \frac{12}{48} + \frac{18}{48} + \frac{28}{48} + \frac{27}{48} = \frac{85}{48} = 1\frac{37}{48}$ hours.

225. C. The percent of increase is equal to the amount of the increase divided by the original price. Therefore, the percent of increase $= \frac{\$60}{\$180} = 0.3333 = 33\frac{1}{3}\%$.

226. A. $x^3 - x^2 + x - 1 = (-1)^3 - (-1)^2 + (-1) - 1 = -1 - 1 - 1 - 1 = -4$.

227. B. An easy way to think about this problem is to assume that Brian earned $1 in the other 11 months and $3 in August. Then, he earned a total of $14, $3 of which was earned in August. His August earnings, then, were $\frac{3}{14}$ of his salary.

228. D. The fraction of fans at the game that were children is $\frac{1}{4} + \frac{1}{3} = \frac{3}{12} + \frac{4}{12} = \frac{7}{12}$.

229. A. This problem becomes easier to think about if you select a value for x. For example, if $x = 20$ minutes, then in 15 minutes, Jimmy can do $\frac{15}{20}$ of the job. It follows that, in x minutes, he can do $\frac{15}{x}$ of the job.

230. D. The volume of the smaller cubes is $\frac{1}{2} \times \frac{1}{2} \times \frac{1}{2} = \frac{1}{8}$. The volume of the larger cube is $2 \times 2 \times 2 = 8$. Thus, the number of small cubes that fit in the larger cube is $\frac{8}{\frac{1}{8}} = 64$.

231. B. If we let x represent the answer to the problem, then $\frac{1}{5} = \frac{3}{4}x$. If both sides of this equation are multiplied by $\frac{4}{3}$, we obtain the answer $\frac{1}{5} \times \frac{4}{3} = \frac{4}{15} = x$.

232. B. The pair that solves both equations at the same time is (3, 0) because $2(3) + 3(0) = 6$, and $3 + 0 = 3$.

233. C. If a square foot of carpeting costs $5, then a square yard costs $5 \times 9 = \$45$. Because 12 square yards are in a 3-yard × 4-yard carpet, the total cost is $\$45 \times 12 = \$540$.

234. B. $\dfrac{\frac{4}{5} - \frac{1}{3}}{\frac{1}{2}} = \dfrac{\frac{12}{15} - \frac{5}{15}}{\frac{1}{2}} = \dfrac{\frac{7}{15}}{\frac{1}{2}} = \frac{7}{15} \times \frac{2}{1} = \frac{14}{15}$.

235. D. If Bobby picks the dime, the quarter, or the half dollar, he is able to buy the gumball. Thus, 3 out of 5 coins are sufficient, and the probability is $\frac{3}{5}$.

236. D. If Susan can type 5 words in 20 seconds, she can type 15 words in a minute. Therefore, it takes her $\frac{600}{15} = 40$ minutes to type the essay.

237. C. Brett earned $\$1,605 - \$1,500 = \$105$ on his investment of $1,500. The interest rate, therefore, was $\frac{\$105}{\$1,500} = 0.07 = 7\%$.

238. B. The amount of the first markdown is $\$6,000 \times 0.30 = \$1,800$. After this markdown, the price becomes $\$6,000 - \$1,800 = \$4,200$. The amount of the second markdown is $\$4,200 \times 0.20 = \$840$, which makes the final price $\$4,200 - \$840 = \$3,360$.

Test 5: Language Skills

239. B. Use a semicolon to join independent clauses.

240. B. *Dogs* requires an apostrophe after the *g* because it is a possessive singular: *dog's*.

241. C. A quotation mark is needed after the word *folks*.

242. D. All answer choices are correct.

243. B. Use an apostrophe to indicate a contraction: *I've*.

244. A. When a noun is used as part of a title, it should be capitalized: *Uncle Fred*.

245. D. All answer choices are correct.

246. B. A comma is needed after *seconds*. Introductory subordinate clauses are followed by a comma.

247. D. All answer choices are correct.

248. C. This is a question and therefore should end with a question mark.

249. B. *Contestants* should be followed by an apostrophe; it is a plural possessive.

250. C. Do not use a comma after a coordinating conjunction that joins two independent clauses.

251. C. *Police* is a collective noun that can be singular or plural depending on the sentence. In this sentence, the plural meaning is clearer, so the verb should be *get*.

252. A. *Different from* is correct usage.

253. D. All answer choices are correct.

254. B. As the sentence is written, the pizza finished the homework.

255. A. Use an adverb, *slowly*, to describe a verb.

256. C. The correct word is *taught*.

257. B. *Dog and cat* is a compound subject, so the plural verb form, *need*, is required.

258. C. After the helping verb *do*, use the base form of the verb: *tell*.

259. A. A compound subject requires a plural verb.

260. A. The verb should agree with its subject, *each*, which is singular.

261. B. The sentence uses a double negative. It should read *I can hardly*.

262. D. All answer choices are correct.

263. B. The family wasn't seven years old. The writer means *when I was seven years old*.

264. A. Do not use the reflexive pronoun when the simple object form is correct.

265. A. The possessive pronoun must agree with its singular antecedent, *each*. Do not be confused by the prepositional phrase and the verb that come between the antecedent and the pronoun. The sentence does not say whether the winners are male or female, so it is uncertain whether *his* or *her* should replace their. The best correction is to make the antecedent plural: *All the winners receive their medals*.

266. C. Who or what was looking under the car? When there is no word or phrase for the opening phrase to describe, the error is called a dangling modifier.

267. B. Do not use double negatives in a sentence.

268. D. All answer choices are correct.

269. A. When the subject follows the verb, as it does in *there is* or *there* are constructions, be sure the verb agrees with the subject. *There are three songs*.

270. C. Did the writer mean to say that the rain was walking?

271. C. Use adverbs to modify verbs: did *well*.

272. B. The second half of the sentence begins in present tense and shifts to past tense for no reason.

273. D. All answer choices are correct.

274. A. Use whom, not which or that, when referring to people.

275. C. Place modifiers as close as possible to what they modify. It is the loans, not the people, that are *of any size*.

276. D. All answer choices are correct.

277. A. According to the sentence, the telephone is preparing dinner.

278. B. *Whose* is the interrogative pronoun. *Who's* means *who is*.

279. C. height.

280. A. tragedy.

281. D. All answer choices are correct.

282. A. environment.

283. D. All answer choices are correct.

284. C. across.

285. A. Committee.

286. C. business.

287. A. parallel.

288. D. All answer choices are correct.

289. B. Choice **A** does not make sense. While choices **C** and **D** are possible, *because* most clearly explains the relationship between the two parts of the sentence.

290. D. Choices **A** and **C** state that the kids are to be put in the freezer. In **B** the grapes are performing an action.

291. D. The dog belonging to the person writing is not an example of a service dog.

292. A. This pair of sentences best states why the march was a major event.

293. C. In **A**, it isn't clear that the leg broke as an immediate result of the fall. In **B**, the leg fell off the horse. **D** has a confusing use of verb tenses.

294. B. Adjectives should be placed as close as possible to the words or phrases they describe to avoid confusing sentences.

295. D. This is the only choice that suggests a danger to the turtles.

296. C. Although commonly heard in speech, it is incorrect to write *on* (**B**) a subject. **A** is unnecessarily wordy. **D** is confusing.

297. B. This sentence provides a phrase to which the pronoun *they* in sentence 2 can refer.

298. B. All the sentences are about an ingredient of pizza, but this choice does not give any nutritional information.